6000
AMAZING
FACTS

6000
AMAZING
FACTS

Miles
Kelly

First published in 2017 by Miles Kelly Publishing Ltd
Harding's Barn, Bardfield End Green, Thaxted, Essex, CM6 3PX, UK

2 4 6 8 10 9 7 5 3 1

Publishing Director Belinda Gallagher
Creative Director Jo Cowan
Editor Becky Miles
Design Manager Simon Lee
Image Manager Liberty Newton
Production Elizabeth Collins, Caroline Kelly
Reprographics Stephan Davis, Jennifer Cozens
Assets Lorraine King

ISBN: 978-1-78617-330-0

Printed in China

British Library Cataloguing-in-Publication Data
A catalogue record for this book is available from the British Library

Made with paper from a sustainable forest

www.mileskelly.net

CONTENTS

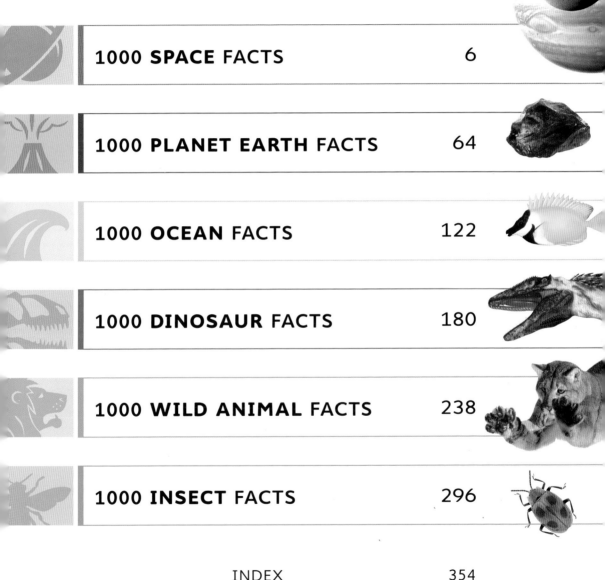

1000 **SPACE** FACTS

Small stars

- **Depending on their colour,** small stars of low brightness are called red, white, brown or black dwarves.

- **Red dwarves are** the most common type of star and make up over two thirds of all stars.

- **They are bigger** than the planet Jupiter, but smaller than the medium-sized star, the Sun. They glow faintly with less than 5 percent of the Sun's brightness.

- **No red dwarf can be seen** with the naked eye – not even the nearest star to the Sun, the red dwarf Proxima Centauri.

- **Red dwarves burn their fuel** more slowly than stars like the Sun, so they last as long as a trillion years.

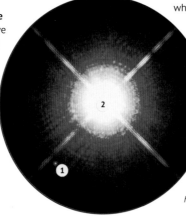

1   *Pup star*
2   *Sirius*

- **White dwarves** are the last stage in the life of a medium-sized star. Although they are even smaller than red dwarves, they contain the same amount of matter as the Sun.

- **The star 40 Eridani** is really three dwarf stars – a white dwarf and a red dwarf circling a small orange star, which can just be seen with the naked eye.

- **Brown dwarves** are cool space objects, a little bigger than Jupiter. They formed in the same way as other stars, but were not big enough to start shining properly. They just glow very faintly with the heat left over from their formation.

- **Black dwarves** will be very small, cold, dead stars. They are either not big enough ever to start shining, or they will burn all their nuclear fuel and stop glowing.

◀ *The night sky's brightest star, Sirius the Dog Star, has a white dwarf companion called the Pup Star.*

Life

- **Life is only known** to exist on Earth. Our planet is suitable for life because of its gas atmosphere, surface water and moderately warm temperatures.

- **Life probably began** on Earth more than 3.5 billion years ago.

- **The first life-forms** were probably bacteria that lived in very hot water around underwater volcanoes.

▼ *This artist's impression shows the Huygens probe plunging through the clouds in Titan's atmosphere in 2005, gathering information as it descends.*

- **Some scientists believe** that life's basic chemicals formed on Earth. Others think that they came from space, maybe on comets.

- **The panspermia theory** says that life exists in many places in the Universe, spread by comets, meteoroids, asteroids and similar space bodies.

- **Basic organic chemicals,** such as amino acids, have been detected in nebulae, meteorites and comets.

- **Huge lightning flashes** may have caused big organic molecules to form on the Earth when it was young.

- **Saturn's icy moon,** Titan, has evidence of organic (life) chemicals, as discovered by the Cassini–Huygens mission, which launched in 1997.

- **Jupiter's moon,** Europa, may have water below its surface, which could spawn life.

Space suits

● **Astronauts wear space suits** for protection when they go outside their spacecraft. The suits are also called EMUs (Extra-vehicular Mobility Units).

● **The outer layers of a space suit** protect against harmful radiation from the Sun and fast-moving particles of space dust called micrometeoroids.

● **The clear, plastic-composite helmet** also protects against radiation and micrometeoroids.

● **Oxygen is circulated** around the helmet to prevent the visor from misting.

● **The middle layers of a space suit** are blown up like a balloon to press against the astronaut's body. Without this pressure, the astronaut's blood would boil.

● **Space suits have a soft inner lining** that contains tubes of water to cool the astronaut's body.

● **The backpack supplies pure oxygen** for the astronaut to breathe, and gets rid of the carbon dioxide that is breathed out. The oxygen tank can supply the astronaut for up to eight hours.

▶ *Crew member and flight engineer Sergey Ryazansky wears the latest version of the Russian Orlan space suit, an Orlan MK. The original Orlan suits date back to 1977.*

● **There are various glove designs.** Some have silicone-rubber fingertips, which allow the astronaut some sense of touch.

● **Various parts in the suit** deal with liquids, including a tube for drinks and another for urine.

● **The full cost of the latest space suit** is more than $10 million (£6.5 million), although about half of this is for the backpack and control module.

Newton

● **Isaac Newton** (1642–1727) discovered laws that govern the force of gravity and motion.

● **Newton's discovery of gravity** showed why planets orbit the Sun.

● **He realized** that a planet's orbit depends on its mass and its distance from the Sun.

● **The farther apart** and the lighter two objects are, the weaker the pull of gravity is between them.

● **To calculate the pull of gravity** between two objects, multiply their masses together, then divide the total by the square of the distance between them.

● **This calculation allows astronomers** to predict the movement of every planet, star and galaxy in the Universe.

● **Using Newton's formula for gravity** (and more lately Einstein's work), astronomers have detected new stars and planets, including Neptune, from the effect of their gravity on other space objects.

● **Newton's three laws of motion** showed how movements of objects in space can be calculated using celestial mechanics. This became known as the 'clockwork Universe', although Einstein's work has replaced some of these ideas.

● **Newton's book** *Philosophiæ Naturalis Principia Mathematica* ('Mathematical Principles of Natural Philosophy') of 1687, usually known as the *Principia*, explained his many theories.

▶ *Newton was made Lucasian professor of mathematics at Cambridge University in 1669, where he studied how and why things in our Universe move as they do.*

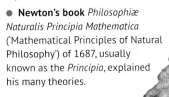
DID YOU KNOW?

Newton's ideas were inspired by seeing an apple fall from a tree in the garden of his home.

Nebulae

● **Any fuzzy patch of light** in the night sky was once called a nebula. Nowadays, many of these are known to be galaxies.

● **A nebula is now defined** as a gigantic cloud of gas and dust.

● **Glowing nebula** give off a dim, red light as the hydrogen gas in them is heated by radiation from nearby stars.

● **The Orion Nebula** (M42 or NGC 1976) is a glowing nebula just visible to the naked eye in the Orion constellation.

● **Reflection nebulae** have no light. They can only be seen because starlight shines off the dust in them.

● **Dark nebulae not only have no light** of their own, they also soak up all light. They can only be seen as patches of darkness blocking out light from the stars behind them.

● **The Horsehead Nebula in Orion** is a well known dark nebula. As its name suggests, it is shaped like a horse's head.

▲ *The Trifid Nebula (M20, NGC 6514) glows as hydrogen and helium gas within is heated by radiation from stars.*

● **Planetary nebulae** are thin rings of gas cloud thrown out by dying stars. Despite their name, they have nothing to do with planets.

● **The Ring Nebula in Lyra** (M57, NGC 6720) is a well known planetary nebula.

● **There may be as many as** 2500 nebulae in the Milky Way alone.

Extraterrestrials

● **Extraterrestrial (ET) means** 'outside the Earth'.

● **Some scientists believe** that ET or alien life could develop anywhere in the Universe where there is a flow of energy.

● **Most scientists believe** that if there is ET life anywhere else in the Universe, it is probably based on organic chemistry, that is, the chemistry of carbon, as life on Earth is. An alternative is silicon.

● **If civilizations exist** elsewhere, they may be on planets circling other stars.

● **The Drake Equation** was proposed by astronomer Frank Drake (1930–) in 1961 to calculate how many civilizations there could be in our galaxy – the figure is millions.

DID YOU KNOW?

Released in 1982, E.T. the Extraterrestrial (Universal Studios) was the biggest earning movie for 11 years (until Jurassic Park, 1993, Universal Pictures)

● **Many stories exist** of people seeing alien spacecraft or other UFOs, encountering aliens, or even being captured by them and visiting their craft or home world.

● **However there is no serious scientific proof** that any ET life-form has ever visited Earth.

● **The space probes** Pioneer 10 and 11 carry metal panels with picture messages about life on Earth into deep space. If found by extraterrestrials, they would regard us as the aliens.

◀ *People have reported spotting UFOs (Unidentified Flying Objects), such as so-called flying saucers, for more than 60 years.*

H-R diagram

● **The Hertzsprung-Russell (H-R) diagram** was devised in about 1910 by Danish astronomer Ejnar Hertzsprung (1873–1967) and US astronomer Henry Russell (1877–1957).

● **An incredibly useful tool** in astronomy and space science, the H-R diagram is a 'scatter graph' that plots the temperature of stars against their brightness or magnitude.

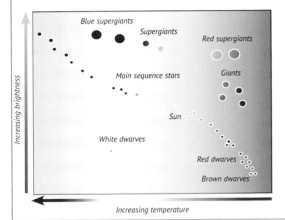

● **The temperature of a star** is indicated by its colour. Cool stars are red or reddish-yellow, medium ones are yellow and hot stars burn white or blue.

● **Medium-sized stars** form a diagonal band called the main sequence across the middle graph.

● **The whiter and hotter a main sequence star is**, the brighter it shines. White stars and blue-white stars are usually bigger and younger.

● **The redder and cooler a star is**, the dimmer it glows. Cool red stars tend to be smaller and older.

● **Giant stars and white dwarf** stars lie to either side of the band of main sequence stars.

● **One use of the H-R diagram** is to show distance. If the star actually looks dimmer for its colour than it should be, it must be farther away from Earth.

◀ *By comparing a star's actual brightness, predicted by the H-R diagram, with how bright it looks from Earth, astronomers can work out how far away it is.*

The Milky Way

● **The faint, hazy band** of light that can be seen stretching right across the night sky is the Milky Way.

● **With binoculars**, thousands of the billions of stars that make up the Milky Way can be seen.

● **The Milky Way** is the view of our galaxy from Earth. We are inside its disc, looking through its thickness.

● **Our galaxy is 100,000 or more light years** across and 1000 light years thick. It is made up of at least 100 billion stars, and possibly five times that many.

● **All of the stars are arranged** in a spiral with a bulge in the middle. The bulge is about 20,000 light years across and 3000 light years thick, with very old stars and little dust or gas.

● **The Sun is just one** of the billions of stars in the Milky Way. It lies about halfway from the centre on one arm of the spiral, the Orion Arm.

● **The Milky Way** is whirling rapidly, spinning our Sun and its Solar System around at 800,000 km/h.

● **Once every 220 million years**, the Solar System and all local stars complete one orbit around the Milky Way centre – a journey of 170,000 light years.

● **At the centre of the Milky Way** is an immensely powerful source of radio energy, Sagittarius A*. It may well be a supermassive black hole.

▼ *The 'arms' at the edge of the Milky Way contain many young, bright stars, while the middle is dust and gas.*

The Universe

● **The Universe** is everything that we can ever know – all of space and all of time. Before the Universe came into existence there was nothingness, no space, no time, no energy and no matter.

● **The study** of the Universe – its history, future, and large-scale features – is known as cosmology.

● **Latest estimates** put the Universe at about 13.8 billion years old.

● **Scientists believe** that the Universe started with an explosion known as the Big Bang.

● **Since the Big Bang** the Universe has been expanding and it still does. The most distant galaxies are moving away from us at about 90 percent of the speed of light.

● **The Universe** was once thought to be everything that could ever exist, but recent theories suggest that our Universe may be just one of countless bubbles of space-time.

● **Although there is no maximum** possible temperature in the Universe, there is a very precise minimum possible temperature. The third law of thermodynamics states that it is impossible for anything to be cooled to absolute zero (−273°C).

▲ *The Universe is getting bigger all the time as galaxies rush outwards in all directions.*

● **Working in specialized laboratories**, scientists have cooled substances to within a billionth of a degree of absolute zero, but they cannot achieve this ultimate low temperature.

● **Matter is not distributed** evenly throughout the Universe. On the largest scale, the Universe consists of thin filaments, each one made up of millions of galaxies, which surround vast voids that contain nothing but clouds of intergalactic hydrogen.

● **The largest structure** yet identified is an extended line of galaxies known as the Great Wall that is located about 500 million light years from our galaxy.

Black holes

● **When a star or galaxy** of a certain size becomes so dense that it collapses under the pull of its own gravity, it becomes a black hole.

● **Gravity is so strong** in a black hole that it sucks in everything, including all matter, radiation and other energy.

● **This immense gravity shrinks** the black hole to an unimaginably small, dense point called a singularity, where vast amounts of matter and energy are squeezed into almost nothing.

● **Around the singularity** is the 'place of no return' for matter and energy falling into the black hole, called the event horizon.

● **Nothing can leave a black hole**, including light – so it is 'black'.

● **However, one theory** says that a certain kind of energy could be emitted from a black hole, called Hawking radiation after famous scientist Stephen Hawking (b. 1942).

● **A stellar black hole**, formed from one collapsed star, has a mass of about 10 to 100 times that of the Sun.

● **Supermassive black holes** with millions – even billions – of stars may exist at the heart of every galaxy.

● **Around the singularity**, gravity is so intense that space-time is bent into a funnel.

● **Matter spiralling into the funnel** and towards the black hole is torn apart and glows so brightly that it creates the most luminous objects in the Universe – quasars.

● **The swirling gases** around a black hole turn it into an electrical generator, spouting jets containing electrons that surge billions of kilometres out into space.

◄ *The gravity of a black hole is so strong that nothing can escape, not even light. Planets, stars, gas and dust are pulled into the hole.*

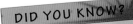
DID YOU KNOW?

The term 'black hole' was first popularized in 1967 by US physicist John Wheeler (1911–2008).

Mercury

● **The nearest planet to the Sun** is Mercury. During its orbit, it is between 46.0 and 69.8 million km away. It has no moons.

● **Mercury has the fastest orbit** – one journey around the Sun takes just 88 Earth days. Its average orbital speed is 47 km/sec.

● **Twice during its orbit**, Mercury gets very close to the Sun and speeds up so much that the Sun seems to go backwards in the sky.

● **Mercury rotates once every 58.6 Earth days**, but the time between one sunrise and the next is 176 Earth days, longer than Mercury's year.

● **Temperatures change** from −190°C at night to more than 430°C (hot enough to melt lead) during the day.

● **The crust and mantle** are made largely of rock, but the core (75 percent of Mercury's diameter) is made from solid iron.

● **Mercury's dusty surface** is pocketed by craters made by space debris crashing into it.

The Caloris Basin is a vast shallow crater, surrounded by mountains 2 km high

A thin crust of rock floats on top of the mantle

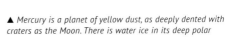

Mercury's huge iron core takes up three quarters of the planet

A layer of rock, called the mantle, surrounds the core

Mercury's surface is wrinkled by long, low ridges that probably formed as the planet's core cooled and shrank

▲ *Mercury is a planet of yellow dust, as deeply dented with craters as the Moon. There is water ice in its deep polar craters, where the Sun never shines.*

● **With less than six percent of Earth's mass**, Mercury is so small that its gravity can only hold on to a very thin atmosphere.

● **Mercury is so small** that its core has cooled and become solid (unlike Earth's). As this happened, Mercury shrank and its surface wrinkled.

● **Craters on Mercury** discovered by the USA's Mariner 10 space probe have names such as Bach, Beethoven, Wagner, Shakespeare and Tolstoy.

▼ *The Sun looks huge as it rises over Mercury. The sunny side of the planet is boiling hot, but the night side is more than twice as cold as Antarctica.*

Copernicus

● **Until the 16th century** most people thought Earth was the centre of the Universe and that everything – the Moon, Sun, planets and stars – revolved around it. This is called the geocentric view.

● **Nicolaus Copernicus** (1473–1543) was the astronomer who first suggested that the Sun was the Solar System's centre, and that Earth went around it. This is known as the heliocentric view.

● **Copernicus had an extensive education** at the best universities in Poland and Italy. He studied astronomy, astrology, various languages, medicine and law.

● **In his book**, *De revolutionibus orbium coelestium (On the Revolutions of the Heavenly Spheres)*, Copernicus described his new ideas.

● **The Roman Catholic Church** banned Copernicus' book for about 140 years.

● **Copernicus' ideas** came mainly from studying ancient astronomy.

● **His main clue** came from the way the planets, seen from Earth, seem to perform a backward loop through the sky every now and then.

● **The first proof of Copernicus' theory** came in 1610, when Galileo saw, through a telescope, moons revolving around Jupiter.

● **The change in ideas** that was brought about by Copernicus is known as the Copernican Revolution.

● **The Copernican Revolution** resulted in scientists and mathematicians rethinking the whole field of physics in the century after Copernicus' death.

▶ *Copernicus was the first to realize that the Sun is at the centre of the Solar System, and the planets orbit around it.*

Day and night

● **A full day** (daytime plus night-time) is the time taken for a planet or similar space object to spin around once on its axis.

● **We are most familiar with Earth's day**, which is approximately 24 hours.

● **Earth turns eastwards** – this means that the Sun rises in the east, as each part of the world spins round to face it.

● **As Earth turns**, the stars come back to the same place in the night sky every 23 hours, 56 minutes and 4.09 seconds. This is a sidereal day.

● **It takes 24 hours** for the Sun to come back to the same place in Earth's daytime sky. This is the solar day, and it is slightly longer than the sidereal day because Earth moves about one degree farther around the Sun each day.

● **For each planet**, the length of day depends on how fast it takes to spin or rotate once, and sometimes its speed in orbit.

● **Mercury spins on its axis** once in every 58.6 Earth days, but its solar day is 176 Earth days because its orbit is near the Sun.

● **A day on Jupiter** lasts less than ten Earth hours because Jupiter spins so fast.

● **A day on Mars** is 24.6 Earth hours.

◀ *When it is daylight on the half of Earth facing towards the Sun, it is night on the half of Earth facing away from it. As Earth rotates, the day and night halves shift gradually around the world.*

Early Moon landings

- **The Moon is the closest large space body** to Earth and so was the first to be visited by space probes, orbiters, landers and rovers.

- **At its closest**, the Moon is 362,600 km away, and at its farthest 405,400 km. This is an average journey of two to five days by most spacecraft.

- **Temperatures typically reach** 105°C at midday on the Moon but plunge to −155°C at night. Lander and rover spacecraft must be tested to withstand such extremes.

- **The first craft to reach the Moon** was Luna 1, a Soviet flyby mission, in January 1959.

- **Luna 1** was intended as an impactor, that is, to crash into the Moon. But a faulty rocket burn made it zoom past, on into space.

- **Luna 2** in September 1959 succeeded in impacting the Moon. It was the first spacecraft ever to reach another celestial body.

- **The first craft to soft-land** on the moon was Luna 9, in 1966. Its landing speed was 6 m/sec. It was the first to send back surface photographs of another space body.

- **The Apollo** missions began in 1961. Of the 11 crewed missions, only six managed to land on the Moon, the first in July 1969.

- **The first rover to move around** on the surface of the Moon was another Soviet mission, Lunokhod 1, in November 1970.

- **Lunokhod 1** was active for almost one year. It travelled a total of 10,000 m and sent back more than 20,000 photographic images.

◄ *This image shows a working model version of Lunokhod 1 being tested on Earth. The actual rover was 2.7 m long and had four cameras, soil-testers, a laser, and detectors for X-rays and cosmic rays.*

The size and shape of the Universe

- **Over the centuries** there have been many proposals for the size and shape of the Universe.

- **Ancient cultures** had many theories but often believed that the Earth was at its centre.

- **These historical ideas** included the belief that the Universe was a ball in the hand of a giant human.

- **Another myth** was that the Universe emerged from a giant egg, laid by a black-winged bird.

- **One modern suggestion** is that it has no measurable size and shape – it goes on forever in all directions.

- **Other proposals** for its shape include an irregular blob, a vast sphere or ball, a flattish slab with rounded corners, and a giant doughnut-like torus.

- **The Universe has four dimensions**, called space-time – three of normal space (up/down, left/right, forward/backward), plus time.

- **Calculations involving space-time** give three possible Universe shapes: flat like a sheet of paper (planar), closed like a ball (spherical) and open curves like the saddle of a horse (hyperbolic).

- **The observable Universe** is what we can detect and estimate from our observations and measurements.

- **Using these estimates** the Universe seems to be about 90 billion light years across, which is 855 billion trillion km.

- **Whatever its size and shape**, it is known that the Universe is expanding, and that its speed of expansion is increasing.

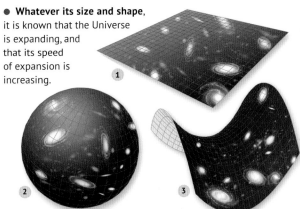

▶ *These images show three likely possible shapes for the Universe. One is the Flat Universe (1) – although it looks thin, its top-bottom distance is many billions of kilometres. The ball shape (2) is known as the Closed Universe. The saddle-like shape (3) with two sets of curves is called the Open Universe.*

Dark matter

● **Space matter that cannot be seen** is called dark matter. Unlike stars and galaxies, it does not give off light.

● **There is much more dark matter** in the Universe than bright. Some scientists think that 97 percent of all matter is dark.

● **Astronomers know about dark matter** because its gravity pulls on stars and galaxies, changing their orbits and the way they rotate.

● **The visible stars in the Milky Way** galaxy are only a thin part, embedded in a big ball of dark matter.

● **Dark matter is of two kinds** – the matter in galaxies (galactic) and the matter between them (intergalactic).

● **Galactic dark matter** may be similar to ordinary matter. However, it burned out early in the life of the Universe.

● **Intergalactic dark matter** is made up of Weakly Interacting Massive Particles (WIMPs).

● **Some WIMPs** are called cold, dark matter, because they are travelling slowly.

● **Other WIMPs** are called hot, dark matter because they are travelling very quickly.

● **The future of the Universe** may depend on how much dark matter there is. If there is too much, its gravity will eventually stop the Universe's expansion, and make it shrink again.

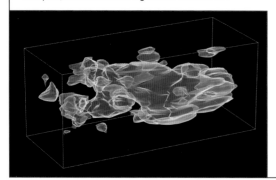

◄ *This 3D map shows how dark matter has formed clumps in the Universe. Since dark matter cannot be detected directly, the map is produced from the effects of gravity and mass on light, and other information gathered by the Hubble Space Telescope. Normal visible matter that forms planets and stars is concentrated in the densest areas of dark matter.*

Orbits

● **An orbit is the path** of one space object around a larger one, held by the pull of gravity. Moons orbit planets and planets orbit stars.

● **Orbits may be circular**, elliptical (oval) or parabolic (open). The orbits of the planets are elliptical.

● **An orbiting space object** is called a satellite.

● **The stars in the Milky Way galaxy** have the longest orbits. They can take up to 200 million years to orbit the galaxy's centre.

● **The force of momentum** keeps a satellite moving through space. The amount of momentum a satellite has depends on its mass and speed.

● **A satellite orbits** at the height where its momentum exactly balances the pull of gravity.

● **If the gravitational pull** is greater than a satellite's momentum, it falls in towards the larger space object.

● **If a satellite's momentum** is greater than the pull of gravity, it flies off into space.

● **The lower a satellite orbits**, the faster it must travel to stop it falling in towards the larger space object.

● **Conversely, the higher a satellite orbits**, the slower it can travel.

● **A satellite in an elliptical orbit** slows down at the farthest distance and speeds up as it gets nearer.

◄ *The planets in the Solar System all move round the Sun in elliptical orbits.*

Venus

- **The second planet from the Sun** is Venus. Its orbit makes it 107.5 million km away at its nearest to the Sun and 109 million km away at its furthest.

- **Venus shines like a star** in the night sky because its thick atmosphere reflects sunlight amazingly well.

- **This planet** is the brightest object in the sky, after the Sun and the Moon.

- **Venus is called the Evening Star** because it can often be seen from Earth in the evening, just after sunset. However, it can also be seen just before sunrise. It is visible at these times because it is quite close to the Sun.

- **The atmosphere of Venus** is mostly carbon dioxide gas with thick clouds containing sulphuric acid, given out by the planet's volcanoes.

- **Venus is the hottest planet** in the Solar System, with a surface temperature of more than 460°C.

- **Venus is so hot** because the carbon dioxide in its atmosphere traps the Sun's heat. This overheating is called a runaway greenhouse effect.

- **The thick clouds hide** its surface so well that until the Russian Venera 9 probe landed on the planet in 1975, it was not known what was beneath the clouds.

- **Atmospheric pressure on the surface of Venus** is 92 times greater than that on Earth.

▲ The thick clouds of Venus are made of carbon dioxide gas and sulphuric acid. They reflect sunlight and make the planet shine like a star. None of its atmosphere is transparent like Earth's, which makes it very difficult to see what is happening on the planet's surface.

- **A day on Venus** (the time it takes to spin around once on its axis) lasts 243 Earth days – longer than its year, which lasts 224.7 Earth days. As Venus rotates backwards, the Sun comes up twice during the planet's yearly orbit – once every 116.8 Earth days.

- **Venus is the nearest planet to Earth** in distance, as near as 38 million km, and in size, at 12,102 km in diameter.

▼ The 8-km-high volcano on the surface of Venus is called Maat Mons. Images have been created on computer using radar data collected by the Magellan orbiter, which reached Venus in the 1990s.

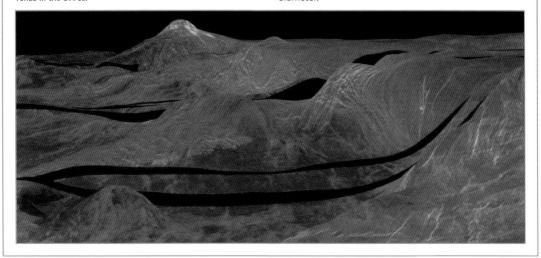

Galileo

● **Galileo Galilei** (1564–1642) was an Italian engineer, mathematician, astronomer, and scientific philosopher.

● **In 1581, Galileo observed how a lamp** in Pisa Cathedral, swinging like a pendulum, took the same time for a small swing as a large one. This began his interest in motion, forces and gravity.

● **Galileo's experiments with balls** rolling down slopes helped us understand how gravity makes things accelerate.

● **When the telescope was invented** in about 1608, Galileo made his own improved versions from 1609. He first looked at the Moon, Venus and Jupiter.

● **Galileo described his observations** of space in a book called *The Starry Messenger*, published in 1610.

● **Through his telescope**, Galileo saw that Jupiter has four moons. He also saw that Venus has phases, as Earth's Moon does.

◄ *Using his own-made telescopes, Galileo made many observations for the first time, such as the Milky Way consisting not of gas but of myriad stars.*

● **Jupiter's moons and Venus' phases** were the first visible evidence of Copernicus' theory.

● **Galileo supported the Copernican theory**, which was declared a heresy by the Catholic Church in 1616.

● **Threatened with torture**, Galileo was forced to deny that the Earth orbits the Sun. He was then kept under house arrest until he died.

● **In 1992**, 350 years after his death, the Catholic Church admitted it had been wrong and apologized for its treatment of Galileo.

● **Galileo has had more than** a dozen moons, asteroids, craters, spacecraft and other astronomical objects named in his honour.

Earth's formation

DID YOU KNOW?

Earth's rotational speed makes it bulge slightly in the middle.

● **The Solar System was created** when the gas cloud left over from a giant supernova explosion began to collapse in on itself and spin.

● **About 4.56 billion years ago**, only a vast, hot cloud of dust and gas circling a new star, the Sun, existed.

● **Earth probably began** when tiny pieces of space debris (called planetesimals) were pulled together by each other's gravity.

● **As Earth formed**, more space debris kept on smashing into it, adding new material. This debris included ice from the edges of the Solar System.

● **About 4.53 billion years ago**, a rock the size of Mars crashed into Earth. The debris joined together to form the Moon.

● **The collision that created** the Moon made Earth very hot. Radioactive decay heated Earth even more.

● **For a long time**, Earth's surface was a mass of erupting volcanoes.

● **Iron and nickel** melted and sank to form the core. Lighter materials, such as aluminium, oxygen and silicon, floated up and cooled to form the crust.

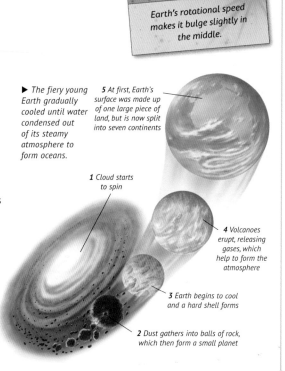

► *The fiery young Earth gradually cooled until water condensed out of its steamy atmosphere to form oceans.*

5 At first, Earth's surface was made up of one large piece of land, but is now split into seven continents

1 Cloud starts to spin

4 Volcanoes erupt, releasing gases, which help to form the atmosphere

3 Earth begins to cool and a hard shell forms

2 Dust gathers into balls of rock, which then form a small planet

Distances

● **The distance to the planets** is measured by bouncing radar signals off them and timing how long the signals take to get there and back.

● **The distance of nearby stars** is calculated by measuring the slight shift in the angle of each star in comparison to faraway stars, as the Earth orbits the Sun. This is called parallax shift.

● **Parallax shift can only be used** to measure nearby stars, so astronomers work out the distance to faraway stars and galaxies by comparing how bright they look with how bright they actually are.

● **For middle distance stars**, astronomers compare colour with brightness using the Hertzsprung-Russell (H-R) diagram. This is called main sequence fitting.

● **Beyond 30,000 light years**, stars are too faint for main sequence fitting to work.

● **Distances to nearby galaxies** can be estimated using 'standard candles' – stars that astronomers know the brightness of, such as supergiants and supernovae.

● **The expected brightness** of a galaxy that is too far away to pick out its stars may be measured using the Tully-Fisher technique, based on how fast galaxies spin.

● **Counting planetary nebulae** (the rings of gas left behind by supernovae explosions) is another way of measuring how bright a distant galaxy should be.

● **A third method** of calculating the brightness of a distant galaxy is to gauge how mottled it looks.

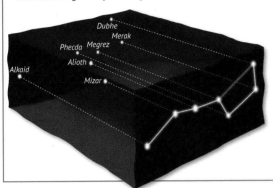

◀ *Seen from Earth, the stars in a constellation (such as this part of the Big Dipper) can appear to be all the same distance away. However, some may be much nearer than others.*

Spacecraft

● **There are three kinds of spacecraft** – artificial orbiting satellites, unmanned probes and manned spacecraft.

● **Almost all spacecraft have double hulls** (outer coverings) for protection against other space objects that may crash into them.

● **Manned spacecraft must also contain** air under pressure to prevent the crew's blood from boiling.

● **Manned spacecraft have life-support systems** that provide oxygen to breathe, usually mixed with nitrogen (as in ordinary air).

● **The carbon dioxide that the crew** breathes out is absorbed by chemicals such as zeolite or lithium hydroxide. The air is refreshed with oxygen made by splitting water (H_2O) using electricity.

● **Spacecraft windows have special filters** to shield astronauts from the Sun's dangerous ultraviolet rays.

● **Radiators on the outside** of the spacecraft remove excess heat from electrical equipment and the crew's bodies.

● **Astronauts use a waterproof shower** that sprays water from all sides and then removes the waste water.

● **Spacecraft toilets** need to get rid of waste in low gravity conditions. Astronauts have to sit on a device that sucks away the waste. Solid waste is dried and returned to Earth.

◀ *Between 1981 and 2011 the US space shuttles, the first and only reusable spacecraft so far, made 135 manned space flights into orbit and back to Earth.*

Earth

● **The third planet from the Sun** is our home planet, Earth. Its average distance from the Sun is 149.6 million km, which is also 1 AU (astronomical unit).

● **The farthest point** of Earth's orbit from the Sun (aphelion) is 151.9 million km, and the nearest (perihelion) is 147.1 million km.

● **Earth is the fifth largest planet** in the Solar System, with a diameter of 12,756 km and a circumference of 40,075 km at the Equator.

● **Along with Mercury, Venus and Mars,** Earth is one of four rocky or terrestrial planets. It is made mostly of rock, with a core of iron and nickel.

● **No other planet in the Solar System** has liquid water on its surface, making Earth uniquely suitable for life.

● **Earth's atmosphere** is a blanket of gases, which we call air, that extends from the planet's surface up to a height of about 10,000 km.

● **The atmosphere is mainly harmless nitrogen** and life-giving oxygen. This oxygen has been made and maintained by plants over billions of years.

● **Near Earth's surface,** our atmosphere consists of 78 percent nitrogen, 21 percent oxygen and small amounts of argon, carbon dioxide and other gases, together with a variable amount of water vapour.

▲ *The International Space Station (ISS) is the largest man-made satellite orbiting Earth. A research lab and observatory, the ISS has had visitors from 15 different countries on Earth.*

● **The air gets progressively thinner** with increasing altitude and above 7000 m there is not enough oxygen for people to breathe.

● **A magnetic field,** stretching 60,000 km out into space, protects Earth from the Sun's radiation.

● **Like the other Solar System planets,** Earth formed about 4.56 billion years ago.

● **Earth's orbit** around the Sun is 940 million km in length and takes 365.242 days.

● **Although Earth is tilted** at an angle of 23.5 degrees, it orbits the Sun on a level plane – the plane of the ecliptic. This is like a giant tabletop on which all the planets move.

● **The Earth is made up** of the same basic materials as meteorites and the other rocky planets – mostly iron (35 percent), oxygen (28 percent), silicon (17 percent), magnesium (15 percent) and nickel (2.7 percent).

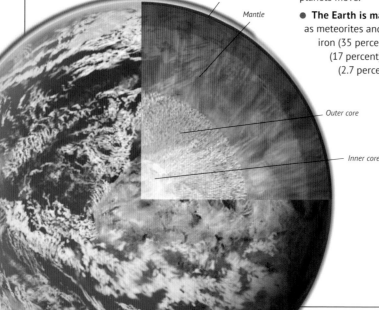

Crust

Mantle

Outer core

Inner core

◀ *The inner core at Earth's centre is made of iron. It is very hot and keeps the outer core as a liquid. Outside this is the mantle, made of thick rock. The thin surface layer is called the crust.*

DID YOU KNOW?

More than 70 percent of the Earth's surface is underwater.

Comets

- **Bright objects with long tails**, comets can sometimes be seen glowing in the night sky – and bright ones can even be seen by day.

- **They may look spectacular**, but most comets are balls of ice, dust and rocky fragments, usually only a few kilometres in diameter.

- **Many comets orbit the Sun**, but their orbits are very long and they spend most of the time in the far reaches of the Solar System. They are seen when their orbits bring them close to the Sun for a few weeks.

- **A comet's tail forms** as it nears the Sun and its head, or nucleus, begins to warm up and outgas (eject gases, vapours and particles).

- **The tail is a vast plume** of gas millions of kilometres long, blown by the solar wind; it shines as sunlight catches it. There may also be a thin atmosphere or coma around the nucleus.

- **Periodic comets** appear at regular intervals. Short-period comets come from the Kuiper Belt and long-period ones come from the Oort Cloud.

- **Some comets reach speeds** of 2 million km/h as they near the Sun. Far from the Sun, they slow down to about 1000 km/h.

- **Comet McNaught** (C/2006 P1) in 2007 was the brightest comet for almost half a century. It was non-periodic, which means it is unlikely to be seen again, or at least, not for many centuries.

- **The Shoemaker-Levy 9 comet** smashed into Jupiter in July 1994, with the biggest space impact ever witnessed, especially by the Galileo space probe. This was an unusual comet in that it orbited Jupiter, not the Sun. It had probably been captured by Jupiter's gravity a few decades earlier.

◄ *Comet West, which visited the Sun in 1976, was bright enough to see in daylight. Its white dust tail and blue gas tail do not trail behind but always point away from the Sun.*

Giant stars

- **Giant stars** are 10 to 100 times as big as the Sun, and 10 to 1000 times as bright.

- **Blue giants are middle-aged stars** that are beginning to run out of hydrogen to burn, which makes them swell and burn blue and hotter than a young star.

- **Red giants are stars** that have swollen 10 to 100 times their former size, as they reach their last stages and their outer gas layers cool and expand.

- **Red giants have burned** all their hydrogen, and so burn helium, fusing (joining) helium atoms to make carbon.

- **The biggest stars** continue to swell after they become red giants. They then grow into supergiants.

- **Supergiant stars are up to 500 times** as big as the Sun.

- **Pressure in the centre** of a supergiant is enough to fuse carbon atoms together to make the metallic chemical element iron.

- **Much of the iron in the Universe** was made in the hearts of supergiant stars.

- **There is a limit to the brightness** of supergiants, so they can be used as distance markers by comparing how bright they look from Earth to how bright they actually are.

- **Supergiant stars** eventually collapse and explode as supernovae.

▶ *Red giant stars expand and eject or 'throw off' matter in cloud-like layers. Our own Sun is about the right size to do this, probably in six or seven billion years, when it will have two-thirds of its current mass – and enlarge to swallow Earth and perhaps Mars.*

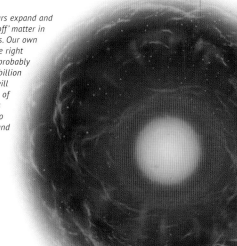

Eclipses

- **When one space object**, such as the Moon, blocks out the light from another, such as the Sun, an eclipse occurs.

- **A lunar eclipse** is when the Moon travels behind Earth, and into Earth's shadow (Earth is between the Moon and the Sun).

- **Lunar eclipses happen** about once or twice a year and last only a few hours.

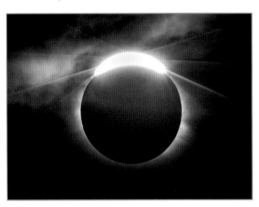

- **In a total lunar eclipse**, the Moon turns rust-red.

- **Lunar eclipses can be seen** from anywhere on the half of Earth facing the Moon.

- **A solar eclipse** is when the Moon comes between Earth and the Sun, casting a shadow up to 270 km wide on to Earth's surface.

- **In a total eclipse of the Sun**, the Moon passes directly in front of the Sun, completely covering it so that only its corona can be seen.

- **There are at least two solar eclipses every year**, but they are only visible from a narrow strip of the world.

- **Totality is when the Moon** blocks out the face of the Sun completely. It only lasts for a few minutes.

- **Solar eclipses are possible** because the Moon is 400 times smaller than the Sun, and is also 400 times closer to Earth. This means the Sun and the Moon appear to be much the same size in the sky.

◀ This solar eclipse in Kenya shows the 'diamond ring' effect, when only one small area of sunlight passes the edge of the Moon, due to its uneven surface, and reaches Earth.

Star brightness

- **Star brightness is measured** on a scale of magnitude that was first devised in 150 BC by the Greek astronomer Hipparchus.

- **The brightest star** that Hipparchus could see was Antares, and he described it as magnitude 1. He described the faintest star he could see as magnitude 6.

- **Using telescopes and binoculars**, astronomers can now see much fainter stars than Hipparchus could.

- **The apparent or relative magnitude scale** describes how bright a star looks from Earth compared to other stars. The further away a star is, the dimmer it looks and the bigger its apparent magnitude is, regardless of how bright it really is.

- **Good binoculars show** apparent magnitude 9 stars, and a home telescope apparent magnitude 10 stars.

- **Brighter stars than Antares** have been identified with apparent magnitudes of less than 1, and even minus numbers. Betelgeuse averages 0.4, Vega 0.03, Alpha Centauri −0.27 and Canopus −0.72.

- **The brightest star visible** from Earth (excluding the Sun) is Sirius, the Dog Star, with a magnitude of −1.46.

▲ To estimate a star's magnitude, its brightness is compared to two stars with known magnitude – one star a little brighter and one a little dimmer.

- **A star's absolute magnitude** describes how bright a star actually is, seen from a standard distance of 32.6 light years, or 10 parsecs.

- **The star Rigel** is more than 200,000 times brighter than the Sun. However, as it is 850 light years away, it looks much dimmer. Rigel's apparent magnitude is 0.13, its absolute magnitude −7.9. This compares with −26.7 and 4.8 for the Sun.

DID YOU KNOW?

The Pistol Star, one of our galaxy's brightest, is absolute magnitude −10.8. But at 25,000 light years away its apparent magnitude is only 6.5.

Herschel

● **William Herschel** (1738–1822) was a German musician who became the King's astronomer in England and built his own powerful telescopes.

● **Until Herschel's time**, astronomers thought that there were only six planets, including Earth, orbiting the Sun.

● **The other five known planets** at that time were Mercury, Venus, Mars, Jupiter and Saturn.

● **Uranus, the seventh planet**, was discovered by William Herschel in 1781.

● **At first Herschel thought** that the dot of light he could see through his telescope was a nebula or comet. When he looked again four days later, it had moved against the background of stars, which meant it must be in the Solar System. He realized that it was a new planet.

● **He wanted to name** the planet George, after King George III, but Uranus was eventually chosen, after the ancient Greek god of the sky.

● **Herschel's sister, Caroline** (1750–1848), was his partner in his discoveries. She was also a great astronomer who discovered eight comets and produced excellent catalogues of stars and nebulae.

● **John, Herschel's son**, catalogued the stars of the Southern Hemisphere.

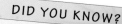

DID YOU KNOW?

Herschel added to his sister's catalogues of nebulae. His 1820 version listed more than 5000 objects.

◄ *Herschel built many telescopes. The biggest was the 'Great 40-foot Telescope' in Slough, Berkshire, UK.*

How rockets work

● **A space launch vehicle** is sometimes called a rocket, but the rocket engine is only one part of this huge and powerful machine.

● **Hot gases** that drive a rocket engine and its launch vehicle upwards are produced when the engine burns propellant.

● **Rocket propellants** come in two parts – a fuel and an oxidizer.

▼ *A US J-2X rocket engine is tested to check its gimbals – swivels or pivots that tilt the nozzle outlet to alter the direction of the thrust and keep the rocket on course.*

● **The fuel is a chemical that burns** or combusts to produce vast amounts of hot gases. These blast out of the engine to provide the pushing force or thrust.

● **The oxidizer** is a chemical that is necessary for the fuel to burn. Combustion is a chemical reaction which needs oxygen. There is no oxygen (or much else) in space, so rocket engines need to take their own supplies.

● **In a solid fuel rocket**, the fuel and oxidizer are chemicals mixed together to make a rubbery substance. Once lit or ignited, it usually burns until it runs out, with little control.

● **In a liquid fuel rocket**, however, the fuel and oxidizer are in liquid form and their flow can be controlled by tap-like valves.

● **Liquid fuel** is sometimes liquid hydrogen, and it is typically used in big rockets. Another form is kerosene or paraffin (as used in homes, lamps and stoves).

● **The oxidizer** may be liquid oxygen, called 'LOx' for short. Other substances that contain a large amount of oxygen include nitrogen tetroxide and hydrogen peroxide.

Satellites

- **Objects that orbit planets** and other space objects are called satellites.

- **Moons are natural satellites** of planets, while planets are natural satellites of their star, such as Earth around the Sun.

- **Spacecraft that orbit Earth**, or the Moon, or another planet or moon, or even an asteroid or a comet, are known as artificial satellites.

- **The first artificial satellite** was Sputnik 1, launched on 4 October 1957.

- **Over 50 artificial satellites** are now launched every year. A few of them are space telescopes or observatories.

- **Navigation satellites** (navsats), such as the 32 satellites involved in the Global Positioning System (GPS), are used by people in ships, planes and vehicles to work out where they are.

- **Communications satellites** (comsats) relay – receive and send on – communications as radio waves or microwaves, including phone calls, computer data, TV and radio, and internet traffic.

- **Weather (meteorological) satellites** (meteosats) measure clouds, rain, snow, temperature, air pressure, waves and other aspects of weather and climate.

- **Survey satellites** measure and photograph Earth's surface in great detail, monitoring events such as earthquakes and tsunamis.

- **Spy satellites** watch developments such as missile movements and listen into all kinds of communications.

◀ *The USA launched five THEMIS satellites in 2007 to study the Earth's magnetic field. Each weighed about 78 kg and all five were packed into the top of a Delta II launcher, inside the streamlined nose cone or fairing.*

Hipparchus

- **Hipparchus of Nicaea** was a Greek astronomer who lived in the 2nd century BC, and died in 127 BC.

- **The framework for astronomy** was created by Hipparchus.

- **Hipparchus' ideas** were almost lost until they were rescued by Greek astronomer, Ptolemy (90–168 AD). They were developed into a system that lasted 1500 years until they were overthrown by the ideas of Copernicus (1473–1543).

- **Ancient Babylonian** records brought back by Alexander the Great from his conquests helped Hipparchus to make his observations of the stars.

- **Hipparchus** was the first astronomer to measure Earth's distance to the Sun.

- **He also made an early star list**, and was the first to identify the constellations systematically and to assess stars in terms of magnitude.

DID YOU KNOW?

The mathematics of trigonometry is thought to have been invented by Hipparchus.

- **Hipparchus discovered** that the positions of the stars on the equinoxes (around 21 March and 21 September) slowly shift around, taking 26,000 years to return to their original place. This is known as precession, due to a slight 'wobble' in the Earth's axis of rotation.

- **Hipparchus carried out** his observations from the Greek island of Rhodes.

- **He was the first** to pinpoint the geographical position of places by latitude and longitude.

◀ *Some of Hipparchus' knowledge of stars came from the Sumerians, who wrote on clay tablets.*

Mars

● **The nearest planet to Earth** after Venus is Mars. It has a daytime temperature and atmosphere more like Earth's than any other planet.

● **Surface temperatures on Mars** range from −140°C in the winter polar regions at night to more than 30°C at the sunny summer equator by day.

● **Mars is called the 'Red Planet'** because it is rust-red in colour. This comes from oxidized (rusted) iron found in its soil.

● **The fourth planet out from the Sun**, Mars orbits at an average distance of 227.9 million km. It takes 687 Earth days to complete its orbit – one Martian year.

● **Mars is 6752 km in diameter** and spins around on its axis once every 24.62 Earth hours. This is almost the same amount of time that Earth takes to rotate once.

● **Olympus Mons**, Mars' volcano, is the biggest in the Solar System. It covers the same area as the UK and is three times higher than Mount Everest.

● **The surface of Mars** is dry, rocky and covered in dust. The wind blows up huge dust storms, sometimes covering the whole planet. Dust devils, similar to small tornadoes, often race across the surface of Mars.

● **Almost all the water on Mars** is frozen into ice. There are ice caps at the poles, and thin clouds made of ice crystals in the sky. Orbiting spacecraft have found ice hidden beneath Mars' surface.

● **Apart from small amounts** of ice crystals, the atmosphere of Mars is almost all carbon dioxide, with about two percent of the gas argon.

▲ *Mars rovers move around the planet's surface exploring its geology. They each have several cameras and regularly transmit data back to Earth.*

● **Mars was probably warmer** and wetter in the past. Spacecraft have spotted many dried-up riverbeds, gullies and lake beds, and the Mars rovers, Spirit, Opportunity and Curiosity, have found minerals that normally form in water.

▶ *Mars is the best known planet besides Earth. Studies have revealed a planet with a surface like a red, rocky desert – but there is also plenty of evidence that Mars was not always so desert-like.*

Light

- **Light**, the fastest thing in the Universe, travels in straight lines.
- **As they pass from one material** to another, light rays change direction. This is called refraction.
- **Colours are different wavelengths** of light.
- **The longest light waves** that can be seen are red, and the shortest are violet.
- **Light is a form** of electromagnetic radiation.
- **Faint light from very distant stars** is often recorded by sensors called CCDs. These count photons from the star as they arrive and build up a picture of the star over a long period of time.

- **The electromagnetic spectrum** includes radio waves, ultraviolet light and X-rays. Visible light is the only part of the spectrum that can be seen by the human eye.
- **Most light is given out by atoms**, and atoms give out light when 'excited', perhaps by radiation.

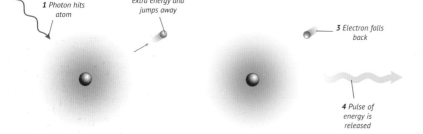

1 Photon hits atom

2 Electron receives extra energy and jumps away

3 Electron falls back

4 Pulse of energy is released

◀ *Light can be viewed as small packets of energy called photons. When a photon hits an atom, energy is produced as light, X-rays or radio waves.*

Magnetosphere

- **Earth's magnetosphere** is the region of space within the influence of Earth's magnetic field. The magnetosphere shields Earth from most of the effects of the solar wind.
- **Despite its name**, the magnetosphere is not spherical. Instead it is shaped like an elongated teardrop.
- **The sunward edge** of the magnetosphere is called the magnetopause and is located 70,000 km from Earth.
- **Immediately to the sunward side** is a shock wave (which is called the bow shock) caused by the solar wind being deflected by the magnetopause.
- **On the side away** from the Sun, the magnetosphere trails away in what is known as the magnetotail.
- **Although the magnetosphere deflects** most of the charged particles coming from the Sun and cosmic rays, some get through and become concentrated in two regions of radiation known as the Van Allen belts.
- **Venus and Mars** are the only planets that do not have their own magnetosphere.
- **Jupiter has by far** the largest magnetosphere and its magnetopause is located about 6 million km from the planet's surface.
- **The magnetism of Earth's Moon** is too weak to produce a magnetosphere, but two of Jupiter's moons, Io and Ganymede, have them.
- **Stars also produce** magnetic fields and have magnetospheres. The Sun's magnetosphere is called the heliosphere.

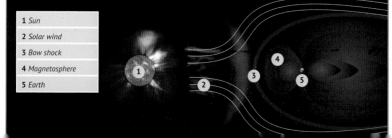

| 1 Sun |
| 2 Solar wind |
| 3 Bow shock |
| 4 Magnetosphere |
| 5 Earth |

◀ *Earth's magnetosphere (shown in blue, with the bow shock in purple) is shaped by the constant pressure of the solar wind.*

Atmosphere

- **The gases held around a planet** or other large space object by its gravity make up its atmosphere.

- **Every planet in the Solar System** has an atmosphere.

- **Each atmosphere** is very different. Earth's atmosphere is the only one that humans can breathe.

- **Atmospheres are not fixed**, but can change rapidly.

- **Moons are generally too small** and their gravity is too weak to have an atmosphere. However, some moons have one, including Saturn's huge moon Titan.

- **The primordial (earliest) atmospheres** came from the cloud of gas and dust surrounding the young Sun.

- **If Earth and the other rocky planets** had primordial atmospheres, they were stripped away by solar wind.

- **Earth's present atmosphere** was first formed from gases pouring out of volcanoes. It has since evolved, becoming enriched with oxygen from plant activity.

- **The atmosphere of Mars** is similar to that of Venus, made mainly of carbon monoxide, but it is much sparser or thinner than that of Venus.

- **Jupiter's atmosphere** is partly primordial, but it has been altered by the Sun's radiation, and the planet's own internal heat and lightning storms.

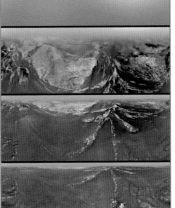

◀ In 2005, the lander Huygens took these images when it floated down through the hazy atmosphere of Saturn's moon Titan, which consists almost entirely of nitrogen with some methane.

DID YOU KNOW?

The oxygen in Earth's atmosphere was formed entirely by plants and microscopic blue-green algae (cyanobacteria).

Cosmic rays

- **Streams of high-energy particles** that strike Earth's atmosphere are called cosmic rays.

- **The lowest-energy cosmic rays** come from the Sun, or are Galactic Cosmic Rays (GCRs) from outside the Solar System.

- **Medium-energy cosmic rays** come from sources within the Milky Way, including powerful supernovae explosions.

- **The highest-energy cosmic rays** may come from outside the Milky Way.

- **About 90 percent of GCRs** are the nuclei of hydrogen atoms stripped of their electron.

- **Most other GCRs** are helium and heavier nuclei, but there are also tiny positrons, electrons and neutrinos.

- **Neutrinos are so small** that they pass almost straight through the Earth without stopping.

- **The study of cosmic rays** provided scientists with most of their early knowledge about high-energy particles.

- **On Earth**, these particles can only be made in huge machines called particle accelerators.

- **Most cosmic rays** are deflected (pushed aside) by Earth's magnetic field or collide with particles in the atmosphere long before they reach the ground.

◀ The Crab Nebula is the result of a supernova or exploding star. Its existence was first written about in 1054. In 1951, it was identified as a powerful source of cosmic rays.

Jupiter

- **The biggest planet in the Solar System,** Jupiter is two-and-a-half times as heavy as all the other planets in our Solar System put together.

- **Jupiter has no surface** for spacecraft to land on because it is made mostly of hydrogen and helium gas. The massive pull of Jupiter's gravity squeezes the hydrogen so hard that it is actually a liquid or even semi-solid at the planet's centre or core.

- **Towards Jupiter's core**, immense pressure makes the liquid hydrogen behave like a metal.

- **The ancient Greeks** originally named the planet Zeus after the king of their gods. Jupiter was the Roman name for Zeus.

- **Jupiter spins around** in only 9.92 Earth hours, which means that its equator is moving at more than 45,000 km/h.

- **It takes Jupiter 11.87 Earth years** to orbit the Sun, at an average speed of 46,800 km/h. Coupled with its very short day, this means one Jovian year lasts almost 10,500 Jovian days.

- **The middle, or equator**, of Jupiter bulges out because the planet spins so fast. It churns up the planet's metal core and generates a magnetic field ten times stronger than Earth's.

- **Jupiter has a Great Red Spot** – a huge swirl of red clouds, measuring more than 40,000 km across. The scientist Robert Hooke first noticed the spot in 1644.

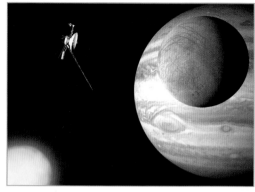

▲ This artist's impression shows a Voyager probe taking pictures of Europa, the fourth largest of Jupiter's 60-plus moons.

- **Jupiter is so big that the pressure** at its core makes it very hot. The planet gives out heat, but not enough to make it glow. If it were 70–100 times bigger, nuclear reactions would occur at its core and turn it into a star.

- **Eight spacecraft** have visited Jupiter. The first were Pioneer 10 and Pioneer 11 and Voyager 1 and Voyager 2, all in the 1970s. The only probe to orbit Jupiter was the US-German Galileo, which arrived in 1995 after a six-year voyage from Earth.

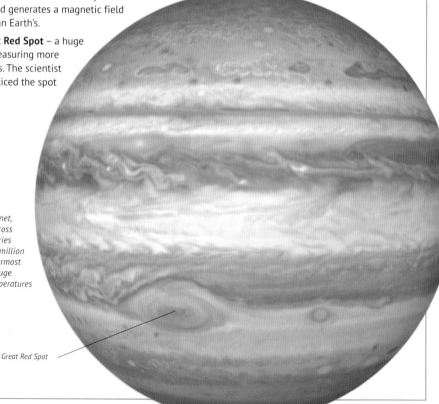

▶ Jupiter is a gigantic planet, measuring 142,984 km across at the equator. Its orbit varies between 740.9 and 815.7 million km from the Sun. The outermost layer is often pierced by huge lightning flashes, and temperatures here plunge to –150°C.

Great Red Spot

Space probes

- **Space can be explored using probes** – unmanned, automatic, robotic, computer-controlled spacecraft.

- **Some probes simply make a flyby** or close approach of a space object. Others, called orbiters, go into orbit around it. Some, known as landers, make a soft touchdown on the surface. A few, called rovers, are able to move around on the surface.

- **The first successful planetary probe** was the USA's Mariner 2, which flew past Venus in 1962.

- **In 1974**, Mariner 10 made a flyby of Mercury.

- **Viking 1 and 2 landed** on Mars in 1976.

- **Voyager 2 has flown** 10 billion km and is heading out of the Solar System after passing close to Jupiter (1979), Saturn (1981), Uranus (1986) and Neptune (1989).

- **To save fuel on journeys** to distant planets, space probes may use a nearby planet's gravity to catapult them on their way. This is called a slingshot.

- **Various orbiters** have visited Venus and Mars, mapping their surfaces in great detail.

- **Rovers have explored** the surface of the Moon and Mars.

▲ *Japan's Hayabusa probe, launched in 2003, had several setbacks on its immense mission. But it also scored several 'firsts', including bringing samples of asteroid Itokawa back to Earth in 2010.*

- **Landers have reached the Moon**, Venus, Mars, Saturn's moon Titan, asteroids Eros and Itokawa, and comet Churyumov–Gerasimenko.

- **The New Horizons probe** was launched in 2006 and reached Pluto in 2015.

Hubble Space Telescope

DID YOU KNOW?

The HST will gradually be replaced by the James Webb Space Telescope probably some time around 2020.

- **The Hubble Space Telescope**, HST, has advanced astronomy and space science more than almost any other single piece of equipment.

- **It is named after** US astronomer Edwin Hubble, and has taken many thousands of images.

- **Hubble was launched** by the space shuttle *Discovery* in 1990 and continues to orbit every 95.6 minutes at an average height of 555 km above sea level.

- **The HST weighs** 11 tonnes and is 13.2 m long and 4.2 m wide.

- **It detects mainly visible light** and the two kinds of radiation either side of those wavelengths, being near infrared (slightly longer waves) and near ultraviolet (shorter).

- **It has a reflecting** telescope with a mirror 2.4 m across.

- **When first used**, astronomers noticed that the images being sent back were slightly blurred. It was discovered that the main mirror had been made slightly to the wrong shape, by about 0.002 mm (2 micrometres). The telescope was in effect 'short-sighted'.

- **In 1993**, during space shuttle mission STS–61, *Endeavour* captured the HST and made alterations needing five long spacewalks. The changes were all successful and the HST could now see into the depths of the Universe.

- **There were another** four servicing missions to the HST, the last in 2009, to install updated cameras and other equipment.

◄ *Shuttle mission STS-61 carried out the first update of the Hubble Space Telescope, in particular to cure its 'short sight'. Here astronaut Story Musgrave on the robot arm installs new magnetometers, with Jeffrey Hoffman in the shuttle's payload bay.*

Meteors

- **Meteoroids are billions** of small rocks that hurtle around the Solar System. Most are no bigger than a pea but a few are several metres across.

- **Most meteoroids that encounter Earth** are very small and burn up when they enter Earth's atmosphere.

- **Streaks of light** seen in the night sky are these burning meteoroids leaving fiery trails, which are known as meteors.

- **The streaks of light** are also called shooting stars, but they have nothing to do with stars.

- **Meteor showers are bursts** of dozens or hundreds of burn-up trails or meteors, often occurring as Earth passes through a dust trail left by an earlier comet.

- **Meteor showers** are named after the constellations they seem to come from, in a radiating pattern like fireworks.

▲ Most meteoroids that enter Earth's atmosphere burn up in the stratosphere to produce bright streaks of light, called meteors or shooting stars.

- **The heaviest showers** are the Quadrantids (3–4 January), the Perseids (12 August) and the Geminids (13 December).

- **Meteorites are larger space rocks** that penetrate through Earth's atmosphere and reach the ground.

- **The largest known Earth meteorite** weighs some 60 tonnes, and is still lying where it fell in Hoba West in Namibia, Africa.

Pulsars

- **A pulsar is a neutron star** that spins rapidly, beaming out regular pulses of radio waves.

- **The first pulsar** was detected by Cambridge astronomer, Jocelyn Bell Burnell (1943–), in 1967.

- **At first, astronomers thought** the regular pulses might be signals from aliens, and pulsars were jokingly called LGMs (Little Green Men).

- **Most pulsars send** their radio pulse about once a second. The slowest pulse is every 10 seconds or more, and the fastest every 1.4 milliseconds, that is, about 715 times per second.

- **As it gets older**, the pulse rate of a pulsar usually slows down.

- **The Crab pulsar** slows by a millionth of a second a day.

- **More than 1500 pulsars** are now known, but there may be 200,000 active in the Milky Way.

- **Pulsars probably result** from a supernova explosion – that is why most are found in the flat disc of the Milky Way, where supernovae occur.

- **Pulsars are not found** in the same place as supernovae because they form after the debris from the explosion has spread into space.

- **Some pulsars emit X-rays**, such as Centaurus X-3 in the constellation Centaurus, confirmed in 1971.

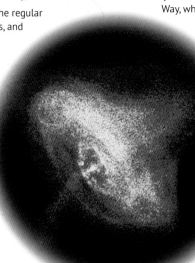

◄ The Crab Nebula is the remnants of a stellar explosion. In this image, taken by the Chandra X-Ray Observatory, the central pulsar is clearly shown.

Elements

- **The basic pure substances** of the Universe are chemical elements. There are no simpler natural substances.

- **An element is formed** entirely of atoms that contain the same number of protons in their nuclei. For example, all oxygen atoms have eight protons.

- **The simplest and lightest elements**, hydrogen and helium, formed very early in the history of the Universe.

- **Other elements form** as the nuclei of light atoms join by the process of nuclear fusion.

- **Nuclear fusion of atoms** happens deep inside stars, especially at the end of their lives.

- **Lighter elements**, such as oxygen and carbon, are the first to form.

- **Helium nuclei fuse** with oxygen and neon atoms to form larger atoms, such as those of the elements silicon, magnesium and calcium.

- **Heavier atoms form** especially when supergiant stars reach the end of their life and collapse, boosting the gravity, pressure and temperature in their core as they explode, as supernovae.

Hydrogen atom

Single electron

Nucleus with single proton

Carbon atom

Nucleus with 6 protons and 6 neutrons

6 electrons

Oxygen atom

8 protons

8 neutrons

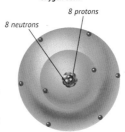

▲ *All the atoms that make up a single element have the same number of protons. All atoms except those of the simplest form of hydrogen also contain neutrons (particles with no electric charge) in their nucleus. Electrons circle the nucleus at different distances depending on how much energy they have.*

Kepler

- **German astronomer Johannes Kepler** (1571–1630) discovered the basic rules that govern the way in which the planets move.

- **Kepler got his ideas** from studying the movement of Mars.

- **Before Kepler's discoveries**, it was thought that the planets moved in circles.

- **Kepler discovered** that the true shape of the planets' orbits is elliptical (a type of oval). This is Kepler's first law.

- **Kepler's second law** is that the speed of a planet through space varies according to its distance from the Sun.

- **A planet moves fastest** when its orbit brings it nearest to the Sun. This point is known as its perihelion. It moves slowest when it is furthest from the Sun, called its aphelion.

- **Kepler's third law** concerns a planet's period, that is, the time it takes to complete its full orbit of the Sun – this is the planet's year. This depends on its distance from the Sun.

- **Kepler's third law also states** that the square of a planet's period is proportional to the cube of its average distance from the Sun.

- **Kepler also believed** that the planets made music as they moved, he called this the music of the spheres.

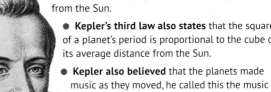

◀ *Despite almost losing his eyesight and the use of his hands through smallpox at the age of three, Johannes Kepler became an assistant to the great Danish astronomer Tycho Brahe, and took over his work when Brahe died.*

Space shuttle

- **A reusable spacecraft**, the space shuttle was made up of a 37.2-m-long orbiter with three main engines, two big Solid Rocket Boosters (SRBs) and a huge external fuel tank.

- **The first shuttle flight** was in April 1981.

- **The shuttle orbiter was launched** into space upright on the SRBs, which fell away to be collected for reuse. When the mission was over, the orbiter landed on a runway like a glider.

- **The orbiter only went as high** as a near-Earth orbit, up to 600 km above the Earth.

▶ *In orbit, the space shuttle circled Earth at a speed of about 28,000 km/h. Its 18-m-long cargo bay could carry a 25,000-kg load.*

Spacelab, a laboratory where the crew carried out experiments

Access tunnel from crew cabin to Spacelab

- **A basic mission** lasted seven days, and the maximum crew was eight.

- **The crew** used a remote manipulator arm to catch satellites for repair.

- **The shuttle programme** was brought to a temporary halt in 1986 when *Challenger* exploded shortly after launch, killing its crew of seven.

- **On 1 February 2003**, *Columbia* broke up when re-entering the atmosphere after a mission, killing the crew. The next shuttle flight was not until 2006.

- **Each shuttle flight** had a mission number. For example, in July 2011, STS–135 (for Space Transportation System) delivered two modules to the International Space Station.

- **The 135th mission**, STS–135 was the last. There are no plans to develop another reusable spacecraft.

Flight deck with pilot's controls

Crew quarters where astronauts ate, slept and worked

Moons

- **Moons are the natural satellites** of planets. Most are small rock globes or lumps that continually orbit the planet, held in place by the planet's gravity.

- **There are more than 150 known planetary moons** in the Solar System, and more that orbit dwarf planets and asteroids.

- **Every planet in the Solar System** has a moon, apart from Mercury and Venus, the two planets nearest to the Sun.

- **New moons are frequently discovered**, as new space probes study the distant planets in more detail, and as the distance we can see using telescopes increases due to technological improvements.

- **Several moons have atmospheres**, including Saturn's moon Titan, Jupiter's Io, and Neptune's Triton.

- **Jupiter's moon Ganymede** is the largest moon in the Solar System, measuring more than 5260 km across – half as wide again as Earth's Moon.

- **Second largest** is Saturn's moon Titan, at 5160 km in diameter. Icy cold, Titan is the only moon with a thick atmosphere of nitrogen gas.

- **The smallest moons** are icy lumps just 1 or 2 km across, rather like asteroids.

- **Saturn's moon Iapetus** is very pale on one side and almost black on the other.

- **Saturn's moon Enceladus** is only 500 km across, and its icy surface reflects almost all the sunlight.

▶ *Enceladus orbits about 240,000 km from Saturn. It is a very active moon with jets and geysers of water vapour and other gases, crystals and various frozen particles. It probably has a hidden ocean of liquid water under the surface.*

Saturn

● **The second biggest planet** in the Solar System is Saturn. It is 764 times as big in volume as Earth and measures an average of 116,465 km in diameter.

● **Saturn takes 29.5 Earth years** to travel around the Sun – that is, Saturn's year is 29.5 Earth years.

● **The planet's average distance from the Sun** is 1.43 billion km and its complete orbit is a journey of more than 4.5 billion km, at an average speed of 34,900 km/h.

● **Winds ten times stronger** than a hurricane on Earth swirl around Saturn's equator, reaching speeds of up to 1800 km/h.

● **Saturn is named after Saturnus**, the ancient Roman god of harvest. He was celebrated in the Roman festival of Saturnalia.

● **Saturn is made up of gases and liquids**, almost entirely hydrogen and helium. Only in the planet's very small core is there any solid material.

● **Since Saturn is so big**, the pressure deep inside is enough to turn hydrogen gas into a liquid. Further down, extreme pressure makes the liquid hydrogen act like a metal.

● **The surface of Saturn appears** smooth because the clouds are hidden under a layer of haze. However, the Cassini probe spotted lightning storms and a huge swirling storm near the pole.

● **Saturn is one** of the fastest-spinning planets. Despite its size, it rotates in just 10.55 Earth hours. This means that its middle, or equator, moves at over 35,000 km/h.

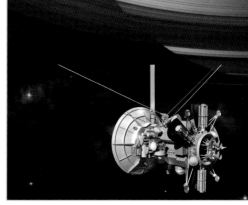

▲ *The Cassini space probe has been studying Saturn since arriving there in 2004.*

● **Like Jupiter**, Saturn's fast rotation makes it bulge at the equator. This means its diameter here is 120,540 km, while the diameter from pole to pole is 108,720 km – smaller by almost the width of the Earth.

● **Saturn has more than** 60 officially described moons, with more than 50 named.

● **The largest of these** is Titan, which is the second biggest moon in the whole Solar System at 5150 km across – half as much again as Earth's Moon.

▼ *Saturn is almost as big as Jupiter, and made largely of liquid hydrogen and helium. It has a smooth surface (clouds of ammonia) and a shimmering halo of rings.*

Saturn's rings are made of many millions of tiny, ice-coated rock fragments

DID YOU KNOW?

Saturn's density is so low that it would float in water.

Space stations

- **A space station** is a man-made structure in space designed for humans (or perhaps animals) to survive for at least days, usually months, even years.

- **Most space stations are designed** to orbit a planet. The only ones built and inhabited so far orbit Earth.

- **There is neither an up nor a down** in a space station, since objects and people are weightless due to the lack of gravity.

- **The first Earth space station** was the *Soviet Salyut 1*, launched in April 1971.

- *Salyut 1* **was occupied** for 24 days by the crew of Soviet spacecraft Soyuz 11. Sadly, they perished as their spacecraft re-entered Earth's atmosphere.

- *Salyut 1* **had a very low orbit** and limited fuel. After the crew disaster, it was de-orbited and itself broke up during re-entry.

- *Skylab* **was the first US space station**. Three crews spent a total of 171 days there in 1973–1974.

- **Launched in 1986**, the Soviet station *Mir* made more than 89,000 orbits of Earth. The last crew left in 2000.

- **The giant International Space Station (ISS)** was built in stages starting in 1998. The first crew boarded in November 2000.

> **DID YOU KNOW?**
> The total living space on the ISS is roomier than the passenger space on a 747 jumbo jet.

▼ *The Columbus module of the ISS is 6.9 m long and was attached in 2008. It was built by the European Space Agency and contains mainly science equipment for experiments and recordings, from the effects of spaceflight on the human body to an incredibly accurate atomic clock that measures if time passes more slowly on board.*

Gravity

- **The attraction**, or pulling force, between all matter is gravity.

- **Gravity holds everything on Earth** on the ground and stops it flying off into space. It holds Earth together, keeps the Moon in orbit around Earth, and Earth and other planets orbiting the Sun.

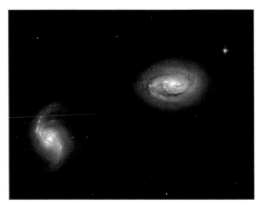

▲ *Giant galaxies are so massive that their force of gravity may pull other, smaller galaxies towards them.*

- **Stars burn by squeezing** their matter together. This is caused by gravity.

- **Gravity acts on all matter** in the Universe, probably in the form of gravitational waves, which were first discovered in 2016.

- **The force of gravity** depends on mass (the amount of matter in an object) and distance.

- **The more mass an object has**, and the closer it is to another object, the more strongly its gravity pulls.

- **Black holes have the strongest** gravitational pull in the Universe.

- **The basic laws of gravity** can be used for anything, including detecting an unseen planet by studying the flickers in another star's light.

- **Einstein's theory of general relativity** shows that gravity not only pulls on matter, but also bends space, and even time itself.

- **Orbits are the result** of a perfect balance between the force of gravity on an object (which pulls it inward towards whatever it is orbiting) and its forward momentum (which keeps it flying straight onwards).

Light years

- **Distances in space** are so vast that the fastest thing in the Universe, light, is used to measure them. The speed of light is about 300,000 km/sec.

- **A light second is the distance** that light travels in one second, that is 300 million km.

- **A light year is the distance** that light travels in one year – 9.46 trillion km.

- **Light years** are one of the standard distance measurements in astronomy.

- **It takes about eight minutes** for light from the Sun to reach Earth.

- **Light takes 4.22 years** to reach Earth from the Sun's nearest star, Proxima Centauri. This means Proxima Centauri is 4.22 light years away – more than 40 trillion km.

- **Viewed from Earth**, Proxima Centauri looks like it did 4.22 years ago because its light takes 4.22 years to reach Earth.

Sirius: 8.6 light years away

◄ *Three of the four telescopes that make up the Very Large Telescope in Chile, South America, gaze at the night sky. Brightest is Sirius, the 'Dog Star', about 8.6 light years distant.*

- **The star Deneb** is 1800 light years away, which means it looks like it did 1800 years ago, when Emperor Septimus Severius ruled Rome (in AD 200).

- **Astronomers use parsecs** to measure distances. They originally came from parallax shift measurements. A light year is 0.3066 parsecs.

Rotation

- **Rotation means spinning** or turning around. Stars spin, planets spin, moons spin and galaxies spin – even atoms spin.

- **Earth takes 23.93 hours** to spin once. This is called its rotation period.

- **The fastest-rotating planet is Jupiter**, which turns around once every 9.9 Earth hours.

- **The slowest-rotating planet is Venus**, the closest planet to Earth, which takes 243.01 Earth days to turn around once.

- **The Sun takes 25.4 Earth days** to rotate, but since Earth is going around the Sun as well, it seems to take 27.27 Earth days.

- **As well as spinning**, space objects also move around each other. This is called orbiting.

- **Moons orbit planets**, planets orbit stars, and stars orbit the centre of galaxies.

- **Earth's movements** are not actually felt because everything is moving with it. However, Earth's spin can be seen as the Sun, Moon and stars move across the sky.

- **Gravity keeps everything** in orbit. The Sun's gravity pulls Earth, and Earth's gravity pulls the Moon.

▼ *Rotating galaxies are just part of the spinning, moving Universe.*

Uranus

● **Uranus is the seventh planet** out from the Sun. Its orbit keeps it 2870 million km away on average and takes 84 Earth years to complete.

● **It tilts so far on its side** that Uranus seems to roll around the Sun. The angle of its tilt is 98 degrees, so its equator runs vertically.

● **This tilt may be** the result of a collision with a meteor or another planet many years ago.

● **In summer on Uranus**, the Sun does not set for 20 Earth years. In winter, darkness lasts for over 20 Earth years. In autumn, the Sun rises and sets every nine Earth hours.

● **Uranus spins around** on its axis once every 17.24 Earth hours.

● **Uranus has more than 25 moons**, all named after characters from William Shakespeare's plays.

● **There are five large moons** – Titania, Oberon, Umbriel, Ariel and Miranda – of which Titania is the largest with a diameter of 1578 km. Ten smaller moons were discovered by the Voyager 2 probe in 1986 and several more have been found since.

● **Since Uranus is so far from the Sun**, it is very cold, with surface temperatures dropping to –225°C. Sunlight takes just eight minutes to reach Earth, but 2.5 hours to reach Uranus.

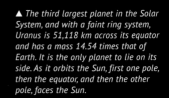

▲ *The third largest planet in the Solar System, and with a faint ring system, Uranus is 51,118 km across its equator and has a mass 14.54 times that of Earth. It is the only planet to lie on its side. As it orbits the Sun, first one pole, then the equator, and then the other pole, faces the Sun.*

▼ *Uranus' five largest moons range in size from Titania, with a diameter of 1578 km, to Miranda, with a diamter of 472 km.*

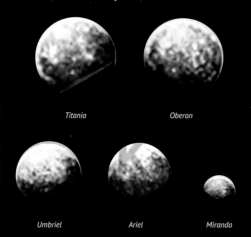

Titania   Oberon

Umbriel   Ariel   Miranda

● **Uranus' icy atmosphere** is made of hydrogen and helium. Wild winds circulate the planet at more than 600 km/h – six times as fast as hurricanes on Earth.

● **The surface of Uranus** is not solid. Green-blue methane clouds surround the planet in an atmosphere of hydrogen and helium gas. Inside Uranus is an icy mixture of water, ammonia and methane, and probably a small, rocky core.

● **Uranus is only faintly visible** from Earth with the naked eye. It looks like a very faint star, and was not identified until 1781.

● **Uranus was named** after the ancient Greek god of the sky.

Solar eruptions

- **Solar flares are sudden eruptions** on the Sun's surface. They flare up in just a few minutes, then take more than half an hour to die away again.
- **Solar flares reach temperatures** of 10 million°C and have the energy of billions of nuclear explosions.
- **As well as heat and radiation**, solar flares also send out streams of charged particles.
- **The solar wind is the stream** of charged particles that shoots out from the Sun in all directions at speeds of over one million km/h. It reaches Earth in several days, but also blows far throughout the Solar System.
- **Every second**, the solar wind carries away over one million tonnes of charged particles from the Sun.
- **Earth is shielded** from the lethal effects of the solar wind by its own magnetic field.
- **Solar prominences** are gigantic arcs of hot hydrogen that sometimes spout out from the Sun. They last from a few days to several weeks, and can reach temperatures of 10,000°C.
- **Magnetic storms** are massive hails of charged particles that hit Earth every few years or so, setting the atmosphere buzzing with electricity.

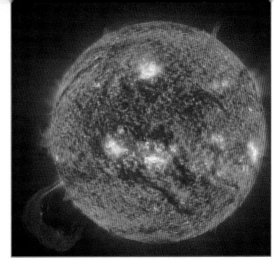

▲ *Solar prominences can loop as far as 200,000 km out from the Sun's surface.*

- **Coronal mass ejections** (CMEs) are gigantic eruptions of charged particles (protons and electrons) from the Sun, creating gusts in the solar wind that set off magnetic storms on Earth.
- **CMEs occur several times daily** when the solar or sunspot cycle is at its peak, but only once a week in between.

Jupiter's Galilean moons

- **The Galilean moons** are the four biggest of Jupiter's 60-plus moons. They were discovered by Galileo in 1610, centuries before astronomers identified the other, smaller ones.
- **Ganymede is the biggest** of the Galilean moons – at 5262 km across, it is larger than the planet Mercury.

▼ *Io's yellow glow comes from sulphur, which is spewed as far as 300 km upwards by the moon's volcanoes.*

- **Ganymede looks solid** but under its shell of ice is 900 km of slushy, half-melted ice and water.
- **Callisto is the second biggest** of Jupiter's Galilean moons, at 4820 km across.
- **Callisto is scarred** with craters from bombardments early in the Solar System's life.
- **Io is the third biggest moon**, at 3642 km across.
- **Io's surface is a mass of volcanoes**, caused by it being stretched and squeezed by Jupiter's massive gravity.
- **The smallest** of the Galilean moons is Europa, at 3138 km across.
- **Europa is covered in ice** and looks like a shiny, honey-coloured billiard ball from a distance – but a close-up view reveals countless cracks in its surface.

DID YOU KNOW?

A crater called Valhalla on Callisto is so big it makes the moon look like a giant eyeball.

Tides

● **Ocean tides are the rise and fall** of the water level in Earth's oceans. They occur about twice each day (24 hours).

● **The gravitational pulls** of the Moon and the Sun create the tides on Earth.

● **The Moon's pull** creates two bulges in the oceans – one below the Moon and one on the opposite side of Earth.

● **As Earth spins**, the tidal bulges seem to move around the world, creating two high tides every day.

● **Spring tides are very high tides** that happen when the Sun and Moon are in line, and their gravitational pulls are combined.

● **Neap tides are small tides** that happen when the Sun and Moon are at right angles to Earth and their pulls are weakened by working against one another.

● **The solid rock of Earth has tides too**, but they are very slight and Earth's surface only moves about 0.5 m.

▶ At high tide, the sea rises and can cut off tidal islands such as St Michael's Mount off the coast of Cornwall, UK. Most coasts have two high tides and two low tides every day.

● **Tides are also any upheaval** created by the pull of gravity, as one space object orbits another.

● **Moons orbiting large planets** undergo huge tidal pulls. Jupiter's moon, Io, is stretched so much by Jupiter's gravity that its interior is heated enough to create volcanoes.

● **Whole galaxies can be affected** by tidal pulls, making them stretch as they are tugged by the gravitational pull of other passing galaxies.

At high tide, the water level rises

At low tide, the water level goes down again

Binary and multiple stars

DID YOU KNOW?

The first binary star to be discovered by telescope was Mizar, in Ursa Major, in 1617.

● **The Sun is alone in space**, but most stars are in groups of two or more.

● **Binaries are double stars** and there are various kinds. True binary stars are two stars that are held together by one another's gravity.

● **Usually one of a binary pair is called A** and one B, such as Mira A, a red giant, and Mira B, a white dwarf.

▼ Most stars are binaries or multiples – two or more stars close together. Their motions depend on their sizes. The left image shows two similar stars following each other in circular orbit, while the right image shows a smaller star orbiting a large star.

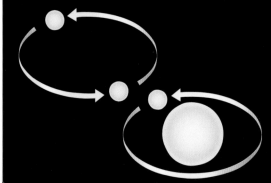

● **Eclipsing binaries are true binary stars** that spin around in exactly the same line of sight from Earth, and keep blocking out each other's light.

● **Spectroscopic binaries are true binaries** that spin so closely together that the only way of knowing that there are two stars is by their changes in colour.

● **Optical binaries** are not binaries at all. They are two stars that look as if they are together because they are in roughly the same line of sight when observed from Earth.

● **The star Epsilon**, in the constellation of Lyra, is called the Double Double because it is a pair of binaries.

● **True multiple stars** have three (triple), four (quadruple) or more stars close together and are bound by their gravity.

● **The closest stars to Earth** form a triple star system. Alpha Centauri A and B are Sun-sized yellow stars, grouped with a red dwarf, Proxima Centauri, which is one seventh the Sun's diameter.

Halley's comet

● **Halley's comet** is named after the British scientist and astronomer Edmund Halley (1656–1742).

● **He forecast that the comet** would return in 1758, which was 16 years after his death. This was the first time a comet's arrival had been accurately predicted.

● **Halley's comet orbits** the Sun on average every 75.3 years.

● **Its innermost orbit loops** between Mercury and Venus, and at its far point stretches out beyond Neptune.

● **Chinese astronomers described** a visit of Halley's comet as long ago as 240 BC.

▲ *Halley's comet came close to Earth in 1986. Its next visit will be in 2061.*

▼ *Halley's comet was embroidered on the Bayeux Tapestry, which shows Harold's defeat by William at the Battle of Hastings in 1066.*

● **Halley's comet** was seen in about 12 BC, so some say it was the Bible's Star of Bethlehem.

● **When Halley's comet** was seen in AD 837, Chinese astronomers wrote that its head was as bright as Venus and that its tail stretched right across the sky.

● **King Harold II of England** saw the comet in 1066. When he was defeated by William the Conqueror a few months later, people interpreted the comet's visit as an evil omen.

● **The comet was examined** at close range by five space probes, called the Halley Armada, when it last came close to Earth in 1986.

Asteroids

● **Lumps of rock that orbit the Sun** are called asteroids. Some were also known as minor planets.

● **Most asteroids are in the Main Asteroid Belt** or Main Belt, which lies between Mars and Jupiter.

● **Some much more distant asteroids** are made of ice and orbit the Sun beyond Neptune.

● **There are more than one million** asteroids bigger than one kilometre across. More than 200 asteroids are more than 100 km across.

DID YOU KNOW?

About every 50 million years, the Earth is hit by an asteroid measuring more than 10 km across.

● **A few asteroids** come near Earth. These are called Near Earth Objects (NEOs).

● **Asteroids were once known** as minor planets. New discoveries are recorded by the Minor Planet Center in Cambridge, Massachusetts, USA, which gives each one a unique catalogue number in addition to any name.

● **In a reorganization of naming** in 2006, the definition of the term asteroid was refined to exclude dwarf planets and certain other objects.

● **The first asteroid to be discovered** was Ceres in 1801. It was detected by Giuseppi Piazzi, one of the Celestial Police, a group of astronomers whose mission was to find a missing planet between Mars and Jupiter.

● **At 940 km across** and 0.0002 percent of the Earth's mass, Ceres was the biggest asteroid. It is now classed as a dwarf planet.

◄ *Impact by an asteroid estimated at 10–15 km across is suspected of wiping out the large dinosaurs, and many other creatures and plants, in the mass extinction of 66 million years ago.*

Solar changes

● **The Sun is about 4.6 billion years old** and halfway through its life – as a medium-sized star it will probably live for around 11 billion years.

● **Over the next few billion years**, the Sun will brighten and swell until it is twice as bright and 50 percent bigger.

▼ *The Sun seems to burn steadily, although its brightness does vary very slightly over decades. Over the next five billion years there will be a long-term trend for it to burn more ferociously.*

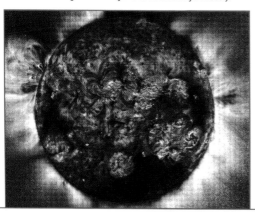

● **In five billion years**, the Sun's hydrogen fuel will have burned out, and its core will start to shrink.

● **As its core shrinks**, the rest of the Sun will swell up and its surface will become cooler and redder. It will be a red giant star.

● **Earth will have burned** out long before the Sun is big enough to expand so much that it completely swallows our planet.

● **The Sun will end** as a white dwarf (the last stage in the life of a medium-sized star).

● **Between 1645 and 1715**, few sunspots were seen on the Sun – this period is called the Maunder minimum. At that time Earth experienced an ice age known as the Little Ice Age, due to less heat from the Sun.

● **More of the chemical carbon-14** is made on Earth when the Sun is less active. The carbon-14 is absorbed by trees, which means scientists can track changes in solar activity in the past by measuring carbon-14 in old wood.

● **The SOHO** (Solar and Heliospheric Observatory) spacecraft is stationed between the Earth and the Sun. It monitors the Sun and changes in solar activity.

Star birth

● **Medium-sized stars** last for about 10 billion years. Small stars may last for 200 billion years. Big stars have comparatively short, fierce lives of up to ten million years.

● **Stars that begin life** in clouds of gas and dust are called nebulae.

● **Inside nebulae**, gravity creates vast dark clumps called evaporating gaseous globules (EGGs). Each clump contains the beginnings of a family of stars.

● **As gravity's attraction squeezes** these globules together, they shrink and form hot, spinning balls of gas and dust.

● **Smaller clumps** do not get very hot, so they eventually fizzle out.

● **If a larger clump** reaches 10 million°C in its core, hydrogen atoms begin to join together or fuse in nuclear reactions and the baby star or proto-star starts to glow.

● **In a medium-sized star**, such as the Sun, the heat of burning hydrogen pushes gas out as fiercely as gravity pulls inwards, and the star becomes stable, giving out radiation at a steady rate.

1 *Clumps of gas in a nebula start to shrink into tight balls that will become stars.*

2 *The gas spirals as it is pulled inwards. Any leftover gas and dust may form planets around the new star.*

3 *Deep in its centre, the new star starts making energy, but it is still hidden by the cloud of dust and gas.*

4 *The dust and gas are blown away and the shining star can be seen.*

▲ *Stars are born and die all over the Universe. By looking at stars at different stages of their life, astronomers have learned about the stages of their existence.*

Neptune

● **The eighth and outermost planet from the Sun** is Neptune. Its distance from Earth varies from 4459 million km to 4537 million km.

● **Neptune was discovered in 1846.** Two mathematicians, Englishman John Couch Adams (1819–1892) and Frenchman Urbain Le Verrier (1811–1877), told astronomers where to look after they worked out where a new planet should be from the effect of its gravity on Uranus.

● **Neptune is so far from the Sun** that its orbit lasts 164.8 Earth years. It has only completed slightly more than one orbit since it was discovered in 1846.

● **Like Uranus**, Neptune is shrouded in blue methane clouds at temperatures as low as −220°C in a deep atmosphere made of hydrogen and helium gas.

● **Unlike Uranus**, which is almost plain blue all over, Neptune has white clouds, created by heat from inside the planet.

● **Neptune has the strongest winds** in the Solar System, blowing at up to 2000 km/h.

● **The Great Dark Spot** on Neptune was a giant storm seen by Voyager 2 in 1989. It then disappeared but other huge spots form and fade.

● **The eight largest moons** of Neptune are named after characters from Greek myths. They are called Triton, Nereid, Naiad, Thalassa, Despina, Larissa, Proteus and Galatea.

● **More than five** additional small moons have been discovered, one as recently as 2013.

▲ *Neptune's moon Triton is green, while its icecaps of frozen nitrogen are pink. It also has volcanoes that erupt fountains of ice. It is one of the coldest places in the Solar System with a surface temperature that goes below −220°C.*

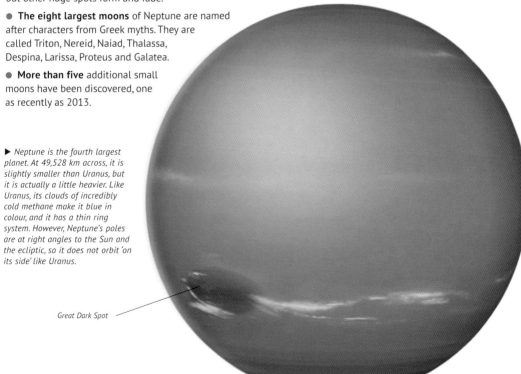

▶ *Neptune is the fourth largest planet. At 49,528 km across, it is slightly smaller than Uranus, but it is actually a little heavier. Like Uranus, its clouds of incredibly cold methane make it blue in colour, and it has a thin ring system. However, Neptune's poles are at right angles to the Sun and the ecliptic, so it does not orbit 'on its side' like Uranus.*

Great Dark Spot

Atoms

- **Matter is made from small particles** called atoms. They are the 'building blocks' of the Universe.

- **Atoms are so small** that one million could fit on the full stop at the end of this sentence.

- **They are the smallest identifiable pieces** of a pure chemical element. There are as many different atoms as there are elements.

- **Atoms are mostly empty space** with tiny subatomic particles (subatomic means smaller than an atom).

- **The core of an atom** is the nucleus, made of two kinds of subatomic particle – protons and neutrons.

- **Whizzing around the nucleus** are even tinier particles called electrons.

- **Electrons have a negative electrical charge**, and protons have a positive charge. Electrons are held near the nucleus by electrical attraction to the protons.

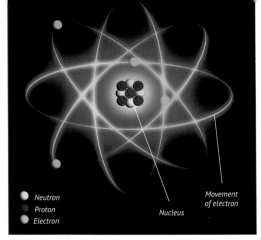

Neutron
Proton
Electron

Movement of electron
Nucleus

▲ *In the centre of the atom is the nucleus, made up of equal numbers of protons and neutrons. These are bonded by a powerful interaction called the strong nuclear force, which can be used to create nuclear energy.*

- **Under certain conditions**, atoms can be split into more than 200 kinds of short-lived subatomic particles. Some of these particles are made from even tinier units – quarks.

- **There are six kinds** of quarks: up, down, strange, charm, top and bottom. Quarks are found with other quarks, forming particles known as hadrons.

DID YOU KNOW?

The basic idea of atoms was proposed by Democritus of ancient Greece, 2400 years ago.

Observatories

- **Observatories are buildings** that house telescopes and other equipment, and from where astronomers study space as well as Earth's atmosphere and weather.

- **For the best view**, most observatories are on mountain tops, far from interference by artificial lights and above some of Earth's blurring atmosphere.

- **In most observatories**, the telescopes are housed in a domed building, which turns around to aim anywhere in the sky.

- **The oldest existing observatory** is thought to be a prehistoric circle built about 7000 years ago in Goseck, Germany.

- **At the Beijing Ancient Observatory**, China, there are 500-year-old bronze astronomical instruments.

- **The first British observatory** was the Royal Greenwich Observatory, London, founded in 1675.

▶ *The Kitt Peak National Observatory is near Tucson, Arizona, USA. It is 2095 m above sea level and houses 24 optical and two radio telescopes and many other kinds of equipment.*

- **The highest observatory** on Earth is 5640 m above sea level, at Cerro Chajnantor in the Atacama Desert of Chile.

- **The lowest 'observatory'** is 1.7 km below sea level, in Homestake Mine, South Dakota, USA. Its 'telescope' is actually tanks of heavy water that trap neutrinos from the Sun.

- **The first photographs** of the stars were taken in 1840 on the then newly invented photographic film.

- **Today, most observatories** rely on sensitive electronic cameras, photographs and computers rather than the eyes of astronomers.

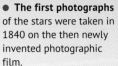

Voyagers 1 and 2

● **The Voyagers are a pair** of unmanned US space probes, launched to explore the outer planets. They are still in space.

● **Voyager 1 was launched** on 5 September 1977. It flew past Jupiter in March 1979 and Saturn in November 1980, then continued on a curved path to take it out of the Solar System altogether.

● **Voyager 2 travelled** more slowly. Although it was launched two weeks earlier than Voyager 1, it did not reach Jupiter until July 1979 and Saturn until August 1981.

● **Both Voyagers used** the slingshot effect of Jupiter's gravity to hurl them on towards Saturn.

◀ *Voyager 2 reached Neptune in 1989, revealing a wealth of new information about this distant planet.*

● **While Voyager 1 headed out** of the Solar System, Voyager 2 flew on and passed Uranus in January 1986.

● **Voyager 2 then passed** Neptune on 25 August 1989. It took close-up photographs of Uranus and Neptune.

● **The Voyagers revealed** volcanoes on Io, one of Jupiter's Galilean moons.

● **Voyager 2 found ten moons** around Uranus.

● **Six moons and five rings** around Neptune were also discovered by Voyager 2.

Space exploration

● **Space is explored in two ways** – by studying it from Earth using powerful telescopes, and by launching spacecraft to get a closer view.

● **Most space exploration** is by unmanned spacecraft, usually called robotic craft or probes.

● **The first living creature** in space was a dog called Laika, who travelled in the Soviet spacecraft, Sputnik 2, in 1957. Although Laika did not survive her mission, she provided scientists with vital information that paved the way for human spaceflight.

● **The first pictures** of the far side of the Moon were sent back by the *Luna 3* space probe in October 1959.

● **Manned missions have only reached** as far as the Moon and no one has been back there since 1972.

● **Astronauts from the US Apollo space programme** took three days to reach the Moon.

● **Apart from Apollo**, a space probe has never come back to Earth's surface from a moon, planet or other space body.

● **However, sample return missions** have brought back rocks, dust and other material from space.

● **This has included rocks from the Moon** brought back by Apollo, comet material brought back by the *Stardust* probe in 2006, and asteroid samples brought back by Japan's *Hayabusa* craft in 2010.

▼ *The first successful planetary probe was the USA's Mariner 2, which flew past Venus in 1962.*

Pluto

- **When it was discovered** in 1930 by US astronomer Clyde Tombaugh (1906–1997), Pluto became the ninth planet – but it was by far the smallest at 2372 km across.

- **Since 2006**, Pluto has been reclassified as a dwarf planet by the International Astronomical Union, IAU.

- **Pluto has a tilted and elongated** orbit that varies from 4437 million km to 7310 million km from the Sun, which is almost 50 times farther out than Earth.

- **This enormous distance** means Pluto is mostly in the region beyond Neptune, called the Kuiper Belt.

- **At this distance**, Pluto takes 248 years to travel once around the Sun, even at its average speed of 16,800 km/h. For 20 years of this time, Pluto is closer than Neptune to the Sun.

▲ *Launched in 2006, the New Horizons space probe finally reached Pluto in January 2015 and took never before seen images of the dwarf planet.*

- **Pluto spins around in 6.4 Earth days**, so its day lasts nearly as long as an Earth week.

- **It is mainly a mix of rock** and frozen substances, such as nitrogen, methane and ammonia.

- **Nitrogen ice** covers most of Pluto's surface.

- **Pluto's very thin atmosphere** contains gases of nitrogen, methane and carbon monoxide.

- **Pluto has five moons**, the first of which was discovered in 1978.

- **Much about Pluto** remained a mystery until it was visited by the New Horizons space probe in 2015.

◄ *Pluto as imaged by the New Horizons probe in 2015. The massive craterless 'Heart' feature lower right is officially named Tombaugh Regio.*

Einstein

- **The great mathematician-scientist** Albert Einstein (1879–1955) is known for devising two theories of relativity.

- **Special relativity** shows that all measurements are relative, including time, space and speed. In other words, time and space and speed depend on where and when they are measured.

- **The fastest thing in the Universe**, light, always travels at the same speed, no matter where you are or how fast you are going.

- **Special relativity** also shows, among other events, that as things travel faster, they seem to become shorter and heavier.

- **Einstein's theory of general relativity** includes the idea of special relativity, but also describes how gravity works. It led to the notion of four dimensions: three of physical space (up-down, left-right, forwards-backwards), and time. This is known as 'space-time'.

- **General relativity predicts** that light rays from stars are bent by the gravitational pull of stars and other huge objects that they pass. The star does this by stretching space-time.

◄ In his later years, Einstein strove to find a 'grand theory of everything'.

- **Evidence for** Einstein's theory of general relativity was proven in 1919, when light rays from distant stars, just grazing the Sun on their way to Earth, were measured during an eclipse and shown to be bent.

- **Einstein overturned the idea** that time is the same everywhere. He was the first to show that time is relative. It depends entirely on how you measure it – and you can only measure it relative to something else. So time can pass faster or slower.

- **Relativity shows that as speed increases**, time slows down. So for astronauts orbiting Earth, time passes very slightly slower than for people on Earth.

Space telescopes

- **In order to study the Universe** without interference from Earth's atmosphere, space telescopes are launched.

- **Some of these space telescopes** are called space observatories since they have so much extra equipment in addition to the telescope itself.

- **Some space telescopes** orbit Earth as satellites, while others orbit the Sun or make their own path through space.

- **Away from Earth's atmosphere**, space telescopes and observatories do not suffer blurring, dust, artificial lights and other problems of the atmosphere.

- **However space brings its own problems** such as risk of collision with meteoroids, huge extremes of temperature, and intense forms of radiation energy.

- **Different space telescopes** study all the different forms of radiation that make up the electromagnetic spectrum.

- **These include** low and high frequency radio waves, low and high frequency microwaves, infrared, visible light, ultraviolet, X-rays and gamma rays.

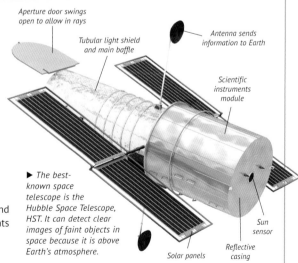

Aperture door swings open to allow in rays

Tubular light shield and main baffle

Antenna sends information to Earth

Scientific instruments module

▶ The best-known space telescope is the Hubble Space Telescope, HST. It can detect clear images of faint objects in space because it is above Earth's atmosphere.

Sun sensor

Reflective casing

Solar panels

- **Some space telescopes** study various kinds of rays and waves, rather than just one kind such as visible light.

- **The first space telescope** was Uhuru, sent up in 1970.

- **Uhuru was first** of several space telescopes designed to map the entire sky for sources of X-rays.

Radio telescopes

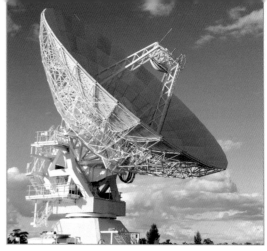

- **Radio telescopes are used** to pick up radio waves and other similar kinds of waves, made of electromagnetic energy, instead of light waves.

- **The first radio telescope** was built by Karl Jansky in New Jersey, USA, in 1932. It looked like a long wire strung on scaffolding.

- **Most modern radio telescopes**, like optical reflecting telescopes, have a big dish to collect and focus data.

- **At the centre of its dish**, a radio telescope has an antenna (aerial or receiver) to pick up radio signals.

- **Radio waves are much longer** than light waves, so radio telescope dishes are very big. They can be up to 100 m or more across.

▲ ATCA, the Australia Telescope Compact Array near Narrabri, New South Wales, has six radio telescope dishes, each 22 m across.

- **Instead of one big dish**, some radio telescopes use a collection of small, linked dishes. The further apart the dishes are, the sharper the image.

- **Radio galaxies are very distant** and only faintly visible (if at all), but they can be detected because they give out radio waves.

- **Radio astronomy** led to the discovery of pulsars and background radiation from the Big Bang.

- **Radio astronomy proved** that the Milky Way is a disc-shaped galaxy with spiralling arms.

DID YOU KNOW?

Jansky's first radio telescope of 1932 turned around on a set of four tyres borrowed from a Ford Model T car.

Astronauts

- **The first astronauts** were jet pilots.

- **In the USA** anyone who has flown at an altitude of more than 80 km above sea level, which includes some aircraft test pilots, is awarded 'astronaut wings'.

- **The US space shuttle carried** three kinds of astronaut – pilots, mission specialists and payload specialists.

▼ Astronauts train for years. They learn to fly in simulators and in training aircraft before dealing with the demands of space missions.

- **A pilot or commander's job** is to be responsible for the mission and to control the spacecraft.

- **Mission specialists** are crew members who carry out specific jobs, such as running experiments or going on space walks.

- **Payload specialists** are not NASA astronauts, but scientists and other onboard guests.

- **Astronauts on long missions** use exercise machines to keep fit and avoid problems such as muscle wasting.

- **The first woman in space** was Soviet cosmonaut Valentina Tereshkova, who completed 48 orbits of the Earth in June 1963.

- **The first space tourist** was American Dennis Tito. He is reported to have paid $20 million to spend nearly eight days aboard a Russian Soyuz spacecraft in 2001. Several other people have subsequently paid their own ticket to get into space.

DID YOU KNOW?

Weightlessness makes astronauts become a few centimetres taller during a long mission.

Space catalogues

● **Since ancient times** astronomers have made lists, charts and other records of stars in the night sky.

● **We now know that some of those light sources** are not stars but other objects, so they have their own kinds of non-stellar (non-star) lists and catalogues.

● **Some of those objects are planets**, and some are comets.

● **Others are galaxies** (vast groups of stars) or nebulae (massive clouds of dust).

● **The first modern catalogue** of non-stellar objects was made by astronomer Charles Messier (1730–1817).

● **One of the main modern lists** of non-stellar objects is the New General Catalogue of nebulae and star clusters (NGC).

● **The advent of radio astronomy** brought a whole new area of catalogues for objects that give out no or little light, but which emit many other kinds of similar electromagnetic energy, such as radio waves, microwaves and X-rays.

● **Radio sources** are listed in some of these catalogues, such as Cambridge University's 3C catalogue.

● **For example**, the first quasar to be discovered was listed as 3C 273. Quasars are immense sources of light, radio and other waves and energy.

▼ *With such a huge number of stars, galaxies and nebulae in the night sky, astronomers need detailed catalogues to locate each kind of object reliably and check whether it has already been identified and investigated.*

Space travel

● **The first artificial satellite**, the Soviet Sputnik 1, was launched into space in 1957.

● **During the late 1960s** and early 1970s, US Apollo astronauts became the first to reach another world when six missions travelled to land on the Moon.

● **The arrival of the US space shuttle** – a reusable spaceplane – in 1981 made working in orbit much easier.

● **Meanwhile the USSR** was focusing on space stations. In 1986 it set up the first large orbiting station suitable for long-term human occupation, called *Mir*.

● **In 1994–1995** Russian astronaut Valeri Poliakov spent 437 days on board *Mir*. This remains the longest continuous stay by a person in space.

● **By the year 2000**, unmanned space probes had visited all of the eight planets in the Solar System, but no humans had ventured beyond the Moon.

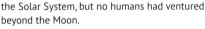

DID YOU KNOW?

In 2003, China became the third nation to launch an astronaut into orbit.

● **Astronauts have lived** on the ISS (International Space Station) since 2001. Some stay for a few weeks, others for six months or more.

● **By the mid 2010s** more than 550 people had travelled into space. An average of 10–12 now go each year.

◄ *One problem facing a spacecraft returning to Earth is the heat produced by friction as it re-enters the Earth's atmosphere. Here you can see scorched, heatproof tiles on the underside of the shuttle.*

Astronomy

- **Astronomy is the study of the night sky** – from the planets and moons to the stars and galaxies.

- **Astronomy** is the most ancient of all the sciences, dating back at least 5000 years.

- **The ancient Egyptians** used their knowledge of astronomy to work out their calendar and to align the pyramids.

- **The word astronomy** comes from the ancient Greek words *astro* meaning 'star' and *nomia* meaning 'law'.

- **Since the early 1600s** astronomers have used telescopes to study objects that are too faint and small to be seen with the naked eye.

- **Space objects** give out other kinds of radiation besides light, such as radio and ultraviolet waves. Astronomers have special equipment to detect this.

- **Professional astronomers today** usually study photographs and computer displays instead of staring through telescopes, because many space objects only show up on long-exposure photographs.

- **Astronomers can spot** new objects in the night sky by laying a current photograph over an old one and looking for differences.

- **Professional astronomy** involves sophisticated equipment costing billions. Yet, amateurs still make important discoveries, even in the 21st century.

- **Amateur astronomers** are usually the first to spot a new comet in the sky. Comets are named after the person who found them.

◄ *Most astronomers work in observatories far from city lights, where they can get a very clear view of the night sky.*

Stars

- **Stars are giant balls of gas**, mainly hydrogen and helium.

- **Nuclear reactions** in the heart of a star generate enormous energy, which the star sends out as heat, light and other forms of radiation, and various particles too.

- **The heart or core of a star** reaches 15 million°C or more. A grain of sand this hot could kill someone from 100 km away.

- **The gas in stars** is in a special hot state called plasma, which is made of atoms stripped of electrons.

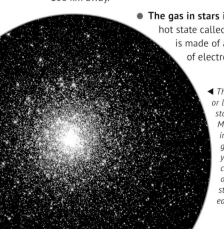

◄ *The globular swarm, or large cluster, of stars known as M80 (NGC 6093), is in the Milky Way galaxy, 32,000 light years from Earth. It contains hundreds of thousands of stars, attracted to each other by gravity.*

- **In the core of a star**, hydrogen nuclei fuse (join together) to form helium. This nuclear reaction is called a proton-proton chain.

- **Stars twinkle** because they are seen through Earth's atmosphere where the air and dust affect their light rays.

- **Astronomers work out the size of a star** from its brightness, colour, temperature and the various types of radiation it emits.

- **The size and brightness** of a star depends on its mass – how much gas it is made of. The Sun is a small-medium star. The biggest stars have up to 200 times the Sun's mass, and the smallest ones about one tenth of its mass.

- **The coolest stars**, such as Arcturus and Antares, glow reddest. Hotter stars are yellow and white. The hottest are blue-white, like Rigel and Zeta Puppis.

- **The blue supergiant Zeta Puppis** has a surface temperature of 42,000°C, while blue-white supergiant Rigel's is 12,000°C.

The Sun

- **A medium-sized yellow star**, the Sun is a fiery ball of gas that measures 1,392,700 km across – 109 times the diameter of Earth.

- **Even though the Sun** is made almost entirely of hydrogen and helium, the lightest gases in the Universe, it weighs 2000 trillion trillion tonnes – about 300,000 times as much as Earth.

- **The Sun's interior** is heated, by nuclear fusion reactions, to temperatures of more than 15 million°C.

- **Energy is produced in the central core** and very slowly works its way outwards through a thick layer of gases. In the outer layer, hot gas rises to the surface where heat and light escape into space.

- **The heat from the Sun's interior** erupts on the surface in patches called granules, and as gigantic arcs of hot gases called solar prominences.

- **The Sun gets hot** because it is so big that the pressure in its core is tremendous – enough to force the nuclei of hydrogen atoms to fuse (join together) to make helium atoms.

- **This nuclear fusion** reaction releases huge amounts of energy.

- **Halfway between its core** and its surface, the Sun is as dense as water. Closer to the surface, it becomes as dense as air.

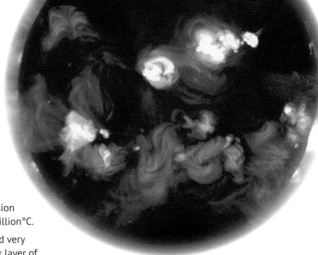

▲ *This artificially coloured photo was taken by a satellite and shows the Sun's surface to be a turbulent mass of flames and tongues of hot gases – very different from the even, yellowish ball we see from Earth.*

- **Nuclear fusion reactions** in the Sun's core convert five million tonnes of gas into energy every second, but the energy takes ten million years to reach the surface.

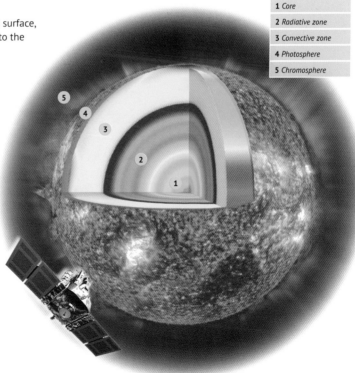

1	Core
2	Radiative zone
3	Convective zone
4	Photosphere
5	Chromosphere

▶ *A cutaway of the Sun shows its layers, and the Solar and Heliospheric Observatory (SOHO) spacecraft, which spent two years gathering information about the Sun.*

DID YOU KNOW?

The Sun has been shining for over 4.5 billion years. Its current surface temperature is about 6000°C.

Nuclear energy

- **The energy released when the nucleus** of an atom is split apart, or when nuclei join, is called nuclear energy.

- **Nuclear energy fuels** nuclear power stations, and every star in the Universe. It can be released either by fission or fusion.

- **Nuclear fusion occurs** when nuclear energy is released as nuclei join together. This occurs inside stars when they are squeezed together by gravity.

- **Usually only tiny nuclei**, such as those of hydrogen and helium, fuse (join). Only under extreme pressure in huge, exploding stars do big nuclei, such as those of iron, fuse.

- **Nuclear fission occurs** when nuclear energy is released by the splitting of nuclei. This is the method used in most power stations and in atomic bombs.

- **Nuclear fission involves** splitting big nuclei, such as uranium-235 and plutonium.

- **When a nucleus splits**, it gives out gamma rays, neutrons and intense heat.

- **In an atomic bomb**, the enormous energy is released in one second.

- **In a power station**, control rods ensure that nuclear reactions are slowed down to release energy gradually.

DID YOU KNOW?

The atomic bomb dropped on Hiroshima in 1945 released 84 trillion joules of energy. A supernova releases 125,000 trillion trillion times as much.

▶ *In a nuclear chain reaction, the products of splitting one nucleus go on to split others, and so on, in an ever-increasing fashion.*

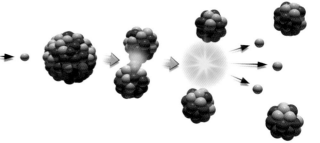

Supernovae

DID YOU KNOW?

Many of the elements that make up the human body were forged in supernovae.

- **A supernova** is the final, gigantic explosion of a supergiant star at the end of its life.

- **A supernova lasts** for just a week or so, but shines as brightly as a galaxy of 100 billion ordinary stars.

- **Supernovae occur when a supergiant star** uses up its hydrogen and helium fuel and shrinks. This boosts pressure in its core, enough to fuse heavy elements such as iron.

- **When iron begins to fuse** in its core, a star collapses at incredible speed – then rebounds in a mighty explosion.

- **Seen in 1987**, SN (supernova) 1987A was the first supernova viewable with the unaided eye since Kepler's 1604 sighting, now called SN 1604.

- **Supernova remnants** (leftovers) are the gigantic, cloudy shells of material swelling out from supernovae.

- **A supernova seen by Chinese astronomers** in AD 185 was thought to be such a bad omen that it sparked a revolution.

- **A dramatic supernova** seen by Chinese astronomers in 1054, now designated M1 or NGC 1952, created the Crab Nebula.

- **Many of the elements heavier** than iron are made in supernovae.

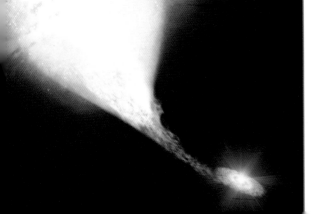

◀ *In this artist's view, one star of a binary (two-star) system is in the process of exploding as a supernova, having added some of its hydrogen gas to its companion blue star, which will endure. This type of 'survivor event' was first seen in 2004.*

Red shift

● **When distant galaxies** are moving away from Earth, the light waves they give off are stretched out behind them. This is because each bit of the light wave is being sent from a little further away.

● **When the light waves** from distant galaxies are stretched out in this way, they look redder. This is called red shift.

● **If a galaxy is moving towards Earth**, the light waves are squashed together and we see them as bluer. This is called blue shift.

● **Red shift was first described** by Austrian mathematician Christian Doppler (1803–1853) in 1842.

● **Edwin Hubble** (1889–1953) showed that a galaxy's red shift is proportional to its distance. The further away a galaxy is, the greater its red shift and the faster it is zooming away from Earth. This is known as Hubble's Law.

● **The increase of red shift** with distance proved that the Universe is growing bigger.

● **Only nearby galaxies** show no red shift at all.

● **The most distant galaxies** have red shifts grades, or values, of up to eight.

▲ *Massive red shifts reveal that the most distant objects in the Universe are flying away from Earth at astonishing speeds – often approaching the speed of light.*

● **Red shift can be caused** by the expansion of the Universe, gravity or the effect of relativity.

● **Black holes may create** large red shifts.

Auroras

● **Auroras** are bright displays of shimmering light that appear on some nights near the North and South poles.

● **The aurora that appears** near the North Pole is the Aurora Borealis, also known as the Northern Lights.

● **The aurora that appears** near the South Pole is the Aurora Australis, or the Southern Lights.

● **Auroras are caused** by streams of charged particles from the Sun, known as solar wind, crashing into the gases of the Earth's atmosphere.

● **Oxygen gas glows yellow-green** when it is hit low in the atmosphere, and glows orange higher up.

● **Nitrogen gas glows bright red** when hit normally, and bright blue when ionized (electrically charged).

● **Haloes of light** permanently exist over each Pole, but they are usually too faint to see. They flare up brightly when extra bursts of energy reach the Earth's atmosphere from the Sun.

● **Auroras only appear** at high latitudes, near the Poles, because there are deep gaps or cracks in the Earth's magnetic field here.

● **Auroras are more spectacular** when the solar wind is blowing strongly.

● **New York, USA, and Edinburgh, Scotland**, get an average of ten aurora displays every year.

▼ *Auroras are among nature's most beautiful sights. This one, above Iceland, looks like a dancing curtain of bright colours.*

The Moon

● **On average, the Moon is 384,400 km** from Earth and, at 3474 km across, it is just over 25 percent of Earth's diameter.

● **Once every month**, the Moon orbits Earth. Each orbit takes 27.3 days. The Moon also spins around once on its axis in exactly the same time, so it always keeps the same half facing Earth.

● **The Moon is the brightest object** in the night sky, but like all planets and moons, it does not give out any light itself. It shines because its surface reflects sunlight from the Sun.

● **One half of the Moon** is lit by the Sun, but as it travels around the Earth, different amounts of this sunlit side are seen. This is why the Moon seems to change shape. These changes are called the phases of the Moon.

● **A lunar month** is the time between one full Moon and the next. This is slightly longer than the time the Moon takes to orbit Earth because Earth is also moving.

● **The Moon has almost no atmosphere** and its surface is simply dust, pitted with craters created by meteorites smashing into it early in its history.

● **On the Moon's surface** are large, dark patches referred to as seas because that is what people once believed they were.

● **These seas are actually** flat plains of hardened lava flows from ancient volcanoes.

● **The Sea of Tranquility** is probably the most famous sea on the Moon. This is where the *Apollo 11* astronauts landed in 1969.

▲ *Unlike Earth's surface, which changes by the hour, the Moon's dusty, crater-pitted surface has remained much the same for billions of years. The only change happens when a meteorite smashes into it and creates a new crater.*

● **The side of the Moon** that is always turned away from Earth is called its far side or, mistakenly, its 'dark' side. This is a mistake because during a new Moon phase this side is almost fully lit by sunlight.

▼ *During the first half of each monthly cycle, the Moon waxes (appears to grow) from a crescent-shaped new Moon to a full Moon. During the second half, it wanes (dwindles) back to a crescent-shaped old Moon.*

New Moon   *Waxing crescent Moon*   *First quarter Moon*   *Waxing gibbous Moon*   *Full Moon*

Quasars

● **The most intense light sources** in the Universe, quasars are no bigger than the Solar System, yet they glow more brightly than 100 galaxies, such as the Milky Way.

● **Quasars are the most distant** known objects in the Universe. Even the nearest is a billion light years away.

● **Quasar is short for** Quasi-Stellar (star-like) Radio Source. This comes from the fact that the first quasars were detected by the strong radio signals they give out, and also because quasars are so small and bright that at first people thought they looked like stars.

● **Less than 10 percent** of the 100,000-plus quasars now known actually beam out radio signals.

● **One of the brightest quasars**, 3C 273, is 2.44 billion light years away. It was the first recorded quasar in 1959.

● **Its mass is** 900 million times that of the Sun and it shines 4000 billion times more brightly than the Sun.

● **Some quasars are so far away** that we see them as they were when the Universe was still in its infancy.

▲ *This artist's impression depicts an active quasar. Winds in the outer regions of the quasar contain dust particles.*

● **One example of this** is the colossally bright quasar, ULAS J1120+0641, which is 13 billion light years away. It is one of the most distant objects ever detected and formed less than one billion years after the Universe itself began.

● **Quasars are at the centre** of 'active galaxies'. Their energy comes from a black hole at their core, which ferociously draws in matter.

● **The energy given out** by this matter heading towards the black hole is radiated as heat, light, radio and other waves, which have enough power to travel across the Universe.

Space walks

● **The technical name** for going outside a spacecraft is Extra-Vehicular Activity (EVA).

● **In 1965, Soviet cosmonaut Alexei Leonov** was the first person to walk in space.

● **During space walks** a cable (called an umbilical) in some space suits keeps the astronauts connected to their spacecraft.

DID YOU KNOW?

Astronauts on space walks may be aided by a flying robot camera the size of a beach ball.

● **A Manned Manoeuvring Unit (MMU)** was a rocket-powered backpack that allowed astronauts to go further from their spacecraft.

● **In 1984, US astronaut Bruce McCandless** was the first person to use an MMU in space.

● **Damage and alterations to various spacecraft**, including the *Skylab* and *Mir* space stations, the Hubble Space Telescope and various satellites, have been repaired by space-walking astronauts.

● **The longest space walks** were 8 hours 56 minutes by US astronauts Susan Helms and Jim Voss in March 2001. They carried out preparations for a new unit to join, or dock with, the ISS.

● **Russian and US astronauts** use robotic arms to help them modify sections of the ISS.

◄ *US astronauts cooperate during a space shuttle mission. The red leg bands identify which astronaut is which.*

The night sky

- **When we look at the night sky** we can see the Moon and many twinkling points of light.

- **Most lights in the sky** are stars. Any moving, flashing lights may be aircraft, weather balloons or Earth-orbit satellites.

- **Often the brightest 'stars'** in the night sky are not actually stars at all, but are the planets, Jupiter, Venus and Mars.

- **A total of 6000 stars** can be seen from Earth with the unaided or naked eye, with 2000 visible from any one place.

- **The pale band across** the middle of the sky is a side-on view of our galaxy, the Milky Way.

- **The pattern of stars** seems to rotate (turn) each night as Earth spins. It takes 23 hours and 56 minutes for the star pattern to return to the same place in the sky.

- **As Earth orbits the Sun** each year, our view of the stars changes and the pattern starts in a different place each night.

- **Different arrangements** of stars are seen in the Northern Hemisphere and the Southern Hemisphere.

- **Over millennia**, the real positions of stars change since they are all moving through the Universe.

◀ *With the unaided eye, about 2000 stars can be seen twinkling in the night sky. Stars twinkle because of the shimmering of heat in the Earth's atmosphere. Some of these stars are trillions of kilometres away and their light takes thousands of years to reach us.*

Water and ice

- **Water is commonly found** as a solid, a liquid and a gas.

- **A compound** of the elements hydrogen and oxygen, water has the chemical formula H_2O.

- **Frozen water**, called water ice, floats because water is the only known substance less dense (heavy) as a solid than as a liquid.

- **However 'ice' may refer to** other frozen substances in very cold places, such as methane ice on Pluto and ammonia ice on Charon (one of Pluto's moons).

- **Water is fundamental** (basic) to all life on Earth. Between 55 and 70 percent of the human body is made up of water.

- **Earth is the only planet** in the Solar System to have liquid water on its surface.

- **Neptune has a deep ocean** of ionized water beneath its atmosphere of helium and hydrogen.

- **Dried-up riverbeds** show that Mars once had surface water. There is ice at both poles and probably underground too.

- **Recently several spacecraft** have discovered signs of ice (frozen water) on the Moon.

▼ *A satellite view of Iceland, which shows the land covered in snow and ice.*

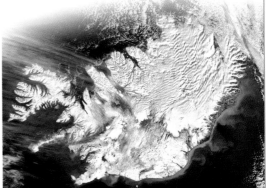

Galaxies

- **Giant groups of millions** or even trillions of stars are called galaxies. Our own local galaxy, containing the Solar System, is called the Milky Way.

- **There are more than 175 billion** galaxies in the known Universe, and possibly more to be discovered.

- **The three galaxies** most visible to the unaided eye from Earth (besides the Milky Way) are the Large and Small Magellanic clouds, and the Andromeda Galaxy.

- **In 1923**, astronomers realized that galaxies are huge star groups. They are vast but so far away that they look like fuzzy clouds.

- **Galaxies are often found** in groups called clusters. One cluster may contain hundreds of galaxies.

- **Spiral galaxies** are spinning galaxies with a dense core and spiralling arms.

- **Barred spiral galaxies** have just two arms. These are linked across the middle of the galaxy by a bar from which they trail.

- **Irregular galaxies** have no obvious shape. They may have formed from the debris of galaxies that crashed into each other.

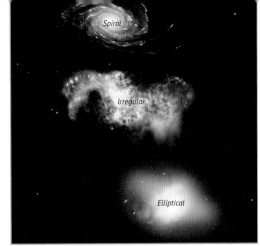

Spiral

Irregular

Elliptical

▲ There are various sizes, types and shapes of galaxies in the Universe. These are some of the main shapes, but there are many others.

- **Elliptical galaxies are vast**, old, egg-shaped galaxies, made up of as many as a trillion stars.

DID YOU KNOW?

About 2400 years ago, Democritus of ancient Greece suggested the band we call the Milky Way (our galaxy) was composed of countless distant stars.

Radiation

- **The energy that is given out** by atoms at high speed is called radiation. There are two main forms – atomic particles and electromagnetic radiation.

- **Electromagnetic radiation either travels** as waves or as tiny particles called photons.

- **Radioactivity is where an atom decays** (breaks down) and sends out gamma rays and particles.

- **Nuclear radiation is generated** by atomic bombs and nuclear power stations.

- **Electromagnetic radiation** is made when electric and magnetic fields move photons in tiny bursts of waves.

- **There are different kinds** of electromagnetic radiation, each with different wavelengths.

- **Gamma rays** are a very short-wave, energetic and dangerous form of electromagnetic radiation.

- **Radio waves** are a long wave, low-energy radiation.

- **In between** radio and gamma waves are microwaves, infrared rays, visible light , ultraviolet rays and X-rays.

- **Together, these forms** of electromagnetic radiation are called the electromagnetic spectrum.

- **All electromagnetic rays** move at the speed of light – 299,792,458 m/sec.

- **Objects in space** can be detected by the radiation they give out, and perhaps by other features such as gravity.

▼ Visible light is the only part of the electromagnetic spectrum that can be seen with the human eye.

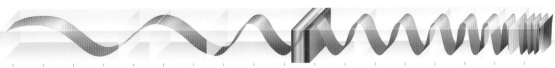

Radio waves   Microwaves   Infrared waves   Visible light   Ultraviolet rays   X-rays   Gamma rays

Missions to Mars

● **As the second-closest** planet to Earth, and one where life has the greatest chance of perhaps existing, Mars has been the target for more than 50 space missions.

● **The former USSR** (Russia and allies) sent two rover missions to Mars in 1971 but both failed.

● **In 1997** the US's Mars Pathfinder landed successfully and released the skateboard-sized rover Sojourner.

● **In 2003** Europe's orbiting Mars Express released Beagle 2, a lander and crawler, but contact was lost.

● **In 2015** images from the multi-purpose Mars Reconnaissance Orbiter showed that Beagle 2's solar panels had not unfolded away from its radio antenna.

● **In 2003** the US sent two Mars rovers, Spirit and Opportunity. They travelled great distances and gathered much information, before Spirit ceased to work in 2010.

● **Opportunity continued its wanderings** and covered over 40 km – more than any other space rover.

● **In 2012** the US's car-sized Curiosity rover arrived as part of the Mars Science Laboratory mission.

▼ *Curiosity is 2.9 m long and 2.2 m tall. It travels up to 200 m each day, depending on rocks, dust and other features of the terrain, and how much information it is gathering.*

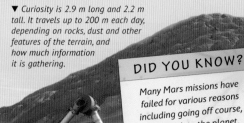

DID YOU KNOW?

Many Mars missions have failed for various reasons including going off course, crashing into the planet, engineering problems and using up fuel.

Telescopes

● **Optical telescopes** magnify distant objects using lenses or mirrors to focus light rays, which makes an enlarged image of the object.

● **Other telescopes detect** radio waves, X-rays or other kinds of electromagnetic radiation.

● **Refracting telescopes** are optical telescopes that use lenses to refract (bend) the light rays.

● **Reflecting telescopes** are optical telescopes that focus light rays by reflecting them off curved, dish-like mirrors. They make the light rays turn back on themselves so they are shorter than refracting telescopes.

● **Most professional astronomers** do not gaze at the stars directly. Their telescopes record light using electronic sensors called Charge-Coupled Devices (CCDs), as in digital cameras and smartphone cameras. The astronomers can then look at the results on a screen later.

● **Most early discoveries** in astronomy were made with refractors.

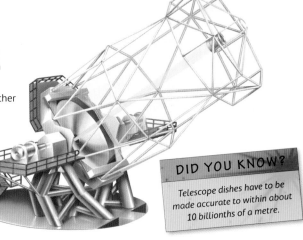

DID YOU KNOW?

Telescope dishes have to be made accurate to within about 10 billionths of a metre.

▲ *The largest telescopes can see about 100 billion galaxies. Most modern optical telescopes are reflectors, and the bigger the mirror, the more light is collected.*

● **Modern observatories** use gigantic reflector dishes made up of hexagons of glass or coated metal.

● **Large telescope dishes** are continually monitored and tweaked by computers to make sure that the reflector's mirrored surface stays completely smooth.

Star charts

● **Plotting the positions** of the stars in the sky is complex because there are vast numbers of them and because they are at hugely different distances.

● **The first modern star charts** were the German Bonner Durchmusterung (BD) charts of 1863, which show the positions of 324,189 stars. The German word *Durchmusterung* means 'scanning through'.

● **Published 1890 to 1945**, the AGK1 chart of the German Astronomical Society showed 200,000 stars.

● **The AGK charts** are now on version AGK3 and remain the standard star chart. They are compiled from photographs.

● **The measurements of accurate places** for huge numbers of stars depends on the careful determination of 1535 stars in the Fundamental Catalog (FK5).

● **Photometric catalogues map** the stars by magnitude and colour, as well as their position.

● **Photographic star atlases** do not actually plot the position of every star on paper, but include photos of them in place instead.

● **Three main atlases** are popular with astronomers – *Norton's Star Atlas*, *Tirion Sky Atlas* and *Photographischer Stern-Atlas*.

● **Celestial coordinates** are the figures that plot a star's position on a ball-shaped graph.

● **The altazimuth system** of coordinates gives a star's position by its altitude (its angle in degrees from the horizon) and its azimuth (its angle in degrees clockwise around the horizon, starting from north).

● **The ecliptic system** does the same, using the ecliptic rather than the horizon as a starting point.

● **The equatorial system** depends on the celestial equator, and gives figures called right ascensions and declination, just like latitude and longitude on Earth.

▼ *A section of an old star chart showing the constellation of Gemini.*

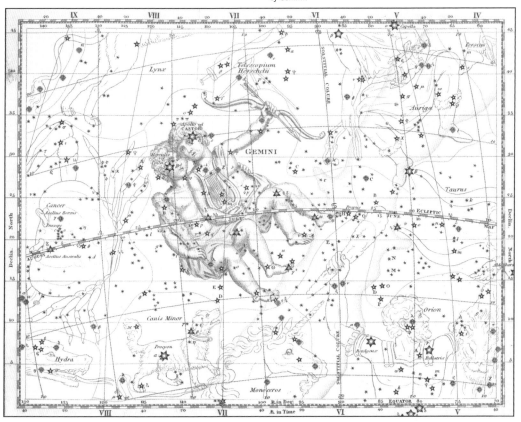

Planets

● **Planets are large globe-shaped objects** that orbit a star. Their gravity and rotation are powerful enough to make them spherical.

● **A planet has no other** large objects nearby, sharing its orbital zone or interfering with its gravity, except for those that the planet dominates by its own gravity, like moons.

◄ Probes, such as the Hubble Space Telescope, are able to give scientists a more detailed view of the planets. Here, on the lower right, the Hubble has detected a storm on Mars.

——— *Storm on Mars*

● **Most planets begin life** at the same time as their star, forming from the leftover clouds of gas and dust.

● **Planets are never** more than about five percent of the mass of their star. If they were bigger, they would be stars themselves.

● **The Solar System's largest planet**, Jupiter, would need to have been 70–100 times bigger than it is to begin nuclear fusion and become a very small star.

● **Thousands of planets** have been detected orbiting stars other than the Sun. These are called extra-solar planets or exoplanets.

● **The Sun contains 99.86 percent** of the total mass in the Solar System. All of the planets only make up a tiny 1/2500th of the Solar System's mass.

● **Terrestrial planets** have a surface made of solid rock.

● **Gas planets** do not have a solid surface, just cloud, although some may have a core of dense liquid, semi-liquid or even solid.

● **The Solar System** has eight planets. Pluto was the ninth, but it is very small and is now classified as a dwarf planet (planetoid).

Clusters

● **The Milky Way** belongs to a cluster of 30 galaxies called the Local Group.

● **The Local Group** measures around 7 million light years across.

● **There are 3 giant spiral galaxies** in the Local Group, plus 15 elliptical galaxies and 13 irregulars, such as the Large Magellanic Cloud.

DID YOU KNOW?

One film of superclusters makes up a vast structure called the Great Wall. It is the largest structure in the Universe – over 700 million light-years long, but just 30 million thick.

● **Beyond the Local Group** are many millions of similar star clusters.

● **The Virgo cluster** is 50 million light years away and is made up of over 1000 galaxies.

● **The Local Group plus millions** of other clusters make up a huge group called the Local Supercluster.

● **Other superclusters** are Hercules and Pegasus.

● **Superclusters** are separated by huge voids (empty space), which the superclusters surround like the film around a soap bubble.

● **The voids between superclusters** measure 350 to 400 million light-years across.

◄ Space looks like a formless collection of stars and clouds, but all matter tends to cluster together.

Variable stars

- **Variable stars** are stars that do not burn steadily like our Sun, but which flare up and down.

- **Pulsating, or intrinsic, variables** are stars that physically expand and contract or otherwise vary in brightness. They include the kinds of stars known as Cepheid variables and RR Lyrae variables.

- **Cepheid variables** are big, bright stars that pulse with energy, flaring up regularly every 1 to 50 days.

- **Cepheid variables** are so predictable in brightness that they make good distance markers.

- **RR Lyrae variables** are yellow supergiant stars near the end of their life that flicker as their fuel runs down.

- **Mira-type variables** are similar to Mira in Cetus, the Whale, and vary regularly over months or years.

- **RV Tauri variables** are very unpredictable, flaring up and down over changing periods of time.

- **Extrinsic variables** are usually steady-glowing stars that are actually eclipsing binaries (pairs of stars). They seem to flare and dim when one star gets in the way of the other.

- **The 'Demon Star'** is Algol in Perseus. It seems to burn fiercely for 59 hours, become dim, then flare up again 10 hours later. It is really an eclipsing binary as part of a triple star system.

- **The 'Vanishing Star'** is Chi in Cygnus, the Swan. It can be seen with the naked eye for a few months each year, but then becomes so dim that it cannot be seen, even with large amateur telescopes.

◀ *The constellation of Cygnus, which contains a vanishing star.*

Take-off

- **When a spacecraft is launched**, it needs to overcome the pull of Earth's gravity by being launched at a particular velocity (speed and direction).

- **The minimum velocity needed** for a spacecraft to combat gravity and stay in orbit around Earth is called the orbital velocity.

- **When a spacecraft at launch reaches** 140 percent of the orbital velocity, it can break free of Earth's gravity. This is called the escape velocity.

- **Earth's escape velocity** is approximately 11.2 km/sec, or 40,300 km/h.

- **The thrust (push) that launches** a spacecraft comes from powerful rocket engines in launch vehicles.

- **Some launch vehicles** are divided into stages, one on top of another, which fall away as their task is done.

- **The first stage lifts** everything off the ground, so its thrust must be greater than the weight of the launch vehicle plus the spacecraft. It falls away a few minutes after take off.

- **A second stage is then needed** to accelerate the spacecraft towards space.

- **After the two launch stages fall away**, there may be a third stage to put or insert the spacecraft into orbit.

- **An alternative design** is to use booster rockets which also fall away, or jettison, from the main vehicle when they finish firing.

▼ *Russia's Soyuz vehicles have been the mainstay of their space programme since the 1960s. This Soyuz FG rocket took a Soyuz TMA-M spacecraft with Yuri Malenchenko, Tim Kopra and Tim Peake to the ISS in 2015.*

Saturn's rings

● **The rings of Saturn** are chunks of water ice (frozen water), dust and tiny rocks that orbit the planet around its equator.

● **When sunlight hits the ice,** the rings seem to shimmer as some parts reflect the light while others are in shadow.

● **The rings may be fragments** of a moon that was torn apart by Saturn's gravity before it formed properly.

● **Galileo was the first** to see Saturn's rings, in 1610. His view through his early telescope was blurred and he said that it was as if the planet had ears.

● **Christiaan Huygens first realized** that these shapes were actually rings in 1659.

● **First described were the two main sets** of rings, A and B.

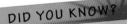

DID YOU KNOW?

Saturn's main rings measure over 900,000 km across, but only 20–50 m in thickness.

● **A third large ring** called the C or crepe ring was identified closer to the planet in 1850.

● **From the 1980s**, space probes revealed many other rings and 10,000 or more ringlets, some just a few metres wide and thick.

▼ *The icy chunks in Saturn's rings range in size from a marble to a truck, each circling the planet in its own orbit.*

● **The A and B rings** are separated by a gap called the Cassini Division, first spotted by Giovanni Cassini in 1675.

Neutron stars

● **Mainly made up of neutrons**, which are parts of an atom's nucleus, neutron stars are incredibly small, super-dense stars with a solid crust made of iron and similar elements.

● **Although neutron stars** weigh as much as the Sun, they are just 20 km across on average.

● **A tablespoon-full of a neutron star** would weigh about one million tonnes.

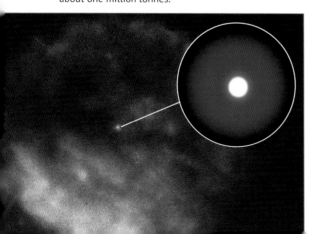

DID YOU KNOW?

The pull of gravity on the surface of a neutron star is more than one billion times stronger than Earth's gravity.

● **Neutron stars form** from the central core of a star that has died in a supernova explosion.

● **To produce a neutron star**, a star must be more than 1.4 times as massive as a medium-sized star, such as the Sun. This is known as the Chandrasekhar limit.

● **A star more than three times** as massive as the Sun would collapse beyond a neutron star to form a black hole. This is called the Oppenheimer-Volkoff limit.

● **The first evidence** of neutron stars came when pulsars (rapidly-spinning neutron stars) were discovered in the 1960s.

● **Some stars giving out X-rays**, such as Hercules X-1, are neutron stars. The X-rays come from nearby stars as material is squeezed on to their surfaces by their gravity.

● **Neutron stars have very powerful magnetic fields**, billions of times stronger than Earth's, which stretch the atoms out into frizzy 'whiskers' on the star's surface.

◀ *The blue dot in the centre of this supernova explosion is probably a neutron star.*

Years

● **A year is the time taken** for a planet to go around, or orbit, its star once.

● **An Earth calendar year is roughly this time** – Earth takes 365 days to travel around the Sun.

● **However Earth actually takes 365.242 days** to orbit the Sun. This is called a solar or tropical year.

● **To compensate for the missing 0.242 days**, the Western calendar adds an extra day in February every fourth (leap) year.

● **When measured by the stars**, not the Sun, Earth takes 365.25636 days to go round the Sun. This is because the Sun also moves a little, relative to the stars. This is called the sidereal (star) year.

● **Earth's perihelion** is the day its elliptical orbit brings it closest to the Sun – 3 January.

● **Earth's aphelion** is the day in its orbit it is farthest from the Sun – 4 July.

● **The planet with the shortest year** is Mercury, which speeds around the Sun in just 88 Earth days.

● **Neptune is the planet with the longest year**. It takes 164.8 Earth years to orbit the Sun.

● **The planet with the year** closest to the length of Earth's is Venus. A Venusian year lasts 225 Earth days.

▼ *The Earth orbits the Sun as though on a flat surface called the ecliptic plane. The planet's axis of rotation (the line around which it spins) is not at right angles to this, but 'leans' at 23.5°. This creates the different seasons.*

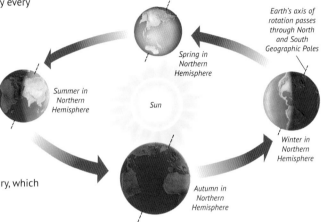

Earth's axis of rotation passes through North and South Geographic Poles

Spring in Northern Hemisphere

Summer in Northern Hemisphere

Sun

Winter in Northern Hemisphere

Autumn in Northern Hemisphere

Zodiac

● **The zodiac is the band of constellations** that the Sun appears to pass in front of during the year as the Earth orbits the Sun. It lies along the ecliptic.

● **The ecliptic is the plane** of Earth's orbit around the Sun. The Moon and all of the other planets lie on this plane.

● **The ancient Greeks divided** the zodiac into 12 parts, named after the constellation (group of stars) they saw in each part. These are the signs of the zodiac.

● **The 12 constellations of the zodiac** are named in Latin and describe how ancient people saw these groups of stars. They are Capricorn, Aquarius, Pisces, Aries, Taurus, Gemini, Cancer, Leo, Virgo, Libra, Scorpio and Sagittarius.

● **The English translations are** Goat, Water-bearer, Fish, Ram, Bull, Twins, Crab, Lion, Maiden, Scales, Scorpion and Centaur (or Archer).

● **Astrology (which is different from astronomy)** believes that the movements of the planets and stars in the zodiac affect events and shape people's lives.

● **For astrologers**, all the constellations of the zodiac are equal in size.

Capricorn   Aquarius   Pisces   Cancer

Leo   Virgo   Aries   Taurus

Gemini   Libra   Scorpio   Sagittarius

▲ *The zodiac signs are imaginary symbols that ancient astronomers linked to star patterns.*

● **However, the Earth has tilted** slightly since ancient times and the constellations no longer correspond to the zodiac. So, the dates that the Sun seems to pass in front of each constellation no longer exactly match the dates astrologers use.

● **The Moon and planets, however**, stay within the band of the zodiac as they move across the sky.

Star names

- **Most of the brightest stars** in the night sky were given individual names by the ancient Greeks. Arabic-speaking astronomers renamed many of these during the Middle Ages.

- **Arcturus means 'bear warden'** in Greek, and the star was given that name because it appears to follow the Great Bear across the sky.

- **The star Beta Orionis** was named Rigel (which means 'the foot' in Arabic) because it forms one of the hunter's feet in the constellation of Orion.

- **Alpha Orionis** has the name Betelgeuse (pronounced 'beetle-juice'), which comes from a mistaken translation of its original Arabic name Yad al-Jawza (which means 'the hand of Orion').

▶ *Canis Major (Great Dog) is a rare example of a constellation name being derived from a particular star name – in this case Sirius, which has long been known as the 'Dog Star'.*

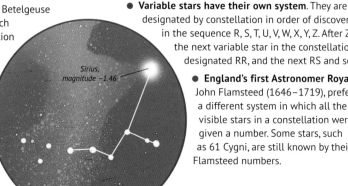

Sirius, magnitude –1.46

- **The constellation of Libra** was once known as the Scorpion's Claws. Consequently, the two brightest stars are Zubenelchemale ('Northern Claw') and Zubenelgenubi ('Southern Claw').

- **In 1603**, the German astronomer Johan Bayer introduced the present system of designating the brightest stars in a constellation by the letters of the Greek alphabet.

- **Variable stars have their own system.** They are designated by constellation in order of discovery in the sequence R, S, T, U, V, W, X, Y, Z. After Z the next variable star in the constellation is designated RR, and the next RS and so on.

- **England's first Astronomer Royal**, John Flamsteed (1646–1719), preferred a different system in which all the visible stars in a constellation were given a number. Some stars, such as 61 Cygni, are still known by their Flamsteed numbers.

X-rays

- **X-rays are electromagnetic rays** with waves shorter than ultraviolet rays and longer than gamma rays.

- **In space,** X-rays may be produced by very hot gases more than one million°C. They are also made when electrons interact with a magnetic field in synchrotron radiation (a kind of radiation).

- **X-rays cannot get through** Earth's atmosphere, so astronomers can only detect them using space telescopes, such as ROSAT, Chandra and XMM.

- **X-ray sources** are stars and galaxies that give out X-rays.

- **The first and brightest X-ray source** found (apart from the Sun) was the star Scorpius X-1 in 1962. Now tens of thousands are known, although most are weak.

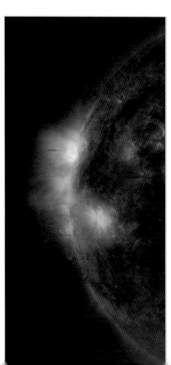

- **Remnants of supernovae,** such as the Crab nebula, are strong sources of X-rays.

- **The strongest sources of X-rays** in the Milky Way are X-ray binaries such as Scorpius X-1 and Cygnus X-1.

- **Some sources of X-rays** in space are thought to indicate to astronomers where there might be a black hole.

- **X-ray binaries** pump out 1000 trillion times as much X-ray radiation as the Sun.

- **Outside the Milky Way,** X-ray galaxies harbouring big black holes are powerful X-ray sources.

◀ *This image of the Sun has two parts. One is a view of the Sun's extreme ultraviolet rays, invisible to our eyes but coloured by computer as orange. Overlaid on this are blue and green areas showing X-rays being given off by the Sun and, again, coloured by computer.*

Sunspots

- **Dark spots on the Sun's photosphere** (surface) are called sunspots. They are 1500°C cooler than the rest of the surface.

- **The dark centre of a sunspot** is the umbra, the coolest part of a sunspot. Around it is the lighter penumbra.

- **Sunspots appear in groups** that seem to move across the Sun over two weeks, as the Sun rotates. Some last less than a day.

- **The number of sunspots** peaks every 11 years on average, varying from 9 to 14 years. This is called the solar or sunspot cycle.

- **The last sunspot** maximum was in 2013–2014.

- **When sunspots are at their maximum**, Earth's weather may be warmer and stormier.

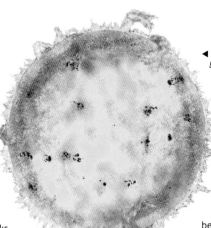

◀ *Sunspots on the surface of the Sun are caused by areas of intense magnetic fields.*

- **Long-term sunspot cycles** last between 80 and 200 years.

- **Observations of the Sun** by satellites, such as Nimbus-7, show that less heat reaches Earth from the Sun when sunspots are at a minimum.

- **The SOHO satellite**, launched in 1995, has revealed whirlpools of gases beneath sunspots.

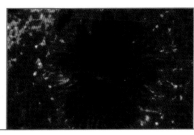

◀ *Infrared photographs reveal the dark sunspots that appear on the surface of the Sun.*

The Big Bang

- **Events happened very quickly** at the beginning of the Universe. In order to explain what happened scientists use measurements of time that are as small as one ten million trillion trillion trillionth of a second.

- **At first the Universe** was indescribably small and hot. It has been getting larger and cooler ever since.

- **In its initial state**, the four fundamental forces (strong and weak nuclear forces, electromagnetism and gravity) were unified into a single force.

- **Gravity** was the first of the four forces to separate, followed by the strong nuclear force. This triggered an event known as inflation and the Universe suddenly became billions of billions times bigger.

- **About one-billionth** of a second after the Big Bang, the Universe consisted of a dense sea of quarks and other particles.

- **About three minutes** after the Big Bang there was a brief period of nucleosynthesis when quarks joined together to form neutrons and protons.

- **For the first 300,000 years** the Universe remained completely opaque. Then it became cool enough for protons and neutrons to capture electrons and form atoms. The Universe was now transparent.

- **About 100 million years** after the Big Bang, the first stars began to shine.

- **There is still much** to be discovered about the Universe and the Big Bang.

- **Scientists** have recently proposed that there must be a fifth fundamental force (known as dark energy or quintessence) that prevents the Universe from collapsing inwards under the force of its own gravity.

◀ *No one knows what the Big Bang looked like 13.8 million years ago, so it is usually shown as some kind of explosion. However at its very beginning, forces and matter were very different. Not even light, as we know it, existed.*

1000 **PLANET EARTH** FACTS

Air moisture

● **Up to 10 km above the ground**, the air is always moist because it contains an invisible gas called water vapour.

● **On average**, air is about one percent water vapour, but the amount varies considerably.

● **Water vapour enters** the air when it evaporates from oceans, rivers and lakes.

● **It is also given off by plants**, especially leaves and grass, and in air breathed out by animals.

● **Water vapour leaves the air** when it cools and condenses (turns to drops of water) to form clouds. Most clouds eventually turn to rain, and the water falls back to the ground. This is called precipitation.

● **Like a sponge**, the air soaks up evaporating water until it is saturated (full). It can only take in more water if it warms up and expands.

● **If saturated air cools**, it contracts and squeezes out the water vapour, forcing it to condense into drops of water. The point at which this happens is called the dew point.

● **Humidity** is the amount of water in the air.

● **Absolute humidity** is the weight of water in grams in a particular volume of air.

● **Relative humidity**, which is written as a percentage, is the amount of water in the air compared to the amount of water the air could hold when saturated.

▼ *When a cold, dry wind blows over a warmish sea, water may evaporate in clouds of steam.*

Lithosphere

● **The outer, rigid layer** of the Earth is called the lithosphere. It consists of the crust and the top of the mantle. It is about 100 km thick.

● **The lithosphere was discovered** by seismology – the study of the patterns of vibrations from earthquakes.

● **It is thickest** – around 120 km – below the continents.

● **The lithosphere is only** a few kilometres thick below the middle of the oceans. Here, the mantle's temperature just below the surface is 1300°C.

● **Fast earthquake waves** show that the top of the mantle is as rigid as the crust, although it is chemically different.

● **Lithosphere** means 'ball of stone'.

● **The lithosphere is broken up** into about 20 slabs called tectonic plates. These are made up of continental plates (under the continents) and oceanic plates.

◀ *The hard, rocky surface of the Earth is made up of 20 or so strong, rigid plates of lithosphere.*

● **Temperatures increase** by 35°C for every 1000 m you move down through the lithosphere.

● **Below the lithosphere**, in the Earth's mantle, is the hot, soft rock of the asthenosphere.

● **The boundary between** the lithosphere and the asthenosphere occurs at the point where temperatures climb above 1300°C.

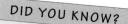

Earthquake waves

● **Earthquake waves** are the vibrations sent out through the ground by earthquakes. They are also called seismic waves.

● **There are two kinds** of deep earthquake wave: primary (P) waves and secondary (S) waves.

● **P waves** travel at 5 km per second and move by alternately squeezing and stretching rock.

● **S waves** travel at 3 km per second and move the ground up and down or from side to side.

● **There are two kinds** of surface earthquake wave: Love (Q) waves and Rayleigh (R) waves.

● **Love waves** shake the ground from side to side in a jerky movement that may topple tall buildings.

● **Rayleigh waves** shake the ground up and down, making it seem to roll.

● **In solid ground**, earthquake waves travel too fast to be seen by the human eye.

● **In unstable ground**, earthquake waves can turn loose sediments into a fluid-like material. They can then be seen rippling across the ground like waves in the sea.

▼ *This shows how the ground is vibrated by waves underground (P and S waves) and on the surface (Q and R waves).*

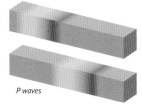
P waves

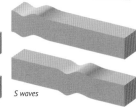
S waves

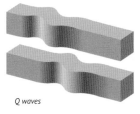
Q waves

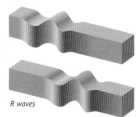
R waves

Caves

● **Caves are giant holes** that run horizontally underground. Holes that plunge vertically are called potholes.

● **The most spectacular caves**, called caverns, are found in limestone. Acid rainwater trickles through cracks in the rock and wears away huge cavities.

● **The world's largest known single cave** is the Sarawak Chamber in Gunung Mulu in Sarawak, Malaysia.

● **The deepest cave** yet found is Krubera Cave in Georgia, 2200 m below the surface.

● **The longest cave system** is the Mammoth Cave in Kentucky, USA, which is 650 km long and not yet fully explored.

● **Many caverns** contain speleothems. These deposits are made mainly from calcium carbonate deposited by water trickling through the cave.

● **Stalactites** are icicle-like speleothems that hang from cave ceilings. Stalagmites grow upwards from the floor.

● **The world's longest stalactite** is 8.2 m in Jeita Grotto, Lebanon.

● **The world's tallest stalagmite** at 70 m is in Son Doong Cave, Vietnam.

◄ *Carlsbad caverns, New Mexico, USA. Caverns can be subterranean palaces filled with glistening pillars.*

Africa

- **Africa is the world's** second largest continent. It stretches from the Mediterranean in the north to the Cape of Good Hope in the south. Its area is over 30,130,000 sq km.

- **It is the world's warmest continent**, lying almost entirely within the tropics or subtropics.

- **Temperatures in the Sahara** are among the highest on Earth, often soaring over 50°C.

Mount Elgon

Great Rift Valley

- **The Sahara** in the north of Africa, and the Kalahari in the south, are the world's largest deserts. Most of the continent in between is savannah (grassland) and bush. In the west and centre are lush tropical rainforests.

- **Much of Africa consists** of vast plains and plateaus, broken in places by mountains such as the Atlas range in the northwest and the Ruwenzori in the centre.

- **The Great Rift Valley** runs 7200 km from the Red Sea. It is a huge trench in the Earth's surface opened up by the pulling apart of two giant tectonic plates.

- **At 69,000 sq km**, Lake Victoria is Africa's largest lake.

- **Africa's highest mountain** is Kilimanjaro, at 5895 m.

- **The world's biggest sand dunes**, over 400 m high, can be found in the Sahara at Erg Tifernine, Algeria.

◀ A satellite view of the Great Rift Valley in Kenya, with the cone of the extinct volcano Mount Elgon on the left.

Ocean deeps

- **The oceans** are over 4000 m deep on average.

- **Along the edge** of the ocean is a ledge of land called the continental shelf. The average water depth here is 130–200 m.

- **At the edge** of the continental shelf the seabed plunges thousands of metres steeply down the continental slope.

- **The gently sloping foot** of the continental slope is called the continental rise.

- **Beyond the continental rise** the ocean floor stretches out in vast plains called abyssal plains. They lie about 4000–6000 m below the water's surface.

- **The abyssal plain** is covered in a thick slime called ooze. It is made from volcanic ash, meteor dust and the remains of dead sea creatures that sink down as 'marine snow'.

- **The abyssal plain is dotted** with huge mountains, thousands of metres high, called seamounts.

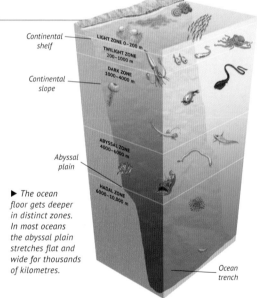

Continental shelf

Continental slope

Abyssal plain

LIGHT ZONE 0–200 m

TWILIGHT ZONE 200–1000 m

DARK ZONE 1000–4000 m

ABYSSAL ZONE 4000–6000 m

HADAL ZONE 6000–10,000 m

▶ The ocean floor gets deeper in distinct zones. In most oceans the abyssal plain stretches flat and wide for thousands of kilometres.

Ocean trench

- **Flat-topped seamounts** are called guyots. They may be volcanoes that once projected above the surface.

- **The deepest places** in the ocean floor are ocean trenches. These are made along subduction zones, where oceanic tectonic plates are driven down into the mantle by continental plates. The deepest is the Mariana Trench in the Pacific.

Changing landscapes

- **The Earth's surface** changes all the time. Most changes take millions of years, but sometimes the landscape is reshaped suddenly by an avalanche, earthquake or volcano.

- **By comparison, the Moon's lanscape** has barely changed over billions of years. The footprints left by Moon astronauts over 40 years ago are still there, perfectly preserved in dust.

- **The huge forces** of the Earth's interior distort and reform the Earth's surface from below.

- **Weather, water, ice** and other 'agents of erosion' mould the Earth's surface from above.

▼ *In southwestern USA, the Colorado Plateau has uplifted and the Colorado River has cut down into it to form a deep canyon.*

- **Most landscapes** are moulded by running water, which explains why hills have rounded slopes. Dry landscapes are more angular, but even in deserts water often plays a major shaping role.

- **Mountain peaks** are jagged because the extreme cold high up causes the rocks to freeze and shatter.

- **American scientist W M Davis** (1850–1935) believed that landscapes are shaped by repeated 'cycles of erosion'.

- **Davis's cycles of erosion** have three stages: Vigorous 'youth', steady 'maturity' and sluggish 'old age'.

- **Observation has shown** that erosion does not become slower as time goes on, as Davis believed.

- **Many landscapes** that exist today have been shaped by forces no longer in operation, or that are now much smaller than they were, such as the moving ice of glaciers during past ice ages.

Earthquake damage

- **Some of the world's major cities** are located in earthquake zones, such as Los Angeles in the USA, Mexico City in Mexico, and Tokyo in Japan.

- **Severe earthquakes** can cause buildings to collapse and rip up roads, rail lines, bridges and tunnels.

- **When freeways collapsed** in the 1989 earthquake in San Francisco, USA, some cars were crushed to just 50 cm thick.

- **The 1906 earthquake** in San Francisco destroyed 400 km of railway track around the city.

- **Some of the worst earthquake damage** is caused by fire, often set off by damage to gas and oil pipes and electrical cables.

- **In 1923**, 200,000 people died in the firestorm that engulfed the city of Tokyo, Japan. The quake hit at noon, toppling thousands of domestic fires that had been lit ready to cook lunch.

- **In the Kobe earthquake** of 1995 in Japan, and the San Francisco earthquake of 1989, some of the worst damage was to buildings built on landfill – loose material thrown into the ground to build up the land.

DID YOU KNOW?

There are probably over one million earthquakes each year, but fewer than 25,000 are detected by scientific instruments.

- **The earthquake that killed** the most people is believed to have hit Shaanxi, China, in 1556. It is estimated to have claimed 830,000 lives.

- **A huge quake in Lisbon**, Portugal, in 1755, caused 5-m-wide cracks in the ground in the city centre.

▼ *This bridge in Santiago, Chile, collapsed after an earthquake with a magnitude of 8.8 hit on 27 February, 2010. At least 82 people were killed.*

Continental drift

● **Continental drift** is the slow movement of the continents around the world.

● **About 220 million years ago** all the continents were joined together in one supercontinent – Pangaea.

● **Pangaea** began to break up about 190 million years ago. The fragments slowly drifted apart to form the continents we know today.

● **South America** used to be joined to Africa. North America used to be joined to Europe.

● **The first hint** that the continents were once joined was the discovery made by German explorer Alexander von Humboldt (1769–1859) that rocks in Brazil (South America) and the Congo (Africa) are very similar.

● **When German meteorologist** Alfred Wegener (1880–1930) first suggested the idea of continental drift in 1923, many scientists were sceptical.

● **Evidence of continental drift** has come from similar ancient fossils found on separate continents. These include the *Glossopteris* fern found in Australia and Asia and *Lystrosaurus* – a reptile-like creature from 200 million years ago – found in Africa, Asia and Antarctica.

● **Satellites provide** incredibly accurate ways of measuring and can record the slow movement of the continents. The main method is satellite laser ranging (SLR), where laser beams are bounced off a satellite from ground stations on each continent. Other methods include the Global Positioning System (GPS) and Very Long Baseline Interferometry (VLBI).

● **Rates of continental drift vary.** India drifted north into Asia relatively quickly. South America is moving 20 cm further from Africa every year. On average, continents move at the same rate as fingernails grow.

● **New York, USA,** is moving about 2.5 cm farther away from London, UK, every year.

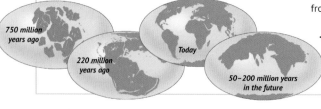

750 million years ago

220 million years ago

Today

50–200 million years in the future

◀ *It is hard to believe that the continents move – over tens of millions of years they move huge distances. The drifting of the continents has changed the map of the world very slowly over the past 200 million years, and will continue to do so.*

Earthquake measurement

● **Earthquakes are measured** with a device called a seismometer (seismograph).

● **The Richter scale** measures the magnitude (size) of an earthquake on a scale of one to ten. Each step up indicates a tenfold increase in energy.

● **The Richter scale** was devised in the 1930s by American geophysicist Charles Richter (1900–1985).

MERCALLI SCALE	
I. Instrumental	Only detected by seismographs.
II. Weak	Felt by only a few people, especially on upper floors.
III. Slight	Felt by some people, especially indoors and on upper floors.
IV. Moderate	Felt by people indoors, some outdoors. Windows and doors rattle. Standing cars rock.
V. Rather strong	Felt by most people. People sleeping wake, small unstable objects fall over. Trees shake.
VI. Strong	Felt by everyone. Difficult to walk. Heavy objects moved. Structural damage is slight.
VII. Very strong	Difficult to stand up. Slight to moderate damage in well-built urban areas. Moderate damage to poorly built structures.
VIII. Destructive	Considerable damage to ordinary buildings, some may partially collapse. Severe damage to poorly built structures.
IX. Violent	Damage great in ordinary buildings, with partial collapse. Buildings shifted off foundations.
X. Intense	Some well-built wooden structures destroyed. Most stone and frame structures with foundations destroyed. Train rails bent.
XI. Extreme	Few structures remain standing. Bridges destroyed. Train rails bent greatly.
XII. Cataclysmic	Damage total. Ground moves in waves and the landscape is altered. Objects thrown into the air.

● **The Modified Mercalli scale** assesses a quake's severity according to its effects.

● **The Mercalli scale** was devised by Italian scientist Giuseppe Mercalli (1850–1914).

● **A Mercalli scale I earthquake** is almost undetectable. A Mercalli scale XII earthquake causes almost total destruction.

● **The modern measuring scale** called the MMS – moment magnitude scale – combines Richter readings with observations of rock movements and measures the amount of energy released. Its numbers are similar to the Richter scale.

● **The most powerful earthquake** ever recorded was the Valdivia earthquake in Chile on 12 May, 1960, measuring 9.5 on the moment magnitude scale.

● **The Indian Ocean earthquake** of December 2004, which set off a tsunami, measured Richter 9.3.

● **Between 10–20 earthquakes** a year reach 7 on the Richter scale.

◀ *The Mercalli scale evaluates the severity of a quake from the damage it does on a scale of one–12 (I–XII).*

Waterfalls

● **When a river plunges vertically**, it is called a waterfall.

● **Waterfalls may form** where the river flows over a band of hard rock, such as a volcanic sill. The river erodes the soft rock below but has little effect on the hard band.

● **If a stream's course** is suddenly broken, for example if it flows over a cliff into the sea, over a fault or over a hanging valley, a waterfall can form.

● **Boulders often swirl** around at the foot of a waterfall, wearing out a deep pool called a plunge pool.

● **Angel Falls** in Venezuela are named after American pilot Jimmy Angel who flew over them in 1935. They have the longest straight drop or plunge at 810 m.

● **Victoria Falls** on the Zambia/Zimbabwe border are 110 m high and known locally as Mosi oa Tunya, which means the 'smoke that thunders'.

● **The roar from Victoria Falls** can be heard 40 km away.

● **Niagara Falls** on the US/Canadian border developed where the Niagara River flows out of Lake Erie.

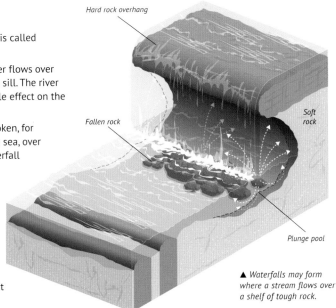

Hard rock overhang

Fallen rock

Soft rock

Plunge pool

▲ *Waterfalls may form where a stream flows over a shelf of tough rock.*

● **Niagara consists of two falls**: Horseshoe Falls, 54 m high, and American Falls, 55 m high.

● **Iguazu Falls** on the Brazil/Argentina border is the largest waterfalls system in the world, consisting of up to 300 waterfalls when the Iguazu River is in full flow.

▼ *In the wet season, over 3000 cubic metres of water flow over Zambia/Zimbabwe's Victoria Falls every second.*

Formation of the Earth

● **The Earth formed** 4.57 billion years ago, probably out of debris left over from the explosion of a giant star.

● **Star debris** spun round the newly formed Sun and clumped into rocks called planetesimals.

● **Planetesimals** were pulled together by their own gravity to form planets including Earth and Mars.

● **At first**, the Earth was a seething mass of molten rock.

● **After 50 million years** a giant rock collided with the newborn Earth. The impact threw out debris, which gradually joined together to become the Moon.

● **The shock of the impact** that formed the Moon made iron and nickel collapse towards the Earth's centre. They formed a core so dense that its atoms fused in nuclear reactions that have kept the inside of the Earth hot.

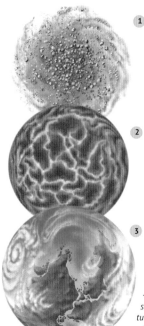

● **Molten rock** formed a mantle about 3000 km thick around the metal core. The core's heat keeps the mantle warm and churning, like boiling treacle.

● **The surface cooled and hardened** to form a thin crust. Then the Late Heavy Bombardment (LHB) of meteorites and asteroids about 3.9 billion years ago smashed the crust.

● **Steam and gases** billowing from volcanoes formed the Earth's first, poisonous atmosphere. The steam condensed to water.

● **By 3.8 billion years ago** the crust cooled again, and land and oceans formed. One Earth day was about 15 hours long.

◀ *When the Earth formed from a whirling cloud of stardust (1), the pieces collided and the young planet turned into a fiery ball (2). It slowly cooled, and the continents and oceans eventually formed (3).*

Antarctica

● **Antarctica is the ice-covered continent** at the South Pole. It covers an area of 14,000,000 sq km.

● **It is the coldest place on Earth.** Even in summer, temperatures rarely climb over −25°C. On 21 July, 1983, the air at the Vostok science station plunged to −89.2°C.

● **Antarctica is one of the driest places** on Earth, receiving barely any rain or snow. It is also very windy.

● **Until about 80 million years ago** Antarctica was joined to Australia.

● **Glaciers began to form** in Antarctica 38 million years ago, and grew rapidly from 13 million years ago. For the past five million years, 98 percent of the continent has been covered in ice.

▲ *Penguins are among the few creatures that can survive the cold of Antarctica all year round.*

● **The Antarctic ice cap** contains 70 percent of the world's fresh water.

● **The ice cap is thickest** – up to 4800 m deep – in deep sea basins far below the surface. Here it is thick enough to bury the Alps.

● **Antarctica is mountainous.** Its highest point is the Vinson Massif, at 5140 m.

● **The magnetic South Pole** – the pole to which a compass needle points – moves 8 km a year.

● **Fossils of tropical plants** and reptiles show that Antarctica was at one time much warmer.

Fog and mist

- **Like clouds**, mist is made up of billions of tiny water droplets floating in the air.

- **Fog forms** close to the surface of the Earth, over bodies of water or moist ground.

- **Mist forms** when the air cools to the point where the water vapour it contains condenses to water.

- **Meteorologists define fog** as a mist that reduces visibility to less than one kilometre.

▶ Mist often forms when cold air sinks into valleys on chilly nights.

- **There are four main kinds** of fog: radiation, advection, frontal and upslope.

- **Radiation fog** forms on cold, clear, calm nights. The ground loses the heat that it absorbed during the day, and cools the air above.

- **Advection fog** forms when warm, moist air flows over a cold surface. This cools the air so much that the moisture it contains condenses.

- **Sea fog** is advection fog that forms as warm air flows out over cool coastal waters and lakes.

- **Frontal fog** forms along weather fronts.

- **Upslope fog** forms when warm, moist air rises up mountains and then cools.

Earthquake prediction

- **One way to predict** earthquakes is to study past quakes.

- **If there has been no earthquake** in a prone area for a while, it is more likely that there will be one soon.

▼ This image of the Hayward Fault, California, uses satellite pictures and radar measurements. It shows the ground movement between 1992 and 1997 (orange and red indicate the most movement).

DID YOU KNOW?

Before an earthquake, dogs are said to start howling, rats and mice scamper from their holes and fish thrash about in the water.

- **The longer the gap** between earthquakes in a prone area, the bigger the next quake will be.

- **Seismic gaps** are places in active earthquake zones where there has been no earthquake activity. This is where a severe earthquake is more likely to occur.

- **Seismologists use ground instruments** and laser beams bounced off satellites to detect tiny distortions in the rock, which may indicate a build up of strain.

- **A linked network** of four laser-satellite stations called Keystone monitors ground movements in Tokyo Bay, Japan, so that earthquakes can be predicted.

- **The level of water** in the ground may indicate strain. The rock can squeeze groundwater towards the surface.

- **Rising surface levels** of the underground gas radon may also indicate that the rock is being squeezed.

- **Other signs of strain** in the rock may show as changes in the ground's electrical resistance or its magnetism.

Metal and mineral resources

- **There are about 91** known metal elements. They are mostly malleable (can be shaped by hammering), fusible (can be fused or melted) or ductile (able to be drawn out into a thin wire).

- **Metals are found** combined with other chemicals in rocks called ores in the Earth's crust. Ores are mined and the pure metals extracted usually by heating. This is called smelting.

- **Minerals are chemical compounds** that make up the rocks of the crust. About 90 percent of them are silicate minerals – made up primarily of silicon and oxygen.

- **Mineral hardness** is measured on the Mohs Scale. The softest, talc, scores 1, quartz (sand) scores 7 and diamond, the hardest, scores 10.

- **The first metals to be mined** were copper and tin about 5000 years ago. Smelted together they made the alloy (metal mixture) bronze, used for tools, weapons and utensils in the Bronze Age.

- **Iron ore was mined** and smelted about 3000 years ago during the Iron Age. Much harder than bronze, iron was used to make tools, weapons, ornaments and vessels.

- **About 95 percent** of all the metal in use in the world today is iron – some two tonnes for every person.

- **Around 98 percent** of all this iron is mixed with carbon, as charcoal or coke, during smelting to make the alloys called steels, which are stronger than pure iron.

- **Steels are used** in buildings, vehicles, railroads, household appliances and all kinds of machines.

- **Brazil produces** the most iron, Australia is second.

◀ *Quarrying and mining are huge businesses. Here, an iron ore rock called haematite is being quarried using excavators, diggers, massive trucks and railroad wagons.*

Deserts

- **Deserts are dry places** where it rarely rains. Many are hot, but one of the biggest deserts is Antarctica. Deserts cover about one-fifth of the Earth's land.

- **Desert that is strewn** with boulders is called hamada. Desert that is blanketed with gravel is called reg.

- **About one-fifth** of all deserts consist of sand dunes. These are known as ergs in the Sahara.

- **The type of sand dune** depends on how much sand there is, and how changeable the wind is.

- **Barchans are moving**, crescent-shaped dunes that form in sparse sand where the wind direction is constant.

- **Seifs are long dunes** that form where sand is sparse and the wind comes from two or more directions.

- **Most streams in deserts** flow only occasionally, leaving dry stream beds called wadis or arroyos. These may fill suddenly to become a flash flood site after rain.

- **In cool, wet regions**, hills are covered in soil and rounded in shape. In deserts, hills are bare rock with cliff faces supported by straight slopes.

- **Mesas and buttes** are pillar-like plateaus that have been carved gradually by water in deserts.

- **Deserts generally get** less than 25 cm of rain a year.

▼ *Sand dunes are sculpted and piled up into different shapes by the different actions of wind.*

| Transverse dune (across prevailing wind) | Seif or longitudinal dune (changing wind direction) | Barchan dune (relatively constant wind direction) | Blow-out dune (scooped out by wind) | Star dune (variable wind direction) |

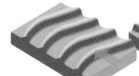
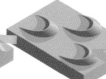

Earthquakes

● **Earthquakes are a shaking of the ground.** Some are slight tremors that barely rock a cradle. Others are so violent they can raze cities and mountains to the ground.

● **Small earthquakes** may be set off by landslides or volcanic eruptions. Large earthquakes are triggered by the grinding together of the tectonic plates that make up the Earth's surface.

● **Tectonic plates** are sliding past each other all the time, but sometimes they get stuck. This causes rock to bend and stretch, until it snaps. This makes the plates jolt, sending out shock waves that cause quakes that can be felt far away.

● **Typically, tectonic plates slide** 4 or 5 cm past each other in a year. In a slip that triggers a major quake they can slip more than one metre in a few seconds.

● **In most earthquakes**, a few minor tremors (foreshocks) are followed by an intense burst lasting just one or two minutes. A second series of minor tremors (aftershocks) occurs over the following few hours.

● **The starting point** of an earthquake below ground where most energy is released is called the focus, or hypocentre.

● **The epicentre** of an earthquake is the point on the surface directly above the focus.

● **An earthquake's effects** are usually strongest at the epicentre and become gradually weaker farther away.

▲ *Earthquakes can cause large cracks to open up in the ground, cutting off towns and villages.*

● **Regions called earthquake zones** are especially prone to earthquakes. Most of these zones lie along the edges of tectonic plates.

● **A shallow earthquake** originates 0–70 km below the ground, and these do the most damage; an intermediate quake begins 70–300 km down, and deep earthquakes start over 300 km down. The deepest ever recorded quakes began more than 600 km below the surface.

▼ *During an earthquake, shock waves radiate in circles outwards and upwards from the focus of the earthquake. The damage caused is greatest at the epicentre, where the waves are strongest, but vibrations may be felt more than 1000 km away.*

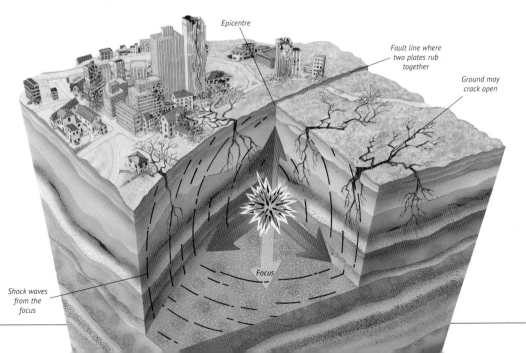

Epicentre

Fault line where two plates rub together

Ground may crack open

Focus

Shock waves from the focus

Climate zones

- **Weather is atmospheric events** over days and weeks, while climate is longer-term conditions over years, decades and centuries.

- **Climates are warmer** near the Equator, where the Sun climbs high in the sky. Its rays pass at a steep angle through the atmosphere, and its heat covers a small area on the ground.

- **Tropical climates** occur in the Tropics, the zones either side of the Equator. Temperatures average 27°C.

- **The climate is cool** near the Poles, where the Sun never climbs high in the sky. Its rays slant through the atmosphere and spread over a wide ground area. Temperatures average −30°C.

- **Temperate climates** occur in the temperate zones between the tropics and the polar regions. They are mild with a summer average of 23°C, and in winter, 12°C.

- **An oceanic climate** is wetter near the oceans, with cooler summers and warmer winters.

- **A Mediterranean climate** is temperate with warm summers and mild winters. It is typical of the Mediterranean, South Africa and South Australia.

North Pole

Tropic of Cancer

Equator

Tropic of Capricorn

South Pole

Tropical   Tropical   Desert   Polar   Mountainous
rainforest

Dry   Wet   Cold   Temperate
temperate   temperate   temperate   grassland

▲ *The coloured rings (left) match the areas on the map. In general, the warmer climates are found close to the Equator.*

- **A monsoon climate** has one very wet and one very dry season – typical of India and Southeast Asia.

- **A continental climate** is dry in the centre of continents, with hot summers and cold winters.

- **Mountain climates** get colder and windier with height.

Weathering

- **Weathering is the gradual breakdown** of rocks when they are exposed to air, water and living things.

- **Weathering affects** surface rocks the most, but water trickling into the ground can weather rocks 200 m down.

- **The more extreme the climate** – very cold or very hot – the faster weathering takes place.

- **In tropical Africa**, the basal weathering front (where weathered meets unweathered rock) is often 60 m down.

- **Weathering works chemically** (through chemicals in rainwater), mechanically (through temperature changes) and organically (through plants and animals).

- **Chemical weathering** is when gases such as carbon dioxide and sulphur oxides dissolve in rain to form weak acids that corrode rocks such as limestone.

- **Organic weathering** is when rocks are broken up by plant roots growing or are dissolved by plant acids.

▶ *The combination of extreme temperatures and the damaging effect of strong winds has created this rock sculpture in the Arizona desert, USA.*

- **The main form of mechanical weathering** is frost shattering. This is when water expands as it freezes in cracks and so splits apart and shatters the rock.

- **Thermoclastis** is when desert rocks crack as they get hot and expand in the day, then cool and contract at night.

- **At −22°C**, ice can exert a pressure of three tonnes on an area of rock the size of a postage stamp.

Gems and jewels

● **Gemstones or jewels** are either precious, such as diamond and ruby, or semi-precious, such as garnet and amethyst, depending on their rarity.

● **Most are mineral crystals** but some, like pearls, amber and jet, come from plant or animal sources.

● **Gems are graded** for value by their colour, clarity and carats (weight). Colour and clarity depend on the arrangement of the crystal's tiniest particles, atoms and molecules, and any traces or impurities.

● **Corundum contains** aluminium and oxygen. With traces of chromium it becomes red ruby, if iron and titanium are involved it becomes blue sapphire.

● **Most opaque gemstones** are polished into dome shapes called cabochons to show off their colour and any internal patterning.

● **Transparent gems** like diamonds have flat faces or facets cut onto their surfaces, which allow the light to sparkle and 'twinkle' as it passes through and reflects.

● **Most gemstones** formed millions of years ago deep in the Earth's crust where they slowly crystallized under great pressure and temperature.

● **The crystals were brought** near to the surface by the slow churning of hot, melted magma, and they are mined from the rocks in which they formed.

● **The largest gem-quality diamond** ever found weighed 3106.75 carats or 621.35 grams. It was found in 1905 in South Africa.

▼ *Clear sparkling diamond and black opaque coal are both forms of the same chemical element, carbon. In diamond the smallest particles, atoms, are arranged in box-like shapes, in coal they are at random.*

Deep ocean currents

● **Ocean surface currents** affect only the top 100 m or so of the ocean. Deep currents involve the whole ocean.

● **Deep currents** are set in motion by differences in the density of sea water. Most move only a few metres a day.

● **Most deep currents** are called thermohaline circulations because they depend on the water's temperature ('thermo') and salt content ('haline').

● **If sea water is cold** and salty, it is dense and sinks.

● **Typically, dense water forms** in the polar regions. Here the water is cold and weighed down by salt left behind when sea ice forms.

● **Dense polar water** sinks and spreads out towards the Equator far below the surface.

● **Oceanographers** call dense water that sinks and starts deep ocean currents 'deep water'.

● **In the Northern Hemisphere** the main area for the formation of deep water is the North Atlantic.

● **Dense salty water** from the Mediterranean sinks quickly – one metre per second – through the Straits of Gibraltar to add to the North Atlantic deep water.

● **Antarctic deep water** is below zero, at –1.9°C, but its salt and movement prevent it freezing solid.

▼ *Deep water circulations begin in the polar regions where cold, dense water sinks, laden with salt left behind as ice forms.*

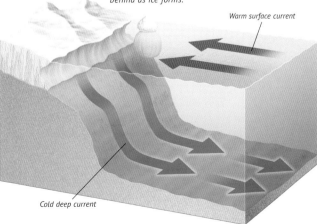

Warm surface current

Cold deep current

Glaciers

● **Glaciers are 'rivers'** of slowly moving ice. They form in mountain regions when it is too cold for snow to melt. They flow down through valleys, creeping lower until they melt in the warm air lower down.

● **When new snow**, or névé, falls on old snow, glaciers are formed. The weight of the new snow compacts the old into denser snow called firn.

● **In firn snow**, all the air is squeezed out so it looks like white ice. As more snow falls, firn gets more compacted and turns into glacier ice that slides slowly downhill.

● **Today, glaciers form** only in high mountains and towards the North and South Poles. In the ice ages, glaciers were widespread and left glaciated landscapes in many places that are now free of ice.

● **Valley glaciers** are glaciers that flow in existing valleys.

● **As glaciers move downhill**, over humps and around bends, they bend and stretch, opening up deep cracks called crevasses. Sometimes these occur where the glacier passes over a ridge of rock.

▲ *The Perito Moreno glacier in Argentina is 30 km in length and flows down from the Andes Mountains.*

● **The biggest crevasse** is often called the bergschrund. It forms when the ice pulls away from the back wall of the hollow where the glacier starts.

● **The underside of a glacier** is warmish (about 0°C). It moves by gliding over a film of water that forms as pressure melts the glacier's base. This is called basal slip.

● **Where the underside** of a glacier is well below 0°C, it moves as if layers were slipping over each other like a pack of cards. This is called internal deformation.

● **Cirque glaciers** are small glaciers that flow from hollows high up.

◀ *Glaciers begin in small hollows in the mountain called cirques, or corries. They flow downhill, gathering huge piles of debris called moraine on the way.*

Névé

Firn

Lateral moraine – debris fallen from the slopes above

Medial moraine – debris from the merging of two glaciers

Cirque

Crevasses

Step in rock floor

Terminal moraine – debris piled up in front of the glacier

Snout

Surface ocean currents

● **Surface ocean currents** are like giant rivers many kilometres wide, on average 100 m deep and flowing at 15 km per hour.

● **The major currents** are split on either side of the Equator into giant rings called gyres.

● **In the Northern Hemisphere** the gyres flow clockwise. In the south they flow anticlockwise.

● **Ocean currents** are driven by a combination of winds and the Earth's rotation.

● **Near the Equator**, water is driven by easterly winds to make westward-flowing equatorial currents.

● **When equatorial currents** reach continents, the Earth's rotation deflects them polewards as warm currents.

● **As warm currents flow polewards**, westerly winds drive them east back across the oceans. When the currents reach the far side, they begin to flow towards the Equator along the west coasts of continents as cool currents.

● **The North Atlantic Drift**, the northern part of the Gulf Stream, brings warm water from the Caribbean to southwest England, so it is warm enough to grow palm trees, yet it is as far north as Newfoundland, Canada.

● **By drying out the air**, cool currents can create deserts, such as the Baja California Desert in Mexico and Chile's Atacama Desert.

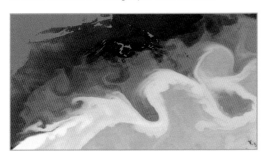

◀ *The warm Gulf Stream current flowing across the Atlantic (light pink) helps to keep the climate of northwest Europe mild.*

Climate change

● **The world's climate** has changed through time, getting warmer, colder, wetter or drier. There are many theories why this happens.

● **One way to see** how climate changed before weather records were kept is by growth rings in old trees. Wide rings show the good growth of a warm summer.

● **Another way of working out** past climate is to examine ancient sediments in lakes and seas for the remains of plants and animals that only thrive in certain conditions.

● **Another method** is to drill ice cores from glaciers and ice caps, where atmospheric gases, pollen and dust from past ages are trapped.

● **One cause** of climate change may be shifts in the Earth's orientation to the Sun. These shifts are called Milankovitch cycles.

● **Among the Milankovitch cycles are**: the change in shape of the Earth's whole orbit around the Sun, in a 100,000-year cycle; the slight increase or decrease in the tilt of the Earth's axis as the Earth orbits the Sun, in a 40,000-year cycle; and the slight wobbling, or precession, of this axis as the planet spins, in a 21,000-year cycle.

● **Climate may be affected** by patches on the Sun called sunspots. These flare up and down every 11 years.

● **Climates may cool** when the air is filled with dust from volcanic eruptions.

● **Local climates may change** as continents drift. Antarctica was once in the tropics, while New York, USA, once had a tropical desert climate.

● **Climates may get warmer** when levels of certain gases in the air increase, for example, with mass volcanic eruptions, and as is happening today with greenhouse gases.

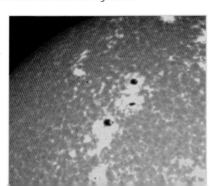

◀ *Some changes in weather are linked to fluctuations in sunspots, dark spots on the Sun. They can cause stormy weather on Earth.*

Clouds

● **Clouds are dense masses** of water drops and ice crystals that are so tiny, they float high in the air.

● **Cumulus clouds** are fluffy and white. They pile up as warm air rises and cools to the point where water vapour condenses.

● **Strong updraughts** create huge cumulonimbus, or thunderclouds.

● **Stratus clouds** are vast, shapeless clouds that form when a layer of air cools to the point where moisture condenses. They often bring long periods of light rain.

● **Cirrus clouds** are wispy, and form so high up, they are made entirely of ice. Strong winds high up blow them into 'mares' tails'.

● **Low clouds** lie below 2000 m altitude. They include stratus and stratocumulus clouds (the spread tops of cumulus clouds).

● **Nimbus are low**, dark clouds that bring rain or other precipitation.

● **Middle clouds** often have the prefix 'alto' and lie from between 2000–6000 m up. They include rolls of altocumulus cloud, and thin sheets called altostratus.

▲ *High level clouds like this are formed more of ice than water. Strong winds high-up create distinctive ripples.*

● **High-level clouds** are ice clouds up to 11,000 m up. They include cirrus, cirrostratus and cirrocumulus.

● **Contrails**, short for condensation trails, are long, thin trails of ice crystals or water droplets made by jet aircraft.

Hot-spot volcanoes

● **About 5 percent of volcanoes** are not near the margins of tectonic plates. Instead, they are thought to be over especially hot regions in the Earth's interior called hot spots.

● **Hot spots** are created by mantle plumes – hot currents that rise all the way from the core, through the mantle.

● **Mantle plumes** are about 500–1000 km across. They rise from as deep as 3000 km and melt their way through the crust to create hot-spot volcanoes.

▼ *Where the Pacific plate has gradually moved over a hot spot, the Hawaiian Island chain has formed.*

Active volcano

Mantle

Hot spot

Tectonic plate

● **Famous hot-spot volcanoes** include the Hawaiian Islands in the Pacific Ocean, and the St Helena chain of seamounts (mountains that are completely submerged underwater) in the Atlantic Ocean.

● **Hot-spot volcanoes** ooze runny lava that spreads out to create shield volcanoes.

● **Hot spots stay** in the same place while the plates slide over the top. At intervals, as the plate moves, a new volcano is created.

● **The Hawaiian Islands** are at the end of a chain of old volcanoes 6000 km long. The chain starts with the Meiji Seamount, which lies northeast of Japan.

● **The geysers**, hot springs and bubbling mud pots of Yellowstone National Park, USA, indicate a hot spot below.

● **Yellowstone** has erupted three times in the past two million years. The first produced over 2000 times as much lava as the eruption of Mount St Helens in 1980.

● **An alternative idea** is that hot spots are not unusually hot. They may be places where the lithosphere is stretched thinner due to tectonic movements, and ordinary mantle material rises through.

Glaciated landscapes

- **Glaciers move slowly** but their sheer weight and size give them enormous power to shape the landscape.

- **Over tens of thousands of years** glaciers carve out winding valleys into huge, straight U-shaped troughs (river valleys are usually V-shaped).

▼ *After an ice age, glaciers leave behind a dramatically altered landscape of deep valleys and piles of debris.*

- **Glaciers may truncate** (slice off) tributary valleys to leave them 'hanging', with a cliff edge high above the main valley. Hill spurs (ends of hills) may also be truncated.

- **Cirques, or corries,** are armchair-shaped hollows carved out where a glacier begins high up in the mountains.

- **Arêtes are knife-edge ridges** that are left between several cirques as the glaciers in them cut backwards.

- **Drift is a blanket of debris** deposited by glaciers. Glaciofluvial drift is left by the water made as the ice melts. Till is left by the ice itself.

- **Drumlins** are egg-shaped mounds of till.

- **Eskers** are snaking ridges of drift left by streams under the ice.

- **Moraine** is piles of debris left by glaciers as they melt and retreat.

Rocks

- **There are three main kinds of rock**: igneous, sedimentary and metamorphic.

- **The oldest known rocks** are in Canada – four-billion-year-old Acasta gneiss, and maybe even older is Nuvvuagittuq greenstone near Hudson Bay.

- **The youngest rocks** form today as molten lava erupts from volcanoes, cools and solidifies into solid rock.

- **The general scientific study** of rocks, their structures, and how they change is known as geology.

- **Petrology** is a specialism within geology that studies the detailed composition and microstructure of rocks, their origins and their fates.

- **Mineralogy** is the scientific study of the minerals that make up rocks, their origins, and how they change or react when rocks change form.

- **Geology** and its allied sciences are vital when surveying or prospecting for mineral wealth such as coal, petroleum oil, natural gas and ores such as those containing metals or sulphur.

- **One of the heaviest** or densest rocks is peridotite, with a density of up to 3.5 gm per cu cm.

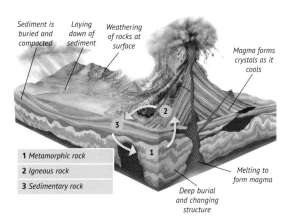

Sediment is buried and compacted *Laying down of sediment* *Weathering of rocks at surface*

Magma forms crystals as it cools

2

3

1

1	Metamorphic rock
2	Igneous rock
3	Sedimentary rock

Melting to form magma

Deep burial and changing structure

▲ *Rocks are continually recycled. They are broken down by weathering and erosion into sediments such as sand and mud. These settle on the beds of seas, lakes and rivers, where they harden to form new rock, in the ongoing process called the rock cycle.*

- **This compares** with the Earth's most dense naturally occurring element or pure chemical substance, the metal osmium, with a density of 22.6 gm per cu cm.

- **Other very dense** or heavy rocks include basalt, diabase and diorite.

Famous eruptions

● **One of the biggest eruptions ever** occurred 2.2 million years ago in Yellowstone, USA. It poured out enough magma to build half a dozen Mount Fujis.

● **In around 1627 BC** the Greek island of Thera erupted, destroying the Minoan settlement of Akrotiri. This may be the origin of the Atlantis myth.

▼ *The eruption of Mount St Helens in Washington, USA on 18 May, 1980 blew away the side of the mountain. It sent out a blast of gas that flattened trees for 30 km around.*

● **On 24 August, AD 79** the volcano Mount Vesuvius in Italy erupted. It buried the Roman town of Pompeii in ash.

● **The remains of Pompeii** were discovered in the 18th century, wonderfully preserved under metres of ash. They provide a remarkable snapshot of ancient Roman life.

● **The huge eruption** of the volcanic island of Krakatoa near Java in 1883 was heard up to 7000 km away.

● **In 1815 the eruption of Mount Tambora** in Indonesia was 60–80 times bigger than the 1980 eruption of Mount St Helens.

● **Ash from Tambora** filled the sky, making the summer of 1816 cool all around the world.

● **J. M. W. Turner's paintings** may have been inspired by fiery sunsets caused by dust from Tambora.

● **During the eruption of Mount Pelée** on Martinique on 8 May, 1902, all but two of the 29,000 townspeople of nearby St Pierre were killed in a few minutes by a scorching flow of gas, ash and cinders.

● **The biggest eruption** in the past 50 years was that of Mount Pinatubo in the Philippines in April 1991.

Ice ages

● **Ice ages** are periods lasting millions of years when the Earth is so cold that the polar ice caps grow huge. There are various theories about why they occur.

● **There have been five ice ages** in the last 1000 million years, including one that lasted 100 million years.

● **The most recent ice age** – called the Pleistocene Ice Age – began about 2.5 mya (million years ago).

● **In an ice age**, the climate varies between cold spells called glacials and warm spells called interglacials.

▼ *California may have looked something like this 18,000 years ago when it was on the fringes of an ice sheet.*

● **There have been** about 15 glacials and interglacials in the last 2.5 million years of the Pleistocene Ice Age.

● **The last glacial** peaked about 25,000–18,000 years ago and ended 12,000–11,000 years ago.

● **Ice covered 40 percent** of the world 18,000 years ago.

● **Glaciers spread** over much of Europe and North America 18,000 years ago. Ice caps grew in Tasmania and New Zealand.

● **About 18,000 years ago** there were glaciers in Hawaii and Australia.

DID YOU KNOW?

Where Washington D.C. and London are today, the ice was 1.5 km thick 18,000 years ago.

Atmosphere

- **The atmosphere is a blanket** of gases that extends to 10,000 km above the Earth. It can be divided into five layers: troposphere (the lowest layer), stratosphere, mesosphere, thermosphere and exosphere.

- **Near Earth's surface the atmosphere is**: 78 percent nitrogen, 21 percent oxygen, one percent argon and carbon dioxide, with tiny traces of neon, krypton, xenon, helium, nitrous oxide, methane and carbon monoxide. It also contains a variable amount of water vapour.

- **It was first created** by the fumes pouring out from volcanoes that covered the early Earth 4000 million years ago. But the atmosphere changed as rocks and seawater absorbed carbon dioxide, and then single-celled bacteria and algae in the sea built up oxygen levels over millions of years.

- **The troposphere** is just 0–20 km thick and yet it contains 75 percent of the weight of gases in the atmosphere.

- **Temperatures in the troposphere** drop with height from an average of 18°C to about –60°C at the top, or tropopause.

- **The stratosphere** contains little water vapour. Unlike the troposphere, which is heated from below, the stratosphere is heated from above as the ozone molecules in it are heated by ultraviolet (UV) light from the Sun. Temperatures rise with height from –60°C at the bottom to 10°C at the top, about 50 km up.

- **The stratosphere** is usually clear and calm, which is why passenger aircraft fly in this layer.

- **The mesosphere** contains few gases but it is thick enough to slow down meteorites. They burn up as they hurtle into it, leaving fiery trails in the night sky. Temperatures drop from 10°C to –120°C about 85 km up.

- **In the thermosphere** temperatures are high, but there is so little gas that there is little heat. Temperatures rise from –120°C to 2000°C about 600 km up.

- **The exosphere** is the highest level of the atmosphere where it fades into the nothingness of space.

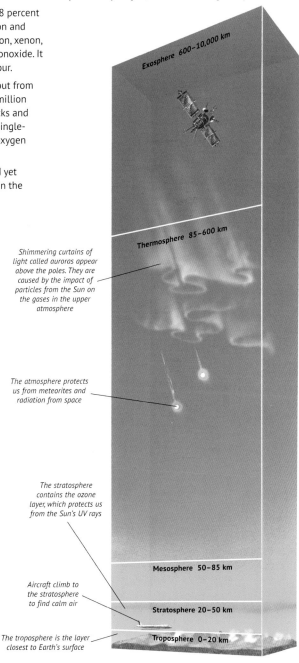

▼ The atmosphere is a sea of colourless, tasteless, odourless gases, mixed with moisture and fine dust particles. It is about 10,000 km deep but has no distinct edge, simply fading away into space. As you move up, each layer contains less and less gas. The topmost layers are very rarefied, which means that gas is sparse.

Exosphere 600–10,000 km

Thermosphere 85–600 km

Shimmering curtains of light called auroras appear above the poles. They are caused by the impact of particles from the Sun on the gases in the upper atmosphere

The atmosphere protects us from meteorites and radiation from space

The stratosphere contains the ozone layer, which protects us from the Sun's UV rays

Mesosphere 50–85 km

Aircraft climb to the stratosphere to find calm air

Stratosphere 20–50 km

Troposphere 0–20 km

The troposphere is the layer closest to Earth's surface

Waves

● **Waves are formed** when wind blows across the sea and whips the surface into ripples.

● **Water particles** are dragged a short distance by the friction between air and water, which is known as wind stress.

● **If the wind continues to blow** long and strong enough in the same direction, moving particles may build up into a ridge of water. At first this is a ripple, then a wave.

● **Waves seem to move** but the water in them stays in the same place, rolling around like rollers on a conveyor belt.

● **The size of a wave** depends on the strength of the wind and how far it blows over the water (the fetch).

● **If the fetch is short**, the waves may simply be a chaotic, choppy sea. If the fetch is long, they may develop into a series of rolling waves called a swell.

● **The biggest waves** occur in the ocean south of South Africa.

● **When waves move** into shallow water, the rolling at the base is impeded by the seabed. The water at the surface piles up, then spills over in a breaker.

● **The tallest breakers** rise to more than 30 m before crashing onto the shore.

◄ *Waves break as the top spills over in shallow water.*

Ecosystems

● **An ecosystem** is a community of living things interacting with each other and their surroundings. Anything from a piece of rotting wood to a swamp can be an ecosystem.

● **When vegetation colonizes** an area, often the first plants to grow are small and simple, such as mosses and lichens. These plants stabilize the soil so that bigger, more complex plants can grow. This is called vegetation succession.

● **Rainforest ecosystems** cover only 8 percent of the world's land, yet they include 40 percent of all plant and animal species.

● **The food chain** is the route linking living things that feed upon each other. The eating interaction between them is rarely simple, so ecologists talk of food 'webs'.

● **Green plants** are autotrophs (producers) – they make their own food.

● **Animals are heterotrophs** (consumers) – they eat other living things.

● **Primary consumers** are herbivore animals (plant-eaters). Secondary consumers are either carnivores (meat-eaters) or omnivores (eat plants and meat).

● **Decomposers or detritivores** include insects, millipedes, worms, bacteria and fungi. They feed on the remains of dead plants and animals. In turn, they prepare the soil for plants and help supply them with nutrients.

● **Every living thing** has its own unique role in the living community, called its niche. Because living species are so interdependent, a problem with one can affect the entire community.

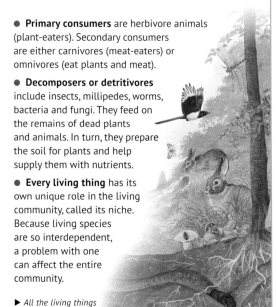

▶ *All the living things in a natural ecosystem, such as a woodland, are dependent on each other.*

Cold landscapes

● **'Periglacial' is used to describe** an area of land that is next to a glacier or ice sheet, or that repeatedly freezes and thaws.

● **Periglacial conditions** are found on the tundra of northern Canada and Siberia and on nunataks, which are the hills that protrude above ice sheets and glaciers.

● **In periglacial areas**, ice melts only in spring at the surface.

● **Where soil stays frozen** for almost the whole year, usually just under the surface, it is known as permafrost.

● **When the ground above** the permafrost melts, the soil twists into buckled layers called involutions.

● **When frozen soil melts** it becomes so fluid that it can creep easily down slopes, creating large tongues and terraces.

● **Frost heave** is the process when frost pushes stones to the surface as the ground freezes.

● **After frost heave**, large stones roll downhill and away, leaving the fine stones on top. This creates intricate patterns on the ground.

● **Pingos are mounds** of soil with a core of ice. They are created when groundwater freezes beneath a lake.

▼ Cold conditions such as on this Arctic tundra create a unique landscape in polar and high mountain regions.

DID YOU KNOW?

In periglacial conditions, temperatures never climb above freezing in winter.

Asia

● **Asia is the world's largest continent**, stretching from Europe in the west to Japan in the east. It has an area of 44,600,00 sq km.

● **Asia has huge climate extremes**, from a cold polar climate in the north to a hot tropical one in the south.

● **Verkhoyansk in Siberia** has had temperatures as high as 37°C and as low as −68°C.

● **The Himalayas** are the highest mountains in the world, with 14 peaks over 8000 m high. To the north are vast, empty deserts, broad grasslands and huge coniferous forests. To the south are fertile plains and valleys and steamy tropical jungles.

● **Northern Asia** sits on one giant tectonic plate.

DID YOU KNOW?

The place on Earth farthest from the ocean is in Xinjiang Province, northwest China, at more than 2500 km from an oceanic coastline.

● **India is on a separate plate** that crashed into northern Asia around 50 million years ago. It is pushing up the Himalayas as it ploughs on northwards.

● **Asia's longest river** is China's Yangtze, at over 6000 km long.

● **Asia's highest mountain** is also the highest in the world – Mount Everest, or Sagarmatha, in Nepal, at 8848 m.

● **The Caspian Sea** between Azerbaijan and Kazakhstan is the world's largest lake, covering 378,400 sq km.

▼ Sometimes called the 'roof of the world', the Tibetan Plateau is on average over 4500 m high and covers an area four times the size of France. The Himalayas border the Tibetan Plateau to the south.

Converging plates

● **In many places** around the world, the tectonic plates that make up the Earth's crust are slowly crunching together with huge force.

● **The Atlantic Ocean** is getting wider, pushing apart the Americas from Europe and Africa. But the Earth is not getting any bigger.

● **As the west edges** of the American plates crash into the Pacific ocean plate, the thinner, denser ocean plate is driven down into the Earth's hot mantle and melted.

● **The process of driving** an ocean plate down into the Earth's interior is called subduction.

● **Subduction creates** deep ocean trenches typically 6–7 km deep. One of these, the Mariana Trench, is 11 km at its deepest point.

● **As an oceanic plate bends down** into the Earth's mantle, it cracks. The movement of these cracks sets off earthquakes originating up to 700 km below the surface. These earthquake zones are called Benioff–Wadati zones after two experts, Hugo Benioff (1899–1968) of the USA and Kiyoo Wadati (1902–1995) of Japan, who discovered them separately in the 1950s.

● **An oceanic plate melts** as it slides down, and creates blobs of magma. This magma floats up towards the surface, pushing its way through weak crust to create a line of volcanoes along the edge of the continental plate.

▼ *This cross-section through the top 1000 km or so of the Earth's surface shows a subduction zone – where an ocean plate is bent down beneath a continental plate.*

▲ *The Aleutians in Alaska are an island arc, a long chain of islands formed by volcanoes above a subduction zone where two tectonic plates converge.*

● **If volcanoes in subduction zones emerge** in the sea, they form a curving line of volcanic islands called an island arc. Beyond this arc is the back-arc basin, an area of shallow sea that slowly fills up with sediments.

● **As a subducting plate sinks**, the continental plate scrapes sediments off the ocean plate and piles them in a great wedge. Between this wedge and the island arc there may be a fore-arc basin, which is a shallow sea that slowly fills with sediment.

● **Where two continental plates collide**, the plates split into two layers: a lower layer of dense upper-mantle rock and an upper layer of lighter crustal rock, which is too buoyant to be subducted. As the mantle rock goes down, the crustal rock peels off and crumples against the other to form fold mountains.

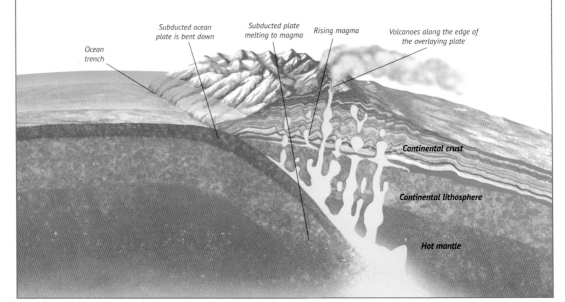

Ocean trench

Subducted ocean plate is bent down

Subducted plate melting to magma

Rising magma

Volcanoes along the edge of the overlaying plate

Continental crust

Continental lithosphere

Hot mantle

Lakes

- **Most of the world's large lakes** lie in regions that were once glaciated. The glaciers carved out deep hollows in the rock in which water collected. The large lakes of the USA and Canada are partly glacial in origin.

- **In Minnesota**, USA, 11,000 lakes were formed by glaciers.

- **The world's deepest lakes** are often formed by faults in the Earth's crust, such as Lake Baikal in Siberia and Lake Tanganyika in East Africa.

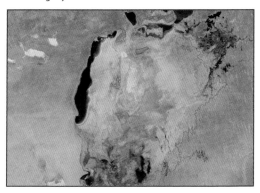

- **The world's largest lake** is the Caspian Sea, in western Asia, which is a saltwater lake.

- **The world's highest large lake** is Titicaca in South America, which is 3812 m above sea level.

- **The world's lowest large lake** is the Dead Sea between Israel and Jordan. It is 399 m below sea level and getting lower all the time.

- **The largest underground lake** in the world is Drauchen-hauchloch or Dragon's Breath, which is inside a cave in Namibia.

- **Most lakes last** only a few thousand years before they are filled in by silt or drained by changes in the landscape.

- **The Aral Sea** in western Asia shrank to only one-tenth of its original size, which was 70,000 sq km, between 1950 and 2000, due to diverting the rivers that fed it to water crops elsewhere.

- **New dam and pipeline projects** hope to refill part of the Aral Sea over the next 50 years.

◄ *About 50 years ago the Aral Sea would have almost filled this photograph's frame. By 2014 it was reduced to two main and several smaller lakes. The whole south and east have become desert.*

Beaches

- **Beaches are slopes** of silt, sand, shingle or pebbles along the edge of an ocean, sea or lake.

- **Some beaches** are made entirely of broken coral or shells.

- **On a steep beach**, the backwash after each wave is strong. It washes material down the beach and gradually makes the beach slope more gently.

- **On a gently sloping beach**, each wave runs in powerfully and falls back gently. Over time, material gets washed up the beach, making it steeper.

- **The slope of a beach** matches the waves, so the slope is often gentler in winter when the waves are stronger.

- **A storm beach** is a ridge of gravel and pebbles flung high above the normal high-tide mark during a storm.

- **At the top of each beach** a ridge, or berm, is often left at high-tide mark.

- **Beach cusps** are tiny bays in the sand that are scooped out along the beach when waves strike it at an angle.

- **Many scientists believe** that beaches are only a temporary phenomenon caused by the changes in sea levels after the last Ice Age.

▼ *The white beach at Cancun, Mexico, is made from the fragments of coral reefs.*

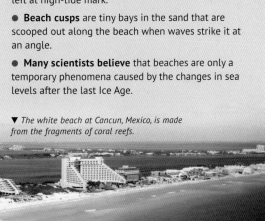

Seasons

● **Seasons are periods** into which the year is divided according to annual shifts in weather patterns.

● **Many places** in the tropics have just two six-month seasons: wet and dry.

● **Outside the tropics** there are four three-month seasons each year: spring, summer, autumn and winter.

● **The changes in the seasons** occur because the tilt of the Earth's axis stays the same as Earth circles the Sun.

● **When the Northern Hemisphere** tilts towards the Sun, it is summer in the north of the world and winter in the south.

● **When the Earth moves** another quarter of its orbit, both hemispheres are equal and it is autumn in the north and spring in the south.

● **After another quarter-orbit**, the Southern Hemisphere is tilted towards the Sun, so the south has summer and the north has winter.

● **As the Earth moves** to its three-quarters orbit around the Sun, the north begins to tilt towards the Sun again. This brings spring weather to the north and autumn to the south.

● **Around 21 March** and 21 September, the night is exactly 12 hours long all over the world. These times are called the vernal (spring) and the autumnal equinox.

● **The day when** nights begin to get longer again is called the summer solstice. This is around 21 June in the north and 21 December in the south.

▼ *As the Earth orbits the Sun it is always tilted the same way. This means that each pole leans towards and then away from the Sun over the year, giving us seasons.*

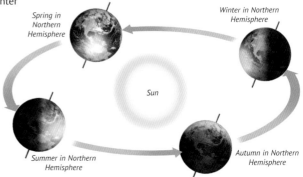

Spring in Northern Hemisphere

Winter in Northern Hemisphere

Sun

Summer in Northern Hemisphere

Autumn in Northern Hemisphere

Global warming

● **The general increase** in average temperatures around the world is called global warming. This increase has been almost 1°C over the last 100 years.

● **Most scientists now think** that global warming is caused mainly by human activities, which have resulted in an increase over and above the Earth's natural greenhouse effect.

● **The greenhouse effect** is how certain gases in the air – notably carbon dioxide, ozone and methane – trap some of the Sun's warmth, like the glass in a greenhouse.

● **The Earth is kept warm** by the natural greenhouse effect, at about 15°C on average, rather than –15°C without a greenhouse effect.

● **If too much heat** is trapped, the Earth may become hotter.

● **Many experts expect** a 4°C rise in average temperatures over the next 100 years.

● **Humans boost** the greenhouse effect by burning fossil fuels, such as coal and oil, which produce carbon dioxide.

▲ *In Antarctica, scientists drill deep into the ice to extract core samples. These hold clues about past changes in weather and climate, and can help us predict how it will change in the future.*

● **Emissions** of the greenhouse gas methane from the world's cattle and other farm livestock add to global warming.

● **Global warming** makes the oceans increase in volume by expansion. It may also melt much of the polar ice caps, flooding large areas of low-lying land in major cities around the world.

● **By trapping more energy** inside the atmosphere, global warming is also predicted to bring climate change and stormier, more extreme weather.

Black smokers

- **Billowing black fumes** of hot gases, particles and scorching water, black smokers are natural chimneys on the seabed.

- **The technical name** for black smokers is hydrothermal vents. They are volcanic features.

- **Black smokers** form along mid-ocean ridges where the tectonic plates are moving apart.

- **When seawater seeps** through cracks in the seafloor, black smokers may form. The water is heated by volcanic magma, and it dissolves the minerals in the rock.

- **Once the water** is superheated, it spews from the vents in scalding, mineral-rich black plumes.

▶ *Black smokers belch streams of superheated water, hot gases and mineral particles into the cold, inky ocean depths.*

- **The plume cools rapidly** in the cold sea, leaving behind thick deposits of sulphur, iron, zinc and copper in tall, chimney-like vents.

- **The tallest vents** can exceed 50 m in height.

- **Water jetting** from black smokers can reach a temperature of 650°C.

- **Smokers are home to a community** of organisms that thrive in the scalding waters and toxic chemicals. The organisms include giant clams, blind crabs, eelpout fish and giant tubeworms.

DID YOU KNOW?

Each drop of sea water in the oceans circulates through a black smoker every ten million years.

Australia, island continent

- **Australia** (with the island of Tasmania) is the smallest of the world's seven continents, with a total land area of 7,700,000 sq km.

- **Australia is part of** the region of Oceania, which also includes New Zealand, New Guinea and the islands of the South Pacific.

- **Until about 95 million years ago** Australia was joined with Antarctica as the southern supercontinent called Gondwana.

- **Australia itself was connected** to Tasmania by dry land during the last Ice Age, about 20,000 years ago, when sea levels were much lower than today.

- **Australia only split** from New Guinea between 8000 and 6500 years ago when sea levels rose again.

- **The tectonic plate** carrying Australia is on the move and heading towards Eurasia at 6–7 cm per year.

- **Australia lies right in the middle** of the Indo-Australian tectonic plate so it has 'quiet' geology. For example, it is the only continent with no active or dormant volcanoes.

- **The continent has been isolated** from the rest of the world for 40 million years, during which time it drifted northwards and became warmer and more arid.

- **Australia has woodland**, rainforest and grassland areas but most of it is desert or semi desert. It is the driest inhabited continent.

- **Also the flattest continent**, the only mountains in Australia are the eastern Great Dividing Range, with few peaks over 2000 m.

◀ *Uluru is a giant exposed sandstone rock formation in central Australia.*

Types of volcano

- **Each volcano** and eruption is slightly different.

- **Shield volcanoes** are shaped like curved shields or low domes. They erupt runny lava, which spreads over a wide area.

- **Fissure volcanoes** are places where floods of lava pour out of long cracks in the ground.

- **Composite volcanoes** are cone shaped. They build up in layers from a succession of explosive eruptions.

- **Cinder cones** are built up from ash, with little lava.

- **Strombolian eruptions** are moderately explosive eruptions of thick, sticky magma. They spit out sizzling blobs of lava called lava bombs.

- **Vulcanian eruptions** are explosive, erupting thick, sticky magma, which clogs the volcano's vent in between cannon-like blasts of clouds of ash and thick lava flows.

- **Peléean or Peléan eruptions** are the most violent, and eject glowing avalanches of ash and gas called *nuée ardentes* (French for 'glowing clouds').

- **Plinian eruptions** are the most explosive type of eruption. They are named after the Roman writer and legal expert Pliny who witnessed the eruption of Vesuvius, in Italy, in AD 79.

- **During Plinian eruptions**, boiling gases blast clouds of ash and volcanic fragments many kilometres up into the atmosphere.

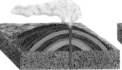

◀ Thick magma creates explosive, cone-shaped volcanoes, made partly of ash, sometimes with a crater. Runnier magma creates flatter volcanoes that ooze lava.

A composite volcano, or stratovolcano, has steep sides built up of layers of lava and ash

A shield volcano has a low, wide shape, with gently sloping sides

A caldera is a huge crater left after an old eruption. New cones often grow again inside

Thunderstorms

- **Thunderstorms begin** when strong updraughts build up towering cumulonimbus clouds.

- **Water drops** and ice crystals in these thunderclouds are buffeted together. This causes them to become charged with static electricity.

- **Negative charges** in a cloud sink and positive charges rise. Lightning is a surge of negative charge travelling towards the positive.

- **Sheet lightning** is a flash within a cloud. Fork lightning is a flash that travels from a cloud to the ground or to another cloud.

- **Fork lightning** begins with a fast, dim flash from a cloud to the ground, called the leader stroke. It prepares the air for a bigger, slower stroke a split second later.

- **Fork lightning travels** at up to 100,000 km per second down a narrow path up to 14 km long. Sheet lightning can be 140 km long.

- **Thunder is the sound** of the shock wave as air expands when it is heated instantly to 25,000°C by the lightning.

- **Sound travels slower than light**, so we hear thunder three seconds later for every one kilometre between us and the storm.

- **At any moment** there are 2000 thunderstorms around the world. Every second, 100 lightning bolts hit the ground.

- **A lightning flash** is brighter than ten million 20-watt low-energy light bulbs. For a split second it has more power than all the power stations in the USA put together.

◀ The tremendous turbulence in a thundercloud builds up an electrical charge that is released in flashes of lightning.

Coasts

● **Coastlines are changing** all the time as waves roll in and out and tides rise and fall. Over longer periods, coastlines are reshaped by the action of waves and the corrosion of salty water.

● **On exposed coasts** where waves strike the high rocks, they undercut the slope to create steep cliffs and headlands. Waves may penetrate into the cliff to form sea caves or arches.

● **When a sea arch collapses**, it leaves behind tall pillars called stacks.

● **Waves reshape rocks** by pounding them with a huge weight of water. Waves also force air into cracks in the rocks, which can split them open.

● **The erosive power of waves** is focused on a narrow band at wave height. As cliffs retreat, the waves slice away a broad shelf of rock called a wave-cut platform.

● **When waves hit a coast** at an angle, they fall back down at a right angle to that first angle. This motion moves material along in a zigzag fashion. This is called longshore drift.

● **Longshore drift** can wash sand or shingle out across bays and estuaries to create long, narrow areas called spits or bars.

▲ *On many coastlines, waves carve away huge amounts of rock to leave isolated stacks like the Apostles on Australia's southern coast.*

▲ *Where hills of tough chalk rock meet the sea, the base is often worn away by waves to form steep cliffs.*

● **Bays are broad indents** in the coast with a headland on each side.

● **A cove is a small bay.** A bight is a huge bay, such as the Great Australian Bight. A gulf is a long, narrow bight.

● **The world's largest bay** by area is the Bay of Bengal, India, which is 2.2 million sq km. Hudson Bay, Canada, has the longest shoreline at 12,268 km.

▼ *Along coastlines, the sea wears away land, but it also deposits particles that settle and gradually form new land. This creates a variety of natural features along coasts.*

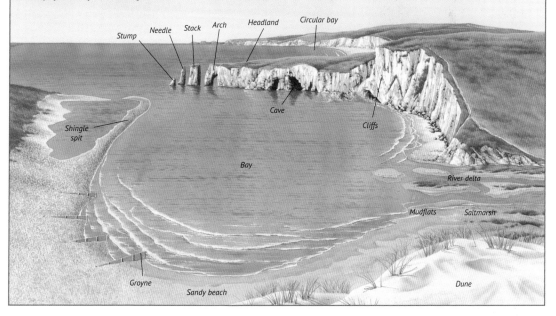

Stump · Needle · Stack · Arch · Headland · Circular bay

Cave

Cliffs

Shingle spit

Bay

River delta

Mudflats · Saltmarsh

Groyne

Sandy beach

Dune

Europe

● **The smallest continent**, Europe has an area of 10,400,000 sq km. For its size, Europe has a very long coastline at over 70,000 km.

● **In the north** of the continent are the ancient glaciated mountains of Scandinavia and Scotland, which were once much higher.

● **Across the centre** are the lowlands of the North European Plain, stretching from the Ural Mountains in Russia to France in the west.

● **Much of southern Europe** has been piled up into young mountain ranges like the Alps, as Africa drifts slowly north.

● **The highest point** in Europe is Mount Elbrus in the Russian Caucasus, at 5642 m high.

● **Northwest Europe** was once joined to Canada. The ancient Caledonian mountains of eastern Canada, Greenland, Scandinavia and Scotland were formed together as a single mountain chain 360–540 million years ago.

● **The Russian islands** of Novaya Zimlya are far into the Arctic Circle and are icebound in winter.

▲ *The Rock of Gibraltar in the far southwest of Europe marks the entrance to the Mediterranean Sea.*

● **Mediterranean Europe** has warm summers and mild winters.

● **Northwest Europe** is often wet and windy. It has mild winters because it is bathed by the warm North Atlantic Drift.

● **The largest lake** is Ladoga in Russia, at 17,600 sq km.

Floods

● **A flood** occurs when a river or the sea rises so much that it spills over the surrounding land.

● **River floods** may occur after a period of prolonged heavy rain or after snow melt in spring.

● **Small floods** are common, but big floods are rare. So, flood size is described in terms of frequency.

● **A two-year flood** is a smallish flood that is likely to occur every two years. A 100-year flood is a big flood that is likely to occur once every century.

▼ *Even when people are rescued, a flood can destroy homes and wash away soil from farmland, leaving it barren.*

DID YOU KNOW?

Not all floods are bad. Before the Aswan Dam was built in 1898–1902, Egyptian farmers relied on the yearly flooding of the Nile to enrich the soil.

● **A flash flood** occurs when a small stream or even dry stream bed changes to a raging torrent after heavy rain during a dry spell.

● **The 1993 flood** on the Mississippi–Missouri river, USA, caused damage of $15 billion and made 75,000 people homeless, despite the massive flood control works built in the 1930s.

● **The Hwang Ho** or Yellow River in China is also known as 'China's sorrow' because its floods are so devastating. In 1887, about one million people died in a flood there.

● **In July/August 2010**, widespread flooding, started by heavy monsoon rains in northern Pakistan, made many millions of people homeless.

● **In 2013**, an estimated 6000 people died in floods in Northern India.

The mantle

- **The mantle**, the layer of rock between the Earth's core and its crust, starts about 35–60 km beneath the Earth's surface and is about 2900 km thick.

- **This is the thickest layer** within the Earth and makes up about 84 percent of the planet's total volume and two-thirds of its mass.

- **Mantle rock** is mainly made up of silicates (silicon and oxygen) rich in iron and magnesium.

- **The boundary between** the mantle and the overlying crust is called the Moho Discontinuity.

- **There are three layers** to the mantle: the upper mantle, the transition zone and the lower mantle.

- **The temperature of the mantle** varies between 500–900°C in its upper regions to 4500°C near its base.

- **Despite these high temperatures** the very high pressures in the mantle increase the melting point of the rock and it remains in a solid/plastic state that flows very slowly.

- **Heat creeps up from great depth**, around the outer mantle and back down again, a circulation called convection currents.

1 Continent
2 Continental crust
3 Oceanic crust
4 Subduction zone (oceanic crust slides under continental crust)
5 Mid-ocean ridge
6 Upper mantle
7 Convection currents in transition zone of mantle
8 Lower mantle
9 Core

▶ This diagram shows the thickness of the Earth's mantle compared to the smaller core and the thin crust. Magma welling up between oceanic plates (5) causes them to move apart, as seafloor spreading.

- **These convection currents** bring rocks to the surface at spreading rifts and carry them down again at subduction zones.

- **The mantle rock** is thought to contain as much water again as is contained in all the oceans.

Arctic Ocean

- **The Arctic Ocean** is the smallest of the world's oceans, at 14,050,000 sq km, and the shallowest, with an average depth of 1040 m.

- **Most of the Arctic Ocean** is permanently covered with a vast floating raft of sea ice.

- **Temperatures are low** all year round, averaging −30°C in winter and sometimes dropping to −70°C.

- **During the long winters**, which last more than four months, the Sun never rises above the horizon.

- **The Arctic gets its name** from *arctos*, the Greek word for 'bear', because the Great Bear constellation is above the North Pole.

- **There are three kinds of sea ice** in the Arctic: Polar ice, pack ice and fast ice.

- **Polar ice** is the raft of ice that never melts. It may be as thin as 2 m in places in summer, but in winter it is up to 20 m thick.

- **Pack ice forms** around the edge of the polar ice and only freezes completely in winter.

- **The ocean swell breaks** and crushes the pack ice into chunky blocks and fantastic ice sculptures.

- **Fast ice forms** in winter between pack ice and the land around the Arctic Ocean. It gets its name because it is held fast to the shore. It cannot move up and down with the ocean as the pack ice does.

▼ Much of the Arctic Ocean freezes over each winter, then melts again in the summer.

Diverging plates

● **Deep down on the ocean floor**, some of the tectonic plates of the Earth's crust are slowly pushing apart. New molten rock wells up from the mantle into the gap between them and solidifies onto their edges. As plates are destroyed at subduction zones, newly made plate spreads the ocean floor wider, known as seafloor spreading.

● **The spreading or divergence** of the ocean floor centres on long ridges along the middle of some oceans, called mid-ocean ridges. Some of these ridges are joined, forming the world's longest mountain range, which winds over 60,000 km beneath the oceans.

● **The Mid-Atlantic Ridge** stretches through the Atlantic Ocean from the North Pole almost to the South Pole. The East Pacific Rise mid-ocean ridge winds under the Pacific Ocean from Mexico to Antarctica.

● **Along the middle** of a mid-ocean ridge is a deep canyon. This is where molten rock from the mantle wells up through the seabed.

● **Mid-ocean ridges** are broken by the curve of the Earth's surface into short, stepped sections. Each section is marked off by a long sideways crack called a transform fault. As the seafloor spreads out from a ridge, the sides of the fault rub together, setting off earthquakes.

● **As molten rock wells up** from a ridge, cools and hardens, its magnetic material solidifies in a certain way to line up with the Earth's magnetic field. Because the field reverses every now and then, bands of material harden with magnetism in alternate directions. This means that scientists can see how the seafloor has spread in the past.

1	Iceland
2	Greenland
3	North Atlantic Ocean
4	Tore-Madeira Rise
5	Romanche Trench
6	South Atlantic Ocean

▲ The Mid-Atlantic Ridge curves almost halfway around the planet from the Arctic Ocean almost to the continent of Antarctica.

● **Rates of seafloor spreading** vary from 1–20 cm a year. Slow-spreading ridges, such as the Mid-Atlantic Ridge, are higher, with sea mounts often topping them. Fast-spreading ridges, such as the East Pacific Rise, are lower, and magma oozes from these like fissure volcanoes on the surface.

● **Hot magma bubbling up** through a mid-ocean ridge emerges as hot lava. As it comes into contact with the cold sea water it solidifies into blobs called pillow lava.

● **Mid-ocean ridges may begin** where mantle plumes rise through the mantle and melt through the seabed. Plumes may also melt through continents to form Y-shaped cracks, which begin as rift valleys and then widen into new oceans.

▼ This cross-section of the top 50 km or so of the Earth's surface shows how the seafloor is spreading away from the mid-ocean ridge.

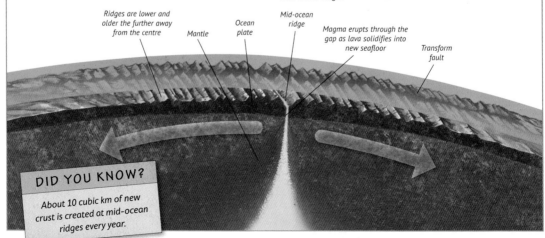

Ridges are lower and older the further away from the centre

Mantle

Ocean plate

Mid-ocean ridge

Magma erupts through the gap as lava solidifies into new seafloor

Transform fault

DID YOU KNOW?

About 10 cubic km of new crust is created at mid-ocean ridges every year.

Rain

- **Rain falls from clouds** filled with large water drops and ice crystals.

- **The technical name** for rain is precipitation, which also includes snow, sleet, hail, frost and dew.

- **Drizzle has drops** 0.2–0.5 mm in diameter and it falls from nimbostratus clouds. Raindrops from nimbostratus are 1–2 mm in diameter. Drops from cumulonimbus (thunderclouds) can be 5 mm in diameter.

- **Rain starts** when water drops or ice crystals inside clouds grow too large for the air to support them.

- **Water drops** in clouds grow when moist air is swept upwards and cools, causing lots of drops to condense and merge. This happens when pockets of warm, rising air form thunderclouds – at weather fronts or when air is forced up over hills.

- **In the tropics**, raindrops grow in clouds by colliding with each other. In cool places, they also grow on ice crystals in the clouds.

- **The world's rainiest place** is Mount Wai-'ale-'ale in Hawaii, where it rains 350 days a year.

▲ *Tall, dark thunderclouds unleash rain in short, heavy showers.*

- **Rainfall estimates** give the wettest place as Lloro in Colombia, which gets more than 1300 cm (13 m) of rain every year.

- **La Réunion island** in the Indian Ocean received 187 cm of rain in one day in 1952.

- **Guadeloupe** in the West Indies received 3.8 cm of rain in one minute in 1970.

How lakes form

- **A lake is a large depression** on land that is usually filled with freshwater that doesn't flow, or flows exceedingly slowly.

- **When tectonic activity** uplifts a mountain range, river water can flood the basins left between the peaks. Lake Victoria in Africa is an example of this.

- **Water sometimes collects** in rift zones where two tectonic plates are separating, as with Lake Baikal in Russia.

▼ *This river in southwest Spain may soon break through the neck of its meander, eventually leaving an isolated oxbow lake.*

- **As glaciers flow** towards the sea they scrape depressions in the land which fill with meltwater; the North American Great Lakes formed this way.

- **If a lake has no inlet** or outlet flow, the water will evaporate until the lake becomes too salty for life. One example of this is the Dead Sea.

- **An oxbow lake** forms when a meandering river takes a new course, leaving behind an isolated crescent-shaped lake.

- **The craters or calderas** of inactive volcanoes soon fill with rainwater, as in Crater Lake, Oregon, USA.

- **Soluble rock**, such as limestone, may collapse and leave a sinkhole lake, such as Lake Jackson in Florida, USA.

- **In cold, mountainous places**, ice and snow can sometimes build up and dam a river, which then forms a proglacial lake behind the blockage. Russell Fjord in Alaska is an example of this.

- **There are many artificial lakes** or reservoirs all over the world where rivers have been dammed to produce hydroelectric power.

Snow and hail

- **Snow is a type of precipitation** made of ice crystals. It falls in cold weather when the air is too cold to melt the ice to rain.

- **Outside of the tropics,** most rain starts to fall as snow but melts on the way down.

- **More snow falls** in the northern USA than at the North Pole where it is usually too cold to snow.

- **The heaviest snow** falls when the air temperature is hovering around freezing.

- **Snow can be hard to forecast** because a rise in temperature of just 1°C can turn snow into rain.

- **All snowflakes have six sides**. They usually consist of crystals that are flat plates, but occasionally needles and columns are found.

▲ *The mist above the hills here is not clouds, but tiny ice crystals blown off the snow.*

- **Wilson Bentley** (1865–1931) was an American farmer who photographed thousands of snowflakes through microscopes. He never found two identical flakes.

- **Hail is in effect frozen raindrops**, usually ball-shaped and larger than 4–5 mm.

- **The balls are called hailstones** and when many fall in a short time this is a hailstorm.

- **Most hailstones have onion-like layers.** These are due to the raindrops freezing then being swept up and down inside a cloud as more water droplets and water vapour condense and freeze onto the ball each time.

Hills

- **Mountains are solid rock,** but hills can be solid rock or piles of debris built up by glaciers, sand or the wind.

- **There is no exact height** when a hill becomes a mountain, but hills are considered to be less tall and less steep than mountains.

- **Hills made of solid rock** are either very old, having been worn down from mountains over millions of years, or they are made from soft sediments that were low hills.

- **In moist climates,** hills are often rounded by weathering and by water running over the land.

- **As solid rock is weathered,** the hill is covered in a layer of debris called regolith, including broken rock, soil, dust and other material.

- **Hills often have** a shallow S-shaped slope, called a 'convexo-concave' slope. There is a rounded convex shape at the top, and a long concave slope lower down.

- **Hill slopes become gentler** as they are worn away because the top is worn away faster. This is called decline.

- **Some hill slopes stay equally steep,** but are simply worn back. This is called retreat.

- **Decline** may take place in damp places; retreat happens in dry places.

- **Some hill slopes wear backwards** as gentler sections get longer and steeper sections get shorter. This is called replacement.

▼ *The contours of hills in damp places have often been gently rounded over long periods by a combination of weathering and erosion by running water.*

Folds

● **Rocks usually form** in flat layers called strata. Tectonic plates can collide with such force that they crumple up these strata.

● **Sometimes the folds** are just tiny wrinkles a few centimetres long. Sometimes they are huge, with hundreds of kilometres between crests (the highest points on a fold).

● **The shape of a fold** depends on the force that is squeezing it and on the resistance of the rock.

● **The slope of a fold** is called the dip. The direction of the dip is the direction in which it is sloping.

● **The strike of the fold** is at right angles to the dip. It is the horizontal alignment of the fold.

● **Some folds** turn right over on themselves to form upturned folds called nappes.

● **As nappes fold on top** of other nappes, the crumpled strata may pile up into mountains.

● **A downfold** is called a syncline. An upfolded arch of strata is called an anticline.

● **The axial plane** of a fold divides the fold into two halves.

▼ *This illustration of a nappe, or overfold, shows the main terms used by geologists to describe a fold.*

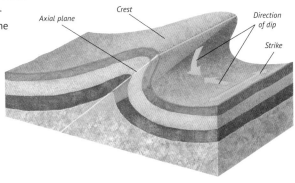

Axial plane

Crest

Direction of dip

Strike

DID YOU KNOW?

Most of the world's oil comes from reservoirs that are trapped in anticlines.

Biomes

● **A biome is a community** of plants and animals adapted to similar conditions in certain parts of the world. They are also known as 'major life zones'.

● **The vegetation or plant life** that grows in a region is mainly influenced by the soil and climate. In turn, plants greatly influence animal life.

● **Since vegetation is closely linked** to climate, biomes usually correspond to climate zones.

● **Most types of biome** occur across several continents.

● **Major biome types** include tundra, boreal (cold) coniferous forests, temperate grasslands (prairies and steppes), savannahs (tropical grasslands), tropical rainforests, deserts, wetlands and mountains.

● **Many plants and animals** have features that make them especially suited to a particular biome.

● **Human activity** is putting many plant and animal species in danger. Forest habitats are lost as trees are cleared for farms and building. Habitats may also be poisoned by pesticides and other pollutants.

● **More than 40 percent** of all plant and animal species are at risk of extinction.

● **A recent survey** by an international team of scientists showed that less than 5 percent of the world's oceans are now entirely undamaged by human activity.

● **The fastest-growing biomes** are deserts, due to desertification, and the urban 'biome' of towns and cities, roads and parks, factories and shopping malls.

▼ *Each different biome has its own range of creatures and plants.*

Desert

Savannah

Rainforest

Sunshine

● **Half of the Earth** is exposed to the Sun at any one time. Radiation from the Sun is the Earth's main source of energy, providing huge amounts of heat and light.

● **'Solar'** means anything to do with the Sun.

● **About 41 percent** of solar radiation is light; 51 percent is long-wave radiation that our eyes cannot see, such as infrared (IR) light, that is, heat. The other 8 percent is short-wave radiation, such as ultraviolet (UV) rays.

● **Only 47 percent** of the solar radiation that strikes the Earth actually reaches the ground. The rest is soaked up or reflected by the atmosphere.

▼ *Snow reflects away a lot of the Sun's heat, so the ground beneath stays cold.*

● **Solar radiation** reaching the ground is called insolation.

● **Insolation is at a peak** in the tropics and during the summer. It is lowest near the Poles and in winter.

● **The air is not warmed** much by the Sun directly, but by heat reflected from the ground.

● **The amount of heat** reaching the ground depends on the angle of the Sun's rays. The lower the Sun is in the sky, the more its rays are spread, and so give off less heat.

● **Some surfaces** reflect the Sun's heat and warm the air better than others. The percentage they reflect is called the albedo.

● **Snow and ice** have an albedo of 85–95 percent and so they stay frozen even as they warm the air.

River channels

● **A channel** is the long trough along which a river flows, often at the base of a river valley.

● **When the channel of a river** winds or has a rough bed, friction slows the river down.

● **A river flows faster** through a narrow, deep channel than a wide, shallow one because there is less friction.

▼ *Where the land is flatter, rivers wind and often divide into separate channels.*

● **All river channels tend to wind**, and the nearer they are to sea level, the more they wind. They form remarkably regular meanders.

● **Meanders seem to develop** because of the way in which a river erodes and deposits sediments.

● **One key factor in meanders** is the ups and downs along the river, called pools (deeps) and riffles (shallows).

● **The distance between pools and riffles**, and the size of meanders, are in close proportion to the river's width.

● **Another key factor in meanders** is the tendency of river water to flow not only straight downstream but also across the channel. Water spirals through the channel in a corkscrew fashion called helicoidal flow.

● **Helicoidal flow** makes water flow faster on the outside of bends, wearing away the banks. It flows more slowly on the inside, building up deposits called slip-off slopes such as sandbars or mudflats.

Volcanoes

● **Volcanoes are places** on the Earth's crust where magma (hot, liquid rock from the Earth's interior) erupts or flows onto the surface.

● **The word 'volcano'** comes from the name of Vulcano, a volcanic island in the Mediterranean. In ancient Roman mythology, Vulcan, the god of fire and blacksmith to the gods, was supposed to have forged his weapons in the fire beneath the mountain on Vulcano.

● **There are many types of volcano.** The most distinctive are cone-shaped composite volcanoes, which build up from alternating layers of ash and lava in successive eruptions.

● **Beneath a composite volcano** there is typically a large reservoir of magma called a magma chamber. Magma collects in the chamber before an eruption.

● **From the magma chamber** a narrow chimney, or vent, leads up to the surface. It erupts through the cone of debris at the peak, built up from previous eruptions.

● **When a volcano erupts**, the magma is driven up the vent by the gases within it. As the magma nears the surface, the pressure on it drops, which allows the gases dissolved in the magma to form bubbles. The expanding gases – mostly carbon dioxide and steam – push the molten rock upwards and out of the vent.

● **If the magma level** in the magma chamber drops, the top of the volcano's cone may collapse into it. This forms a crater called a caldera, which is Spanish for 'boiling pot'.

● **The world's largest caldera** is Toba on the island of Sumatra, Indonesia, which is 1775 sq km.

● **When a caldera subsides**, the whole cone may collapse into the old magma chamber. The caldera may fill with water to form a crater lake, such as Crater Lake in Oregon, USA.

● **Not all of the magma gushes** up the central vent. Some exits through branching side vents, which often have their own small 'parasitic' cones on the side of the main one.

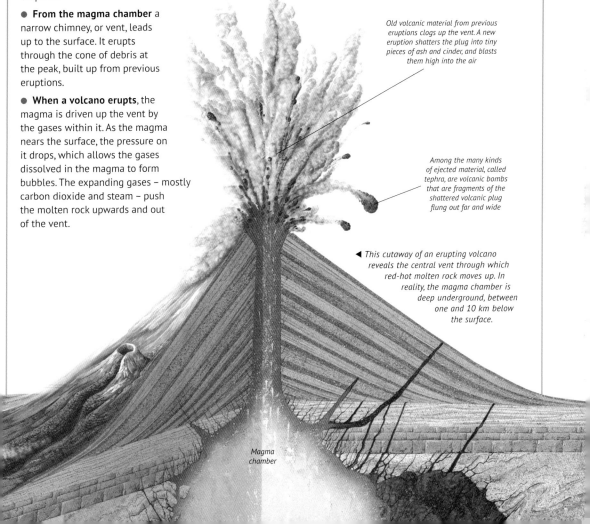

Old volcanic material from previous eruptions clogs up the vent. A new eruption shatters the plug into tiny pieces of ash and cinder, and blasts them high into the air

Among the many kinds of ejected material, called tephra, are volcanic bombs that are fragments of the shattered volcanic plug flung out far and wide

◀ *This cutaway of an erupting volcano reveals the central vent through which red-hot molten rock moves up. In reality, the magma chamber is deep underground, between one and 10 km below the surface.*

Magma chamber

Hurricanes

● **Hurricanes are powerful**, whirling tropical storms. They are also called cyclones (in the Indian Ocean and southwest Pacific) or typhoons (in the northwest Pacific). In the Atlantic and Northeast Pacific, they are simply known as hurricanes.

● **In late summer**, Atlantic hurricanes develop as clusters of thunderstorms build up over warm seas that are at least 27°C.

● **As hurricanes grow**, they tighten into a spiral with a calm ring of low pressure, called the 'eye', at the centre.

● **Hurricanes move westwards** in the Atlantic at about 20 km/h. They strike east coasts of the Caribbean and North America, bringing torrential rain and winds gusting up to 360 km/h.

▶ *Satellite technology allows hurricanes to be tracked minute by minute. This image shows Hurricane Ivan of 2004.*

● **A hurricane is a storm** with winds exceeding 119 km/h.

● **Each hurricane is given a name.** Every year these run in alphabetical order, from a list of six sets of names issued by the World Meteorological Organization.

● **So the first storm of the year** has a name beginning with 'A': Alberto in 2012, Andrea in 2013, then Arthur, Ana, Alex, and Arlene in 2017. The next storm of the season starts with 'B' and so on.

● **The names of hurricanes** that cause huge damage and loss of life, such as Andrew in 1992 and Katrina in 2005, are 'retired' and replaced by new ones.

● **The most fatal cyclone** ever struck Bangladesh in 1970. The flood from the storm surge killed 266,000 people.

Pollution

● **Air pollution comes mainly** from vehicle exhausts, waste burners, factories, power stations and the burning of oil, coal and gas in homes.

● **Pesticide crop sprays**, farm animals, mining and heavy industries also contribute to air pollution.

● **Some pollutants**, such as soot and ash, are solid as tiny particles or particulates, but many more pollutants are gases.

● **Air pollution can spread** huge distances. For example, pesticide traces have been discovered in Antarctica where they have never been used.

● **Most fuels are made up** of chemicals called hydrocarbons (hydrogen and carbon). Any hydrocarbons left unburned in vehicle exhausts can react in sunlight to form toxic ozone at ground level.

● **When exhaust gases react** in sunlight to form ozone, they may create a harmful photochemical smog.

● **Air pollution** is probably a major cause of global warming and has harmed the ozone layer of the Earth's atmosphere, which protects the Earth's surface from the Sun's harmful ultraviolet rays.

● **Breathing polluted air** in big cities is thought to be as harmful as smoking 20 cigarettes a day.

● **Air pollution affects** children more than adults as children breathe more air for their body size and spend more time playing outside.

● **Before a major clean up** the city of Benxi in China produced so much smoke it was invisible to satellites.

▶ *Most gas emissions from power station stacks or chimneys (upper right) are now filtered or 'scrubbed' to reduce pollution.*

Tsunamis

- **Tsunamis are huge waves** that are triggered when the seafloor is shaken violently by an earthquake, landslide or volcanic eruption.

- **In deep water**, tsunamis travel almost unnoticed below the surface. However, once they reach shallow coastal waters they rear up into waves 30 m or higher.

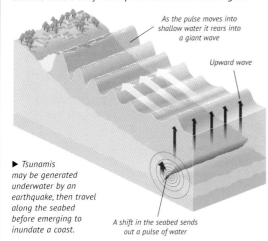

As the pulse moves into shallow water it rears into a giant wave

Upward wave

▶ *Tsunamis may be generated underwater by an earthquake, then travel along the seabed before emerging to inundate a coast.*

A shift in the seabed sends out a pulse of water

- **Often called 'tidal waves'**, tsunamis are nothing to do with tides. The word tsunami (pronounced 'soo-nah-mee') is Japanese for 'harbour wave'.

- **Tsunamis usually come** in a series of a dozen or more waves, anything from five minutes to one hour apart.

- **Before a tsunami hits**, the sea may recede, moving back away from the beach.

- **Tsunamis can travel** along the seabed as fast as a jet plane, at 700 km/h or more.

- **On 26 December, 2004**, an earthquake beneath the sea off Sumatra, Indonesia, generated a huge tsunami that spread across the Indian Ocean. It is now known as the Asian or Indian Ocean tsunami.

- **The Asian tsunami** was 30 m high and travelled 8000 km to South Africa. Over 225,000 people in 14 countries were killed.

- **On 11 March, 2011** a huge earthquake off the east coast of Japan generated tsunami waves that reached more than 40 m high in places.

- **The Japanese tsunami** waves travelled more than 10 km inland and killed more than 15,000 people.

Indian Ocean

- **The Indian Ocean** is the third largest ocean. It covers one-fifth of the world's ocean area at 73,500,000 sq km.

- **The average depth** of the Indian Ocean is 3890 m.

- **The deepest point** is the Java Trench off Java, in Indonesia, which is 7450 m deep. It marks the line where the Australian plate is being subducted under the Eurasian plate.

- **The Indian Ocean** is 10,000 km across at its widest point, between Africa and Australia.

- **Scientists have calculated** that the Indian Ocean began to form about 200 million years ago when Australia broke away from Africa, followed by India.

- **Every year** the Indian Ocean gets 20 cm wider.

- **The Indian Ocean is scattered** with thousands of tropical islands such as the Seychelles and Maldives.

- **The Maldives** are so low-lying that they may be swamped if global warming melts more polar ice.

- **Unlike other oceans**, currents in the Indian Ocean change course twice a year. They are blown by monsoon winds towards Africa in winter, and then in the other direction towards India in summer.

- **At the Rodrigues Triple Point** in the southern Indian Ocean, three tectonic plates – African, Indian-Australian and Antarctic – all move away from each other due to seafloor spreading.

▼ *The Maldives are some of many island groups in the Indian Ocean formed by coral on top of undersea volcanoes.*

Rivers

● **The water that fills rivers** comes from rainfall running directly off the land, from melting snow or ice, or from a spring bubbling out water that has soaked into the ground.

● **High up in mountains** near their sources (starts), rivers are usually small and steep. They tumble over rocks through narrow valleys, which they have carved out over thousands of years.

● **All the rivers** in a particular area, called a catchment area, flow down to join each other, like branches on a tree. The branches are called tributaries. The bigger the river, the more tributaries it is likely to have.

● **As rivers flow downhill**, they are joined by more tributaries and grow bigger.

● **In its lower reaches** a river is often wide and deep. It winds back and forth in meanders (bends) across floodplains made of silt.

● **Rivers flow fast** over rapids in their upper reaches.

● **The banks and beds** of rivers are worn away by gravel and sand, and the force of the moving water.

● **Every river carries sediment**. This consists of sand, large stones that are rolled along and fine silt that is suspended in the water.

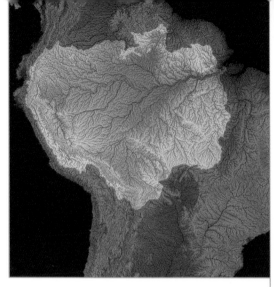

▲ *A computerized satellite image reveals the fantastic dendritic, or branching, network of the river Amazon and its tributaries.*

● **The discharge** of a river is the amount of water flowing past a certain point each second (in cubic metres per second).

DID YOU KNOW?

Intermittent rivers only flow after rain. Rivers that flow all year round are perennial – they are fed by water flowing underground, as well as by rain.

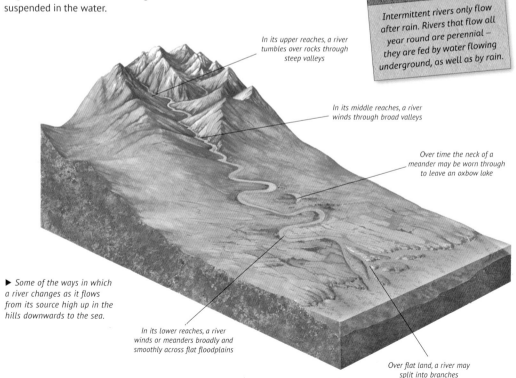

In its upper reaches, a river tumbles over rocks through steep valleys

In its middle reaches, a river winds through broad valleys

Over time the neck of a meander may be worn through to leave an oxbow lake

▶ *Some of the ways in which a river changes as it flows from its source high up in the hills downwards to the sea.*

In its lower reaches, a river winds or meanders broadly and smoothly across flat floodplains

Over flat land, a river may split into branches

Tornadoes

- **Tornadoes, or twisters**, are tall funnels of violently spiralling winds beneath thunderclouds.

- **A tornado can roar** past in just a few minutes, but it can cause severe damage.

- **Wind speeds** inside tornadoes are difficult to measure, but they are believed to be over 400 km/h.

- **Tornadoes form** beneath huge thunderclouds, called supercells, which develop along cold fronts.

- **England has more tornadoes** per square kilometre than any other country, but they are usually very small and mild.

- **In the USA**, Tornado Alley is centred on the states of Kansas and Oklahoma, and has about 1000 tornadoes a year. Some of them are incredibly powerful.

- **A tornado may be rated** on the Fujita scale, from F0 (F zero, gale tornado) to F6 (inconceivable tornado).

- **An F5 tornado** (incredible tornado) with wind speeds of 420–510 km/h can lift up a house and carry a bus hundreds of metres.

- **In 1990**, a Kansas tornado lifted an 88-carriage train from the track and dropped it in piles, four cars high.

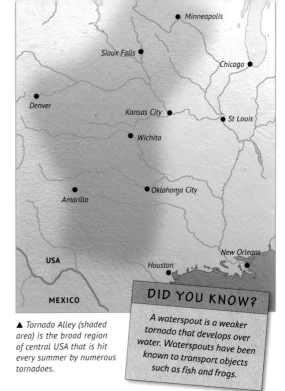

▲ Tornado Alley (shaded area) is the broad region of central USA that is hit every summer by numerous tornadoes.

DID YOU KNOW?

A waterspout is a weaker tornado that develops over water. Waterspouts have been known to transport objects such as fish and frogs.

The crust

- **The Earth's crust** is its hard outer shell.

- **The crust is a thin layer** of dense, solid rock that floats on the mantle. It is made mainly of silicate minerals (minerals made of silicon and oxygen) such as quartz.

- **There are two kinds of crust** – oceanic and continental.

- **Oceanic crust** is the crust beneath the oceans. It is much thinner – just 7 km thick on average. It is also young, with none being over 200 million years old.

- **The crust beneath** the continents is called continental crust. It is up to 80 km thick and mostly old.

- **Continental crust** is mostly crystalline 'basement' rock up to 3800 million years old. Some geologists think at least half of this rock is over 2500 million years old.

- **One cubic kilometre** of new continental crust is probably being created each year.

- **The 'basement' rock** has two main layers: an upper half of silica-rich rock, such as granite, schist and gneiss, and a lower half of volcanic rock, such as basalt, which has less silica. Oceanic crust is mostly basalt.

- **Continental crust** is created in the volcanic arcs above subduction zones. Molten rock from the subducted plate oozes to the surface over a period of a few hundred thousand years.

- **Almost one half** (47 percent) of the crust by mass is the chemical element oxygen, and more than one-quarter (28 percent) is silicon.

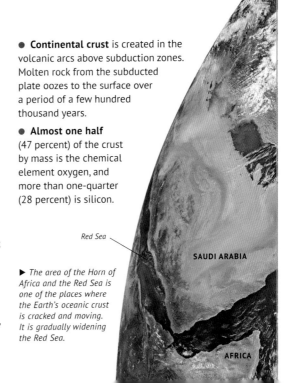

▶ The area of the Horn of Africa and the Red Sea is one of the places where the Earth's oceanic crust is cracked and moving. It is gradually widening the Red Sea.

Tectonic plates

● **The Earth's surface** is divided into thick slabs called tectonic plates. Each plate is a fragment of the Earth's rigid outer layer, or lithosphere.

● **There are about** ten larger plates, and dozens of smaller ones.

● **The biggest** is the Pacific plate, which lies beneath the whole of the Pacific Ocean.

● **Tectonic plates are moving** all the time, by an average of about 10 cm per year. Over millions of years they move vast distances. Some have moved halfway around the globe.

● **Continents are embedded** within most of the plates and move with them.

● **The Pacific plate** is the only large plate with no part of a continent situated on it.

● **The movement of tectonic plates** accounts for many geological events, including the patterns of volcanic and earthquake activity around the world.

● **There are three kinds** of boundary between plates: convergent, divergent and transform.

North American plate

Pacific plate

Eurasian plate

African plate

Pacific pl

South American plate

Indo-Australian plate

Antarctic plate

▲ *This map shows the major tectonic plates. Most of their boundaries have 'side branches' called transform faults, shown right. Smaller plates include the Cocos and Caribbean plates between North and South America.*

▲ *The boundaries between plates are usually broken into short stretches called transform faults. Here, the jagged edges of the plates rub past each other in opposite directions.*

● **Tectonic plates** are probably driven by convection currents of molten rock that circulate within the Earth's mantle (the layer between the Earth's crust and its core).

● **The lithosphere** was too thin for tectonic plates to form until 500 million years ago.

Vanishing resources

● **Naturally occurring** resources are substances people use for energy, food or manufacturing. Some are renewable, some are not.

● **Solar and wind power** and geothermal energy are not vanishing resources, they are naturally renewed.

● **Energy resources** such as coal and oil may last for only another one or two centuries at current rates of use.

● **Poor farming practices** may mean food production cannot be maintained because the land, another natural resource, has lost its fertility.

● **Another food resource** at risk is fish. Overfishing means fish are unable to reproduce fast enough to recover numbers. The Atlantic cod fisheries collapsed by 90 percent by the 1990s and show little signs of recovery.

● **Clean freshwater**, used for drinking, washing, watering animals and irrigation, may eventually become very scarce. Up to one-quarter of the world's population may not have access to clean drinking water by 2050.

● **Clean air is a resource** that will not run out in the long term. But air can become so polluted that it causes illnesses and prevents the growth of food plants.

● **Metals come from rocks** called ores that are found in the ground and which are not renewable. Iron, for example, may run out in 100–150 years at the rate it is currently used.

● **Phosphate is an essential element** that is used to make fertilizers for growing crops. There may only be enough for another 100–200 years.

● **Certain chemical elements** called rare earths, essential for today's electrical devices from smartphones to wind turbines, also have a limited supply, estimated at 250 years or less.

▼ *In Mato Grosso state, Brazil, workers install a tank to store clean water pumped up from a new well. Local surface water can be very polluted from mining and farming.*

Minerals

- **Minerals are the natural chemicals** from which rocks are made. Some rocks are made from crystals of just one mineral, but many consist of several.

- **Most minerals** are made up of two or more chemical elements, but a few, such as gold and copper, consist of just one element.

- **There are over 2000 minerals**, and around 30 of these are very common.

- **Most of the less common minerals** are present in rocks in minute traces. They may become concentrated in certain places by geological processes.

- **The Earth's surface** contains an enormous wealth of mineral resources, from clay for bricks to precious gems.

- **Silicates make up** the largest group of minerals. They form when metals join with oxygen and silicon. The most common silicates are quartz and feldspar, which are rock-forming minerals.

- **Other common minerals** are oxides such as haematite and cuprite, sulphates such as gypsum and barite, sulphides such as galena and pyrite, and carbonates such as calcite and aragonite.

▲ *Materials such as limestone and clay are taken from large, deep pits in the ground (quarries) in huge quantities for building.*

- **Some minerals**, like amber and opal, do not have a microcrystal structure and are called mineraloids.

- **Fossil fuels** – oil, coal and natural gas – formed from the remains of plants and animals that lived millions of years ago. The remains changed into fuel by intense heat and pressure. Coal formed from plants that grew in huge, warm swamps. Oil and natural gas form from the remains of tiny marine plants and animals.

- **Ores are the minerals** from which metals are extracted. Bauxite is the ore for aluminium, chalcopyrite for copper, galena for lead, haematite for iron and sphalerite for zinc.

Pacific Ocean

DID YOU KNOW?

There are more seamounts (undersea mountains) in the Pacific than any other ocean.

- **The world's largest ocean** is the Pacific. It is twice as large as the Atlantic and covers over one-third of the Earth, with an area of 165,200,000 sq km.

- **The Pacific is over 24,000 km across** from the Malay Peninsula to Panama – more than halfway round the world.

▼ *Easter Island, in the remote Central Pacific, is easily recognized by the great stone head statues called moai, made between 1200 and 1500.*

- **The word 'pacific' means peaceful**. The ocean was was given its name by 16th-century Portuguese explorer Ferdinand Magellan (1480–1521) who was lucky enough to find gentle winds when he first sailed there.

- **Thousands of islands** are dotted within the Pacific Ocean. Some of them are the peaks of undersea volcanoes. Others are coral reefs on top of the peaks.

- **The Pacific has some of the world's greatest tides**, over 9 m off Korea. Its smallest tide, just 0.3 m, is on Midway Island in the middle of the Pacific.

- **On average**, the Pacific Ocean is 4280 m deep.

- **Around the rim** there are deep ocean trenches including the world's deepest, the Mariana Trench at almost 11 km deep.

- **A huge undersea mountain range** called the East Pacific Rise stretches northwards from Antarctica all the way to Mexico.

- **The floor of the Pacific** is spreading along the East Pacific Rise at the rate of 12–16 cm per year.

Volcanic eruptions

- **Volcanoes erupt** because of magma – the hot, liquid rock beneath the Earth's surface. Magma is less dense than the rock above, and so it 'floats' or moves up towards the surface.

- **When magma is runny**, eruptions are 'effusive', which means they ooze lava all the time.

- **When magma is thick and sticky**, eruptions are explosive. Magma clogs up the volcano's vent until enough pressure builds up to blast it out, like a popping cork.

- **An explosive eruption** blasts globs of hot magma, ash, cinder, gas and steam high up into the air.

- **Shattered fragments** of the volcanic plug that are blasted out are called pyroclasts, from the ancient Greek for 'fire broken'.

- **Volcanoes usually erupt** again and again. The interval between eruptions varies from a few minutes to thousands of years.

- **The gas inside magma** can expand hundreds of times in just a few seconds.

- **Volcanoes that erupt regularly** are known as active, and those that are inactive but could erupt in the future are dormant or 'sleeping'.

- **The Volcanic Explosivity Index (VEI)** measures the power of eruptions from VE1 (Gentle) to VE8 (Mega-colossal). Each stage represents a ten-fold increase in explosivity.

- **A volcano that is old and dead**, with no future eruptions possible, is called extinct.

◀ *The 1980 eruption of Mount St Helens in Washington, USA, measured 5 on the VEI.*

Mountain ranges

- **Great mountain ranges**, such as the Andes in South America, usually lie along the edges of continents.

- **Most mountain ranges** are formed by the folding of rock layers as tectonic plates move together.

- **Mountain building** is very slow because rocks flow like thick treacle. Rock is pushed up like the bow wave in front of a boat as one tectonic plate pushes into another.

- **High mountain ranges** are geologically young because they are not yet worn down.

- **Many ranges** are still growing. The Himalayas grow a few centimetres each year as the Indian plate pushes into Africa.

▶ *Mountain ranges such as the Alps in Europe are thrown up by the crumpling of rock layers as the tectonic plates crunch together.*

- **Satellite techniques** show that the central peaks of the Andes and the Himalayas are rising. The outer peaks are sinking as the rock flows slowly away from the 'bow wave'.

- **Mountain building** is very active during orogenic (mountain forming) phases, which last millions of years.

- **The process by which mountains form** makes the Earth's crust especially thick beneath them, giving mountains deep 'roots'.

- **As mountains are worn down**, their weight reduces and the 'roots' float upwards. This is called isostasy.

- **The Himalayas** are home to the world's highest peak, the 8848-m Mount Everest, and 13 other mountains that are more than 8000 m tall.

Weather fronts

- **A weather front** is where a large mass of warm air meets a large mass of cold air.

- **At a warm front**, the mass of warm air is moving faster than the cold air. The warm air slowly rises over the cold air, sloping gently up to 1.5 km over a distance of 300 km.

- **At a cold front**, the mass of cold air is moving faster. It undercuts the warm air, forcing it to rise sharply and creating a steeply sloping front. The front climbs to 1.5 km over a distance of about 100 km.

- **In the mid-latitudes**, fronts are linked to vast spiralling weather systems called depressions, or lows. These are centred on a region of low pressure where warm, moist air rises. Winds spiral into the low – anticlockwise in the Northern Hemisphere, clockwise in the Southern.

- **Lows start along** the polar front, which stretches around the world. Here, cold air from the poles meets warm, moist air moving up from the subtropics.

- **Lows develop as a kink** in the polar front. They then grow bigger as strong winds in the upper air drag them eastwards, bringing rain, snow and blustery winds. A wedge of warm air intrudes into the heart of the low, and the worst weather occurs along the edges of the wedge. One edge is a warm front, the other is a cold front.

- **The warm front arrives first**, shown by feathery cirrus clouds of ice high in the sky. As the front moves over, the sky fills with slate-grey nimbostratus clouds that bring steady rain. As the warm front passes away, the weather becomes milder and skies may briefly clear.

- **After a few hours**, a build-up of thunderclouds and gusty winds warn that the cold front is on its way. When it arrives, the clouds unleash short, heavy showers, and sometimes thunderstorms or even tornadoes.

- **After the cold front passes**, the air grows colder and the sky clears, leaving just a few fluffy cumulus clouds.

DID YOU KNOW?

Meteorologists think that depressions are linked to strong winds, called jet streams, which circle the Earth high above the polar front.

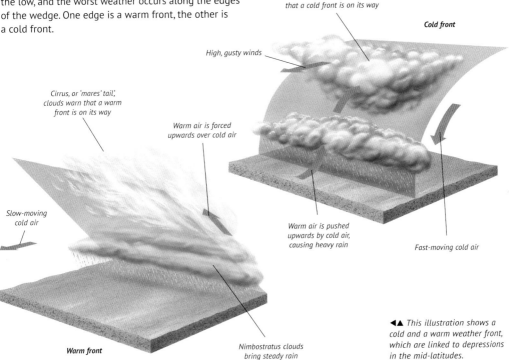

Cumulonimbus thunderclouds warn that a cold front is on its way

Cold front

High, gusty winds

Cirrus, or 'mares' tail', clouds warn that a warm front is on its way

Warm air is forced upwards over cold air

Slow-moving cold air

Warm air is pushed upwards by cold air, causing heavy rain

Fast-moving cold air

Warm front

Nimbostratus clouds bring steady rain

◀▲ This illustration shows a cold and a warm weather front, which are linked to depressions in the mid-latitudes.

Southern Ocean

● **The fourth largest ocean** is the Southern or Antarctic. Its boundaries with the Pacific, Atlantic and Indian Oceans have been debated but are generally considered to be latitude 60 degrees South.

● **It is a deep ocean**, between 4000 and 5000 m over most of its area, and 7236 m at its deepest.

● **The Southern Ocean** stretches all the way around Antarctica, and has an area of 20,330,000 sq km. It is the only ocean that goes all around the world.

● **In winter** over half the Southern Ocean is covered with ice and icebergs that break off from the Antarctic ice sheet.

● **Sea ice** forms in round pieces called pancake ice.

● **The East Wind Drift** is a current that flows anticlockwise around Antarctica close to the coast.

● **Further out from the coast** of Antarctica, the Antarctic Circumpolar Current flows in the opposite direction – clockwise from west to east.

● **The Antarctic Circumpolar Current** carries more water than any other current in the world.

● **The latitudes just below** 60° South are called the 'Screaming Sixties', due to the fierce westerly winds that blow unobstructed for weeks at a time, all around the planet.

● **In this region**, sustained winds exceeding 150 km/h whip up waves more than 15 m high.

▼ *Blocks and chunks of ice continually break off into the Southern Ocean from the ice shelves and glaciers spreading outwards from Antarctica. Some of the largest are bigger than small countries.*

North America

● **The world's third largest continent** is North America. It has an area of 24,700,000 sq km.

● **North America's long north side** is bound by the icy Arctic Ocean, and its short southeast side by the Gulf of Mexico.

● **The north lies inside** the Arctic Circle and is icebound for much of the year.

▼ *A herd of bison moves among the billowing steam and spurting hot water of geysers, caused by underground 'hot spot' rocks in Yellowstone National Park in the USA.*

● **Death Valley**, in the southwestern desert in California and Nevada, holds the record as the hottest place on the Earth, at 56.7°C.

● **Mountain ranges** run down each side of North America – the ancient, worn-down Appalachians in the east and the younger, higher Rockies in the west.

● **In between the mountains** lie vast interior plains. These are based on very old rocks, the oldest of which are in the Canadian Shield in the north.

● **Most of North America** sits on the North American tectonic plate. There are three hot spots beneath it at Yellowstone, Anahim and Raton, generating volcanic activity.

● **The Grand Canyon** is one of the world's most spectacular gorges. It is 446 km long, and 1800 m deep in places.

● **The longest river** in North America is the Mississippi–Missouri, at 5970 km long.

● **The highest mountain** is Mount McKinley in Alaska, at 6194 m.

Weather forecasting

- **The scientific study** of the atmosphere, including weather and climate, is called meteorology.

- **Weather forecasting** relies partly on powerful computers, which analyze the Earth's atmosphere.

- **One kind of weather prediction** divides the air into 'parcels'. These are stacked in columns above grid points spread throughout the world.

- **There are over one million grid points**, each with a stack of at least 30 parcels above it.

- **Weather stations** take millions of measurements of weather conditions at regular intervals each day.

- **Every few hours**, more than 15,000 land-based weather stations record conditions on the ground.

- **Also every few hours**, balloons carry instruments up into the atmosphere to record conditions high up.

- **Meteosats**, or meteorological satellites, give an overview of developing weather patterns.

- **Infrared satellite images** show temperatures on the Earth's surface, on land and water, and in the atmosphere.

- **Supercomputers allow** the weather to be predicted accurately three days in advance, and for up to 14 days in advance with some confidence.

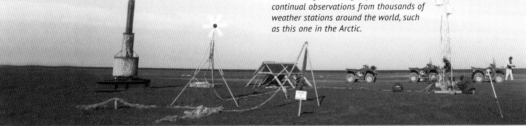

▼ Weather forecasting depends on continual observations from thousands of weather stations around the world, such as this one in the Arctic.

River valleys

- **Rivers carve out valleys** as they wear away their channels.

- **High up in the mountains**, much of a river's energy is spent on carving into or eroding the riverbed. The valleys there are deep, with steep sides.

- **Farther down towards the sea**, more of a river's erosive energy goes into wearing away its banks. It carves out a broader valley as it winds back and forth.

> **DID YOU KNOW?**
>
> The world's rivers wear the entire land surface down by an average of 8 cm every 1000 years.

- **Large meanders** normally develop only when a river is crossing broad, flat plains in its lower reaches.

- **Incised meanders** are those that have been carved into deep valleys. These meanders form when a river flows across a low plain. The plain is lifted up and the river cuts down into it, keeping its meanders.

- **The Grand Canyon** is made of incised meanders. They were created as the Colorado River cut into the Colorado Plateau after it was uplifted 17 million years ago.

- **The shape of a river valley** depends partly on the structure of the rocks over which it is flowing.

- **Some valleys** seem far too big for their river alone to have carved them. Such a river is 'underfit' or 'misfit'.

- **Many large valleys** with misfit rivers were carved out by glaciers or glacial meltwaters.

◄ Rivers carve out valleys over hundreds of thousands of years as they grind material along their beds.

Earth's interior

◀ The Earth's interior is made up of many layers – solid and molten. The inner core is solid metal, and the mantle is more semi-molten or 'plastic'.

● **The Earth has three main layers** inside. Outermost is the crust, a thin, hard shell of rock, which is a few dozen kilometres thick.

● **The crust's thickness** in relation to the size of the whole Earth is about the same as the skin on an apple.

● **Under the crust**, there is a deep layer of hot, soft rock called the mantle.

● **Beneath the mantle** is an outer core of hot iron and nickel that is mostly semi-molten or melted.

● **The inner core** contains 1.7 percent of the Earth's mass, the outer core 30.8 percent, the core–mantle boundary 3 percent, the lower mantle 49 percent, the upper mantle 15 percent, the ocean crust 0.099 percent and the continental crust 0.374 percent.

● **Satellite measurements** are so accurate they can detect slight lumps and dents in the Earth's surface. These indicate where gravity is stronger or weaker because of differences in rock density. Variations in gravity reveal features such as mantle plumes (upwellings of unusually hot rock within the mantle).

● **Our knowledge** of the Earth's interior comes mainly from studying how earthquake waves vibrate through the Earth.

● **Analysis of how** earthquake waves are deflected reveals where different materials occur in the interior. S (secondary) waves pass only through the mantle. P (primary) waves pass through the core as well.

● **As P waves pass through** the core they are deflected, leaving a shadow zone where no waves reach the far side of the Earth.

● **The speed at which** earthquake waves travel reveals how dense the rocks are. Cold, hard rock transmits waves more quickly than hot, soft rock.

High mountains

● **A few high mountains**, such as Africa's Kilimanjaro, are lone volcanoes that are built up by eruptions.

● **Some volcanic mountains**, such as Japan's Mount Fuji, are in chains in volcanic arcs.

● **Most high mountains** are part of great mountain ranges stretching over hundreds of kilometres.

● **Some mountain ranges** are huge slabs of rock called fault blocks. They were forced up by quakes.

● **Other mountain ranges**, such as the Himalayas in Asia and the Andes in South America, are fold mountains.

● **The height of mountains** used to be measured on the ground, using levels and sighting devices to measure angles. Now, mountains are measured accurately using satellite techniques.

● **Temperatures drop** 0.6°C for every 100 m you climb, so mountain peaks are very cold and often covered in snow.

● **Air is thinner** high up on mountains, so the air pressure is lower.

● **There is also less oxygen** in the thinner air. Animals that live here are specially adapted with larger lungs and extra blood cells.

● **Climbers may need** oxygen masks to breathe, especially above 8000 m.

◀ High peaks such as Mount Everest are jagged because massive folding fractures the rock and makes it vulnerable to the sharp frosts and erosion.

Limestone weathering

● **Streams and rainwater** absorb carbon dioxide gas from soil and air, turning them into weak carbonic acid.

● **Carbonic acid corrodes** (wears away by dissolving) limestone in a process called carbonation.

● **When limestone rock** is close to the surface, carbonation can create spectacular scenery.

● **Corroded limestone** scenery is often called karst. This is because a very good example of it is the Karst Plateau near Dalmatia, in Bosnia.

● **On the surface**, carbonation eats along cracks to create 'pavements', with slabs called clints. The slabs are separated by deeply etched grooves called grykes.

● **Limestone rock** does not soak up water like a sponge. It has massive cracks called joints, and streams and rainwater trickle deep into the rock through these cracks.

● **Streams drop down** into limestone through sinkholes, like water down a plughole. Carbonation eats out such holes to form giant shafts called potholes.

● **Some potholes** are eaten out to create great funnel-shaped hollows called dolines, up to 100 m across.

● **Where water streams** out along horizontal cracks at the base of potholes, the rock may be etched out into caverns.

● **Caverns may be eaten out** so much that the roof collapses to form a gorge or a large hole called a polje.

▼ *The acidity of rainwater has etched out the cracks in limestone to create a limestone 'pavement' on The Burren, Ireland.*

Icebergs

● **Icebergs are big lumps** of floating ice that calve, or break off, from the ends of glaciers or polar ice caps.

● **The calving of icebergs** occurs mostly during the summer when warm conditions partially melt the ice.

● **Around 15,000 icebergs a year** calve in the Arctic.

● **Arctic icebergs** vary from car-sized blocks, to those the size of mansions. The biggest, which was 11 km long, was spotted off Baffin Island in 1882.

● **The Petterman and Jungersen** glaciers in northern Greenland form big table-shaped icebergs called ice islands. They are like the icebergs found in Antarctica.

▼ *Rocked by the waves, chunks of ice break off Antarctic glaciers and ice sheets to form fantastically shaped icebergs.*

● **Antarctic icebergs** are much bigger than Arctic ones. One of the biggest, which was 300 km long, was spotted in 1956 by the icebreaker USS *Glacier*.

● **Another 300-km iceberg**, B-15, came from the Ross Ice Shelf in Antarctica in 2000.

● **The ice of Arctic icebergs** is 3000–6000 years old.

● **Each year 500 or so icebergs** drift from Greenland into the shipping lanes off Newfoundland. They are a major hazard to shipping in that area.

DID YOU KNOW?

The International Ice Patrol was set up in 1914 to monitor icebergs after the liner RMS Titanic sunk in 1912, when it hit an iceberg off Newfoundland.

Atlantic Ocean

● **The Atlantic Ocean** is the world's second largest ocean, with an area of 106,400,000 sq km. It covers about one-fifth of the world's surface.

● **At its widest point**, between Spain and Mexico, the Atlantic is 9600 km across.

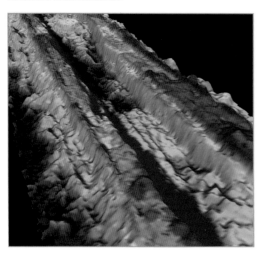

● **The Atlantic was named** by the ancient Romans after the Atlas Mountains of North Africa. The Atlas were at the limit of the Romans' known world.

● **There are very few islands** in the middle of the Atlantic Ocean. Most lie close to the continents.

● **On average**, the Atlantic is about 3600 m deep.

● **The deepest point** in the Atlantic is the Puerto Rico Trench off Puerto Rico, which is 8648 m deep.

● **The Mid-Atlantic Ridge** is a great undersea ridge that splits the seabed in half. Here, the Atlantic is growing wider by 2–4 cm every year.

● **Islands in the mid-Atlantic** are volcanoes that lie along the Mid-Atlantic Ridge, such as the Azores and Ascension Island.

● **The Sargasso Sea** is a huge area of water in the western Atlantic. It is famous for its floating seaweed.

● **The Atlantic** is a young ocean, less than 150 million years old.

◄ *This computer model, built from sonar data, reveals the great ridge that winds along the floor of the Atlantic Ocean.*

Wind

● **Wind is moving air**. Strong winds are fast-moving air and gentle breezes are air that moves slowly.

● **Air moves** because the Sun warms some places more than others, creating differences in air pressure.

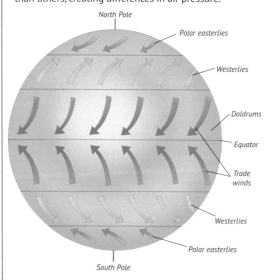

North Pole

Polar easterlies

Westerlies

Doldrums

Equator

Trade winds

Westerlies

Polar easterlies

South Pole

● **Warmth makes air expand** and rise, lowering air pressure. Cold makes air heavier, raising pressure.

● **As air warms and rises**, cooler air flows along to take its place, creating winds.

● **Winds blow** from areas of high pressure, called highs, to areas of low pressure, called lows.

● **The sharper the pressure difference**, or gradient, the stronger the winds blow.

● **In the Northern Hemisphere**, winds spiral clockwise out of highs, and anticlockwise into lows. In the Southern Hemisphere, the reverse occurs.

● **A prevailing wind** is one that blows frequently from the same direction. Winds are named by the direction they blow from. A westerly wind blows from the west.

● **In the tropics** the prevailing winds are warm and dry. They blow from the northeast and the southeast towards the Equator.

● **In the mid-latitudes** the prevailing winds are warm, moist westerlies.

◄ *The most common or 'prevailing' wind direction is different in the tropics, in the mid-latitudes and in the polar regions.*

South America

▲ *The high Andes Mountains have many glaciers, such as Perito Moreno glacier in southern Argentina. The glacier is 30 km long and covers more than 250 sq km. It flows downwards 1800 m, east into Lake Argentina.*

● **The world's fourth largest** continent, South America has an area of 17,830,000 sq km.

● **The Andes Mountains,** which run over 4500 km down the west side, are the world's longest mountain range.

● **The heart of South America** is the vast Amazon rainforest around the Amazon River and its tributaries.

● **The southeast** is dominated by the huge grasslands of the Gran Chaco, the Pampas and Patagonia.

● **No other continent** reaches so far south. South America extends to within 1000 km of the Antarctic Circle.

● **Three-quarters of South America** is in the tropics. In the high Andes are large zones of cool, temperate climate.

● **Quito, in Ecuador**, is called the 'Land of Eternal Spring' because its temperature never drops below 8°C at night, and never climbs above 22°C during the day.

● **The highest volcanic peak** is Aconcagua, at 6962 m.

● **Eastern South America** was joined to western Africa until the Atlantic began to open up 90 million years ago.

● **The Pantanal** in southwest Brazil, Paraguay and Bolivia, is the world's biggest tropical wetland, covering over 180,000 sq km in the wet season.

▶ *The jaguar is South America's largest big cat. It is at home in the swampy regions of the Amazon and Pantanal, where it swims well to catch fish and turtles.*

Ice and cold

● **Winter is cold** because the days are short. In winter, the Sun moves across the sky at a low angle, so its warmth is spread out.

● **The coldest places** in the world are around the North and South poles. Here, the Sun shines at a low angle even in summer, and in winter it does not rise for days on end.

● **The average temperature** at Polus Nedostupnosti (Pole of Cold) in Antarctica is −58°C.

● **The coldest temperature** ever recorded was −89.2°C at Vostok in Antarctica on 21 July, 1983.

● **The interiors of the continents** can get very cold in winter because land loses heat rapidly and there are no warmer oceans nearby.

● **When air cools below freezing point** (0°C), the water vapour in it may freeze without turning first to dew (water drops that form on cool surfaces). It covers the ground with crystals of ice or frost.

● **Fern frost** is feathery tails of ice that form on cold glass as dew drops freeze bit by bit.

● **Hoar frost** forms as spiky needles when damp air blows over cold surfaces and freezes onto them.

● **Rime is a thick coating** of ice that forms when drops of water in clouds and fogs remain as liquid well below freezing point. The drops freeze instantly when they touch a surface.

● **Black ice forms** when rain falls on freezing road surfaces.

◀ *A sudden plunge in temperature turns a waterfall into a curtain of icicles.*

Tides

● **Tides are the way** the sea rises a little and falls back every 12 hours or so.

● **When the tide is flowing** it is rising. When the tide is ebbing, it is falling.

● **The pull of gravity** between the Earth, Moon and Sun causes tides. Ocean waters flow freely over the Earth to create two tidal bulges (high tides) of water. One bulge is below the Moon, the other is on the opposite side of the Earth.

● **The Sun is much farther away** than the Moon, but it is so huge that its gravity affects the tides.

DID YOU KNOW?

On very gently sloping shores like mudflats, the rising tide water's edge moves faster than a person can run.

● **As the Earth turns**, and the Moon orbits, the two bulges stay in line with the Moon, so they move around the Earth to create two high tides a day. But the Moon's slight movement means they occur every 12.5 hours, not 12 hours.

● **The continents get in the way** of the movement of tides, and as a result their timing and height varies. In the open, tides rise one metre or so, but in enclosed spaces such as the Bay of Fundy, Canada, they rise over 15 m.

● **The Moon and the Sun** line up at a Full and a New Moon, creating high spring tides twice a month. (They have nothing to do with the season of spring.)

● **When the Moon and the Sun pull** at right angles at Half Moon, they cause neap tides, which are lower than normal tides.

● **The mutual pull** of the Moon's and the Earth's gravity also stretches the Earth slightly into an egg shape.

◀ *As the tide goes out here in St Ives in southwest England (and other places in the world) it is flowing in as a high tide at other locations around the globe.*

The Ages of the Earth

● **The Earth formed** 4570 million years ago (mya), but the first animals with shells and bones appeared less than 600 mya. With the help of these fossils, geologists have learned about the Earth's history since then. We know very little about the 4000 million years before, known as the Precambrian Eon.

● **Geologists divide** the Earth's history into time periods. The longest are eons, thousands of millions of years long. The shortest are chrons, a few thousand years long. In between come eras, periods, epochs and ages.

● **The years since the Precambrian Eon** are split into three eras: Palaeozoic, Mesozoic and Cenozoic.

● **Different plants and animals** lived at different times, so geologists can tell from the fossils in rocks how long ago the rocks formed. Using fossils, they have divided the Earth's history since Precambrian time into 12 periods.

● **Layers of rock form** on top of each other, so the oldest rocks are usually at the bottom, unless they have been disturbed.

● **The order of layers** from top to bottom is known as the geological column.

● **By looking for certain fossils** geologists can tell if one layer of rock is older than another, and place it in the geological column.

● **Fossils can show** only if a rock is older or younger than another, they cannot give a date in years. Also many rocks, such as igneous, contain no fossils. To give an absolute date, geologists may use radiocarbon and other similar radio-dating methods.

● **Radio-dating** allows the oldest rocks on Earth to be dated. After certain substances, such as uranium and rubidium, form in rocks, their atoms slowly break down and they give off radioactivity. By assessing how many atoms have changed, geologists work out the rock's age.

● **Breaks in the sequence** of the geological column, called unconformities, can help to build up a picture of an area's geological history.

▼ *This sequence shows the main geological periods and events in Earth's history, from the most recent (top) to the most ancient.*

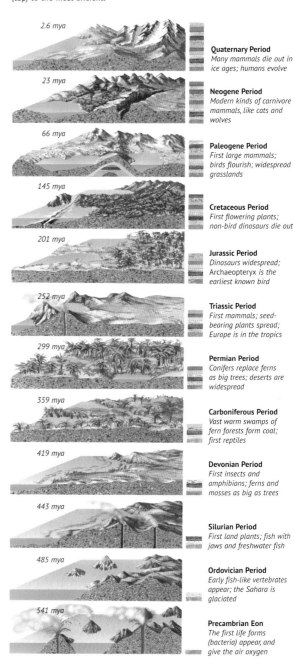

2.6 mya

Quaternary Period
Many mammals die out in ice ages; humans evolve

23 mya

Neogene Period
Modern kinds of carnivore mammals, like cats and wolves

66 mya

Paleogene Period
First large mammals; birds flourish; widespread grasslands

145 mya

Cretaceous Period
First flowering plants; non-bird dinosaurs die out

201 mya

Jurassic Period
Dinosaurs widespread; Archaeopteryx is the earliest known bird

252 mya

Triassic Period
First mammals; seed-bearing plants spread; Europe is in the tropics

299 mya

Permian Period
Conifers replace ferns as big trees; deserts are widespread

359 mya

Carboniferous Period
Vast warm swamps of fern forests form coal; first reptiles

419 mya

Devonian Period
First insects and amphibians; ferns and mosses as big as trees

443 mya

Silurian Period
First land plants; fish with jaws and freshwater fish

485 mya

Ordovician Period
Early fish-like vertebrates appear; the Sahara is glaciated

541 mya

Precambrian Eon
The first life forms (bacteria) appear, and give the air oxygen

Fossils

● **Fossils are the remains** of living things that have been preserved for millions of years, usually in stone.

● **Most fossils** are the remains of living things such as bones, shells, claws, teeth, leaves, bark, cones and seeds.

● **Trace fossils** are fossils of signs left behind by creatures, such as footprints and scratch marks.

● **Palaeontologists** (scientists who study fossils) can tell the age of a fossil from the rock layer in which it is found. They can also measure how the rock has changed radioactively since it was formed (radio-dating).

● **The oldest fossils** are called stromatolites. They are fossils of big colonies of microscopic bacteria over 3500 million years old.

● **The biggest fossils** are conyphytons. These are 2000-million-year-old stromatolites over 100 m high.

● **Not all fossils are stone**. Mammoths have been preserved by being frozen in the permafrost of Siberia.

● **Insects have been preserved** in amber, the solidified resin of ancient trees.

● **Certain widespread**, short-lived fossils are very useful for dating rock layers. These are known as index fossils.

● **Index fossils include** shellfish such as brachiopods, belemnites and ammonites, also trilobites, graptolites and crinoids.

◀ *Transformed into hard, new minerals, remains of living things can be preserved for hundreds of millions of years, although fossils as good as these ancient fish are rare.*

Lava and ash

● **When a volcano erupts** it sends out a variety of hot materials, including lava, rock fragments, cinders, ash and gases.

● **Lava is the name** for hot molten rock once it has been erupted. It is called magma while it is still underground.

● **Tephra is the material** blasted into the air by an eruption. It includes pyroclasts and volcanic bombs.

● **Pyroclasts are large fragments** of solidified volcanic rock that are thrown out by explosive volcanoes when the plug in the volcano's vent shatters. Pyroclasts are usually 0.3–1 m across.

● **Large eruptions** can blast pyroclasts weighing one tonne or more up into the air at the speed of a jet plane.

● **Cinders and lapilli** are types of small pyroclasts. Cinders are 6.4–30 cm in diameter, lapilli are 0.1–6.4 cm.

▶ *Island volcanoes often ooze chunky lava, called 'aa' lava, like this flow on the island of Réunion, in the Indian Ocean.*

DID YOU KNOW?

Pumice rock is made from hardened lava froth – it is so full of air bubbles that it floats.

● **Volcanic bombs** are blobs of molten magma that cool and harden as they fly through the air.

● **'Breadcrust' bombs** have a hard crust. The expanding hot centre makes the crust crack, like a loaf of bread.

● **Around 90 percent** of the material ejected by explosive volcanoes is not lava, but tephra such as ash.

Air pressure

● **Air is light,** but there is so much that it can exert huge pressure at ground level. Air or atmospheric pressure is the constant bombardment of billions of air molecules as they move around.

● **Air pushes in all directions** at ground level with a force of over one kilogram per square centimetre – that is the equivalent of an elephant standing on a coffee table.

● **A device called a barometer** measures air pressure in units called millibars (mb).

● **Air pressure varies constantly** in different places and at different times. This is because the Sun's heat varies too, making air expand to get thinner and lighter, or contract to get thicker and heavier.

● **Normal air pressure** at sea level is 1013 mb, but it can vary between 800 mb and 1050 mb.

● **Air pressure is shown** on weather maps by lines called isobars, which link together locations that have equal pressure.

● **High-pressure zones** are called anticyclones. Low-pressure zones are called cyclones or depressions.

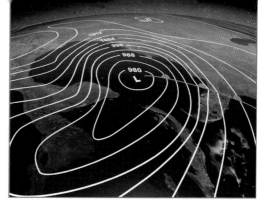

▲ *Familiar from weather charts and forecast maps, these white lines are isobars. They represent places of equal air pressure (iso = same or equal, bar = pressure). So the 980 line shows all places with an air pressure of 980 millibars. The closer the isobars, the stronger the winds in that area. 'L' signifies the middle of this low pressure system – a hurricane in the Gulf of Mexico.*

● **Barometers help to forecast** weather because changes in air pressure are linked to changes in weather.

● **A sudden, sharp fall** in air pressure warns that stormy weather is on its way because depressions are linked to storms.

● **Steady high pressure** indicates clearer, calm weather.

The Earth's chemistry

● **The bulk of the Earth** is made from iron, oxygen, silicon and magnesium.

● **More than 80 chemical elements** occur naturally in the Earth and its atmosphere.

● **The crust** is made mostly from oxygen and silicon, with aluminium, iron, calcium, magnesium, sodium, potassium, titanium and traces of 64 other elements.

▼ *This diagram shows the percentages by mass (weight) of the chemical elements that make up the Earth.*

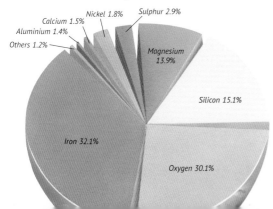

Calcium 1.5%
Nickel 1.8%
Sulphur 2.9%
Aluminium 1.4%
Others 1.2%
Magnesium 13.9%
Silicon 15.1%
Iron 32.1%
Oxygen 30.1%

● **The upper mantle** is made from iron and magnesium silicates. The lower is silicon and magnesium sulphides and oxides.

● **The core is mostly iron,** with a small amount of nickel and traces of sulphur, carbon, oxygen and potassium.

● **Evidence for the Earth's chemistry** comes from analyzing its density with the help of earthquake waves, and from studying stars, meteorites and other planets.

● **When the Earth was still semi-molten,** dense elements such as iron sank to form the core. Lighter elements such as oxygen floated up to form the crust.

● **Some heavy elements,** such as uranium, ended up in the crust because they make compounds easily with oxygen and silicon.

● **Large amounts** of elements that combine easily with sulphur, such as zinc and lead, spread through the mantle.

● **Elements that combine** easily with iron, such as gold and nickel, sank to the core.

Volcano zones

● **Worldwide,** there are over 1500 volcanoes; 500 of these are active. A volcano can have a lifespan of a million years and not erupt for several centuries.

● **Volcanoes are said to be active** if they have erupted recently. The official Smithsonian Institute list of active volcanoes includes any that have erupted in the past 10,000 years. Extinct volcanoes will never erupt again.

● **Volcanoes occur** either along the margins of tectonic plates, or over hot spots in the Earth's interior.

● **Some volcanoes** erupt where the plates are pulling apart, such as under the sea along mid-ocean ridges.

● **Some volcanoes** lie near subduction zones, forming either an arc of volcanic islands or a line of volcanoes on land, called a volcanic arc.

● **Subduction zone volcanoes** are often explosive, because their magma is sticky and gassy. It clogs up volcanic vents then blasts its way out.

● **Around the Pacific** there is a ring of explosive volcanoes called the Ring of Fire. It includes Mount Pinatubo in the Philippines, and Mount St Helens in Washington State, USA.

▲ *One of the many volcanoes in the Ring of Fire around the Pacific Ocean is Mount Fuji in Japan.*

● **Away from subduction zones** magma is basaltic. It is runny and low in gas, so the volcanoes here gush lava.

● **Effusive volcanoes** pour out lava frequently but steadily and relatively slowly.

● **Detailed 3D imaging** from satellites may pick up the minutest swelling on every active volcano in the world. In this way it helps to predict eruptions.

The shape of the Earth

● **The study of the shape** of the Earth is called geodesy. In the past, geodesy depended on ground-based surveys. Today, satellites play a major role.

● **The Earth is not a perfect sphere**. It is a unique shape called a geoid, which means 'Earth-shaped'.

● **At the Equator**, the Earth spins faster than at the Poles. This is because the Equator is farther from the Earth's spinning axis.

● **The extra speed** at the Equator pushes the Earth out in a bulge, while it is flattened at the Poles.

● **This Equatorial bulge** was predicted in 1687 by English scientist Isaac Newton (1642–1727).

● **The Equatorial bulge** was confirmed 70 years after Newton, by French surveys in Peru by explorer and mathematician Charles de La Condamine (1701–1774), and in Lapland by mathematician and philosopher Pierre de Maupertuis (1698–1759).

● **The Earth's diameter** at the Equator is 12,758 km. This is longer – by 43 km – than the vertical diameter from the North Pole to the South Pole.

● **The official measurement** of the Earth's radius at the Equator is 6,376,136 m, plus or minus one metre.

● **The LAGEOS** (Laser Geodynamic) series of satellites, first launched in 1976, reflect laser beams to make very accurate measurements of the Earth. They can measure movements of the Earth's tectonic plates as small as a centimetre.

● **The Seasat satellite** of 1978 confirmed the ocean surfaces are geoid. It took millions of measurements of the height of the ocean surface, accurate to within a few centimetres.

◄ *The ancient Greeks realized that the Earth is a globe. Satellite measurements show that it is not quite perfectly round.*

Drought and desertification

- **A drought is** a long period when there is too little rain.

- **During a drought** the soil dries out, streams stop flowing, groundwater levels of the water table sink, and plants die.

- **Deserts suffer** from permanent drought. Many tropical places have seasonal droughts, with long dry seasons.

- **High temperatures** often accompany droughts. This increases water loss through evaporation.

- **In North America**, the Great Drought of 1276–1299 destroyed the cities of the native civilizations of the southwest, called the ancient Pueblo culture, and many were abandoned.

- **In the 1870s** severe drought in China killed crops and livestock, and an estimated nine million people died.

- **Between 1931 and 1938**, drought reduced the Great Plains of the USA to a dustbowl, as the soil dried out and became windblown dust.

- **Desertification** is the spread of desert conditions into surrounding grassland. It is caused by climate changes and related human activities such as too many livestock and trying to grow too many crops.

▲ In severe droughts, even waterholes dry out, leaving nothing but cracked mud.

- **Combined with increased numbers** of livestock and people, drought has put pressure on the Sahel region, south of the Sahara, in Africa, causing widespread desertification. It has also brought famine to the region, especially in Sudan and Ethiopia.

- **Drought in the Sahel** may be partly triggered by El Niño – a reversal of the ocean currents in the Pacific Ocean, off Peru, which happens every two to seven years.

Seas

- **Seas are small oceans**, enclosed or partly enclosed by land.

- **There are no major currents** flowing through seas and they are shallower than oceans.

- **In the Mediterranean** and other seas, tides can set up a seiche – a standing wave that sloshes back and forth like a ripple running up and down a bath.

- **If the natural wave cycle** of a seiche is different from the ocean tides, the tides are cancelled out.

- **If the natural wave cycle** of a seiche is similar to the ocean tides, the tides are magnified.

- **About 6 million years ago**, the Mediterranean was cut off from the Atlantic and water evaporated, leaving a desert with just a few very salty lakes.

- **Then about 5.3 million years ago**, in the Zanclean flood, an earthquake allowed the Atlantic to gush through the land where the Straits of Gibraltar are now, filling the Mediterranean again.

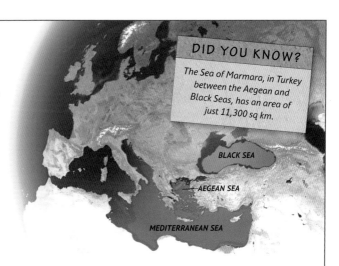

DID YOU KNOW?
The Sea of Marmara, in Turkey between the Aegean and Black Seas, has an area of just 11,300 sq km.

BLACK SEA

AEGEAN SEA

MEDITERRANEAN SEA

▲ The Mediterranean is the world's largest sea, covering 2.5 million sq km.

- **Warm seas such as the Mediterranean** lose much more water by evaporation than they gain from rivers. So a current of water flows into it steadily from the Atlantic Ocean.

- **Warm seas lose** so much water by evaporation that they are usually saltier than the open ocean.

Faults

● **A fault is a fracture** in rock along which large blocks of rock have slipped past each other.

● **Faults usually occur** in fault zones, which are often along the boundaries between tectonic plates. Faults are typically caused by earthquakes.

● **Single earthquakes** rarely move blocks more than a few centimetres. Repeated small earthquakes can shift blocks hundreds of kilometres.

● **Compression faults** are caused by rocks being squeezed together, perhaps by converging plates.

● **Tension faults** are caused by rocks being stretched, perhaps by diverging plates.

● **Normal, or dip-slip, faults** are tension faults where the rock fractures and slips straight down.

● **A wrench, or tear, fault** occurs when plates slide past each other and make blocks slip horizontally.

● **Large wrench faults**, such as the San Andreas Fault in California, USA, are called transcurrent faults.

● **Rift valleys are huge**, trough-shaped valleys created by faulting, such as Africa's Great Rift Valley. The valley floor is a depressed block called a graben. Some geologists think they are caused by tension, others by compression.

● **Horst blocks** are blocks of rock thrown up between normal faults, often creating a high plateau.

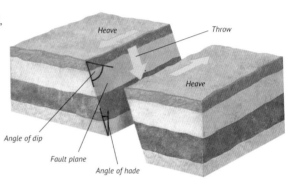

Heave

Throw

Heave

Angle of dip

▶ *Geologists who study faults describe their movement using the terms illustrated here.*

Fault plane

Angle of hade

Famous earthquakes

● **The palaces of the Minoan people** on the island of Crete were destroyed by an earthquake and tsunami around 1650 BC.

● **The earliest well-documented earthquake** hit the ancient Greek town of Sparta in 464 BC, killing 20,000 people.

● **In July 1201** an earthquake rocked every city in the eastern Mediterranean. It is estimated to have killed up to one million people.

● **In 1556** an earthquake thought to have been 8.3 on the Richter scale hit the province of Shaanxi in China.

● **The 1755 Lisbon earthquake** prompted the French writer Voltaire to write *Candide*, a book that inspired the French and American revolutions.

● **In 1906**, the US city of San Francisco was shaken by an earthquake that lasted three minutes. The earthquake started fires that burned the city almost to the ground.

● **The Tangshan earthquake** of 1976 in China was the deadliest of the 20th century. It killed over 250,000 people, as the entire city of Tangshan was levelled.

● **The powerful 7.0 magnitude** earthquake that hit the Caribbean country of Haiti on 12 January, 2010 took the lives of up to 230,000 people and made more than one million people homeless.

● **In 2013** a 7.7 magnitude quake hit Balochistan, Pakistan and killed over 800 people.

▼ *In January 2010, a powerful earthquake hit the city of Port-au-Prince in Haiti with devastating effects.*

Swamps and marshes

● **Wetlands are areas of land** where the water level is mostly above the ground.

● **The main types of wetland** are bogs, fens, swamps and marshes.

● **Bogs and fens** occur in cold climates and contain plenty of partially rotted plant material called peat.

● **Swamps and marshes** are found in warm and cold places. They have more plants than bogs and fens.

● **Marshes are in** permanently wet places, such as shallow lakes and river deltas. Reeds and rushes grow in marshes.

● **Swamps develop** where the water level varies – often along the edges of tropical rivers where they are flooded, notably along the Amazon and Congo. Trees such as mangroves grow in swamps.

● **Half the wetlands in the USA** were drained before their value was appreciated. Almost half of the 1200 sq km area of Dismal Swamp, North Carolina, has been drained.

● **The Pripet Marshes** on the borders of Belorussia are the biggest in Europe, covering 270,000 sq km.

● **Floods are controlled by wetlands** since they act like sponges, soaking up heavy rain then releasing the water slowly.

● **Wetlands also act to top up supplies** of groundwater and even have an effect on the local climate, helping to reduce the extremes of heat and cold.

▼ *Mangrove swamps are created by the unique ability of mangrove trees to live in salt water*

Acid and ozone

● **All rain is slightly acidic**, but air pollution can turn rain into harmful, corrosive acid rain.

● **Acid rain forms** when sunlight makes sulphur dioxide and nitrogen oxide combine with oxygen and moisture in the air.

● **Sulphur dioxide** and nitrogen oxide come mainly from burning fossil fuels – coal, oil and natural gas.

● **In some developed regions** such as Europe and North America, acid rain has been cut dramatically by government regulations to reduce sulphur dioxide emissions from power stations.

● **Acid rain damages** plants by taking nutrients from leaves and blocking the plants' uptake of nitrogen.

● **Twenty percent** of trees in Europe, and up to 50 percent of trees in some places, were damaged by acid rain.

● **Life on Earth** depends on the layer of ozone gas in the air, which shields the Earth from the Sun's ultraviolet (UV) rays.

● **In the early 1980s**, scientists noticed a loss of ozone over Antarctica, which peaked each spring.

● **The loss, depletion or thinning** of ozone was caused mainly by manufactured gases, notably chlorofluorocarbons (CFCs).

● **Most CFCs were banned** in the 1990s, and the ozone layer is now mending itself naturally very slowly.

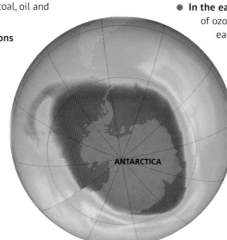

ANTARCTICA

◀ *The ozone thinned area (blue) is loss of ozone density over the South Pole. In recent years it has stabilized and may be fading.*

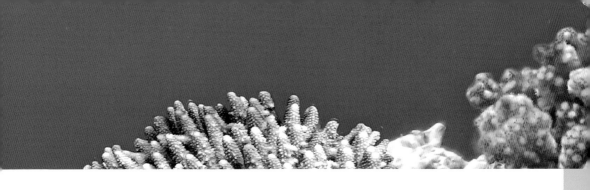

1000 **OCEAN** FACTS

A world of water

● **Water covers** over 360 million sq km of the Earth's surface. It has been divided into five major ocean basins.

● **The five basins** are the Pacific, Atlantic, Indian, Arctic and Antarctic (Southern) oceans.

● **The Arctic Ocean** surrounds the North Pole and is largely frozen.

● **The Pacific Ocean** is 165.2 million sq km, more than twice the size of the Atlantic Ocean.

● **The average depth** of the Pacific is more than 4000 m, making it the world's deepest ocean.

● **With an area** of over 73 million sq km, the Indian Ocean is bounded by Asia, Africa and Oceania.

● **The Arctic Ocean**, at 14 million sq km, is both the smallest and shallowest ocean. The deepest point in the Arctic Ocean is only 5450 m.

● **Seas are smaller than oceans** and are usually close to, or surrounded by, land. There are about 100 seas in the world. The largest are the South China Sea, the Caribbean Sea and the Mediterranean Sea.

● **The Southern Ocean** has the longest ocean current, the Antarctic circumpolar current, which is 21,000 km long and constantly moves east around Antarctica.

▶ *Oceans cover about 70 percent of the Earth's surface.*

Studying the oceans

● **The study of oceans** and their ecosystems is called oceanography.

● **Oceanography comprises** marine geology, physical oceanography, chemical oceanography, marine biology and meteorological oceanography.

▼ *Fish biologists on a fish survey in Tabuaeran (Fanning) Island, Kiribati, in the Pacific Ocean.*

● **Marine geology** is the study of tectonic plates. Marine geologists involved in offshore oil exploration and drilling also study how sediments and minerals are formed.

● **Physical oceanography** is the study of physical processes such as currents, temperature and tides.

● **Chemical oceanography** is the study of chemicals in the oceans.

● **Marine biology** is the study of ocean life – about 80 percent of our planet's life is found in the oceans.

● **Meteorological oceanography** is the study of atmospheric reactions above the oceans and the influence of the oceans on global weather.

● **Less than ten percent** of the oceans have been explored.

● **In 1960**, the bathyscaphe ('deep boat') *Trieste* reached the deepest part of the oceans, some 10,900 m beneath the surface of the Pacific, in the Mariana Trench.

● **It took the** *Trieste* four hours and 48 minutes to reach the ocean floor.

Icebergs

- **In winter,** seawater close to land can become frozen. The ice melts in summer and huge chunks, called icebergs, break off the ends of ice sheets, ice shelves and glaciers and float into the sea.

- **The process by which icebergs** break away from ice on land and move into the ocean is called calving.

- **Icebergs float** because ice is lighter, or less dense, than water. However 85 to 90 percent of the iceberg is below the water level.

- **The smallest icebergs** are called growlers. They are less than one metre high and less than 5 m long. The largest icebergs are over 75 m high and over 213 m long.

- **The tallest known iceberg** was the height of a 55 storey building. The largest iceberg ever recorded broke off from the Ross Ice Shelf in Antarctica in 2000. It had an area of 11,000 sq km.

- **The word 'iceberg'** comes from the Dutch word igsberg, which means 'ice mountain'.

- **When an iceberg melts,** tiny air bubbles trapped in the ice make a fizzing sound. These air bubbles also reflect the light, giving the iceberg a dazzling look and sometimes unusual colours, such as bright blue.

- **In April 1912,** the luxury cruise ship *Titanic* sank after hitting an iceberg, which probably came from a glacier in Greenland. Over 1500 passengers and crew members lost their lives in the disaster.

- **In 1987,** a huge flat-topped Antarctic iceberg, 155 km long and 230 m thick, was estimated to contain enough water to provide everyone on Earth with two glasses of water daily for about 2000 years.

> **DID YOU KNOW?**
>
> James Cameron's 1997 movie Titanic starred Leonardo DiCaprio and Kate Winslet. It was nominated for 14 Academy Awards, and won 11.

▶ *Icebergs are carved into ice sculptures by the wind and the waves and change shape as they gradually drift into warmer waters and melt.*

Fact file: Arctic Ocean

● **The Arctic Ocean** surrounds the North Pole. Unlike the South Pole, there is no landmass around the North Pole.

● **The maximum depth** of the Arctic Ocean is 5450 m but the average depth is 1040 m.

● **The Arctic Ocean** is partly frozen throughout the year. At least half the ice melts in summer and large chunks, called icebergs, break off and float away.

● **About two percent** of the water leaving the Arctic Ocean does so in the form of icebergs.

● **The water** in the Arctic may be freezing cold, but it is still home to a huge variety of marine life. Whales, sharks, jellyfish, squid, seals, polar bears and seabirds can be found living in and around this ocean.

● **An underwater ridge**, the Lomonosov Ridge, some 1750 km long, divides the Arctic basin in two – the Eurasian and the Amerasian basins.

● **The Arctic Ocean** is linked to the Atlantic Ocean via the Greenland Sea, a narrow, deep-water gap between Greenland and Svalbard. It is linked to the Pacific Ocean via the Bering Straits.

● **The landmasses** of Europe, North America and Greenland almost completely surround the Arctic Ocean.

● **The coastline** of the Arctic Ocean stretches for some 45,390 km and its total area is 14 million sq km.

● **The Arctic** is the least salty of all the five oceans, because of all the freshwater from rivers and streams that flow into it, and the low rate of water evaporation due to the extreme cold. It also has limited connections to other saltier oceans.

▼ *Polar bears are powerful predators, and hunt for seals beneath the ice covering the Arctic Ocean.*

Fact file: Southern Ocean

● **In 2000**, the Southern Ocean was officially confirmed as the world's fourth-largest ocean by the International Hydrographic Organization (IHO).

● **It has a total area** of some 20.3 million sq km.

● **The waters of the Southern Ocean** encircle the Antarctic continent, which surrounds the South Pole.

● **The Southern Ocean** extends from the coast of Antarctica to 60 degrees south latitude, where it merges with the Atlantic, Pacific and Indian oceans.

● **The typical depth** of the Southern Ocean is between 4000 and 5000 m.

● **The greatest depth** is 7236 m, which is at the bottom of the Sandwich Trench.

● **The Southern Ocean** formed about 30 million years ago, when South America moved away from Antarctica.

● **It has the strongest** average winds on Earth.

● **The water temperature** in the Southern Ocean varies from –2°C to 10°C.

● **The area of the Southern Ocean** covered by sea ice increases over seven times in winter, from 2.6 million sq km to 18.8 million sq km.

▼ *Penguins catch fish in the cold waters of the Southern Ocean and breed on the Antarctic continent and islands.*

Fact file: Pacific Ocean

● **The Pacific covers an area** of around 165.2 million sq km, about 15 times the size of the USA.

● **Larger than the total land area** of the world, the Pacific Ocean contains some 724 million cubic km of water. That is more than twice as much water as the Atlantic Ocean.

● **More than 80 percent** of the world's active volcanoes are found in the Pacific. They encircle the ocean along the continent margins to form the 'Ring of Fire'.

● **The average depth** of the Pacific Ocean is 4280 m, but the Mariana Trench and the Tonga Trench reach depths of over 10.5 km – more than twice the average depth of the ocean.

● **One hundred million years ago**, the Pacific Ocean was much larger than it is today. It has been decreasing in size as the Atlantic and Indian oceans have been increasing in size.

● **The name Pacific means** 'peaceful' because European explorers thought that this ocean had a gentler climate than the others.

● **The Pacific Ocean** contains many thousands of islands, including Japan, Taiwan, Borneo, New Guinea, Tahiti, Easter Island and the Galápagos Islands.

● **The North Equatorial current** of the Pacific Ocean is the longest westerly current in the world. It runs for 14,484 km from Panama to the Philippines.

● **A warm water current** called El Niño flows at regular intervals off the coast of Peru in the South Pacific Ocean, causing rainstorms and floods in Central and South America and bad weather in Asia.

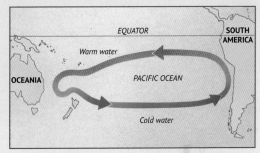

▲ Winds and the shapes of the continents make currents on the surface of the oceans flow in great circles, called gyres. The gyre in the South Pacific Ocean is one of three in the Southern Hemisphere.

▼ The Great Barrier Reef is a huge coral reef off the coast of northeastern Australia in the warm waters of the Pacific Ocean.

DID YOU KNOW?

The Great Barrier Reef is longer than the west coast of the USA. It is the largest living structure on Earth.

Fact file: Atlantic Ocean

● **The Atlantic Ocean** is the world's second largest ocean at 106.4 million sq km.

● **Its average depth** is 3646 m, but the deepest point is the Puerto Rico Trench, at 8648 m beneath the surface.

● **The Atlantic** is expanding at a rate of about 2–4 cm per year.

● **The floor** of the Atlantic Ocean is divided in two by an underwater mountain range, which extends from north of Iceland down to the edge of the Southern Ocean.

◀ *In the North Atlantic Ocean, warm water circulates round and round, flowing westwards from Africa to Central America and eastwards (as the Gulf Stream) from North America to Europe.*

● **The Gulf Stream** is a North Atlantic current that carries warm water from the Caribbean and the Gulf of Mexico up the east coast of North America and across to western Europe, keeping the climate of western Europe warmer than it would otherwise be.

● **These mountains** are twice as wide as the Andes Mountains of South America.

● **Most of the Atlantic's mountains** lie beneath the waves but the Azores, Ascension Island and Tristan da Cunha are the tops of some of these mountains.

● **The Atlantic Ocean** receives water from about half the world's land area, including many of the world's great rivers, such as the Amazon.

● **Formed about** 150 million years ago, the Atlantic is the youngest of the world's oceans.

Fact file: Indian Ocean

● **The Indian Ocean** covers about 20 percent of the global ocean between Africa, Asia, Australia and Antarctica.

● **At 73.5 million sq km**, it is nearly eight times the size of the USA.

● **The average depth** of the Indian Ocean is 3890 m but its deepest point is the Java Trench, which is 7450 m.

▼ *One feature of the Indian Ocean is coral islands, such as the Seychelles. The beautiful beaches are popular tourist destinations.*

● **Two of the world's largest rivers**, the Indus and the Ganges-Brahmaputra, flow into the Indian Ocean, depositing fans of sediment where they enter the ocean.

● **The surface** of the Indian Ocean is dominated by monsoon winds, which blow in opposite directions during the monsoon seasons.

● **During the northeast monsoon**, the surface waters are driven away from India and towards the African coast.

● **During the southwest monsoon**, the surface waters of the Indian Ocean are driven back towards India again.

● **The floor** of the Indian Ocean is divided by a mid-ocean ridge of undersea mountains, which form an upside-down Y shape.

● **The subcontinent** of India divides the northern Indian Ocean into two, with the Arabian Sea to the west and the Bay of Bengal to the east.

● **In December 2004**, a huge tsunami in the Indian Ocean caused massive waves and flooding that devastated 11 countries and killed 283,000 people.

Ocean floor

● **The surface of the land** under the oceans is called the ocean floor. Its landscape is varied with mountain ranges, valleys, deep canyons and wide, flat plains.

● **The ocean floor** is divided into the continental shelf, the continental slope and the deep ocean floor.

● **The continental shelf** is an underwater extension of the coast. The outer rim of islands and continents gently slope into the surrounding water to form it.

● **The average width** of the continental shelf is about 65 km but some, such as the Siberian Shelf in the Arctic Ocean, can extend up to 1500 km.

● **This area contains** large deposits of petroleum, natural gas and minerals. It receives the most sunlight.

● **The continental slope** is the point where the shelf starts to plunge towards the ocean floor. The ocean floor is marked by deep canyons.

● **Below continental slopes**, sediments often collect to form gentle slopes called continental rise.

● **In many places** the ocean floor forms vast expanses that are flat and covered with sediment. These regions are called abyssal plains.

● **Abyssal plains** are broken by mid-ocean ridges, such as the Mid-Atlantic and the East Pacific rise, and trenches such as the Mariana Trench in the Pacific.

▼ *Underwater ocean features include (1) Continental shelf, (2) Abyssal plain, (3) Guyot, (4) Seamount, (5) Mid-ocean ridges, (6) Deep-sea trench, (7) Continental slope.*

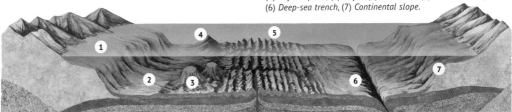

Trenches and ridges

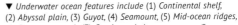

DID YOU KNOW?

The Hawaiian Islands are a chain of seamounts.

● **Ocean floor structures** include trenches (similar to valleys) and ridges (similar to mountain chains).

● **The Earth's crust** is made up of huge rock segments (tectonic plates) that move against each other.

● **Ridges and trenches** are formed by the movement of these plates.

● **The Mariana Trench** is one of the deepest trenches. It is in the Pacific Ocean.

● **Challenger Deep**, in the Mariana Trench, is the deepest point in the Earth – it is 11,033 m deep.

● **The mid-ocean ridge** in the Atlantic is the longest mountain chain on Earth, at over 50,000 km long.

● **Most of the crests** of these mountains lie nearly 2500 m below the ocean surface.

● **Sometimes the mid-ocean ridge** rises above the sea level. Iceland is located on a crest of the mid-Atlantic ocean ridge.

● **Seamounts are underwater** volcanoes. A flat-topped seamount is known as a guyot, while those with peaks are known as seapeaks.

▼ *Ridges (1) form when two plates drift apart and magma oozes through the cracks and cools. Trenches (2) form when an ocean plate collides with a continental plate and the ocean plate is forced down into the mantle in a process called subduction.*

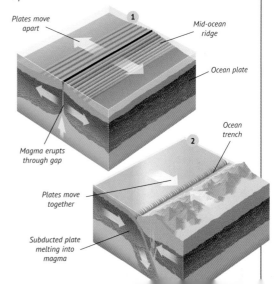

Plates move apart

1

Mid-ocean ridge

Ocean plate

Magma erupts through gap

Ocean trench

Plates move together

2

Subducted plate melting into magma

Hydrothermal vents

● **Hot springs** (hydrothermal vents) are also found on the sea floor along the mid-ocean ridge. They are formed when water seeps into the crust as two plates pull apart. This water is heated by the magma and shoots up through cracks in the ocean floor.

● **The water temperature** in and around a vent can reach 400°C. It is rich in minerals and the gas hydrogen sulphide.

● **The scalding water** mixes with the surrounding cold water to create jets of warm water. These are often black because of the mineral content in the water, so they are also called black smokers.

● **Hydrothermal vents** were first discovered in 1977 near the Galápagos Islands, along the eastern Pacific Ocean basin.

● **Some vents** form chimneys as minerals in the vent fluid are deposited around the jets of water. These chimneys can be over 60 m high and grow as fast as 30 cm a day.

● **Vents may last** from 100 to perhaps as long as 100,000 years, although they are probably destroyed sooner than this as the Earth's tectonic plates move and volcanoes erupt under the sea.

● **The water** at the deep-ocean floor is too cold for creatures to survive, but hydrothermal vents are like underwater oases. Long tube worms and other life forms that are not found anywhere else in the world thrive near these vents.

● **Vent communities** feed on bacteria, which use the minerals from the vents (especially sulphur) to make food. This is very different from most food chains, which depend on the Sun's energy to make food, and may provide clues to the scientific origin of life on Earth.

● **Giant tube worms** that live around deep-sea vents can be over 2 m long. They do not have a mouth or digestive system, but absorb food directly from the billions of microscopic bacteria living inside them.

● **An unusual worm**, called the Pompeii worm, lives right inside some of the growing vent chimneys, surviving temperatures as high as 80°C.

DID YOU KNOW?

Godzilla, a vent chimney in the Pacific Ocean, reached the height of a 15-storey building before it toppled over. It is now growing upwards again.

▼ Giant tube worms breathe through red gills, which emerge from the top of their tubes. Rattail fish use their fleshy barbels to detect small creatures in the black water.

1 Cloud of hot water rich in minerals
2 Rocky chimney made from a build up of minerals
3 Rattail fish
4 Giant tube worms
5 Giant clams

Islands

- **An island** is an area of land that is surrounded by water. Rising sea levels can create islands by cutting off a piece of land from the mainland.

- **The world's four largest islands** are Greenland, New Guinea, Borneo and Madagascar. Unique wildlife, such as lemurs, evolved on Madagascar after it broke away from the African mainland some 165 million years ago.

- **The island of Surtsey** was created by the eruption of Sutur, an underwater volcano near Iceland, which erupted for four months, from 1964–1965.

- **The 16 Galápagos Islands** are the tops of volcanoes that rose from the ocean floor and have never been connected to the mainland. The oldest islands are probably no more than five million years old and some are still forming.

- **The Maldives**, in the Indian Ocean, are made up of 1190 coral reef islands that have grown on top of an underwater mountain chain.

- **An atoll** is a coral reef surrounding a lagoon. The formation of atolls can take millions of years.

▲ *Only 200 of the Maldive Islands are inhabited. The highest point on the islands is only 2.4 m above sea level.*

- **Atoll formation** begins with the creation of a coral reef around a volcanic island. Wind and waves erode the island and it begins to sink. The reef grows upwards to form a barrier separated from the island by a lagoon. At this stage the island is called a barrier reef island.

- **The barrier reef island** sinks until submerged. The reef around the island continues to grow upwards to form a ring around a lagoon. This is called a coral atoll.

- **Coral atolls are formed** mostly in the warm, shallow waters of the Indian and Pacific oceans.

- **Waves and wind** may deposit bits of coral and sand on top of reefs. Over time, this piles up to form low-lying islands called cays.

Volcanic islands

- **Undersea volcanoes** often lead to the formation of volcanic islands. Some form around one or two volcanic vents, others can be made up of a series of vents.

- **Volcanic activity** often occurs at the point between two tectonic plates.

- **Sometimes**, volcanoes are formed away from the plate boundaries, near fixed points of volcanic activity located beneath tectonic plates (hot spots).

- **Molten magma** from deep within the mantle forces its way through fissures (gaps) in the plate and flows out to form seamounts.

- **Over millions of years**, magma oozes out of these seamounts, which rise above the ocean surface as islands. These islands are called oceanic high islands.

- **Volcanic activity** on an island stops when it is carried away from the hot spot when the tectonic plates move.

- **Then another island is created** at the hot spot. This continues until a chain of islands, such as the Hawaiian Islands, is created.

- **Big Island in Hawaii** has five volcanoes. They are Kilauea, Mauna Loa, Mauna Kea, Hualalai and Kohala. Kilauea is the most active volcano in the region.

- **The hot spot** in the Pacific Ocean is currently under Big Island – the largest among the Hawaiian Islands.

- **Iceland was formed** by volcanic activity near the ocean ridge. It is the only part of the mid-oceanic ridge that emerges from the surface.

▼ (1) *Molten magma breaks through Earth's crust.* (2) *More lava is deposited on the seabed, so a cone shape builds up.* (3) *When this breaks the water's surface, a new island appears.*

Waves, tides and currents

● **Oceans are continually** rocked by movements such as waves, currents and tides.

● **Most movements** are caused by wind. Waves are created by winds blowing over the surface of the oceans.

● **The water in a wave** moves in circles. As a wave nears land it slows. The top part continues and crashes on the shore as a breaker.

● **The shape and size** of waves differ. A steep, choppy wave is one that formed near the coast, while slow, steady waves are those that formed out in the ocean.

● **The regular rise and fall** of the oceans are called tides. They are caused by the gravitational pull of the Moon.

● **The period of high water level** is called high tide and the period of low water level is called low tide.

● **An ocean current** is a mass of water moving continuously in one direction.

● **Surface currents** are caused by winds and the rotation of the Earth.

● **Underwater currents** are caused by differences in temperature and salt content.

● **When the Sun, Moon and Earth** are aligned, their combined gravities cause very high tides (spring tides). Smaller tides (neap tides) occur at times when the Moon is at a right angle to the Sun and the Earth.

▼ *High tide occurs in those areas that are closest to and farthest away from the Moon. As the Earth turns about six hours later, the water subsides and low tide occurs.*

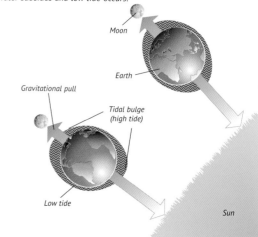

Moon

Earth

Gravitational pull

Tidal bulge (high tide)

Low tide

Sun

Danger at sea

● **The oceans** can wreak havoc in the form of tsunamis, whirlpools and hurricanes.

● **Tsunamis are massive waves** generated by certain natural disturbances. They lash against the shore with great force and can cause a lot of damage.

● **Usually created by earthquakes**, tsunamis can also be generated by landslides and undersea volcanic eruptions.

● **Most tsunamis** originate along an earthquake-prone zone known as the Ring of Fire, around the Pacific.

● **Hurricanes are cyclones** arising in tropical or sub-tropical waters. These powerful storms often travel onto land where they cause floods and devastate towns.

● **A typical hurricane** is about 500 km wide. At the centre is a small circular area with no clouds.

● **This is called the 'eye'**, and it's completely calm and quiet.

● **A whirlpool is created** when opposing currents meet. Most whirlpools are not dangerous, but some are powerful enough to destroy small boats.

● **Mokstraumen** off the coast of Norway and Old Sow near Deer Island in Canada are two of the world's most powerful whirlpools.

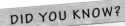

◀ *In 2005, Hurricane Katrina flooded 80 percent of the city of New Orleans, USA. Over 1800 people lost their lives.*

DID YOU KNOW?

El Niño is a warming of surface waters in the eastern Pacific near the Equator. It can lead to flooding and drought around the world.

Coastlines

● **A coast** is a continuous stretch of land that borders an ocean. The outline of the coast is called a coastline.

● **Hard rocks** along the coastline withstand the waves and erode slowly, forming headlands.

● **A cliff is formed** by the pounding of waves on weak spots on the rock face.

● **Continuous erosion** leads to the creation of hollows (sea caves). Sometimes waves pound the headland from both sides, causing two caves to form back-to-back.

● **When two caves meet**, a sea arch forms. The top of the arch links the headland to the mainland. After years of erosion, sea arches cave in and leave a sea stack – a column of rock in the sea.

● **The best known natural structure** formed by waves is the beach. Waves lose much of their power in shallow waters and instead of eroding, they deposit sand and shingle along the coast. These deposits eventually become the beach.

● **Longshore drift** is the term used to describe the movement of beach material along the shore when waves strike the beach at an angle.

● **A spit is formed** by longshore drift. It is a long, thin ridge of sand, shingle or mud, which is joined to the coast at one end but extends out into the sea. Spits often curve at the end because the waves push them back towards the coast.

● **A lagoon** is a coastal lake cut off from the sea by a bar of sand or mud (perhaps a spit joining two headlands) or a coral reef.

▼ *Towering sea cliffs on the Hawaiian Islands are among the tallest in the world, and are as high as a 300-storey building.*

▼ *The wind can create sand dunes on beaches, which may be covered with grass and other plants. The dunes help to protect the coastline from erosion.*

Life on the seashore

● **Creatures such as periwinkles** and limpets can survive out of water for long periods at low tide. They live high up on a rocky shore.

● **Animals and plants** that need to be underwater most of the time, such as starfish, topshells and kelp seaweeds, live low down on a rocky shore.

● **The middle of a rocky** shore is underwater half the time. Animals such as barnacles and mussels survive well here, as well as seaweeds such as wracks.

● **Buried under a sandy shore** are burrowing animals such as worms and shellfish (razor shells and tellins) that feed on food particles brought in by the tide.

● **The South African plough snail** 'surfs' up the beach to feed on decaying matter and creatures stranded by the high tide. It has a muscular foot that it uses as a plough-shaped 'surf board'.

● **Rockpool fish** such as lumpsuckers and clingfish have suckers to help them stick to rocks when waves crash into their pools or the tide drains away.

● **To protect themselves** from drying out at low tide, sea anemones pull their tentacles inside their hollow bodies so they look like blobs of jelly.

● **Mudskippers** are named after their habit of 'skipping' across muddy shores by wriggling their tails. They burrow into the mud to escape danger and drying out at low tide.

● **Mangrove trees** shield tropical shores from storms and hurricanes and also build up the shoreline by trapping mud among their thick, tangled roots.

▲ *At low tide, the roots of mangrove trees look like legs supporting the trees.*

1	Anemone	8	Sponge
2	Goby	9	Bladderwrack seaweed
3	Starfish		
4	Hermit crab	10	Shore crab
5	Limpet	11	Prawn
6	Mussel	12	Topshell
7	Sea urchin	13	Razor shell

▼ *Large rockpools shelter a variety of life, from seaweeds and shellfish to starfish and crabs.*

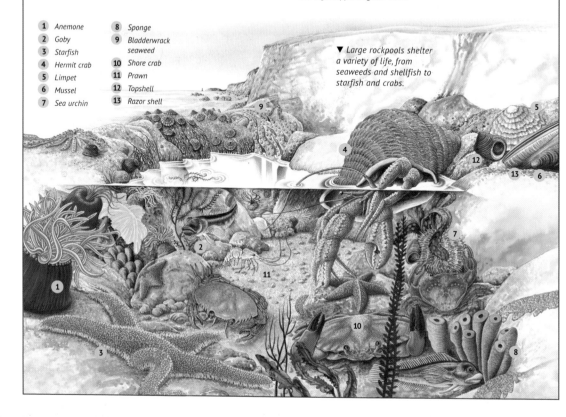

Cephalopods

- **Octopuses, squid, cuttlefish and nautiluses** make up a group of molluscs called cephalopods, which have a large head, well-developed eyes and long arms with lots of suckers.

- **The nautilus** is the only cephalopod with an external shell.

- **Cuttlefish have an internal shell**, or cuttlebone, which is often washed up on the shore. The cuttlebone contains spaces filled with gas, which helps the cuttlefish to float.

- **Cephalopods swim** by jet propulsion. They squirt a jet of water out of a funnel called a siphon, which makes them shoot forwards through the water.

- **Cephalopods can change colour** almost immediately to startle predators, blend in with the background or send messages to others of their own kind.

- **The bright blue** colour of the blue-ringed octopus warns that it has a deadly bite. The rings turn blue when the octopus is threatened. A bite from this octopus can kill a person.

◀ *Squid are predators of fish, crustaceans and other squid. Their streamlined body shape helps them to swim fast and their long tentacles are used to catch food.*

- **The giant squid** is the largest invertebrate, with a body 2–4 m long and tentacles reaching lengths of 25 or 30 m. Its eyes are the largest of any living creature and can grow to the size of dinner plates.

- **Many cephalopods** can produce light so they glow in the darkness of the deep sea. They use their glowing lights to communicate with others or to attract prey.

- **If it is disturbed**, an octopus can shoot a cloud of murky ink called sepia into the water. This confuses the predator or sometimes has a numbing effect, giving the octopus time to escape.

- **Cephalopods** very similar to the nautilus of today swam in the oceans millions of years ago. Nowadays, the nautilus is very rare and is a kind of 'living fossil'. Its arms do not have suckers.

Coral reefs

- **Corals are ancient animals** that have been around for 400 million years.

- **Coral reefs** are formed by colonies of coral polyps – tiny animals that use minerals in the sea to produce their protective outer skeletons. These skeletons form hard and branching structures – the coral reefs.

- **The polyps** use their tentacles to capture tiny creatures called zooplankton, and also eat algae.

- **Coral reefs are home** to many creatures such as starfish, reef sharks, sponges, crabs, lobsters, anemones and a huge variety of fish.

- **The reefs** are found in warm and shallow waters, usually within 30 degrees north and south of the Equator.

- **There are three kinds** of coral reef – fringing and barrier reefs, and coral atolls.

- **Fringing reefs** extend from the land into the sea. Barrier reefs are found further from the shore, separated from the mainland by a lagoon.

- **The Great Barrier Reef** in the Coral Sea off the northeastern coast of Australia is the biggest coral reef in the world. It is just over 2000 km long.

- **Reefs are also found** in the Indian Ocean and the Red Sea. Some also stretch along the Atlantic Ocean from Florida in the United States to the Caribbean Sea and Brazil.

DID YOU KNOW?

Most coral reefs are in the Pacific Ocean and they are home to about 25 percent of all ocean life.

▶ *A single coral reef may be home to as many as 3000 species of living things.*

Crabs and other crustaceans

● **Crustaceans are named** after their hard, tough outer casings, or exoskeletons, which are made of chalky plates that cover their bodies like a crust.

● **As well as lobsters and crabs**, the crustacean group includes shrimps, prawns, krill, barnacles and sea slaters (relatives of woodlice).

● **Many crustaceans** start life as microscopic larvae that drift with the plankton, which forms the start of most ocean food chains.

● **In the Southern Ocean**, a shrimp-like crustacean called krill is a vital source of food for many sea animals, from whales and seals to penguins and other seabirds.

● **The decorator crab** is camouflaged by seaweed, sponges and other small animals, which cover its body and are held in place by tiny hooks.

▶ *A lobster uses its big claws for gripping and shredding its food. As well as its two front claws, it has eight walking legs.*

● **Goose barnacles** may drift thousands of kilometres across the oceans attached to pieces of driftwood or rafts of bubbles, which they make themselves. Most barnacles stay fixed to rocks when they are adults.

● **In autumn**, West Indian spiny lobsters migrate to deeper water to avoid storms on the coast. They march across the seabed in long lines for up to 15 km a day.

● **The Japanese spider crab** is the largest crustacean, with legs spanning over 4 m. These crabs have poor balance and live in still waters, hunting slow-moving prey such as other crustaceans, starfish, worms and shellfish.

● **Some crabs**, such as boxer crabs, grab hold of sea anemones with their pincers and wave them about to scare away their enemies.

Worms

● **Ocean worms** include flatworms, ringed or segmented worms, tube-making worms, peanut worms, ribbon worms, beard worms and arrow worms.

● **Ragworms are named** after the ragged fringe of flat legs along the sides of their bodies. They use their legs for crawling, swimming and breathing.

● **The sea mouse** is a worm that is covered in bristles that look like fur. It lives on coasts near the low tide line.

● **The peacock fanworm** lives inside a tube of mud and sand, pushing a fan of feathery tentacles out of the top of the tube to breathe and catch food particles.

● **Lugworms** live in U-shaped burrows under sandy or muddy shores, swallowing the sand or mud and extracting food particles.

● **Their waste** piles up at the exit to their burrows like heaps of 'sand spaghetti'.

● **The palolo worm** of the Pacific Ocean reproduces by breaking off a special 'tail' filled with eggs and sperm, which wriggles on its own to the surface.

● **Peanut worms** are named after their shape. They have a proboscis (tubular sucking organ), which they use for feeding.

● **Giant tube worms** that live around hydrothermal vents grow up to 2 m long in the deep sea, but in shallow water, they are only as long as your hand.

● **Bloodworms** live in tubelike structures built on rocks underwater. Up to 37 cm in length, they have strong jaws with poison glands, which they use to kill prey. Their poisonous bite is painful to humans.

◀ *Feather duster worms filter food from the water with their fan-shaped tentacles.*

Jellyfish

● **Jellyfish have inhabited** the oceans for more than 650 million years. They were living on Earth long before the dinosaurs and still survive today.

● **These creatures are not fish**, instead they belong to a group of animals called cnidarians (or coelenterates), which also includes sea anemones and corals. Most cnidarians live in the oceans.

● **A group of jellyfish** is called a smack.

● **A jellyfish** is made up of 90–95 percent water. It needs water to support its delicate body and stay alive. It will dry up and die out of water.

● **Jellyfish open and close** their umbrella-shaped 'bell' to force water out behind their bodies and push themselves along. They also drift on ocean currents.

● **Jellyfish do not have a brain**, heart, blood, head, eyes ears or bones. They can, however, detect light and dark, and scents in the water.

● **To capture prey** such as small fish, shrimps or tiny sea creatures, jellyfish use stinging cells on their tentacles. The stings inject poison to paralyze or kill prey.

▲ *A jellyfish has a bell-shaped body and long, trailing tentacles.*

● **The stings of some jellyfish**, such as the box jellyfish or sea wasp, are strong enough to kill a person. The box jellyfish has about 5000 stinging cells on each tentacle.

● **The world's largest jellyfish**, the Arctic lion's mane jellyfish, has tentacles up to 30 m long.

● **Jellyfish do not have** gills or lungs. Oxygen is absorbed and carbon dioxide is released through their membrane-like skin.

Sponges

● **Sponges are animals** with no brain or body parts.

● **There are about 10,000 species** of sponge. Some grow to more than one metre wide and the largest (Monoraphus) grows to about 3 m in width.

● **Most sponges** are attached to a surface. They often form a thin crust, but some are shaped like tubes, cups or fans.

● **The breadcrumb sponge** grows in flat mats over rocks. If it is touched, it crumbles into small pieces, like breadcrumbs.

● **Most sponges** have an internal skeleton made of rod- or star-shaped parts called spicules, made from calcium carbonate or silica. This skeleton helps to support the sponge's body.

● **In the Venus's flower-basket sponge**, the spicules are fused to form a delicate, basket-like structure.

● **Bath sponges** have a very dense and elastic skeleton made of a substance called spongin. They do not have a spicule skeleton like most other sponges.

● **If part of a sponge** breaks off, it can grow into a new sponge.

● **Many sponges** give off poisonous substances to defend themselves. Some of these substances may be used by people as medicines.

● **Sponges** are filter-feeders. They strain bacteria and food particles from the water using tiny tentacles, which line chambers inside their bodies.

▼ *Yellow tube sponges usually grow in groups, building tubes at least 60 cm high.*

Starfish, sea urchins and sea cucumbers

- **Starfish, sea urchins and sea cucumbers** belong to the echinoderm group of animals.

- **Echinoderms**, which also include brittle stars and sand dollars, are not fish and their name means 'spiny skinned'. There are about 7000 species of echinoderms.

- **They have a skeleton** made of hard plates, covered by a layer of skin. In some species the plates are joined to long spines.

- **All echinoderms live in the sea**, in both shallow and deep water.

- **A starfish** has rows of tube feet underneath its arms. By pumping water into these tubes, it can crawl along. The feet are also used for feeding and breathing.

- **Many starfish** have five arms, but some have as many as 50. If one arm breaks off, starfish can generate a new one to replace it.

- **Brittle stars** are relatives of starfish, with thinner arms that break off easily if they are touched. They usually hide during the day and come out to feed at night-time.

- **Sea cucumbers** live on the ocean floor, using a set of sticky tentacles to trap particles of food. Some can produce poisonous, sticky threads to trap predators.

- **Sea urchins** are protected by their poisonous spines. Underneath the spiny body is a mouth with five pointed teeth for scraping food from the rocks.

- **Sea lilies** are echinoderms that are fixed to the sea floor by a long stalk. Their five feathery arms collect food particles from the water.

◀ *Starfish are active predators. They can even push their stomachs out of their mouths to digest large prey that is too big to swallow.*

Molluscs

- **Molluscs that live** in the oceans include a variety of shellfish (such as clams or cowries) as well as sea snails, chitons, octopuses, squid and cuttlefish.

- **Chitons have** one muscular foot and a rasping tongue (like snails and slugs) but their shell is made up of eight overlapping plates.

- **Many sea slugs** have bright colours to warn of the poisons in their bodies. Some kinds steal poisonous stinging cells from sea anemones and use them for their own defence.

- **Sea snails**, such as whelks, breathe oxygen from the water by means of gills. They draw water over their gills using a tube called a siphon.

- **Scallops are a sort of bivalve** – a mollusc with a shell made of two hinged plates, called valves. Scallops swim by 'clapping' the two halves of their shell together, forcing out a jet of water that pushes them along.

- **Pearls may grow** inside oyster shells if a piece of grit gets trapped between the shell and the thin layer lining the shell. Pearls grow at a rate of about one millimetre in five years.

- **Giant clams** can grow as large as one metre across and live for up to 100 years. The clam has rows of tiny eyes along the edge of its shell to detect danger. It heaves its shell slowly shut if danger threatens.

- **Cone shells use a tiny**, poisonous 'harpoon' to paralyze their prey, such as small fish or worms. Some cone shells can kill people.

- **Purple dye** produced from some murex shells was used to dye the cloth worn by the rich in ancient Rome.

- **Mussels produce** tough, silky threads to anchor themselves to the rocks.

▼ *Sea slugs have feathery plumes called ceratia on their backs to absorb oxygen from the water.*

Living links

● **Ocean plants and animals** are linked by the way they feed on each other. Each plant or animal is like a link in a chain, so a series of feeding links is called a food chain.

● **Most ocean food chains** start with tiny drifting plants and animals called plankton. Plant plankton is called phytoplankton and animal plankton is called zooplankton.

● **An example** of an ocean food chain is: phytoplankton – zooplankton – mackerel – humans.

● **An example** of a seashore food chain is: seaweed – periwinkle – crab – octopus.

● **Some ocean animals** help each other to survive by living together. This is called symbiosis. Tiny green plants called algae grow on the edge of a giant clam's shell. They feed on the clam's waste and, in return, the clam feeds on some of the algae.

▲ Clown fish clean up the anemones they live with by feeding on leftover food scraps.

● **Clown fish** are protected from predators by hiding in an anemone's stinging tentacles. The clown fish covers itself in slimy mucus so it is not harmed by the poisonous stings. The bright colours of the fish may warn predators that the anemone is dangerous so that both animals are more likely to survive.

● **Cleaner wrasse fish** feed on the pests and dead skin of larger fish – they even work down a shark's throat.

● **Remora fish** are the hitch-hikers of the oceans, sticking to larger fish with a sucker on their head. When the larger fish finds food, the remora lets go and feeds on the scraps.

● **Male anglerfish** attach themselves to the larger females because it is so difficult to find a mate in the darkness of the deep ocean. They live off the blood supply of the female and are ready to fertilize her eggs whenever she lays them.

▲ The basking shark is the world's second-largest fish, but feeds on microscopic plankton that drifts near the surface of the ocean.

DID YOU KNOW?

The banded coral shrimp cleans the needle-sharp teeth of moray eels, and gets a free meal into the bargain.

▼ Cleaner wrasse fish gather around the gills and mouth of a shark. The shark is cleaned up and the wrasse get protection and an easy meal.

Fish

● **Fish are vertebrates**, so they have a backbone. They live in water, breathe through their gills and have scales. Most fish live in oceans – only one in five lives in freshwater.

● **Fish are cold-blooded**, meaning their body temperature changes with their surroundings.

● **There are two** main groups of fish – jawed and jawless. Jawless fish, such as lampreys and hagfish, have a sucker-like mouth with horny teeth.

● **Jawed fish** are further divided into cartilaginous and bony fish. The skeletons of cartilaginous fish are made of tissue called cartilage. Sharks, rays and chimaeras are cartilaginous fish.

● **The skeletons** of bony fish are made of bone. They are the most common fish species. Most have a gas-filled swim bladder that controls buoyancy.

● **Two of the largest fish** in the oceans, the whale shark and the basking shark, feed on microscopic plankton.

● **Fish are important** to humans as food. Excessive fishing has endangered some species, while others are already extinct.

● **Some fish of the Southern Ocean** have a natural anti-freeze in their blood to keep their bodies working in freezing cold water.

● **Fish sense vibrations** caused by currents, predators and prey by means of a lateral line of nerve cells that runs along each side of the body under the skin.

▼ *Cod are active hunters, catching molluscs, crabs, starfish, worms, squid and small fish.*

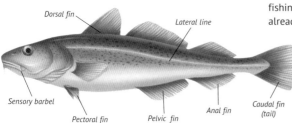

Dorsal fin

Lateral line

Sensory barbel

Pectoral fin

Pelvic fin

Anal fin

Caudal fin (tail)

Coral reef fish

● **There are more species** of fish on a coral reef than in any other place in the oceans.

● **The Great Barrier Reef** is be home to more than 1500 different kinds of fish.

● **Blue tuskfish** grow up to one metre long and are strong enough to lift rocks aside with their mouths to reach crabs hiding underneath.

▼ *A variety of fish live on coral reefs because there is plenty to eat and lots of places to hide and shelter.*

● **Manta rays** are common in the waters around coral reefs. They 'fly' underwater on their huge wing-like fins. A giant manta ray can weigh up to 2 tonnes.

● **If a porcupine fish** is threatened, it puffs its body up with water, making its spines stand out.

● **Surgeonfish are named** after the sharp scale at the base of the tail, which is like the sharp scalpel used by surgeons during operations.

● **Butterfly fish have long snouts** to help them to reach into small cracks and crevices in the coral to search for food. The long-snouted butterfly fish has a particularly long nose.

● **Cowfish or boxfish** are protected by bony plates in their skin, which act like a suit of armour. They also have strong 'horns' and skin poisons to keep predators away.

● **If triggerfish are chased**, they will swim into a hole and lock a spine on their back in an upright position so predators cannot pull them free.

● **Scorpionfish are well camouflaged** as they lie still among the corals, waiting for prey to pass by close enough to catch.

Seahorses

- **There are about** 35 different species of seahorse, which are named after their horse-shaped heads.

- **These fish** range from less than one centimetre to about 30 cm long.

- **Seahorses swim** by fluttering the small fin on their back, which beats up to 35 times a second. Side fins help them to steer through the water.

- **A seahorse has no teeth** and sucks up small fish, shrimps and plankton with its long, hollow jaws. It can eat up to 3000 shrimps a day.

- **Instead of scales,** seahorses have a series of rectangular bony plates. These protect them from predators, such as crabs.

- **The female lays** up to 2000 eggs in a pouch on the male's body. The male carries the eggs until they hatch and the young are able to swim out.

- **Seahorses can change** colour to match their surroundings by expanding or contracting cells full of coloured pigment in their skin.

- **The pencil-shaped pipefish** belongs to the same family as the seahorse. It can grow to 50 cm in length.

- **The seahorse family** also includes seadragons, shrimpfish, sea moths and trumpet fish.

> **DID YOU KNOW?**
> Food passes through the digestive system quickly as the seahorse has no stomach. It has to keep eating all the time to stay alive.

▲ *Seahorses have a gripping or prehensile tail, which they wrap around corals and seaweeds. This stops them being battered by waves or washed away by currents.*

Sharks and rays

- **Sharks and rays** are cartilaginous fish that belong to the same animal family. They have skeletons made of cartilage instead of bone.

- **There are over 460 species** of shark but only four regularly attack humans: the tiger, great white, bull and whitetip shark.

- **Sharks range in size** from the 23-cm pygmy shark to the 14-m whale shark, which is the world's largest fish.

- **The skin of a shark** is not covered with smooth scales like bony fish. Instead, it is covered with tiny, tooth-like structures called dermal denticles.

- **The diet of sharks** includes seals, squid, fish and other marine creatures.

- **Rays are found** in all the oceans. Most live near the seabed. They bury themselves in the sand when threatened.

- **These fish have** broad, flat bodies. Their eyes are located on the upper surface of the body, while the mouth and gills are on the lower side.

- **Rays are usually brown** or black in colour, with a light underside. Some species can change their colour to match the surroundings.

- **Some species** of ray are less than 10 cm in width, while others measure over 6 m across.

> **DID YOU KNOW?**
> The largest electric rays can give shocks of up to 220 volts. These stun or kill predators or prey, and may also be used for communication.

▶ *Most sharks such as this Caribbean reef shark have torpedo-shaped bodies and large tail fins that give them extra power. They are very efficient swimmers.*

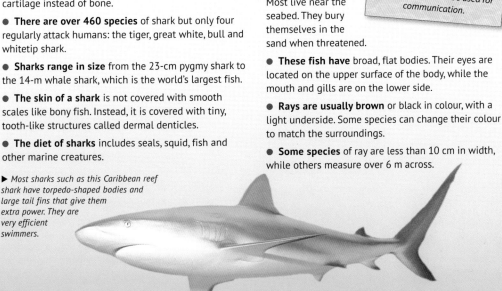

Predatory sharks

- **Sharks are excellent hunters** – they have keen senses that help them hunt and travel great distances.

- **Teeth** are a shark's most powerful weapon. A shark can have as many as 3000 teeth, in three rows.

- **It is thought** that almost one-third of a shark's brain is devoted to detecting smell.

DID YOU KNOW?

Some sharks have special eyelids called nictitating membranes. These close to protect the eyes from being damaged.

- **Some sharks** have whisker-like projections on their snouts (nasal barbels) to help them feel for prey.

- **Sharks also have** good eyesight. Most of them hunt at night and have enhanced night vision.

- **The ears of a shark** are inside its head. Each ear leads to a small sensory pore on the shark's head.

- **It is believed** that sharks can hear sounds over a distance of 250 m.

- **Sharks have an extra sense organ** called the lateral line. It runs down each side of the body, under the skin.

- **As a shark swims**, ripples pass over the lateral line through its skin. Tiny hairs inside sense the ripples and send signals to the shark's brain.

◄ One of the fastest sharks, the mako can swim at speeds of over 48 km/h. It often jumps out of the water, sometimes as high as 6 m.

Great white shark

- **The great white** is the largest predatory fish. It has a pointed snout and a large tail fin.

- **Commonly found** in temperate waters, great white sharks are grey in colour, with a white underbelly.

- **The great white** is normally about 4.5 m in length, but it is thought that some grow as long as 6 m.

- **The 3000 teeth** of great whites have saw-like (serrated) edges, and can grow up to 7.5 cm long.

- **This shark** hunts sea lions, seals and sea turtles. Young great whites eat fish, rays and small sharks.

- **Without a swim bladder** to keep them afloat, great whites have to swim continuously or else they sink.

- **Unlike other sharks**, the great white does not have a protective membrane to cover its eyes. When it attacks, the shark rolls its eyes back in their sockets for protection.

- **The great white** usually approaches prey from below. Sometimes it will jump out of the water. This is called breaching.

- **Female great whites** give birth to live young.

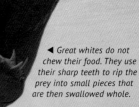

◄ Great whites do not chew their food. They use their sharp teeth to rip the prey into small pieces that are then swallowed whole.

Hammerhead shark

- **Hammerhead sharks** have a wide, hammer-shaped head. Their eyes are located on either side of this 'hammer'.

- **The head contains** tiny receptors that detect prey. Its unusual shape also helps the shark to take sharp turns.

▲ *The hammerhead is an excellent hunter. It uses its highly developed senses of smell and direction to track prey.*

- **The hammerhead is common** in tropical and temperate waters. This shark migrates towards warmer waters near the Equator in winter.

- **It is grey or brown** in colour, with an off-white belly.

- **The first dorsal fin** of the hammerhead, located on its back, is large and pointed. Like most sharks, it can be seen cutting through the surface as the shark swims.

- **The great hammerhead** is the largest member of the hammerhead family. It can reach up to 6 m in length. Bonnethead sharks are smaller and have heads shaped like shovels.

- **Hammerheads feed** on fish, smaller sharks, squid and octopuses. Stingrays are their favourite food.

- **Large teeth** enable the great hammerhead to bite big chunks off its prey.

- **Other varieties of hammerhead** include the scalloped and the smooth hammerhead. Both types are found in moderately temperate waters.

- **Most hammerheads are harmless**, but the great hammerhead is one of the few dangerous species. It is known to have attacked humans.

Whale shark

- **Although they are the largest fish** in the world, whale sharks are not aggressive and pose no threat to humans.

- **Whale sharks live** in warm, tropical waters.

- **The average length** of a whale shark is about 14 m, but some have been known to grow to over 18 m long.

- **An average** adult whale shark weighs about 15 tonnes.

▼ *Grey or brown in colour with an off-white underside, the whale shark has white dots and lines on its back.*

- **Owing to their size**, these sharks cannot move fast. They swim by moving their bodies from side to side.

- **Although whale sharks** are usually solitary, they have been observed swimming in schools.

- **The mouth of the whale shark** is enormous and can be as wide as 2–3 m. It contains around 300 rows of tiny, hook-like teeth in each jaw.

- **As they swim** with their mouths open, whale sharks suck in water. Bristles on their gills filter their tiny prey, while water passes out through the gill slits.

- **The diet of whale sharks** consists mainly of plankton, sardines, krill and anchovies.

- **Whale sharks** are known to wait at fish breeding grounds to capture freshly laid eggs to eat.

Deep-sea fish

● **Over 300 species of fish** live in the deep ocean at depths below 1000 m, where they never see sunlight.

● **The greatest depth** at which a fish has been recorded is 8372 m in the Puerto Rico Trench, the boundary between the Caribbean Sea and Atlantic Ocean. This fish has been named *Abyssobrotula galatheae* but very little is known about its biology.

● **Food is hard to find** in the deep ocean so fish have to rely on fragments of food floating down from above ('marine snow') or eat other deep-sea creatures.

● **Deep-sea fish** usually have big mouths, long, sharp teeth and stretchy, expandable stomachs to help them catch as much food as possible when they do find a meal.

● **As there is no light** in the deep ocean, many fish produce their own light to help them find a mate or attract prey. This production of biological light is called bioluminescence.

● **The deep-sea anglerfish** has a 'fishing rod' growing out of its head, which glows in the dark because it contains luminous bacteria.

● **The gulper eel** has huge hinged jaws, which allow it to swallow prey much larger than itself.

● **The viperfish** is named after the long fangs that stick out from its jaws, like the fangs of snakes, called vipers. The teeth point backwards to form a cage, so that fish cannot escape once they are caught.

● **Deep-sea hatchet fish** have large, tubular eyes that point upwards to look for food falling from above. They migrate to shallower waters at night to hunt for small fish and plankton.

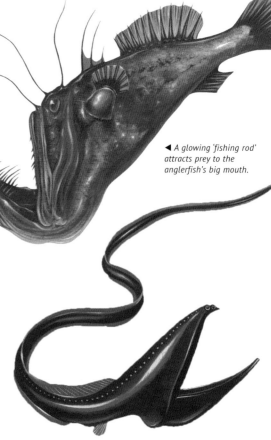

◀ *A glowing 'fishing rod' attracts prey to the anglerfish's big mouth.*

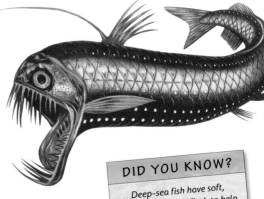

▲ *The gaping mouth and stretchy stomach of the black swallower allow it to eat fish much larger than itself.*

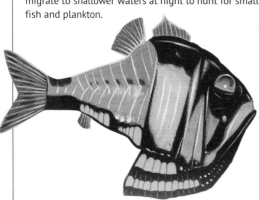

▲ *Hatchet fish have light organs on their body called photophores. These help with camouflage and flash on and off in a special pattern during courtship.*

▲ *Viperfish are fierce predators of the deep sea. Their long, needle-like teeth are used to trap prey.*

DID YOU KNOW?

Deep-sea fish have soft, flabby bones and flesh to help them withstand the enormous water pressure.

Barracuda

● **Barracuda are powerful predators** – in some coastal regions, they are more feared than sharks. There are about 25 species of barracuda and they live for about 10–15 years.

● **These fish have** long heads and slender bodies. They vary from 40 cm to almost 2 m in length.

● **Powerful swimmers**, barracuda are found in the tropical waters of the Pacific, Atlantic and Indian oceans.

● **The mouth contains** a number of fang-like teeth. These predators have a forked tail, and their dorsal fins are widely separated.

● **The great barracuda**, found in the Pacific and Atlantic oceans, grows to a length of 1.8 m and can weigh as much as 41 kg. Also called the 'tiger of the sea', this aggressive predator is known to attack divers and swimmers.

● **The diet of barracuda** includes sardines, anchovies, mullet, bream, grunts, groupers, snapper and squid.

▲ *Barracuda are fearsome predators. They seize, maim and tear up other fish with their fang-like teeth.*

DID YOU KNOW?

The flesh of some barracuda species is toxic to humans because the fish they feed on are poisonous. The barracuda are immune to this poison.

● **Smaller barracuda** swim and hunt in schools, while larger ones hunt alone.

● **Barracuda make** surprise attacks on their prey, relying on sudden bursts of speed to catch a meal. They can swim at speeds of up to 45 km/h.

● **Few predators** are large and fast enough to catch the great barracuda, but sharks and tuna feed on small adult barracuda.

Swordfish

● **Found in tropical** and temperate waters, swordfish are mostly dark in colour, with a lighter-coloured belly.

● **Swordfish get their name** from their upper jaw, which extends to form a long, sword-like snout with a sharp point. This jaw does not have teeth.

● **Swordfish can grow** over 4 m in length. The 'sword' accounts for about one-third of this.

● **The snout is used** for both defence and attack. Swordfish probably dash into schools of fish to injure or spear their prey.

● **The jaws of a young swordfish** are equal in length. The upper jaw grows longer with age.

● **Mackerel,** herring and other small fish that swim in schools are the usual prey of swordfish. They may also dive deep in search of sardines.

◄ *The 'sword' of a swordfish can be up to 1.4 m long.*

● **Like marlin and sailfish**, swordfish are powerful swimmers. They swim long distances to catch prey.

● **The crescent-shaped tail** is characteristic of fast swimmers belonging to the same family. Swordfish do not have pelvic fins.

● **Swordfish can swim** at speeds of up to 100 km/h. Some gather together in schools, but most are solitary.

● **Females are larger** than the males and produce tens of millions of eggs at a time. Adult swordfish live for around nine years.

Herring

- **Herring are often found** in the waters of the North Atlantic and the North Pacific oceans.
- **There are over 360 species** in the herring family, which includes sardines, anchovies and shad.
- **Sardines are named** after Sardinia, an island in the Mediterranean where the fish were once abundant.
- **Herring species vary** in size from the Baltic herring, which is 14–18 cm long, to the Pacific herring, which is 38 cm long, and the Atlantic herring, which reaches about 46 cm in length.
- **Herring feed on** small fish and plankton. They are an important part of the diet of larger creatures such as sharks, seals, whales and seabirds.
- **A female herring** produces up to 40,000 eggs each year.
- **The wolf herring** is the largest of the herring family. It is a fierce hunter and can grow to one metre in length.
- **They also have no lateral line** to sense vibrations in the water.
- **Unlike most fish,** herring have soft dorsal fins that have no spines.

▲ *Herrings have streamlined bodies and usually swim in large schools.*

- **Herring are processed** and sold in several forms. They can be smoked, dried, salted or pickled. Kippers are split and smoked herrings, a bloater is a whole smoked herring and rollmops are pickled herring fillets.

Tuna and mackerel

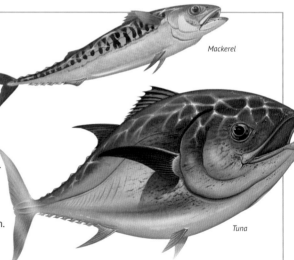

Mackerel

Tuna

- **Tuna and mackerel** belong to the Scombridae family of fish.
- **These fish** are fast swimmers. Their torpedo-shaped bodies and crescent tails help them thrust through the water at great speeds.
- **Mackerel** have sleek, shiny bodies and large mouths. The head does not have any scales.
- **Found in cool waters** around the northeast United States, Canada, Great Britain and Norway, mackerel remain close to the surface and eat small crabs and fish.
- **The Atlantic mackerel** is the most common variety. It is blue and silver in colour and can grow up to half a metre in length.
- **Tuna need lots of oxygen** so they swim with their mouths open, shooting jets of water over their gills. Oxygen is extracted from this water.
- **This method of breathing** means that tuna can never stop swimming.
- **Tuna are not cold-blooded,** instead their bodies keep a few degrees warmer than the water.

▲ *A mackerel's back shows a greeny-blue sheen, but its underside is pale, allowing it to camouflage itself and surprise its prey. Tuna are more rounded and sleeker than mackerel.*

- **Schools of tuna** can travel long distances. They come to coastal areas to lay their eggs. The eggs usually hatch within 24 hours.
- **Bluefin tuna** are large marine fish. Adults weigh over 680 kg and can swim at a speed of about 90 km/h.

Flying fish

- **Flying fish** do not actually fly. They leap into the air and glide for short distances.

- **The average length** of a flying fish is around 20–30 cm. The California flying fish, found in the Pacific Ocean, is the largest species. It can grow up to 45 cm in length.

- **The pectoral fins** of flying fish have similar functions to a bird's wings. The two-winged flying fish have very large pectoral fins that they stretch out to soar.

- **Some flying fish** have four 'wings'. In addition to large pectoral fins, these species also have large pelvic fins.

- **When threatened**, flying fish build up speed under the water's surface by thrashing their tails and holding their fins close to the body. The fish then leap into the air and glide for about 45 seconds.

- **Flying fish can leap** to a height of 1.2 m and cover a distance of over 200 m. In between glides, they return to the water to gain speed.

▲ *Flying fish use their gliding ability effectively to escape predators.*

- **These fish can glide** at double the speed they swim, and are known to accelerate from 30 km/h in water to 60 km/h in air.

- **Young flying fish** look very different from their parents. They have whiskers on their lower jaw, which disappear as they mature.

- **Usually, flying fish** swim in schools. Sometimes a whole school leaps into the air and glides together.

- **The ability to glide** helps flying fish escape from sea predators such as tuna and mackerel. But once in the air, they become the target of seabirds.

Eels

- **Eels are snake-like fish** that live in shallow waters. Most live in the sea, but a few are found in freshwater.

- **Most species of eel** are around one metre long. However, the conger eel can grow up to 3 m in length.

- **Eels are normally found** among coral reefs and on the ocean floor. There are about 700 eel species. The most common include the conger, moray and gulper.

- **A species of moray eel** found in the Pacific Ocean has been known to grow over 4 m in length. There are about 200 different species of moray eel.

- **Eels do not have a tail fin** as their dorsal fin, which runs along the top of the body, provides them with the power to swim.

- **Some species** have scales, but the bodies of most eels are covered with a slippery layer of mucus.

- **Eels are graceful swimmers** but are not very fast. Some species, like the American eel, can breathe through their skin and can survive for some time out of water.

- **Eels have over 100 bones** (vertebrae) in their spine, which makes their bodies very flexible.

▲ *Fan-like structures on the nose of a blue ribbon eel probably help it to sense an approaching meal.*

- **There are about 20 species** of garden eels, which live in colonies in shallow water. Their heads poke out of the seabed like walking sticks to catch food drifting past in the water. In the densest colonies, there may be as many as one eel every 50 cm.

- **Adult European eels** live in rivers but migrate to the Sargasso Sea, in the North Atlantic Ocean, to breed. Their eggs hatch into leaf-shaped larvae, which drift about the oceans for three to four years. When the larvae mature into young eels they swim back into the rivers until it is time for them to breed.

Sea turtles

- **There are only seven species** of marine turtle. They are found in tropical and sub-tropical waters around the world.

- **The leatherback turtle** is the largest. The other species are loggerhead, hawksbill, olive ridley, Kemp's ridley, flatback and green turtle.

- **A hard shell** covers and protects all sea turtles except the leatherback. These shells are flat and streamlined to allow water to flow over them easily.

- **The shell of the leatherback** turtle is made of a thick, rubbery substance that is strengthened by small bones. This turtle is named after its unusual shell.

- **The front limbs** of sea turtles are larger than the back. These flipper-like limbs help turtles to 'fly' through the water, although moving on land is quite awkward.

- **Sea snakes and sea turtles** are the only reptiles that spend most of their lives in the ocean. Female turtles swim ashore for a few hours each year to lay eggs.

- **Females prefer to lay their eggs** at night. They dig a pit in the sand with their flippers then lay about 50–150 eggs, and cover the nest with sand.

▲ *A female green turtle covers her eggs. Green turtles are named after the colour of their body fat, which is green due to their diet.*

- **Once the eggs hatch**, the young turtles struggle out of their sandpit and make their way to the sea. On the way, many babies fall prey to seabirds, crabs, otters and other predators.

- **The diet of sea turtles** differs from species to species. Leatherbacks prefer jellyfish, while olive ridleys and loggerheads eat hard-shelled creatures such as crabs. Sponges are a favourite of hawksbills.

- **Most turtle species** are under threat because they are hunted for their eggs, meat and shells. The trade in turtles has been declared illegal in most countries, but people continue to kill them.

Sea snakes

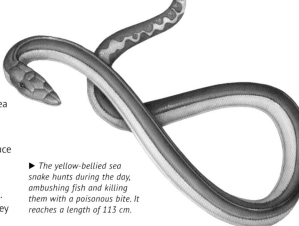

- **Sea snakes** are commonly found in the warm waters of the Indian and Pacific oceans. Their venom is more powerful than that of most land snakes.

- **Fish, eels and fish eggs** are the preferred diet of sea snakes. They use their venom to kill prey and then swallow it whole.

- **Sea snakes are covered** in small scales. These reduce friction, helping the animal to swim faster. A flat, paddle-like tail aids swimming.

- **To breathe**, sea snakes have to come to the surface. They can stay underwater for long periods because they absorb some oxygen from the water and have an extra-large lung.

- **A gland under the tongue** helps a sea snake get rid of excess salt from seawater. It also has highly developed nostril valves that can be closed while underwater.

- **Most sea snakes** never leave the water. Females give birth to live young in the water.

- **Five species** (the sea kraits) lay eggs on land instead of giving birth to live young.

▶ *The yellow-bellied sea snake hunts during the day, ambushing fish and killing them with a poisonous bite. It reaches a length of 113 cm.*

- **Sea kraits** have coloured bands on their bodies. Unlike true sea snakes, sea kraits have wide scales on their bellies that help them to move on land.

- **The yellow-bellied sea snake**, named after its bright yellow underside, is the most recognizable true sea snake. It is poisonous, but attacks only when disturbed.

- **The fastest swimmer**, the yellow-bellied sea snake can reach a speed of 3.6 km/h. It can stay underwater for three hours before coming to the surface to breathe.

Marine iguanas

● **The marine iguana** of the Galápagos Islands in the Pacific Ocean is the only ocean-going lizard in the world.

● **These unusual lizards** live on rocks around the coasts, diving into the sea to feed on underwater algae and seaweed. Their short, blunt snouts and razor-sharp teeth help them to scrape their food off the rocks.

● **Marine iguanas** dive to depths of more than 15 m and stay underwater for up to an hour, although dives of 5–10 minutes are more common.

● **The sea around the Galápagos** is cold, so the marine iguana slows its heart rate when it dives, to stop it losing too much heat through its skin.

● **Long, sharp claws** help the marine iguanas to cling to slippery rocks on the shore, or hold onto underwater rocks in the strong currents around the Galápagos Islands.

DID YOU KNOW?

To get rid of excess salt, marine iguanas sneeze. The expelled salt covers their heads like a white wig.

● **Strong swimmers,** marine iguanas lash their tails from side to side to push through the water.

▲ Marine iguanas bask on the rocks to warm up in the sun. Their bodies need to be warm to digest their food and their dark colour helps them to absorb heat rapidly.

● **In the breeding season,** males defend groups of females against rival males.

● **Breeding males** develop colourful patches of red and green skin, which help them to attract females.

● **At night,** marine iguanas huddle together to sleep in groups. This helps them to keep warm and save energy.

Saltwater crocodiles

DID YOU KNOW?

Saltwater crocodiles are increasingly threatened by habitat loss, pollution and illegal hunting.

● **The saltwater crocodile,** or 'saltie', is the largest crocodile in the world, reaching a length of up to 7 m and weighing up to one tonne.

● **Salties** are the world's heaviest living reptiles.

● **These crocodiles live in rivers,** estuaries and oceans over a wide range, from southern India and other parts of Southeast Asia to northern Australia and the island of Fiji in the Pacific Ocean.

● **Excellent swimmers,** saltwater crocodiles have been spotted hundreds of kilometres out at sea.

● **These crocodiles** can reach swimming speeds of 24–29 km/h in short bursts, but generally cruise at 3–5 km/h. They prefer to drift in calm water near the shore rather than swimming in stormy seas.

● **Saltwater crocodiles** try to use as little energy as possible. This helps them to survive for months at a time without eating when food is scarce.

● **Compared to other crocodilians,** the saltwater crocodile has less armoured scales on its neck and back. This makes it easier for the crocodile to bend its huge body when swimming. Heavy scales would also weigh it down too much out at sea.

● **These huge crocodiles** feed on a variety of animals including fish such as sharks, turtles, birds and even mammals.

● **Saltwater crocodiles** have efficient salt glands to help get rid of the extra salt from seawater before it is absorbed into their bodies.

◄ Saltwater crocodiles warm up by basking in the sun and cool down by swimming or floating in the water.

Albatrosses

● **The three great albatrosses** – royal, wandering and Amsterdam – are the largest of all the seabirds. They weigh up to 10 kg.

● **Albatrosses live** in all oceans except the North Atlantic, but 17 out of the 22 species live only in the area covered by the Southern Ocean.

● **The wandering albatross** has the greatest wingspan of any bird, measuring about 3.4 m from one outstretched wingtip to another. That's more than three times the distance between your outstretched arms.

● **Most albatrosses** are white or pale grey in colour, with black wing tips. Some have brown feathers.

● **Albatrosses have a sharp bill** with a hooked upper jaw. They also have tubular nostrils and webbed feet. Their long, narrow wings make them powerful gliders.

● **Squid**, cuttlefish and small marine creatures are the favourite prey of albatrosses.

● **Of all seabirds**, albatrosses spend the most time at sea. They even sleep while floating on the surface of the ocean. They come ashore only to breed.

● **Albatrosses nest in colonies** on remote islands. Many have complex mating dance rituals.

● **These birds can travel** thousands of kilometres over the oceans in search of food for their chicks. The parents swallow the prey and regurgitate (cough up) the food into the chick's bill when they get back to the nest.

● **There is a superstition** among sailors that killing an albatross brings bad luck. This belief forms the theme of Samuel Taylor Coleridge's famous poem 'The Rime of the Ancient Mariner'.

◄ *The black-browed albatross is named for its dark eye stripe. It has a wingspan of 2–2.4 m.*

Gulls

● **Many birds** live around the oceans. The most common are gulls (seagulls), which are migratory.

● **There are about 43 species** of gull. Gulls range in length from 28–80 cm.

● **Most have a white** and grey plumage. Some have black markings on the back, wings and head.

● **The plumage** changes colour throughout the gull's life, and some have winter and summer plumage.

● **Many gulls** are great scavengers and feed on dead matter along seashores.

● **Black-headed gulls** have dark heads and red bills in summer. In winter their heads turn white with a grey spot. It is thought that this gives better camouflage.

● **Gulls are able to fish** in shallow waters and often prey on the eggs of other seabirds.

● **Some gulls nest** on ledges in cliffs. However most make simple grass-lined nests, mostly on flat ground in isolated areas on beaches.

● **A sharp, hooked bill** helps gulls to kill small birds and other prey. They have webbed feet to paddle on the water's surface, but they cannot dive underwater.

◄ *This herring gull is using the wind to stay aloft without flapping its wings.*

Cormorants and shags

● **There are about 40 species** of cormorant and shag.

● **They range in size** from the pygmy cormorant at 45 cm to the flightless cormorant, which reaches about one metre in length.

● **These birds live in coastal areas** rather than the open ocean and occur all over the world, except on islands in the middle of the Pacific Ocean.

● **Cormorants and shags** have a long, thin, hooked bill for catching fish and even water snakes.

● **To catch prey**, these birds dive underwater and use their webbed feet to propel themselves along. They stay underwater for more than a minute, reaching depths of up to 30 m.

● **Strong fliers**, cormorants and shags usually move low over the water with rapid wingbeats and necks outstretched.

● **In the breeding season**, some cormorants and shags develop brightly coloured patches of skin on their faces to help them attract a mate.

▲ *After fishing, cormorants hold out their wings to dry. Their feathers are not as well waterproofed as those of other birds, and this helps them to swim underwater.*

● **These birds nest in colonies** on trees, cliffs or rocky islands, where they are safe from predators.

● **The flightless cormorant** lives only on some of the Galápagos Islands in the Pacific Ocean. It has very small wings and is unable to fly. In order to feed, it dives into the sea from rocks along the shore.

Pelicans

● **Pelicans are easily identified** by their long bill and massive throat pouch. They are the largest diving birds.

● **Adult pelicans** grow up to 1.8 m in length and weigh 4–7 kg. Males are larger than females. Their wingspan can measure up to 3 m.

● **There are seven species** of pelican. Most can live near bodies of freshwater, as well as oceans.

● **Most pelicans are white**, but Brown and Peruvian pelicans are dark in colour, and American white pelicans have black wing tips.

● **In some species**, the colour of the bill and pouch changes during the mating season.

● **Groups of up to 40,000 pelicans** can come together on isolated shores or islands to breed.

● **The female pelican** builds a nest by digging a hole in the ground. She lines the hole with grass and feathers. Three days later, she lays her eggs in her new nest.

● **While fishing**, pelicans use their pouch to catch prey. Once the prey is caught, the pelican draws the pouch close to its chest to empty the water out and swallows the prey.

● **Brown and Peruvian** pelicans dive headlong into the water to catch fish.

● **Most other pelicans** swim and then pounce on their prey. Some fish in groups and drive the fish towards shallow waters where it is easier to capture them.

● **Pelicans feed** on small fish and crustaceans.

▶ *The Peruvian pelican can reach a weight of 7 kg and is 1.5 m in length. It lives along the west coast of South America.*

Gannets and boobies

● **The nine species** of gannets and boobies live in temperate, sub-tropical and tropical oceans all over the world. They do not live in the Southern Ocean around Antarctica.

● **These seabirds** have a narrow, streamlined body, long wings and a pointed tail. Their feet are webbed for swimming and their feathers are waterproof.

● **The largest species** is the northern gannet, which is up to one metre in length. The smallest is the Abbot's booby at 71 cm long.

● **These birds have** a strong and pointed bill with serrated edges for gripping fish.

● **To catch fish**, these birds plunge-dive into the sea from heights of about 30 m. They are travelling at about 100 km/h when they hit the water, which means they can catch food at greater depths.

● **Gannets and boobies** do not have external nostrils. Instead the nostrils are in the roof of the mouth, as in cormorants.

▶ *To cushion the impact of a dive, gannets have air sacs under the skin of the face and chest.*

● **Their eyes are at the base** of the skull so the birds can scan the surface before plunging into the water.

● **They can stay underwater** for 5–30 minutes, reaching depths of 30 m and eating prey while still submerged.

● **Blue-footed boobies** lift and spread their bright blue feet in a courtship dance to impress their partners. The name 'booby' comes from the Spanish word 'bobo', meaning 'clown'.

● **Most gannets and boobies** lay one egg each year. Chicks are fed on food regurgitated (coughed up) by the parents.

Waders

● **There are over 200 species** of waders or shorebirds living in shorelines or waterways around the world.

● **Waders are usually small** or medium-sized birds with long legs and long, sensitive bills.

● **They use their bills** to probe in the mud or sand for worms, shellfish or other small animals to eat.

● **Different species** have different lengths and shapes of bill, enabling them to feed at different depths and allowing a variety of species to feed in one area.

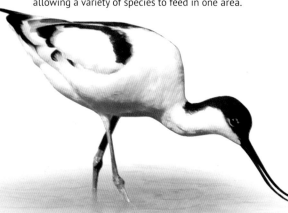

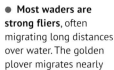

DID YOU KNOW?

The smallest wader is the least sandpiper, at 13 cm long. The largest is the far eastern curlew, at 63 cm long.

● **Most waders are strong fliers**, often migrating long distances over water. The golden plover migrates nearly 4000 km over the Atlantic Ocean, from the coast of Canada to Brazil, where it spends the winter.

● **Nearly all waders** nest on the ground, often with little or no nesting material.

● **The eggs of waders** are often camouflaged with spots or patterns because they are not hidden in a nest.

● **Some oystercatchers** use their bills to hammer open mussels and cockles and pull out the flesh inside. Others have pointed bills to pull worms from the sand.

● **The red-necked phalarope** is an unusual bird – the male sits on the eggs and takes care of the chicks. For most birds, the female does this. In the winter, red-necked phalaropes migrate to tropical oceans.

◀ *Avocets sweep their upturned bills from side to side in shallow water, grabbing worms or small water creatures that they find. They often nest on islands, where their young are safer from attack by predators.*

Nesting seabirds

● **Nearly 95 percent** of the world's seabirds nest in large colonies for protection. The birds can warn each other of danger and help to drive attackers away from the nests and eggs.

● **Even though steep cliffs** are dangerous places for nests, it is harder for predators to reach the eggs and young.

● **Different species** nest at different levels on the same cliff, sharing out the nesting space.

▼ *Guillemots breed in tightly packed colonies on rocky islands or steep cliff faces.*

● **At the bottom of a cliff** nest cormorants and shags. Guillemots, razorbills and kittiwakes nest in the middle, and gannets, gulls and puffins nest near the top.

● **Murres and guillemots** lay their eggs on rocky cliff ledges. The eggs are sharply pointed at one end so they spin round instead of rolling off the cliff and into the sea.

● **Razorbill chicks** leave their nesting ledges when they are only two weeks old, but their parents feed them out at sea until they are old enough to feed themselves.

● **Kittiwakes are unusual** cliff-nesters because they build cup-shaped nests for their eggs, gluing them to cliff ledges with sticky mud and droppings.

● **Large colonies of little terns** nest on sandy beaches in summer. Members of the colony help each other by dive-bombing predators from above.

● **Puffins use their powerful bills** to dig nesting burrows on grassy cliff-tops.

Penguins

● **Penguins are big seabirds** that cannot fly. There are 17 species, most of which live in the Antarctic. Some kinds of penguins are found as far north as the Galápagos Islands, while smaller species are found in warmer waters.

● **Larger penguins are better** at retaining heat, so they can live closer to the South Pole.

● **The emperor penguin** is the tallest at 1.2 m. The smallest is the fairy penguin (or little blue penguin), at less than 40 cm tall.

● **Penguins have a thick layer** of fat that protects them from the freezing temperatures of the region. Their feathers are waterproof.

● **These flightless birds** have black heads and wings, and a white underside. They also have sharp bills and short tails.

● **The wings of penguins** act like flippers, which help the birds to swim. Penguins are good divers and can move in water at great speeds.

● **On land**, penguins move clumsily. They are often seen sliding down slopes on their bellies.

▲ *Emperor penguin chicks huddle together in groups, called crèches, from when they are about 50 days old. Parents recognize their own chicks from the high-pitched calls that they make.*

● **Adélie penguins waddle** over 100 km every year to reach their breeding grounds. They depend on the Sun to navigate across the ice, so once the Sun sets they are at risk of losing their way.

● **Rockhopper penguins** have a tuft of yellow feathers on their head. They are named because they often jump from rock to rock.

● **Penguins have been hunted** extensively by humans for their fat and skin. Their natural enemies are sharks, whales and leopard seals.

Seals

- **Seals are marine mammals** that belong to the pinnipeds group along with walruses and sea lions.

- **There are two families** of seals: true seals and eared seals. While both have ears, true seals do not have external ear flaps.

- **There are 19 species** of true seals. Eared seals consist of sea lions and fur seals.

- **The limbs of seals** are modified into powerful flippers. Their torpedo-shaped bodies and ability to store oxygen in their muscles make them superb swimmers.

- **True seals** use their back flippers for swimming, while eared seals use their strong front flippers to row themselves through the water.

- **Seals spend** most of their lives in water, coming ashore to breed and nurse their young. Some live at sea for months at a time, while others return to the shore every day.

- **Most species live in cold regions**, so they have a thick layer of fatty blubber under the skin to provide warmth and energy.

▲ *Baby harp seals are born on the ice and have snowy-white coats, which act as camouflage. Mothers identify their pups by their scent.*

- **Southern elephant seals** can dive to depths of up to 1500 m and can stay underwater for up to two hours. The huge males have fierce fights in the breeding season to win a group of females for mating.

- **The diet of seals** consists mainly of fish, squid, crabs and shellfish. Leopard seals are among the most aggressive hunters.

- **Killer whales**, sharks and polar bears are the natural predators of seals. Many seals are threatened by pollution, hunting and competition with the fishing industry for food resources.

Sea otters

- **The smallest ocean mammal**, the sea otter grows up to 1.4 m long. It lives in shallow coastal waters of the north Pacific Ocean, from California to Alaska.

- **This mammal** has a long, flat, rudder-like tail and large, webbed back feet, which act as flippers.

- **Sea otters spend** most of their time in the water, often floating on their backs at the surface. They even sleep like this, anchoring themselves to giant seaweeds called kelp to prevent themselves from drifting away on currents.

- **The fur of sea otters** is fine and dense, and consists of about 100,000 hairs per square centimetre to keep the animal warm.

- **Hunted for their fur** until almost extinct, sea otters are now protected and numbers have increased to about 100,000–150,000. They are still threatened by pollution and coastal development.

- **These mammals** constantly groom their fur with their teeth and paws to keep it clean and waterproof.

- **Sea otters** dive to depths of up to 75 m to gather food such as mussels, snails, crabs and urchins.

- **Social animals**, sea otters live in groups of between ten and 100 or more, called rafts.

- **Sea otters** give birth in the water. Females usually have one pup and carry it on their chest.

- **Pups stay at the surface** while their mother dives for food, but learn to follow her and find food for themselves.

▼ *Sea otters are one of the few mammals to use tools. They float on their back, place a rock on their chest and smash shellfish against the rock to break them open so they can eat the flesh.*

Whales and dolphins

● **Whales belong to a group** of mammals called cetaceans, which includes the small whales we call dolphins and porpoises. Cetaceans range in size from the vaquita, or gulf porpoise, which is less than 1.5 m long, to the blue whale, which can reach a length of over 30 m.

● **Whales hold their** breath underwater. They come up to the surface to breathe air through nostrils called blowholes on the top of the head. The blowholes stay closed underwater.

● **The spout** (blow) that can be seen rising from the blowhole is exhaled air that condenses and vaporizes the moment it is released into the atmosphere.

● **Whales are divided** into two main groups: toothed whales and baleen whales. Together, these groups contain about 80 known species.

● **Toothed whales** have small teeth, which they use to kill prey such as squid. This group includes dolphins, killer whales, sperm whales, beluga whales and porpoises.

● **Toothed whales emit sound waves** that are bounced off an object, revealing its size, shape and location. This is known as echolocation.

▲ *Dusky dolphins are very agile and acrobatic.*

● **Whales and dolphins** can even use echolocation to distinguish between prey and non-prey objects.

● **Baleen whales** are toothless. They trap prey in sieve-like structures hanging from their upper jaws. Bowhead whales have the longest baleen, which reaches a length of about 4 m.

● **The blue whale** has a call that is louder than a jet plane. It reaches a level of 188 decibels, whereas a jet plane only reaches 140 decibels. A blue whale's call travels long distances through the oceans, perhaps for hundreds of kilometres.

DID YOU KNOW?

The heart of a blue whale is the size of a small car, but its eye is only as big as a teacup.

▶ *A female grey whale and newborn calf. If threatened, a mother will defend her calf fiercely from predators.*

Killer whale

- **Despite their name**, killer whales, also known as orcas, are the largest members of the dolphin family.

- **They have** a black body with white patches on their underside and behind each eye.

- **Found in oceans** across the world, killer whales prefer to live in colder waters.

- **They do not migrate** in summer like great whales, and often live close to the coast.

▶ *Killer whales swim almost onto the beach to try to catch sea lions.*

- **Killer whales** reach lengths of 8–10 m. They have sharp, hooked teeth, which are used to rip prey apart.

- **The diet** of killer whales is varied. They largely prey on fish, squid, sharks and warm-blooded animals such as seals, seabirds and larger whales.

- **Also known** as the 'wolves of the sea', killer whales hunt in groups (pods) and can tackle prey of any size.

- **Killer whale pods** are divided into resident and transient pods.

- **Resident pods** consist of between 5–50 members that communicate with whistles and high-pitched screams.

- **Transient pods** have a maximum of seven members that feed mainly on marine mammals. They do not communicate frequently with each other.

Baleen whales

- **The baleen whales** include the largest whales, such as the blue, humpback, grey, fin, sei, minke, bowhead and right whales.

- **The largest family of baleen whales** is the Balaenopteridae, also known as the rorqual family.

- **These whales have** 25–100 throat grooves, which look like pleats and allow the throat to expand as the whales feed.

- **Baleen is a strong**, flexible material made of keratin, the material that your fingernails and hair are made of.

- **When a whale is born**, the baleen is soft and short, but it grows and thickens.

- **Baleen grows** throughout a whale's life and the ends wear down all the time.

- **The outer edge** of a baleen plate is smooth, but the inner edge is frayed to form a fringe. This overlaps to sieve fish, crustaceans and plankton from the water.

- **Some baleen whales** feed by gulping large amounts of water and then using their tongue to force the water out between their baleen plates.

- **Other baleen whales** swim along with their mouths wide open, skimming and filtering food as they go.

- **Baleen whales** have two blowholes. When the whales surface, they expel stale air through these blowholes, which makes a V-shaped pattern in the air.

◀ *Baleen whales, such as this bowhead whale, have hundreds of baleen plates in their jaws – bowhead whales have about 350 pairs of plates.*

Blue whale

- **Blue whales** are the largest creatures ever to have lived on Earth.

- **Their average length** is 25 m but some can grow to more than 30 m.

- **These whales** are blue-grey in colour with light patches on their backs.

- **The body is streamlined** with a large tail fin. The dorsal fin is small, while the tail is thick and large. Blue whales have splashguards in front of their blowholes.

- **Blue whales** are migratory animals. They live near the tropics during winter and migrate towards icy waters in summer.

- **The diet of a blue whale** consists of small fish, plankton and krill in enormous quantities. They can eat over 4 tonnes of krill every day.

- **Blue whales** have been known to gather in groups of 60 or more. However, they are largely solitary animals.

- **Blue whales** are relatively slow swimmers. However, if threatened, these animals can swim at a speed of up to 50 km/h.

- **Merciless hunting** over several decades has caused the blue whale population to decline drastically.

- **It is currently** an endangered species, and between 10,000 and 25,000 are thought to exist worldwide.

▲ *An adult blue whale weighs about 160 tonnes – that's the combined weight of 30 big bull elephants.*

Humpback whale

- **Humpbacks** are large baleen whales. They are one of the most active whales and often leap out of the water. Found in most parts of the world, humpbacks migrate to icy waters in the north and south during summer. In winter, they breed in tropical waters.

- **Humpbacks have a flat head** that has fleshy bumps (tubercles). The body is dark, with white patches. The underside is off-white in colour.

- **The humpback grows** up to 15 m in length. It is named after a hump on which the whale's dorsal fin is located.

▼ *Humpback whales scoop up food from the water with their huge mouths.*

> **DID YOU KNOW?**
>
> Humpbacks travel over 8000 km on their migration from Antarctica to Central America each year.

- **The tail fin** measures nearly 5.5 m across and has black-and-white patterns. These patterns are unique to each whale, so scientists use them to identify and monitor humpbacks.

- **Humpbacks feed on** shrimps, krill and small fish. They have various methods of feeding.

- **When lunge-feeding**, the humpback opens its mouth wide and swims through a group of prey.

- **When tail-flicking**, the whale lies with its belly below the surface using its tail to flick prey into its mouth.

- **Bubble-netting** is a spectacular feeding habit. The humpbacks submerge and swim in circles as they blow out air around a school of fish. This creates a wall of bubbles, forcing the fish to move to the surface, which makes them easy prey.

- **Male humpbacks** are known for their songs. The sounds vary from squeaks to wails. They are usually heard in the breeding season.

Fin whale

- **After the blue whale**, the fin whale is the second-largest animal in the world.

- **It can reach** a huge 27 m in length.

- **Fin whales eat krill**, but also include small fish in their diet. They trap food between their baleen plates.

- **Fin whales** have an unusual lower jaw, which is white on the right side and grey-black on the left side. The colour of the baleen plates is the same as that of the jaw.

- **Groups of 100** or more fin whales may gather at feeding grounds. They have 50–200 pleats on their lower jaw, which expand to gulp in water and prey.

- **Males make** long, low sounds during the breeding season. This calls are extremely loud, reaching 184–186 decibels.

- **Calves are born** after a gestation of 11–12 months. They double in size during the last two months of development inside their mother.

▲ *Fin whales are the fastest whales, with swimming speeds of up to 56 km/h when hunting small fish.*

- **Fin whale calves** are about 6 m long when born and weigh about 2 tonnes.

- **Commercial whaling** in the 20th century killed off about 70 percent of the world's fin whales. There are no reliable estimates of global numbers at the moment but these magnificent whales are an endangered species.

DID YOU KNOW?

When a fin whale comes to the water's surface and breathes out, its spout can reach heights of 10–15 m.

Minke whale

- **The second-smallest** of the baleen whales (after the pygmy right whale), the minke (pronounced 'minkey') whale grows to between 8 and 10 m long.

- **They are the most common** of the baleen whales, with a population of some 665,000. Minke whales escaped much of the 20th century whaling due to their smaller size.

- **Minke whales** feed mainly on krill in the Southern Hemisphere and fish such as capelin, cod and herring in the Northern Hemisphere.

- **They are usually solitary** but may gather in groups at feeding areas.

- **Food is filtered** from the water with baleen plates hanging down from either side of the whale's top jaws.

- **Minke whales** are a type of rorqual whale, with 50–70 pleats or grooves in the throat. This allows the throat to expand widely when feeding, enabling them to take in large quantities of water and food.

- **Males make sounds** as loud as 152 decibels, which is louder than a jet taking off. Sound travels well through the ocean waters, allowing the whales to communicate with others of their kind.

- **Calves are born** after a gestation period of about ten months and are about 3 m long at birth. They drink their mother's milk for about five months.

- **Minke whales** are found in all oceans but often prefer icy waters and the open sea.

- **In the Northern Hemisphere**, minke whales have a white band on each flipper. Those living in Antarctic waters have grey flippers, and are probably a different species.

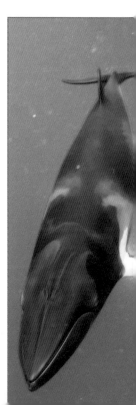

▶ *A slender whale with a pointed snout, the minke whale can reach speeds of 30 km/h and dive for up to 20 minutes.*

Right whale

- **The three species** of large baleen whales called right whales are among the most endangered.

- **Right whales live** in the North Atlantic, the eastern North Pacific and the Southern Ocean.

- **The name 'right'** was given to these great whales by early whalers because they were the 'right' whales to hunt. They were easy to catch as they were slow swimmers, lived close to shore, floated when killed and contained a lot of valuable oil in their blubber.

▶ *Right whales are almost black and have massive, rounded bodies. Their flippers are wide and the tail may reach 7 m across.*

DID YOU KNOW?
Unlike other baleen whales, the right whale does not have a grooved throat.

- **These huge whales** can reach 18 m in length and weigh up to 100 tonnes.

- **Right whales have** rough patches of skin on the head, called callosities. These are often colonized by whale lice. Individual whales can be recognized from the pattern of their callosities.

- **Right whales filter plankton**, krill and crustaceans from the ocean with 200–300 baleen plates, which reach up to 10 m in length.

- **Calves are born** after a gestation period of about a year and measure 4–5 m in length.

- **They stay** with their mothers for a year before becoming independent.

- **The northern right whale** and the North Pacific right whale are probably the most endangered of the great whales, with only a few hundred individuals remaining. Even the southern right whale has only 3200 mature females in its population.

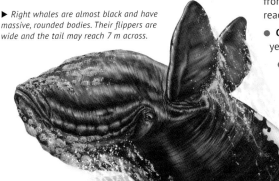

Toothed whales

- **There are over 70 species** of toothed whale, which make up almost 90 percent of the cetacean group.

- **Toothed whales** are generally smaller than baleen whales and include dolphins, porpoises, pilot whales, beluga whales, narwhals, beaked whales, killer whales and sperm whales.

- **The largest toothed whale** is the sperm whale, which reaches lengths of 18 m.

- **Toothed whales** have one blowhole in the top of the head, whereas baleen whales have two.

▶ *Male narwhals fight with their tusks in the breeding season.*

- **Active hunters**, toothed whales have peg-like teeth to grip prey such as fish, squid and, in some cases, seals or other whales.

- **Toothed whales** have a larger throat than baleen whales and swallow food whole or in large pieces.

- **Most species** of toothed whale have a waxy organ, called a melon in the forehead. This helps to focus the clicking sounds the whales make for echolocation.

- **Echolocation is a method** of locating prey by sending out sounds and listening for the echoes that bounce back.

- **Narwhals have only two teeth** in the top jaw. In most males, and some females, one of these teeth develops into a 2–3-m-long, spiral tusk, growing out through a hole in the top lip.

- **One large family** of toothed whales (over 20 species) is the beaked whales. Beaked whales are almost toothless, although males have one pair of teeth, which they may use to fight for females.

Sperm whale

● **The sperm whale** is the world's largest toothed animal. Males are 16–18 m long, while females reach lengths of 12–14 m. Males weigh about 50 tonnes, about twice as much as females.

● **Males reach full size** at 50 years old and live for up to 80 years.

● **The sperm whale** has a very large head, which takes up about one-third of its length.

● **The spout** of a sperm whale reaches up to 15 m above the surface and is angled to the left.

● **Sperm whales** were once hunted for the oil that was obtained from their blubber and a part of their head called the spermaceti organ. Scientists are not sure what this organ does. It may help the whale to make deep dives or focus the sounds made during echolocation.

● **By slowing their heart rate** and directing blood to the brain and other essential organs, sperm whales may stay underwater for up to two hours.

▲ *Sperm whales dive to depths of up to 3000 m to hunt for giant squid.*

● **In the gut** of sperm whales, a substance called ambergris forms around the beaks of the squid they have eaten. This was once used to make perfume and was one reason so many sperm whales were killed between the 17th and 20th centuries. They are still endangered today.

● **Sperm whales** have 20–26 pairs of cone-shaped teeth in the bottom jaw but do not seem to use their teeth for feeding.

● **Males may use** their teeth to fight rivals.

● **Calves are born** after a gestation period of at least a year. They are 4 m long at birth and weigh one tonne.

Dolphins

● **Dolphins are small toothed whales** and there are about 37 species. They have a beak-shaped snout and are very active and playful mammals.

● **Found in all oceans**, dolphins are powerful swimmers. They are often spotted riding on waves, probably to conserve energy.

● **Dolphins may take** deep dives, but usually swim just a few metres beneath the surface of the water. They usually stay underwater for just a few minutes but can remain submerged for up to half an hour.

● **Like all toothed whales**, dolphins have only one blowhole in the top of the head for breathing air.

● **Dolphins use echolocation** to hunt and navigate through cloudy waters. They emit a series of high-pitched sound pulses, which bounce off prey or obstacles, enabling dolphins to locate them.

● **These animals hunt in groups** by chasing their prey. They then surround it and catch it with their powerful jaws.

● **A dolphin's brain**, in relation to the size of its body, is larger than the brains of humans, chimpanzees and other great apes. Dolphins are very intelligent mammals and may even have a language of their own.

● **A baby dolphin** is born tail first. The mother is often helped by another female dolphin during the birth. The calf stays with its mother for two to three years.

● **Wild dolphins can live** to be 50 years old, although their average lifespan is 17 years. Members of dolphin groups (called pods) form strong bonds with each other and may even support sick or dying pod members.

▼ *Some dolphins swim at up to 40 km/h, which is more than three times faster than the fastest human swimmers.*

Porpoises

● **Porpoises are small**, toothed whales. They are close relatives of dolphins.

● **Usually smaller than dolphins**, porpoises rarely grow to more than 2.2 m. They are grey, blue or black in colour.

● **Unlike most dolphins**, porpoises do not have a pointed snout. A porpoise's head is blunt and rounded.

● **Porpoises have a triangular fin** mid-way down the back, whereas dolphins have a curved fin.

● **Another difference** between porpoises and dolphins is their teeth. Porpoises have spade- or shovel-shaped teeth, whereas dolphins have teeth shaped like cones.

● **The Asian finless porpoise** has a ridge of small, rounded bumps just behind the area where other porpoises have a triangular fin on the back.

● **Dall's porpoise** is known for the splash it makes with its tail. This is called a 'rooster-tail', and has earned this species its other name of 'spray porpoise'.

● **The harbour**, or common, porpoise has the shortest lifespan of all cetaceans – up to 20 or 25 years. Most only survive about ten years in the wild.

● **Spectacled porpoises** are found in the South Atlantic. The upper part of their body is bluish black, while the lower half is white.

● **They have black patches** around their eyes, which are surrounded by a white line. These resemble spectacles.

▼ *The spectacled porpoise has distinctive colouration. It lives in the Southern Ocean, around the lower tip of South America and near islands such as the Falklands and South Georgia.*

Beluga

● **Beluga whales** have a playful nature and this, along with their unusual colour, makes them popular attractions in aquariums. They are related to dolphins.

● **As they have narrow necks**, belugas can nod and shake their heads from side to side.

● **The beluga's scientific name**, *Delphinapterus leucas*, means 'white dolphin without wings', referring to the absence of a dorsal fin.

● **The beluga's diet** consists of crabs, squid, shrimps and fish.

● **They use their teeth** to grab prey rather than to chew it.

● **Highly social animals**, belugas tend to travel in groups of 5–20 members, usually led by a single male.

● **These whales emit** various sounds, from whistles to chirps and squeaks. They are the most vocal whales, earning them the nickname of sea canaries.

● **During migrations**, groups can exceed 10,000 members.

● **Belugas are hunted** by killer whales. The young are often killed by polar bears. It is not uncommon to find adult belugas bearing scars from polar bear attacks.

▼ *The milky-white colour of the beluga matches its habitat, in the icy Arctic Ocean. Young belugas are born grey, turning white as they get older.*

Sea lions

● **Sea lions are eared seals** – unlike true seals, they have external ear flaps and their flippers are quite big.

● **These extremely vocal animals** make a roaring noise, which gives them their name. They are brownish in colour, with males being darker than females.

● **Sea lions use their flippers** to swim and paddle in water as well as to walk on land.

▼ *Australian sea lions are very social animals, gathering in large groups, especially in the breeding season. There are just 3000–5000 animals surviving, and they breed only on mainland Australia and nearby islands.*

● **Being highly social creatures**, sea lions swim in large groups.

● **Steller's sea lion** is the largest sea lion – males can grow up to 3 m in length. They are found in the northern waters of the Pacific Ocean.

● **Adult male** Steller's sea lions have a thick neck covered by long, coarse hair.

● **The diet of a sea lion** includes mainly fish, crabs, squid, octopus and clams. Steller's sea lion also feeds on seals and small otters.

● **Unlike other sea lions,** California sea lions do not have lion-like manes. They can swim at top speeds of 40 km/h and stay underwater for nearly ten minutes before surfacing to breathe.

● **A large number of sea lions** die as a result of getting caught in fishing nets, and there are now laws restricting the hunting of them. Steller's sea lion has been declared endangered.

DID YOU KNOW?

Killer whales are the biggest enemies of sea lions. Sharks are also known to hunt California sea lions.

Sea cows

● **There are four species** of sea cows alive today, one species of dugong and three species of manatee.

● **Sea cows** are also called sirenians, after the sirens (mermaids) of Greek mythology. It is thought that sailors mistook sea cows for creatures that were half-human and half-fish, giving rise to the mermaid legends.

● **Dugongs are found** in the tropical waters of the Indian and Pacific oceans.

● **Manatees** are found off the Caribbean islands, the southeast coast of the United States and West Africa.

● **Steller's sea cow,** one of the largest species, is now extinct. It was hunted for its meat and skin.

● **Sea cows breathe** through two nostrils at the end of their muzzle. They can close off the nostrils with a flap of skin when they are underwater.

● **Manatees have long,** rounded bodies and their average length is 3.5 m. They are mostly grey in colour.

● **Manatees and dugongs** are slow swimmers.

▶ *Sea cows feed on sea grasses, using lip pads to grip plants and rows of stiff bristles under the lips to guide food to the mouth.*

● **Dugongs are quite strong swimmers,** with a forked tail similar to that of a dolphin.

● **Manatees have a paddle-shaped tail** and can roll and spiral in the water by curling and twisting the edges of their tail.

Finding the way

- **Marine navigation** involves guiding a boat or ship safely through the waters to its destination.

- **When they ventured** into open seas, these early seafarers used the positions of the Sun, stars and planets to determine directions. Several instruments, including the sextant, were designed for this purpose.

- **Modified versions** of some of the navigational tools from the past are still in use. The best known is the magnetic compass, which determines direction at sea.

- **A compass consists** of a moving needle that points automatically towards the Earth's magnetic north. They have been in use since the 12th century. The mariner's compass was an early form of the magnetic compass.

- **A mariner's compass** consisted of an iron needle and a lodestone. The needle was rubbed against the stone, then stuck in a piece of straw and floated in a bowl of water. The needle would come to rest pointing north.

- **Other primitive tools** of navigation included the jackstaff. This instrument was used to measure the Pole Star's distance from the horizon and thus determine the position of the vessel at sea.

DID YOU KNOW?
In ancient times, mariners stayed close to the shore so they would not lose their way. Sailors kept in sight of land and used landmarks as reference points.

- **Ancient navigators** also used a line with a piece of lead on one end to measure the depth of the water, thereby determining how far into the sea the vessel has sailed.

- **Dead reckoning** was another popular method of determining the position of a vessel. For this, navigators calculate the ship's position, or the 'fix', with its speed, time and direction.

- **Nautical charts** provided details about bodies of water, like the depth of the water and the location of islands, shores, rocks and lighthouses.

▶ *A compass was used by the ship's captain to show his bearing, or direction. A telescope allowed mariners to spot things far in the distance.*

Ships and boats today

- **Modern ships** and boats are highly developed compared to those used in ancient times. Today, we have a wide choice of ships and boats suited for all purposes, from pleasure boats to cargo ships and battleships.

- **Sailboats** of the past have given way to sophisticated fuel-driven vessels. Iron, steel and fibreglass hulls have replaced wooden ones to provide greater speed and durability.

- **Modern commercial ships** are of various types. However, they are broadly classified into cargo and passenger ships. Cargo ships are used to transport goods, while passenger liners carry people.

- **Among the different kinds** of cargo ships, tankers are most widely used. Tankers transport petroleum, crude oil or chemicals, and are the largest ocean-going vessels.

- **Reefers**, or refrigerated container ships, transport perishable goods, such as fruit, vegetables and meat.

- **Boats**, too, are of different types, including high-speed jet boats, motorboats, iceboats, rowboats and sailboats.

- **Oars and sails** are still extremely popular. However, motorboats are more common now.

- **Modern navies** have a variety of warships. These include cruisers, destroyers, aircraft carriers, frigates and various support vessels.

- **Our knowledge** of marine life and resources depends heavily on research vessels. Fitted with state-of-the-art equipment, these ships undertake study expeditions.

- **Specialized ships** and boats are used for fishing, patrolling, repairing and rescue operations. Modern vessels such as trawlers, long liners, seiners and lobster boats that use a variety of fishing gear have replaced old wooden fishing boats.

▼ *This luxury powerboat has a motor engine that enables it to travel at high speeds.*

The first boats

● **Based on drawings and models** found in Egypt, there is evidence that boats date back to 6000 BC. In fact, recent studies suggest that boats were common in Asia and Africa even before that.

● **Wood was** the most popular material used to build boats in ancient times. In some cases, boats were made of animal skin stretched over bones.

● **Later, coracles,** or round boats covered with animal skin, were developed. These boats had wicker frames and were used mainly for fishing.

● **Kayaks** were another type of skin boat. They were used by the Inuit in Greenland for whaling. Kayaks are still used today, mostly for recreation.

● **Dugouts** soon replaced skin boats. At first, dugouts were just hollowed-out tree trunks. Later, these were made watertight by either inserting a separate piece of wood on both ends, or by sealing the ends with clay.

● **The early Egyptians** built rafts by tying papyrus reeds together. These lightweight boats were used for fishing and for transporting light goods on the Nile.

▶ *In ancient Egypt the first boats were made from bundles of papyrus reeds tied together.*

● **Later Egyptian rafts** were made from planks of wood tied together. They were not very sturdy and were only used for trips along rivers and coasts.

● **Gradually sails** were developed, which could harness wind energy and move boats at a greater speed. Sails were first developed by the Egyptians.

● **The Phoenicians** developed the sail further. They were mainly traders and travelled long distances. During the period 1500–1000 BC, they developed excellent sail boats.

● **Shipbuilding** got a boost during the age of exploration, from AD 1000 to 1500. The Vikings and Portuguese and Spanish sailors went on long voyages, which required fast, sturdy and dependable ships.

Ancient cargo ships

● **In ancient Mesopotamia** there were three types of boats – wooden boats with triangular sails, tub-shaped boats made from reeds and animal skins, and rafts made of timber and inflated animal skins, called *kalakku*.

● **A *kalakku*** did not have sails, but relied on currents to float downstream.

● **Massive clay pots** were once used as floats. Animal skins were stretched across the surfaces of the pots to keep them waterproof.

● **The earliest wooden boats** were simple structures. They were either pieces of log tied together or hollowed-out tree trunks.

● **With the need to transport** more cargo, the simple wooden boats were modified. Sails were first developed in Egypt in about 3500BC and were used in reed boats built to transport large stones.

● **The invention of the sail** revolutionized shipbuilding. People could now move boats with big hulls enabling the transportation of large quantities of cargo at a time.

▶ *Ancient Phoenician trading ships had broad beams, a sail and two stern oars.*

DID YOU KNOW?

Chinese cargo ships called 'junks' are known to have travelled as far as Africa.

● **The Phoenicians** were the most skilled shipbuilders of ancient times. They made huge merchant vessels, with strong wooden hulls, capable of carrying large amounts of cargo.

● **While most ancient boats** were small and used to transport cargo down rivers, ocean-going vessels were being made in Asia.

● **People of the Indus Valley civilization** are believed to have used ships to trade with other civilizations such as Mesopotamia.

Sailing ships

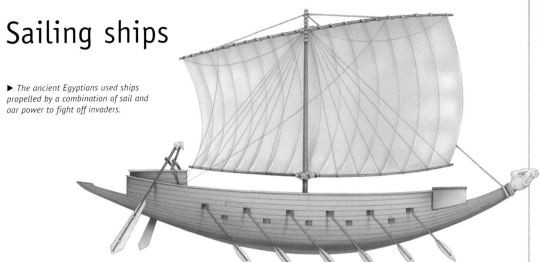

▶ *The ancient Egyptians used ships propelled by a combination of sail and oar power to fight off invaders.*

● **Sailing ships** use the energy of the wind to move. A sail is made up of pieces of cloth stitched together and tied to long poles called 'masts'.

● **Egyptians are believed** to have first developed sails. Their reed boats were simple flat-bottomed structures with a huge square sail. Since these vessels did not have a keel, the mast was attached to the edge, or the gunwale, of the boat.

● **The Phoenicians**, from 1500–1000 BC, modified sailboats further. They also created a space in the hull, called the 'deck,' to protect sailors from bad weather.

● **New sailing vessels** were developed for use at war. These were known as 'galleys' and had rows of oarsmen as well as sails.

● **These galleys** gave way to the bireme, a big vessel that had two decks of oarsmen, followed by the trireme, which had three.

● **In China**, shipbuilders built a superior cargo boat called the 'junk'. This boat had a number of sails and was steered by rudders, or movable blades on the stern.

● **The Vikings** developed the longship, which was later replaced by 13th-century cargo vessels, called 'cogs', as the major carrier of goods in Europe.

● **In the 15th century**, sturdy boats called 'caravels' were developed in Spain and Portugal. They had four sails and were up to 25 m long.

● **Galleons had long, slender hulls** and were quite fast. The Spanish Armada of 1588 used this vessel. The famous *Mayflower*, which took pilgrims to America in 1620, was also a galleon.

▶ *Sir Francis Drake took three years to sail around the world (1577–1580) in his favourite galleon, the* Golden Hind.

● **With the British Empire** beginning to spread its wings in the 19th century, ships became larger and more fortified. They often carried riches back from India and Africa.

● **The advent of steam ships** gradually led to the demise of sailing ships. Sailing is now a leisure activity, and sailboats are used for cruising, racing or fishing.

Modern navigation

● **The navigation equipment** used in the early days of seafaring has undergone major change. Electronic navigation has replaced manual techniques, and advanced high-tech gadgets are now used worldwide.

● **Modern navigational tools** are more accurate than ancient methods. Some of the most important are radio direction finding, long-ranging navigation and radar.

● **One of the first forms** of radio navigation was radio direction finding, or RDF. With this method, navigators tuned in to a particular radio frequency to determine their position.

● **Long-range navigation,** or Loran, helps to fix the position of the ship by measuring the time taken by different radio signals to reach the receiver from fixed onshore transmitters.

● **The most popular form** of Loran is Loran-C, which uses two land transmittors simultaneously. This is now being replaced by the global positioning system, or GPS.

▲ *GPS is used for a variety of purposes such as measuring the movement of polar ice sheets and finding the best route between two points, at sea and on land.*

● **With this system**, the navigator has a GPS receiver. A control device keeps track of the satellites, which send signals and the exact time. Comparing data from more than one satellite, the receiver calculates the ship's exact position.

● **The traditional dead-reckoning system** (DRS) has been modified into the inertial guidance system. This has the same function as the earlier DRS, but is more accurate.

● **Radio detection and ranging**, popularly called radar, is another commonly used navigational technique. Radar helps to locate faraway objects by bouncing radio waves off them.

● **A radar uses a scanner** to determine the location of objects, and has a display that shows its findings. It locates the presence and position of an object, as well as its shape, size, speed and direction of movement.

DID YOU KNOW?

GPS is a type of modern satellite navigation, or satellite positioning system. It uses 32 artificial satellites orbiting the Earth, the first of which was launched in 1978.

Luxurious liners

● **Until the invention** of the aeroplane, ships were the only way that people could cross the seas to new lands.

● **Ships that carry people** are called 'passenger ships'. Smaller vessels are used for shorter journeys, while large ships with lavish amenities, called cruise ships, are used for longer pleasure trips.

● **Cruise ships** appeared in the latter half of the 20th century. Before that, intercontinental voyages were made in large, motorized ships known as ocean liners.

● **Ocean liners** thrived towards the end of 19th century, when millions emigrated from Europe to the USA.

● **The increased use** of ocean liners led to the setting up of several shipping companies. The better known of these included the White Star Line and the Cunard line.

● **The Cunard Line** is a British company that today owns the famous cruise ships, *Queen Elizabeth 2* and *Queen Mary 2*.

● **The first regular steamship** service between Europe and the US was the Cunard Line. Two huge Cunard liners, *Mauretania* and *Lusitania*, were launched in 1906. The *Lusitania* was sunk by a German submarine in 1915.

● **The Cunard liners** were not the fastest or the largest. The company's rival, the White Star Line, owned the fastest ships of that time. However, Cunard ships were known for their safety.

● **World War I** (1914–1918) disrupted the transatlantic service. Some liners were taken over and used to transport troops. After the war, the transatlantic services recovered and boomed.

● **France launched the** *Normandie*, a luxury liner famous for its modern art. The revival, however, did not last long. World War II (1939–1945) and the advent of jet aeroplanes in the 1950s effectively put an end to the transatlantic ocean liners.

◄ *The* Queen Mary *was 310 m long. It was launched by the Cunard line to compete with France's* Normandie.

The Titanic

● The *Titanic* was the pride of the White Star Line, a British shipping company. Built in Belfast, Northern Ireland, in 1911, the luxury ocean liner was one of the largest passenger steamships of the time.

● **The ship belonged to** the company's Olympic-class liners. The others in this line were the *Olympic* and *Britannic*. The *Britannic* sank in 1916 after striking a German mine in the Aegean Sea.

● **Like all transatlantic liners**, the *Titanic* was meant to transport passengers between Europe and the United States. It was about 260 m long and 28 m wide.

● **The ship had about 900** crew members and could carry over 3000 passengers. Since the *Titanic* also carried mail, it was categorized as a Royal Mail Steamer, or RMS.

● **The *Titanic*** was the ultimate name in luxury at the time. Its most striking feature, the grand staircase, was immortalized in James Cameron's 1997 epic film of the same name. The ship had 16 watertight compartments in its hull and was thought to be unsinkable.

● **At noon on 10 April, 1912**, the *Titanic* began her maiden voyage. She set sail from Southampton, England, towards New York, United States. Among the passengers were several famous personalities including the American businessmen Benjamin Guggenheim and John Jacob Astor IV, and the writers Jacque Futrelle and Francis Davis Millet.

● **Four days later**, on 14 April, the ship struck an iceberg off the coast of Newfoundland. It was almost midnight.

● **The iceberg** ripped through the hull, causing the first six watertight compartments to flood. The ship broke in two and the bow sank almost immediately. It was followed by the stern, which hit the ocean bottom at high speed, severely damaging the hull.

● **Another steamship**, *Californian*, was anchored nearby. The crew members saw white rockets being fired from the *Titanic*, but failed to recognize these as distress signals and didn't come to the ship's aid.

▼ *After its collision with an iceberg, the* Titanic *took only three minutes to break apart and start sinking.*

Diving deep

● **People crossed the oceans** to reach new lands. Soon, the oceans themselves drew their interest. Adventurers began exploring the depths. This quest produced some great divers and explorers in the 20th century.

● **Charles William Beebe** (1872–1962) was a famous deep sea explorer. In 1934, he set a record by diving to a depth of over 920 m off Nonsuch Island, Bermuda.

● **The simple** deep-sea diving vessel that Beebe used was called the bathysphere. It was invented by Otis Barton, a wealthy engineer, who accompanied Beebe in one of the most dangerous expeditions ever.

● **Another renowned** deep sea explorer is Dr Robert Ballard. He has discovered two of the most famous wrecks – the *Titanic*, in 1985, and the *Bismarck*, in 1989.

● **With over 100** deep-sea expeditions to his name, Ballard also found *Yorktown*, the American aircraft carrier sunk in the Battle of Midway during World War II.

● **Ballard led the team** that discovered hydrothermal vents in the seafloor off the Galapagos Islands in 1977. In 1999, he found two Phoenician ships off the Israeli coast. Dating back to about 750 BC, these are the oldest shipwrecks ever found.

▲ *A scientist taking photographs of a great white shark.*

● **Marine biologist** Sylvia Earle is famous for her expeditions that research marine ecosystems. She holds the depth record for solo diving by a woman.

● **Emile Gagnan and Jacques Cousteau** contributed to the field of deep-sea exploration through their 1943 invention, the aqualung. This device helped divers stay underwater for several hours.

● **Hans Hass** was a pioneer in underwater expeditions and scuba diving. His film, *Red Sea Adventure*, won best underwater documentary at the 1950 Venice Film Festival.

● **Undersea photographers** and filmmakers such as David Doubilet, Stan Waterman, Michele Hall and Howard Hall have also contributed to our knowledge of the ocean depths.

Diving through time

● **It is believed** that around the 5th century BC, a man named Scyllias, from the Greek city of Scione, saved the Greeks from Persian attack by diving beneath the sea and cutting off the anchors of the Persian ships.

● **The history of diving** goes back to the time of Alexander the Great. Greek philosopher Aristotle wrote about a diving bell being used during Alexander's reign.

● **In ancient times**, the diving bell consisted of divers placing inverted buckets and cauldrons over their heads before going underwater.

● **These inverted objects** trapped air inside them, allowing the diver to breathe. They gradually gave way to a more sophisticated bell-shaped wooden barrel that was placed over the diver's head.

● **Air was passed** into the bell through tubes that went all the way up to the surface. Over the years the bell was enlarged to allow for more air.

▶ *In the early days of diving, air was passed to the divers through long tubes that went up to the water's surface.*

● **A more advanced version** of the diving bell is still used today. Modern bells are made of steel and can withstand huge amounts of pressure.

● **Divers in ancient Rome** were called urinatores, derived from the Latin word *urus*, meaning 'leather bag', because they carried one while diving. These divers recovered treasures from sunken ships. They used heavy stones to help them dive to depths of 30 m.

● **It is said that** around the first century BC urinatores salvaged a cargo of ancient wine jars from the Roman merchant ship, *Madrague de Giens*.

● **Divers** were also a major force in naval battles. According to historical accounts, Alexander the Great had to contend with diving warriors during the siege of Tyre in 332 BC.

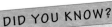
DID YOU KNOW?

In his account of the Athenian attack on Syracuse, the Greek historian, Thucydides, recounts how soldiers fixed wooden poles underwater to block entry into the harbour. These unseen poles caused immense damage to Athenian ships.

Shipwrecks

● **In modern times**, sophisticated navigational equipment has greatly reduced the number of shipwrecks. But until the 20th century, seafarers were completely dependant on 'dead reckoning' (calculating by estimating direction and distance travelled) and the magnetic compass.

● **One of the best known** shipwrecks is the *Titanic*. It sank after colliding with an iceberg in 1912. Today, with the aid of navigational instruments like GPS and radar, such disasters can be averted.

● **Wars have claimed** many ships. Both naval and civilian vessels have been sunk by torpedoes fired from warships and submarines. In fact, the majority of the existing wrecks around the world are a direct result of war. Most of them were sunk during World Wars I and II by German submarines.

● **One of the famous casualties** of war was the *Lusitania*. This passenger liner was sunk during the World War I by a torpedo from a German submarine off the coast of southern Ireland. Around 1200 people were killed.

● **On 19 July, 1545**, the English Tudor warship *Mary Rose* sank unexpectedly during a battle with the French. The ship went down at Solent, near Portsmouth, killing almost all its crew.

● **The actual reasons** behind the sinking of the *Mary Rose* continue to be a mystery. But it is believed that overloading and human error, not French cannons, could have sealed the ship's fate.

▶ *Water pours into the hull as the* Mary Rose *keels over. At this point, there was so much water inside that sinking was unavoidable.*

● ***Bismarck***, the pride of the German navy during World War II, was responsible for several attacks on both merchant and naval vessels. The most noteworthy of these was the sinking of the British warship *Hood*, in May 1941.

● **The *Bismarck***, in turn, was sunk by British ships hungry for revenge. After a long battle, it finally sank three days after the *Hood*, taking with it over 2000 sailors. The remains of the *Bismarck* were discovered in 1989, off the coast of Ireland.

● **The USS *Arizona*** was bombed when the Japanese attacked Pearl Harbor on 7 December, 1941, leading to the USA entering World War II. The *Arizona* exploded and sank, killing 1177, and still lies at the bottom of the sea.

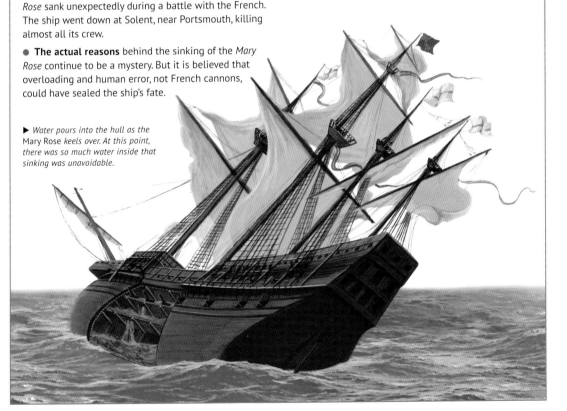

Fishing

- **People use a variety** of fishing methods – from hand, spear or bow fishing to netting, fishing hooks and lines, trapping or dredging, and even explosions.

- **Fishing nets** are made by knotting a fine thread to form a mesh, which traps the fish. In gill nets, fish are caught when their gill covers catch in the mesh.

- **Trawlers tow** heavy conical nets (trawls) through the seawater or along the seabed. The mouth of the net stays open while it is being towed, scooping up shoals of fish, which are then lifted with winches onto the trawler.

- **Longline fishing** uses long strings of baited hooks, which may be up to 20 km long with up to 12,000 hooks.

- **Purse seining** is a way of catching fish in mid-water or near the surface in a deep curtain of netting that is supported at the surface by floats. Unlike trawl nets, the mouths of seiner nets are drawn together (like closing a purse) before they are hauled on board.

- **A large purse seine net** can be one kilometre long and 200 m deep.

▲ *Fishermen aboard the Breton trawler* Amaryllis *haul in their catch from the Greenland Sea, off the coast of Iceland.*

- **Creels and pots** are small baited traps that attract prey such as crabs and lobsters. They are set down on the seabed, often in long strings, with floating buoys attached to show where they are.

- **Dredges are used** to collect scallops or oysters from the seabed but the process destroys sea creatures. They may also be farmed or collected by divers.

- **At least 43 percent** of fish supplies around the world come from fish farms, which cause problems such as pollution of the surrounding waters and the spread of disease to wild fish.

- **Modern fishing vessels** are so efficient that their use has greatly reduced the fish populations in many regions. Many countries regulate hauls to slow the decrease in fish populations.

Fishing vessels

- **People have used boats** for fishing since the beginning of civilization. Commercial fishing may be carried out by a single fisherman who takes his boat out to sea, or by huge fishing fleets.

- **Fishermen** in some countries still go out to sea in small wooden boats to cast their nets and wait for the catch. However, traditional fishing boats and methods have given way to bigger, more advanced vessels and new techniques that produce a very large haul.

- **There are three main** fishing vessels that can be found across the world. These are trawlers, seiners and long liners. All these vessels are more than 40 m long.

- **Trawlers**, also known as 'draggers', drag heavy nets, called trawls, across the seabed or through the water. These vessels are mainly used to catch shrimp, salmon and other edible marine creatures.

▶ *Trawlers have refrigeration facilities, allowing them to keep the catch fresh. Hence these vessels can also stay out at sea for several days.*

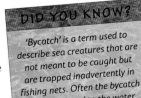

DID YOU KNOW?

'Bycatch' is a term used to describe sea creatures that are not meant to be caught but are trapped inadvertently in fishing nets. Often the bycatch is not returned to the water despite the fact that it is unsuitable for commercial use.

- **Whereas earlier trawlers** had sails, the modern ones are powered by diesel. They are often large and can measure up to 120 m in length.

- **Unlike trawls**, the mouths of seiner nets are closed before hauling them aboard. Seiners target fast-swimming fish like tuna and herring. The nets are allowed to float on the water to catch these fish.

- **Long liners** do not use nets at all. Instead, they have long lines with numerous baited hooks along their length. These lines trail behind the ship, hooking tuna, cod and even small sharks.

- **Other less common** fishing vessels include shrimp or lobster boats, head boats and dive boats.

Submersibles

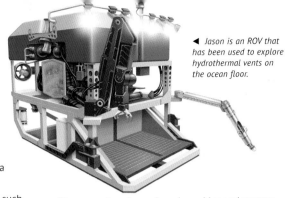

◀ Jason is an ROV that has been used to explore hydrothermal vents on the ocean floor.

- **A submersible** is an underwater research vessel. It is primarily used to conduct scientific research and for military and industrial purposes.

- **Submersibles help with the studies** of undersea geological activity, marine life and mineral deposits. They also help to check on oil rigs. Those involved in research often accompany a research vessel.

- **Navies use submersibles** for a variety of tasks, such as submarine rescue and repair, and mine detection.

- **Wreck divers** use submersibles for salvage operations, such as recovering planes or equipment that have sunk to the ocean depths.

- **Pressurized submersibles** are designed to operate in very deep waters, and are capable of withstanding extreme pressure.

- **An ROV** (Remotely Operated Vehicle) is a robot submersible that is tethered to a ship by a thick cable and controlled by a 'pilot' on board the ship. The biggest ROVs are lifted in and out of the water by cranes.

- **ROVs are used** for pipeline and oil rig inspections.

- **They can also** clear mines, lay cables and recover ships or planes from the seabed.

- **ROVs are equipped with lights**, cameras, underwater microphones, thrusters (to move position) and instruments such as temperature sensors and depth sensors. Some ROVs have a robot arm for moving or cutting things or taking scientific samples.

- **Scientists use ROVs** to explore the oceans in areas where it is difficult for people to go, such as under the Antarctic ice sheets or in particularly deep water.

- **Mini and micro ROVs** can be used by one person on a small boat. A mini ROV weighs about 15 kg and a micro ROV can weigh as little as 3 kg or less.

Minerals

- **Oceans contain minerals** that form in the oceans themselves, as well as those that wash into the water from the land.

- **Seawater contains** about 3.5 percent dissolved solids, including more than 60 chemical elements, such as potassium, magnesium and manganese.

- **Extraction** of minerals from the oceans depends on cost, ownership and technology.

▼ Salt is one mineral obtained from the oceans. It can be extracted by evaporating the water to leave the salt behind.

- **The International Seabed Authority**, which is part of the United Nations, controls mining in international waters. It aims to protect the ocean from the harmful effects of mining, such as pollution.

- **Magnesium is the only metal** extracted directly from seawater. It can also be obtained by mining minerals such as magnesite or dolomite from ancient ocean deposits.

- **Huge deposits of manganese nodules** have been discovered on the seabed. These nodules primarily consist of manganese and iron. Traces of copper, cobalt and nickel can also be found in them.

- **In 2009**, advances in technology made it possible to extract minerals from the deep ocean floor, about 1.6 km below the surface.

- **Deep-sea mines** are likely to cause noise, waste and pollution as well as damaging ecosystems such as hydrothermal vent communities.

Fossil fuels

● **Fossil fuels,** such as petroleum, coal and natural gas, are extracted from the fossilized remains of animals and plants. These remains have been buried under layers of sediment, rock and soil for millions of years ago.

● **Crude oil,** which is refined to make petroleum, is formed from tiny plants and animals that lived in the ancient oceans. Sediment settled on the mud, and heat and pressure turned it into crude oil.

● **Natural gas** is primarily formed by the decaying of dead plankton that has accumulated on the ocean floor.

● **Crude oil and natural gas** fill porous (reservoir) rocks. As reservoir rocks are normally filled with water, the fuel, which is lighter than water, travels up until it reaches non porous rocks. These trap the fuel to create a reservoir of fuel.

● **Since natural gas** is lighter than crude oil, it is found in a layer above the oil. Crude oil forms in the middle layer with water as the bottom layer.

● **Coal is a fossil fuel** formed from decomposed plants. Like oil and gas, coal can also be found under the ocean floor.

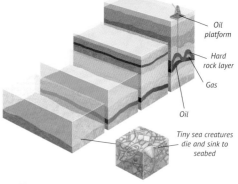

Oil platform

Hard rock layer

Gas

Oil

Tiny sea creatures die and sink to seabed

▲ *The remains of tiny sea creatures sink to the seabed and are buried under sediments. Slowly they turn into oil or gas by heat and pressure.*

● **About half of the carbon dioxide** released into the atmosphere by humans burning fossil fuels has dissolved in the oceans. This makes them more acidic, which, in turn, could have a serious impact on ocean food chains.

● **Acidic oceans** make corals grow more slowly or their skeletons become less dense. The corals are worn away, threatening the ecosystem.

● **Some scientists** have suggested storing carbon dioxide beneath the seabed. The carbon dioxide would be pumped down in liquid form and take millions of years to leak out.

Drilling for oil

● **The search for oil** in the oceans is increasing. Natural resources found in the seabed are extracted and refined to produce fuel.

● **Oil companies** usually build offshore drilling rigs to extract resources from the seabed. Rigs are platforms set up in the sea, some distance from the shore.

● **Oil rigs are** made of steel or concrete that can withstand huge waves and storms. Alaskan oil rigs also have to withstand icy waters and ice floes.

● **Rigs are equipped** with drills that tunnel several hundred metres into the ocean floor.

● **Once the presence** of crude oil is confirmed, it is extracted and sent to refineries where it is processed into petroleum and petroleum products, such as kerosene.

● **Some oil rigs** are huge platforms that drop an anchor and float on the water. These platforms have air-filled supports and are called semi-submersible rigs.

▶ *Drilling rigs are built to extract oil and gas from rocks beneath the ocean. Stormy weather at sea often makes this a dangerous and expensive activity.*

● **Permanent oil rigs** are built in areas where production is high and multiple oil wells can be drilled.

● **Sometimes pressure builds up** in the underground wells, causing blow-outs. When a blow-out occurs the drilling hole explodes, spilling oil into the water.

● **Blow-out preventers** control pressure in underwater wells while drilling.

● **One oil rig** can be linked to as many as 80 wells and reach over 1.6 km beneath the surface of the oceans.

Oil spills

- **Less than eight percent** of the oil spills in the oceans come from leaking ships, oil tankers or ocean-based oil wells.

- **Most waste oil** comes from oily water washed into the oceans from farms, factories and cities (including waste oil from car engines), routine maintenance of ships and recreational boating.

- **Oil spills happen** when people are careless or do not respect the law. Wars, terrorists or natural disasters, such as hurricanes, may also cause oil spills.

- **The damage caused** depends on the amount and type of oil and the location of the spill, as well as temperature, wind and weather.

- **Oil spills harm all ocean life**, from plankton, seaweed and fish to birds, sea otters and whales. Oil may block a whale's blowhole or poison the fish or plankton it eats.

- **To stop the spread** of an oil spill, booms can be placed around a tanker to contain and absorb oil. The oil can then be skimmed or burned off, or chemicals can be used to break it up.

▲ If seabirds get covered in oil, their feathers no longer keep them warm and waterproof. The birds may also eat the oil and poison themselves.

- **High-pressure hoses** help to clean up beaches if oil washes ashore.

- **In 1989**, the *Exxon Valdez* oil tanker ran aground at Prince William Sound in Alaska, spilling enough oil to fill about 125 Olympic-sized swimming pools. About 2800 sea otters and 250,000 seabirds died. It took 10,000 workers four summers to clean up the spill.

- **Two major spills** occured in the 1990s. The *Braer* tanker spilled 26 million tonnes of oil off the Shetland Islands (Scotland, UK) in 1993 and the *Sea Empress* spilled 18 million tonnes off Wales (UK) in 1996.

Ocean pollution

- **Excessive human activity** in coastal areas has increased pollution and caused damage to ocean life.

- **The discharge** of industrial waste and human sewage into the sea is the most common form of pollution. This affects marine life and makes the sea unfit for bathing.

- **The pollution** that enters oceans can be categorized as coming from 'point sources' and 'non-point sources'.

- **Sewer pipes** and industrial waste pipes are examples of point sources, as the discharge is from a single, identifiable point.

▼ Pipes discharging untreated sewage onto beaches are a major problem for people and ocean life.

- **Non-point sources** of pollution are harder to tackle. They include water or sewage from farms containing fertilizers with a high chemical content.

> **DID YOU KNOW?**
>
> Eighty percent of ocean pollution comes from sources on land, such as cars and farms.

- **Some chemicals** found in pesticides are biodegradable, and their effects are minimal. Others remain dangerous for a long time.

- **Petroleum and oil products** enter the water through spills from ships and leakages from pipelines and storage tanks.

- **Power stations** are a major source of pollution. The water they discharge is usually hot and so it alters the temperature of the water, adversely affecting marine life in the area.

- **Many beaches** have become tourist attractions. Plastic litter left on beaches is a hazard to marine life.

- **Metals such as copper** and lead enter the oceans from dumped industrial waste and automobile emissions. These metals can lead to health problems in animals and in people.

Sea levels

- **Sea levels have risen** and fallen for millions of years, due to changes in climate or movement inside the Earth, causing the ocean floor to move up or down.

- **During the last Ice Age**, sea levels fell by about 90 m because so much water was frozen as ice sheets on land.

- **The melting of the ice caps** at the end of the last Ice Age caused sea levels to rise about 120 m.

▼ *Sea levels are thought to have risen by about 10–25 cm over the past 100 years.*

- **Valleys in Norway and Alaska** that had once been filled by glaciers became flooded. These watery valleys are called fjords.

- **A rise in sea level** is partly caused by melting snow, glaciers and ice sheets when the Earth's temperature increases.

- **Sea levels also rise** because the oceans expand and take up more space as the sea warms up.

- **Some scientists estimate** that sea levels could rise by up to 1.5 m by the year 2100. Other estimates suggest a smaller rise of about 28–43 cm.

- **About 80–90 percent** of Bangladesh is within a metre of sea level, and islands in the Pacific, such as the Maldives, are just a few metres above sea level.

- **The Thames Barrier** was built across the river Thames in London to stop the city being flooded by high tides and storm waves from the North Sea.

- **Rising sea levels** would threaten other coastal cities around the world, such as New York, Los Angeles, Lagos, Shanghai, Rio de Janeiro and Tokyo.

Ocean power

- **The energy** of movement in the ocean's waves, tides and currents can be used to produce electrical power.

- **The moving water** is used to push a turbine wheel around and this movement energy can be converted into electrical energy inside a generator.

- **A tidal power station** is built inside a dam or barrage across a narrow bay or the mouth of a river where it meets the ocean. As the tide flows in and out of the dam, it generates electricity.

- **Underwater turbines** can be used to collect the energy in ocean and tidal currents.

- **Some wave-power devices** are fixed to the ocean floor where they are less likely to be damaged by storms and strong winds and cause less visual pollution than if they were on the surface.

- **Other wave-energy systems** include devices that use the rise and fall of the waves inside a concrete chamber, and shoreline devices that channel waves into reservoirs to concentrate wave power.

▶ *Offshore wind farms could produce more energy than those based on land, but they are more costly.*

- **Groups of large windmills**, or wind turbines, called wind farms can be built in the oceans near the shore, where they generate energy from the winds moving over the waves. These wind farms may disturb the ocean currents and marine ecosystems.

- **In the future**, it may be possible to generate power from the temperature differences between the ocean's warm surface waters and the icy cold water in the deep ocean.

Coastal defences

- **There are two** ways that coasts are defended against erosion and flooding – these are called hard engineering and soft engineering.

- **Hard engineering** includes defences such as sea walls and breakwaters (offshore sea walls), cages of boulders (gabions), heaps of rocks and stones piled against the bases of cliffs (riprap), slatted barriers (revetments) and groynes.

- **Hard engineering solutions** are designed to stop waves hitting the shore but are expensive and often cause problems further along the coast. They need regular maintenance and take away from the natural beauty of beaches.

- **Soft engineering** uses natural processes to manage coasts and sometimes lets the sea erode coasts rather than trying to fight nature.

- **In tropical areas**, mangrove swamps protect coasts from storms and floods. The roots of mangrove trees also trap mud, helping to build up the coastline.

- **When beach material** is washed away, more mud or sand can be added to build up the beach and protect the land behind the beach from flooding.

- **Plants such as marram grass** can be planted on sand dunes to stop them being blown away. The grass roots bind the sand together and protect the dunes, which provide a defence against floods.

- **Planting salt marshes** on the shoreline helps to protect the beach and slow down erosion by the waves. It also creates a habitat for wildlife, such as wading birds.

▲ *Groynes are low wooden fences on beaches. They are placed at right angles to the coast and help to stop beach material from being washed along the coast by the waves.*

Global warming

- **Global warming** is a rapid rise in the average temperature of the whole planet as a result of the greenhouse effect.

- **The greenhouse effect** is the process by which certain gases in the Earth's atmosphere trap some of the heat given off by the Earth and keep the planet warm enough for life to survive.

- **Greenhouse gases** include water vapour, carbon dioxide, methane, nitrous oxide, CFCs and ozone. Water vapour is the most common of these, and is responsible for about 60 percent of the natural greenhouse effect.

- **Without greenhouse gases**, the Earth's average temperature would be −18°C, which is too cold for life.

- **Most scientists** think that deforestation and pollution have increased the amounts of greenhouse gases in the atmosphere, causing the planet to warm up faster than it would do naturally.

- **In the last 150 years**, the amount of carbon dioxide in the atmosphere has increased by about one third.

- **Scientists predict** that global temperatures could rise by 2–5°C by the end of the 21st century.

- **This would make the world** world hotter than it has been for more than 100,000 years.

- **Global warming** is already causing problems, such as rising sea levels, flooding, droughts, wildfires, extreme weather and the spread of diseases such as malaria.

- **One hundred million people** live in places that are only one metre above sea level, so they are very vulnerable to even small rises in sea levels.

◀ *The Maldives could sink beneath the waves within 100 years as a result of global warming. Wave breakers have been built as a protective measure.*

Coral reef threats

- **The impact of global warming** on the oceans is most visible in the bleaching (die-off caused by stress) of coral reefs.

- **Reefs are very delicate structures**, formed by tiny creatures called coral polyps. The main food source of polyps is the unicellular algae, called zooxanthellae, which live within their tissues.

- **The algae** feed on nitrogen waste produced by corals.

- **They also produce** food using sunlight (photosynthesis). The corals rely on this to survive.

- **As well as providing food**, the algae also give the reefs their colour, which attracts many other marine creatures.

- **Reefs lose colour and die** when the algae are damaged. This is known as 'bleaching'.

- **Global warming** is the main cause of bleaching. A rise in ocean temperatures interferes with the photosynthetic process, poisoning the algae.

- **Corals expel** the dead algae, along with some of their own tissue. Once the algae are expelled, the corals lose their colour and main source of food.

▲ *Without the algae that give them colour, corals look white or 'bleached'.*

- **Bleached coral reefs** take years to recover. Bleaching affects not only the coral reefs, but also a large number of marine creatures that depend on them for food.

- **Coral reefs** can also be smothered by silt or sewage draining off the land from buildings operations. If the algae have no light to make food, the corals die.

- **Reefs are often** damaged by heavy anchors from boats used by tourists, or by divers hunting for souvenirs for the tourist trade.

Fragile islands

- **Many threatened species** live on islands, where they are at risk from expanding human populations, global warming and introduced species, such as cats.

- **Island species** are vulnerable because their populations are small and they are often unable to compete with new species that arrive on their island.

- **The dodo bird** lived on Mauritius, an island in the Indian Ocean. It was wiped out by sailors killing it for food, and by introduced species such as rats and monkeys eating its eggs. The last dodo died in 1681.

▼ *Tourists watching Galápagos sea lions. Tourism has helped to fund conservation projects on the Galápagos Islands, but it could also destroy this fragile ecosystem.*

- **The kakapo** is an almost flightless parrot. Only about 40 live in the wild on two small islands off the coast of New Zealand. All predators have been removed from these islands and human access is controlled.

- **The biggest lizard**, the Komodo dragon, lives on the island of Komodo and a few smaller islands north of Australia. It is threatened by illegal hunting and the spread of human settlements.

- **Lemurs live** on Madagascar, off the coast of Africa. They are threatened by deforestation and also hunted for food and captured for the pet trade or zoos.

- **The Galápagos Islands**, off the coast of Ecuador, are home to many rare species, such as giant tortoises, flightless cormorants and Galápagos finches. The growing human population and introduced plants and animals threaten the survival of this unique ecosystem.

- **Many thousands of bird species** have become extinct on the 4000 or so islands of Micronesia and Polynesia in the South Pacific Ocean. The introduction of the common rat when humans colonised these islands is one of the biggest contributing factors.

Endangered species

● **Endangered species** are animals and plants that are facing extinction. These species will die out if nothing is done to keep them alive.

● **Ocean species are** becoming endangered because of habitat destruction, coastal development, tourism, illegal hunting, overfishing, pollution, climate change, disease, alien or invasive species and increased predation.

● **Endangered ocean animals** include the coelacanth, southern bluefin tuna, leatherback turtle, blue whale, whale shark, great white shark and dugong.

● **All seven species of sawfish** are threatened and the smalltooth sawfish is now endangered.

● **Adult sawfish** are hunted for their 'saw' – a long flat snout edged with sharp teeth. Young sawfish are very sensitive to habitat destruction.

● **The numbers of baleen whales**, such as right whales and blue whales, were greatly reduced by hunting in the 1700s to 1900s. Numbers are still low, even though most hunting is now illegal.

▶ *Coelacanths are very rare. It is illegal to trade them and if caught, they should be released back into the wild.*

● **The Mediterranean monk seal** is one of the most endangered mammals. There are less than 500 left due to tourism, illegal hunting and pollution.

● **Dugongs** are close to extinction due to collisions with boats, being accidentally caught in nets, illegal hunting and the destruction of the seagrass beds where they feed.

● **The coelacanth is a deep-water fish** that has lived on Earth for about 400 million years, but less than 1000 are probably alive today.

● **Southern bluefin tuna** have been overfished to the brink of extinction. Their numbers have been reduced by about 97 percent and this fish is critically endangered.

Whales in danger

● **For hundreds of years**, people hunted whales for their meat, bones and blubber (fat).

● **Whale oil**, made from blubber, was used in lamps and candles and to make margarine, soap, machine oil and cosmetics.

● **Even the baleen** (whalebone) was used to make tennis racquets, umbrellas and corsets.

● **At first**, people hunted whales from sailing ships and rowing boats. They killed them with spears called harpoons, thrown by hand. The whaling industry expanded after the invention of an exploding harpoon in the 1860s. This could kill even the biggest whales.

● **Commercial whaling** in the 19th and 20th centuries almost wiped out the world's whale populations.

DID YOU KNOW?

Seven out of the 13 great whales are still endangered, despite being protected.

● **In 1946**, the International Whaling Commission (IWC) was established to try to stop whales becoming extinct. It regulated the hunting of whales, but whales continued to be killed in large numbers.

● **In 1986**, whale numbers were so low that the IWC banned commercial whaling completely.

● **Today**, some aboriginal peoples still hunt small numbers of whales for food and essential materials. Also, Norway still hunts minke whales in the north Atlantic, and Japan kills hundreds of whales each year for their controversial scientific research programme.

● **Threats to whales** include noise pollution, climate change, illegal trade in whale meat, entanglement in fishing nets (especially for small whales, such as dolphins), collisions with ships, pollution, habitat degradation and oil and gas exploration.

◀ *Whale bones were used as building materials and tools and to make glue and fertilizer.*

Turtles in trouble

● **Six out of the seven** types of sea turtle are defined as endangered or critically endangered, including Kemp's ridley, hawksbill, green, leatherback and loggerhead turtles.

● **Several million green turtles** once swam in the oceans, but today less than 200,000 nesting females survive in the wild.

● **Populations of leatherback** turtles have dropped, with numbers estimated at less than 100,000. On one Mexican beach, there were 6500 nests in 1986, but only 50 in 1993.

● **Leatherbacks are killed** for their oil, which is used in lamps and to make ships watertight and also for medicines. These turtles eat a lot of jellyfish and often die after mistaking floating plastic debris for food.

● **Female sea turtles** return to the same nesting beaches each year. They are disturbed by the noise and lights from hotels. Tourists also crush eggs buried in the sand.

● **On some beaches**, nests are protected and people carry the hatchlings to the sea.

▲ *The shell of the hawksbill turtle has been highly prized for thousands of years, and this reptile is now critically endangered.*

● **Poachers may steal** turtles' eggs or cut out the cartilage (calipee) from between the bones of the bottom shell and sell it for making turtle soup.

● **Parts of the shell** of hawksbill turtles are used to make combs, jewellery and spectacle frames.

● **Sea turtles** are an important part of ocean food chains and help to attract ecotourists to tropical beaches.

● **The money raised** from tourists supports conservation work and provides employment for coastal communities.

Penguins in peril

● **Four species of penguin** are endangered – Galápagos, yellow-eyed, erect-crested and northern rockhopper penguins.

● **Seven other species** face a high risk of extinction and two more are threatened.

● **Emperor penguins** may be seriously threatened in the future due to melting sea ice.

● **Northern rockhopper** penguin populations have declined by about 90 percent in the last 50 years. Scientists think this is probably connected with hunting, climate change, overfishing and wild dogs eating the penguins' eggs.

◀ *Over the past 45 years, numbers of erect-crested penguins have declined by 50 percent for reasons that are not fully understood.*

● **In the past**, people have collected penguin eggs to eat and killed adults for their meat and the oil in their blubber.

● **In 2000**, almost 40 percent of the African penguin population was covered in oil after a tanker sank. Penguins are especially vulnerable to oil pollution on the water's surface as they have to surface to breathe air.

● **African penguin** numbers have declined from 1.5 million breeding pairs 100 years ago to only 63,000 pairs today.

● **Yellow-eyed penguins** of New Zealand are endangered by the destruction of the forests where they nest. Predators such as stoats and ferrets feed on the chicks.

● **Yellow-eyed penguins** also get entangled in fishing nets and drown when they cannot surface to breathe.

● **The Humboldt penguin** is threatened by over-harvesting of the deep piles of guano (penguin droppings) in which they dig their nesting burrows.

The last ice bears

● **Polar bears roam** across the sea ice that covers the Arctic Ocean.

● **They catch seals** by waiting next to their breathing holes in the ice and killing the seals when they pop up to breathe.

● **There are about** 20,000 to 25,000 polar bears left in the Arctic but they are in grave danger of extinction.

● **The greatest threat** to polar bears used to be hunting but now they are mainly threatened by global warming, which is causing the sea ice to melt.

DID YOU KNOW?

The Arctic sea ice is melting so fast that most of it could be gone by 2040.

● **As the sea ice melts** earlier in summer as a result of global warming, this shortens the winter hunting season for the polar bears. They cannot build up enough fat reserves to last them through the summer when they can't catch seals, and they have to find whatever food is available on land.

● **With less food**, polar bears will not reproduce as often. Their cubs will be smaller and less likely to survive.

● **As well as melting ice**, polar bears are also threatened by poisons in the snow and ice, mining in the Arctic, shipping, tourists, drilling for oil and gas, and illegal hunting or over-hunting for sport.

● **An oil spill in the Arctic** would expose both polar bears and their seal prey to the dangers of oil pollution.

● **Oil exploration and development** could disturb pregnant females choosing a den to give birth to their cubs as well as mothers looking after newborn cubs.

◀ *Global warming is melting the sea ice where the polar bears hunt for ringed and bearded seals.*

Saving the oceans

● **Ocean resources** need to be managed sustainably to avoid destroying habitats, forcing species into extinction and polluting the seas.

● **Less than one percent** of the world's oceans are now marine protected areas (MPAs).

● **Expanding these areas**, where fishing, mining and dredging are prohibited, would protect habitats and species.

● **Coastal areas** can be protected by managing the land use based on scientific knowledge so that areas are set aside for different types of activity.

● **The Marine Stewardship Council** (MSC) label provides a way of identifying sustainable fisheries that are not wiping out fish stocks and still allow fishermen to maintain their livelihoods.

● **Many fishing methods** trap and kill other wildlife, such as seabirds and mammals. Different fishing techniques could reduce or avoid this bycatch.

● **To avoid polluting the oceans**, we must reduce the waste we produce, recycle more, control illegal dumping of waste and change dangerous waste into safer waste.

● **Fighting global warming** involves using less energy and developing more sources of alternative energy that do not harm ocean environments.

● **The introduction** of invasive species needs to be avoided as they can disrupt the ocean ecosystem by multiplying rapidly and upsetting the balance of life.

● **Sustainable tourism** is an important part of protecting oceans, coasts and cultures of local people.

▼ *More scientific research into ocean ecosystems and endangered species will help conservation projects to be more effective.*

1000 **DINOSAUR** FACTS

Age of Dinosaurs

● **The Age of Dinosaurs** corresponds to the time period that geologists call the Mesozoic Era, from about 252–66 mya (million years ago).

● **The Mesozoic Era** is divided into three shorter time spans – the Triassic, Jurassic and Cretaceous Periods.

● **In the Triassic Period,** 252–201 mya, the dinosaurs began to evolve.

● **During the Jurassic Period** – about 201–145 mya – many dinosaurs reached their greatest size.

● **The Cretaceous Period** is when dinosaurs were at their most varied – about 145–66 mya.

● **All through the Mesozoic Era,** and before and since, the major landmasses gradually moved across the globe in a process known as continental drift.

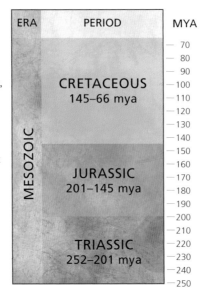

ERA	PERIOD	MYA
MESOZOIC	CRETACEOUS 145–66 mya	— 70 — 80 — 90 — 100 — 110 — 120 — 130 — 140 — 150 — 160
	JURASSIC 201–145 mya	— 170 — 180 — 190 — 200 — 210
	TRIASSIC 252–201 mya	— 220 — 230 — 240 — 250

◀ *Dinosaurs ruled the land for 185 million years – longer than any other animal group.*

● **In the Triassic Period,** all the continents were joined as one supercontinent – Pangaea.

● **In the Jurassic Period,** Pangaea separated into two huge landmasses – Laurasia in the north and Gondwana in the south.

● **In the Cretaceous Period,** Laurasia and Gondwana split, and the continents began to take the positions that we know today.

● **The joining and separating** of the continents affected which kinds of dinosaurs lived where.

Legs and posture

● **All dinosaurs had four limbs.** Unlike some other reptiles, such as snakes and slow-worms, they did not lose their limbs through evolution.

● **Some dinosaurs,** such as the massive, plant-eating sauropod *Janenschia*, stood and walked on all four legs nearly all the time.

● **The all-fours method** of standing and walking is called 'quadrupedal'.

● **Some dinosaurs,** such as the nimble, meat-eating dromaeosaur *Deinonychus*, stood and walked on their back limbs only.

● **The back-limbs-only method** of standing and walking is called 'bipedal'.

● **Some dinosaurs,** such as the hadrosaur *Edmontosaurus*, could move on all four limbs or just on their back legs if they chose to.

● **The two- or four-legs method** of standing and walking is called 'bipedal/quadrupedal'.

● **Reptiles such as lizards** and crocodiles have a sprawling posture, in which the upper legs join the body at the sides.

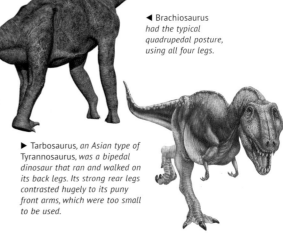

◀ *Brachiosaurus had the typical quadrupedal posture, using all four legs.*

▶ Tarbosaurus, *an Asian type of Tyrannosaurus, was a bipedal dinosaur that ran and walked on its back legs. Its strong rear legs contrasted hugely to its puny front arms, which were too small to be used.*

● **Dinosaurs had an upright posture,** with the legs directly below the body.

● **The more efficient upright posture** and gait may be one major reason why dinosaurs were so successful compared to other animals of the time.

Lesothosaurus and Fabrosaurus

● **There has been much confusion** between two very small plant-eating dinosaurs, *Lesothosaurus* and *Fabrosaurus*.

● **Their fossils come from South Africa** and date back to the Early Jurassic Period, 200–190 mya.

● *Fabrosaurus* **was named** in 1964 from just one fossil specimen of three teeth set in part of a jawbone.

● **Comparing this specimen** with similar fossils from other regions, these indicated a dinosaur plant-eater about one metre long.

● *Lesothosaurus* **received its name** in 1978. Its more plentiful fossils showed a similar one-metre plant-eater to *Fabrosaurus*.

● **Slim and lightly built**, *Lesothosaurus* was only one metre long from nose to tail-tip and would have stood knee-high to an adult human being.

● **Its long, slim back legs** and long toes indicate that *Lesothosaurus* was a fast runner.

● **Teeth and other fossils** of *Lesothosaurus* show that it probably ate low-growing plants such as ferns.

● **The rear teeth were set** inwards slightly from the sides of its skull, suggesting fleshy cheek pouches for storing or chewing food.

● **It is possible that** *Lesothosaurus* and *Fabrosaurus* were the same type of dinosaur. If so, all the fossils should receive the name given first – *Fabrosaurus*.

● **But the remains of** *Fabrosaurus* are so limited, some experts say that it should not even exist as an official name.

● *Lesothosaurus* **may be** a very early type of ornithischian or 'bird-hipped' dinosaur, perhaps on the way to becoming an ornithopod like *Iguanodon* – or a stegosaur or ankylosaur.

◀ Lesothosaurus *may have stood on hind legs to spot danger, much like the mammals called meerkats in the region today.*

Ancestors

● **Experts have many opinions** about which group (or groups) of reptiles were the ancestors of the dinosaurs.

● **Very early dinosaurs** walked and ran on their strong back limbs, so their ancestors probably did the same.

● **One group name** for the dinosaurs' ancestors was the thecodonts, or 'socket-toothed', but this is no longer regarded as a true scientific grouping.

● **However there are several kinds** of small, slim, bipedal (walking on back legs), sharp-toothed reptiles that could show what the dinosaurs' ancestors looked like.

● *Largerperton*, 70 cm long, lived about 240 mya in Argentina, South America.

● *Marasuchus* was a similar creature but even smaller, less than 50 cm in length, also from Argentina.

● *Lagosuchus* was another small predator about 30 cm long from the same area, although it may have been the same as *Marasuchus*.

● *Euparkeria* from South Africa dates from 235 mya, but its rear legs were not as well developed.

DID YOU KNOW?

The earliest known dinosaurs came from South America, so their ancestors probably did, too.

◀ Euparkeria, *or 'Parker's good animal', was named in 1913. It was about 60 cm in total length, slim and agile, and resembled the creatures from which dinosaurs probably evolved.*

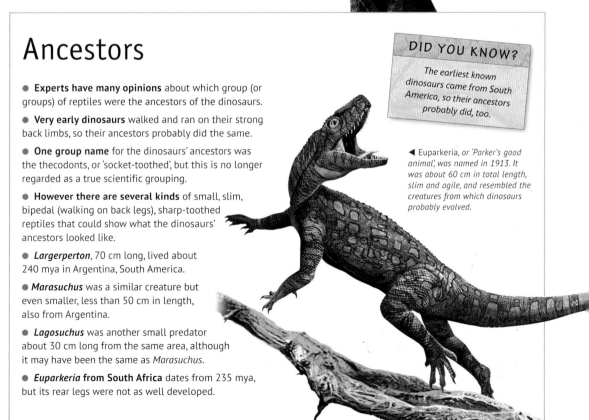

Prosauropods

● **The first big dinosaurs** were the prosauropods, also called plateosaurids. Most lived between 230 and 180 mya.

● **They were plant-eaters**, with small heads, long necks and tails, wide bodies and four sturdy limbs.

● **One of the first prosauropods** was *Plateosaurus*, which lived in Europe between about 215 and 205 mya.

● *Plateosaurus* **walked on all fours**, but may have reared up on its back legs to reach leaves. It was up to 9 m long, and weighed as much as 3 tonnes.

● **Another prosauropod** was *Riojasaurus*. Its fossils are about 220–215 million years old, and come from Argentina.

● *Riojasaurus* **was 10 m** long and weighed about 2 tonnes.

● **Over 20 fossil skeletons** of the prosauropod *Sellosaurus* have been found in Europe, dating from 215–210 mya.

● *Lufengosaurus* was an early Jurassic prosauropod from China, measuring up to 9 m in length. It was the first complete dinosaur skeleton to be restored in that country.

● **The sauropods followed** the prosauropods and were even bigger, but had the same basic body shape, with long necks and tails.

DID YOU KNOW?

A similar dinosaur and close relative to Riojasaurus was Melanorosaurus from Africa – South America and Africa were once joined together as part of Gondwana, 200 mya.

◀ Riojasaurus was South America's first big dinosaur.

Horns

DID YOU KNOW?

Dinosaurs may have used their horns to push over plants or dig up roots for food.

● **A dinosaur's horns got bigger** as the animal grew.

● **Each horn** had a bony core and an outer covering of a tough material formed mainly from keratin – the same substance that makes up human hair and fingernails.

● **Horns were most common** among plant-eating dinosaurs. They were probably used for defence and to protect young against predators.

● **The biggest horns** belonged to the ceratopsians or 'horn-faces', such as *Triceratops*.

● **In some ceratopsian horns**, the bony core alone was about one metre long. This did not include the outer sheath, so the whole horn would have been longer.

● **The ceratopsian** *Styracosaurus*, or 'spiked reptile', had a series of long horns around the top of its neck frill, and a very long horn on its nose.

● **Horns may have been used** in head-swinging displays to intimidate rivals and make physical fighting less likely.

● **In battle**, male dinosaurs may have locked horns in a trial of strength, as antelopes do today.

● **Armoured dinosaurs** such as the nodosaur *Panoplosaurus* had horn-like spikes along the sides of the body, especially in the shoulder region.

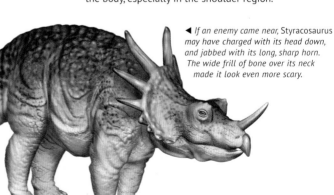

◀ *If an enemy came near*, Styracosaurus may have charged with its head down, and jabbed with its long, sharp horn. The wide frill of bone over its neck made it look even more scary.

Tyrannosaurus

● **Tyrannosaurus is not only** one of the most famous dinosaurs, it is also one about which a great deal is known. Several discoveries have revealed fossilized bones, teeth and whole skeletons.

● **Tyrannosaurus lived** at the end of the Age of Dinosaurs, about 68–66 mya. It was 12 m long and weighed 7 tonnes.

● **Its full name** is *Tyrannosaurus rex*, which means 'king of the tyrant reptiles'.

● **The head was 1.2 m long** and had more than 50 dagger-like teeth, some longer than 15 cm.

● **Tyrannosaurus fossils** have been found at many sites in North America, including Alberta and Saskatchewan in Canada, and Colorado, Wyoming, Montana and New Mexico in the USA.

● **The arms and hands** of *Tyrannosaurus* were so small that they could not pass food to its mouth, and may have had no use at all.

● **The rear feet were enormous**, each set of three toes supporting some 3–4 tonnes.

● **Recent fossil finds** of a group of *Tyrannosaurus* include youngsters, suggesting that they may have lived as families in small herds or packs.

● **Tyrannosaurus may have been** an active hunter, pounding along with long strides after its fleeing prey,

● **Or it may** have been a skulking scavenger that ambushed old and sickly victims.

● **Until the 1990s**, *Tyrannosaurus* was known as the biggest meat-eating dinosaur, and the biggest meat-eating animal ever to walk the Earth, but its size record was broken by *Giganotosaurus* and then *Spinosaurus*.

▼ Tyrannosaurus'
massive, powerful rear legs contrasted greatly with its puny front limbs or 'arms'. As it ran, its thick-based tail balanced the horizontal body and head, which was held low.

DID YOU KNOW?

Tyrannosaurus, when fully grown, was about 12–13 m long and stood taller than a two-decker bus. It weighed 6–7 tonnes.

Raptors

● 'Raptors' is a name for the dromaeosaur group. It is variously said to mean 'plunderer', 'thief' or 'hunter' (birds of prey are also called raptors).

● Dromaeosaurs were medium- to large-sized, powerful, agile, meat-eating dinosaurs that lived about 110–66 mya.

● Most dromaeosaurs were 1.5–3 m from nose to tail, weighed 20–60 kg, and stood 1–2 m tall.

● Velociraptor lived 75–70 mya, in what is now the barren scrub and desert of Mongolia in Central Asia.

● Like other raptors, Velociraptor probably ran fast and could leap great distances on its powerful back legs.

● The dromaeosaurs are named after the 1.8-m-long Dromaeosaurus from North America – one of the least known of the group, from very few fossil finds.

● The most-studied raptor is probably Deinonychus.

● The large mouths of dromaeosaurs opened wide and were equipped with many small, sharp, curved teeth.

● Most raptors probably had feathers, although for some there is no direct fossil evidence.

◀ Velociraptor, the 'speedy thief', was a typical dromaeosaur. Fossils of it were found in Central Asia.

DID YOU KNOW?

On each second toe, a dromaeosaur had a large, curved claw that it could swing in an arc to slash through its victim's flesh.

Tails

● All dinosaurs evolved with tails – though some individuals may have lost theirs in attacks or accidents.

● The length of the tail relative to the body, and its shape, thickness and special features, gives many clues as to how the dinosaur used it.

● The longest tails, at more than 17 m, belonged to the giant plant-eating sauropods such as Diplodocus.

● Some sauropods had a chain of more than 80 separate caudal vertebrae (bones in the tail) – more than twice the usual number.

● Sauropods may have used their tails as a whip to flick at enemies.

● Many meat-eating dinosaurs that stood or ran on their back legs had thick-based tails to balance the weight of their bodies.

● Small meat-eaters, such as Compsognathus, used their tails for balance when leaping and darting about.

● The meat-eater Ornitholestes had a tail that was more than half of its 2-m length. It was used as a counterbalance and rudder to help it turn corners at speed.

● Armoured dinosaurs called ankylosaurs had two huge lumps of bone at the end of their tails, which they swung at their enemies like a club.

● The tails of duckbilled dinosaurs (hadrosaurs) may have been swished from side to side in the water as an aid to swimming.

◀ Compsognathus had a long tail that helped it to balance and turn quickly when running fast.

Gobi Desert

- **The Gobi Desert** covers much of southern Mongolia and parts of northern China.

- **The first fossil-hunting expeditions** to the Gobi Desert took place in 1922–25, and were organized by the American Museum of Natural History.

- **The expeditions** set out to look for fossils of early humans, but instead found amazing dinosaur remains.

- **The first fossil dinosaur eggs** were found by the 1922–25 expeditions.

- **Russian expeditions** to the Gobi Desert in 1946 and 1948–49 discovered new armoured and duckbilled dinosaurs.

- **More expeditions** in the 1960s–70s found the giant sauropod *Opisthocoelicaudia* and the helmet-headed *Prenocephale*.

DID YOU KNOW?

Velociraptor, Avimimus and Pinacosaurus were discovered in the Gobi.

- **Other Gobi dinosaurs** include *Gallimimus* and *Oviraptor*. In the 1990s–2000s more expeditions uncovered therizinosaur fossils.

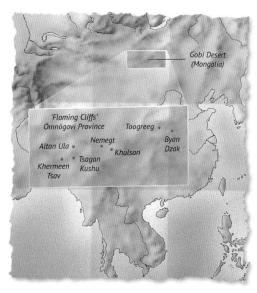

Gobi Desert
(Mongolia)

'Flaming Cliffs'
Ömnögovi Province   Toogreeg
        Nemegt   Byan
Altan Ula   Khulsan   Dzak
        Tsagan
Khermeen   Kushu
Tsav

▲ *The Gobi's fossil sites are far from any towns or cities. Searching for fossils is hard work in extreme temperatures and dust storms that affect this area.*

Brachiosaurus

- *Brachiosaurus* **lived about 155–150 mya** and its fossils have been found at several sites in North America.

- **Fossils of a similar dinosaur** from Africa, previously thought to have been *Brachiosaurus*, have been renamed *Giraffatitan*.

- **At 25 m in length** from nose to tail, *Brachiosaurus* was not one of the longest dinosaurs, but it was one of the heaviest. Its weight has been estimated between 20 and 50 tonnes.

- *Brachiosaurus* **fossils** were first found in 1900 and the dinosaur was named the year after.

- **The name** *Brachiosaurus* means 'arm reptile' – it was so-named because of its massive front legs.

- **With its huge front legs** and long neck, *Brachiosaurus* could perhaps reach food more than 13 m from the ground.

- **Its teeth were small** and chisel-shaped for snipping leaves from trees. The nostrils were positioned high on its head.

- **Although weighing** up to ten times more than an elephant, fossil footprints show that *Brachiosaurus* could run quite fast – nearly as fast as a human.

◀ Brachiosaurus *had similar body proportions to a giraffe, but was more than twice as tall and 50 times heavier.*

Europe

- **The first dinosaur fossils** ever discovered and given official names were found in England in the 1820s.

- **One of the first** almost complete dinosaur skeletons found was that of the big plant-eater *Iguanodon*, in 1871, in southern England.

- **Some of the most numerous** early fossils found were those of *Iguanodon*, discovered in the Belgian village of Bernissart in 1878.

- **About 155–145 mya**, Solnhofen in southern Germany was a mosaic of lush islands and shallow lagoons – ideal for many kinds of life.

- **At Solnhofen**, amazingly detailed fossils of tiny *Compsognathus* and the first-known bird *Archaeopteryx* have been found preserved in sandstone.

- **Fossils of *Compsognathus*** were also found near Nice in southern France.

- **Many fossils** of *Plateosaurus* were recovered from Trossingen, Germany, in 1911–12, 1921–23 and 1932.

- **Some of the largest fossil eggs**, measuring 30 cm long, were thought to have been laid by *Hypselosaurus* near Aix-en-Provence in southern France.

▲ *The dots indicate just a few of the dinosaur fossil sites found in Europe.*

- **The Isle of Wight** off the coast of southern England has provided so many dinosaur fossils that it is sometimes known as 'Dinosaur Island'.

- **Fossils of *Hypsilophodon*** have been found in eastern Spain, and those of *Camptosaurus* have been found on the coast of Portugal.

Dinosaur names 1

- **Every dinosaur** has a scientific name, usually made up from Latin or Greek place names or person names, and is written in italics.

- **Many dinosaur names** end in '-saurus', which some scientists say means 'reptile' and others say means 'lizard' – but dinosaurs were not lizards.

▼ *In 1988, an almost complete specimen of the meat-eater Herrerasaurus was excavated in Argentina. It was named after Victorino Herrera, the farmer who discovered it.*

- **Names often refer** to a unique feature a dinosaur had. *Baryonyx*, for example, means 'heavy claw', from the massive claw on its thumb.

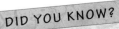

DID YOU KNOW?

Some dinosaur groups are named after the first discovered or major one of its kind, such as the tyrannosaurs or stegosaurs.

- **Many dinosaur names** are real tongue-twisters, such as *Opisthocoelicaudia*, pronounced 'owe-pis-thowe-see-lee-cord-ee-ah'. The name means 'posterior tail cavity', and refers to the joints between the backbones in the dinosaur's tail.

- **Some dinosaurs** are named after the place where their fossils were found. *Minmi* was found near Minmi Crossing, Queensland, Australia.

- **The fast-running ostrich dinosaurs** are named ornithomimosaurs, which means 'bird-mimic reptiles'.

Biggest dinosaurs

- **Dinosaurs can be measured** by length and height, but 'biggest' usually means heaviest or bulkiest.

- **The sauropod dinosaurs** of the Late Jurassic and Early–Mid Cretaceous Periods were the biggest animals to walk on Earth, as far as we know.

- **However, today's biggest whales**, and maybe the huge sea reptiles (pliosaurs) of the Dinosaur Age, rival them in size.

- **For any dinosaur**, enough fossils must be found for scientists to be sure it is a distinct type before they can give it a scientific name. They must also be able to estimate its size. With some giant dinosaurs, not enough fossils have been found.

- **Remains of *Supersaurus*** found in Colorado, USA, suggest a dinosaur similar to *Diplodocus*, but perhaps even longer, at 35 m.

- ***Diplodocus hallorum* fossils** found in 1991 in the USA may belong to a 35-m-long sauropod.

- ***Ultrasaurus* fossils** found in South Korea suggest a dinosaur similar to *Brachiosaurus*, but smaller. However these fossils are fragmentary and some experts disagree with their naming.

- ***Argentinosaurus***, from South America, is known from a few fossils, mainly backbones, found in the early 1990s. It may have weighed up to 100 tonnes.

▼ *Seismosaurus was named in 1991, but further studies in the 2000s show it was probably one of the species of* Diplodocus, *now known as* Diplodocus hallorum *or* Diplodocus longus.

Long neck for reaching high leaves

Hips

- **All dinosaurs are classified** in one of two large groups, according to the design and shape of their hip bones.

- **One of these groups** is the Saurischia, meaning 'lizard-hipped'.

- **In a saurischian dinosaur**, the pubis bones (the lower front pair of rod-shaped bones in the pelvis) project down and forwards.

- **Almost all meat-eating dinosaurs** belonged to the Saurischia.

- **The biggest dinosaurs**, the plant-eating sauropods, also belonged to the Saurischia.

- **The second group** is the Ornithischia, meaning 'bird-hipped'.

- **In an ornithischian dinosaur**, the pubis bones project down and backwards, lying parallel with another pair, the ischium bones.

- **All dinosaurs** in the Ornithischia group, from small *Heterodontosaurus* to huge *Triceratops*, were plant-eaters.

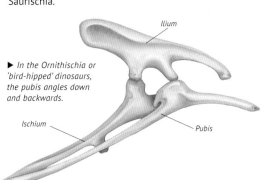

Ilium

▶ *In the Ornithischia or 'bird-hipped' dinosaurs, the pubis angles down and backwards.*

Ischium

Pubis

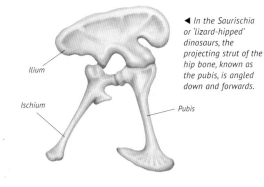

◀ *In the Saurischia or 'lizard-hipped' dinosaurs, the projecting strut of the hip bone, known as the pubis, is angled down and forwards.*

Ilium

Ischium

Pubis

Ostrich dinosaurs

- **'Ostrich dinosaurs'** is the common name of the ornithomimosaurs, because of their resemblance to today's largest bird – the flightless ostrich.

- **These dinosaurs** were tall and slim, with two long, powerful back legs for running fast.

- **The front limbs** were like strong arms, with grasping fingers tipped by sharp claws.

- **The eyes were large** and set high on the head.

- **Some ostrich dinosaurs** could reach speeds of up to 70 km/h when running.

- **Ostrich dinosaurs** lived towards the end of the Cretaceous Period, about 100–66 mya, in North America and Asia.

- **Fossils** of the ostrich dinosaur *Struthiomimus* from Alberta, Canada, suggest it was almost 4 m in total length and stood about 2 m tall – the same height as a modern ostrich.

- **The ostrich dinosaur** *Gallimimus* was almost 8 m long and stood nearly 3 m high.

- **Ostrich dinosaurs** probably ate seeds, fruits and other plant material, as well as small animals such as worms and lizards, which they may have grasped with their powerful clawed hands.

- **Other ostrich dinosaurs** included *Dromiceiomimus*, at 3–4 m long, and the slightly bigger *Ornithomimus*.

> **DID YOU KNOW?**
>
> Huge fossils of front limbs found in 1965, and named *Deinocheirus*, indicate a massive ostrich dinosaur 10 m long, 4 m high and weighing up to 5 tonnes.

◀ *Like all ostrich dinosaurs,* Ornithomimus *had a toothless mouth similar to the long, slim beak of a bird.*

Sauropelta

- *Sauropelta* **was a nodosaur** – a type of armoured dinosaur.

- **The name** *Sauropelta* means 'shielded reptile', from the many large, cone-like lumps of bone – some almost as big as dinner plates – on its head, neck, back and tail.

- **The larger lumps of bone** on *Sauropelta* were interspersed with smaller, fist-sized bony studs.

▼ *If attacked,* Sauropelta *probably crouched down low to protect its soft belly.*

- *Sauropelta* **was about** 5 m long, including the tail, and probably weighed almost 2 tonnes.

> **DID YOU KNOW?**
>
> *Sauropelta* lived 115–110 mya, in present-day Montana and Wyoming, USA.

- *Sauropelta* **had a row** of sharp spikes along each side of its body, from just behind the eyes to the tail. The spikes decreased in size towards the tail.

- **It may have** swung its head to jab enemies with its long neck spikes.

- **The armour** of *Sauropelta* was flexible, almost like lumps of metal set into thick leather, so the dinosaur could twist and turn, but was unable to run fast.

- **Pillar-like legs** supported *Sauropelta's* weight.

- **Using its beak-like mouth,** *Sauropelta* probably plucked its low-growing plant food.

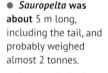

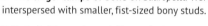

Fossil formation

● **Most of the information we know**, or guess, about dinosaurs and other ancient life comes from fossils.

● **Fossils are the remains** of once-living things that have been preserved in rocks and turned to stone, usually over millions of years.

● **Many kinds of living things** from prehistoric times have left fossils, including mammals, birds, lizards, fish and insects as well as plants such as ferns and trees.

● **Using a dinosaur as an example** of fossil formation, the flesh, guts and other soft parts of the dead body were probably eaten by scavengers, or rotted away, so these parts rarely formed fossils.

● **Fossils usually formed** when a dinosaur's remains were quickly covered by sediments such as sand, silt or mud, especially along the banks of a river or lake, or on the seashore.

● **The sand or other sediment** around a dinosaur's remains was gradually buried deeper by more sediment, squeezed under pressure, and cemented together into a solid mass of rock.

● **As the sediment turned** to rock, so did the dinosaur remains encased within it.

● **It is extremely rare** to find all the parts of a dinosaur arranged as they were in life.

● **Information about dinosaurs** comes not only from fossils of their body parts, but also from 'trace' fossils. These were not actual parts of their bodies, but other items or signs of their presence.

● **Trace fossils** include eggshells, footprints, marks made by claws and teeth, and coprolites – fossilized dinosaur droppings.

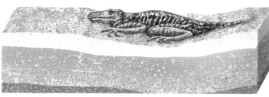

1 *Dinosaur dies and its soft parts are scavenged or rot away*

◀ *Fossil formation is a very long process, and extremely prone to chance and luck. Only a tiny fraction of dinosaurs that ever lived have left remains preserved by this process. Because of the way fossils are formed, dinosaurs that died in water or along banks and shores were most likely to become fossilized.*

2 *Sand, mud or other sediments cover the hard parts, such as the claws, teeth or bones*

3 *More layers build up as the minerals in the bones and other hard parts turn to rock*

DID YOU KNOW?

The hard parts of a dinosaur's body were the most likely parts to form fossils, especially teeth, bones, claws and horns.

4 *Erosion (wearing away) of upper rock layers exposes the fossil, which is now solid stone*

Stegosaurus

● *Stegosaurus* **was the largest** of the stegosaur group. Its fossils were found mainly in present-day Colorado, Utah and Wyoming, USA.

● **Like most of its group**, *Stegosaurus* lived towards the end of the Jurassic Period, about 155–150 mya.

● *Stegosaurus* **was about 8–9 m** long from nose to tail and probably weighed more than 4 tonnes.

● **Its most striking features** were the large, roughly diamond-shaped, leaf-shaped or triangular bony plates along its back.

● **The name** *Stegosaurus* means 'roof reptile'. This is because it was first thought that its bony plates lay flat on its back, overlapping like the tiles on a roof.

● **It is now thought** that the back plates stood upright in two long rows.

● **The plates may have been** for body temperature control, allowing the dinosaur to warm up quickly if it stood side-on to the sun's rays.

● **The back plates** may have been covered with brightly coloured skin, possibly to intimidate enemies – they were too flimsy to provide much protection.

● **Armed with large spikes**, *Stegosaurus* probably used its tail for swinging at enemies in self-defence.

DID YOU KNOW?

When Stegosaurus fossils were first unearthed in 1876–77, they were thought to be from a large sea turtle, with the back plates lying flat to form its protective shell.

◄ Stegosaurus' *short front limbs meant that it ate low-growing plants.*

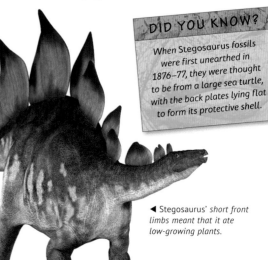

Carcharodontosaurus

● *Carcharodontosaurus* was one of the biggest meat-eating dinosaurs and land predators ever, rivalling *Tyrannosaurus* and similar types.

● **Some of its fossils** are very detailed, with the cavity inside its skull showing the shape of the dinosaur's brain, including the parts dealing with sight and smell.

● *Carcharodontosaurus'* teeth were about 20 cm long and triangular in shape.

● **The whole dinosaur** was about 13 m in total length and very powerfully built, with a weight of perhaps 10 tonnes.

▲ Carcharodontosaurus *was not the largest predator of its time and place, since the even greater* Spinosaurus *roamed the same region some 100 mya.*

DID YOU KNOW?

Carcharodontosaurus was named 'ragged tooth reptile' after the great white shark, Carcharodon carcharias, due to similar jagged serrations along its tooth edges.

● **Putting together** several specimen finds shows the skull was up to 1.7 m long.

● *Carcharodontosaurus* lived in North Africa about 100–95 mya, when the region had rivers, lakes, swamps and forests.

● **Its first fossils were dug up** in 1925, but more, larger specimens unearthed in the 1990s showed its true size.

● *Carcharodontosaurus* **belonged** to the group known as Carnosauria, which used to include all kinds of big meat-eaters but has recently been restricted to just a few kinds.

● **A cousin of** *Carcharodontosaurus* may have been *Allosaurus* from North America, which lived about 50 million years before and was almost as large.

Claws

● **Like reptiles today**, dinosaurs had claws or similar hard structures at the ends of their digits (fingers and toes).

● **Dinosaur claws** were probably made from keratin – the same hard substance that formed their horns, and from which our own fingernails and toenails are made.

● **Claw shapes and sizes** relative to body size varied greatly between dinosaurs.

● **In many meat-eating dinosaurs** that ran on two back legs, the claws on the fingers were long and sharp, similar to a cat's claws.

● **A small, meat-eating dinosaur** such as *Troodon* probably used its finger claws for grabbing small mammals and lizards, and for scrabbling in the soil for insects and worms.

● **Larger meat-eating dinosaurs** such as *Allosaurus* may have used their hand claws to hold and slash their prey.

● **Huge plant-eating sauropods** such as *Diplodocus* had claws on its elephant-like feet that resembled nails or hooves.

● **Many dinosaurs** had five-clawed digits on their feet, but some, such as *Tyrannosaurus*, had only three.

● **The largest animal claws** belonged to the 'scythe lizards' or therizinosaur dinosaurs – some were more than one metre long.

● ***Deinonychus* had long claws** on its hands and feet that it used to slash at prey. Its name means 'terrible claw' and it lived in the Mid-Cretaceous Period.

▼ *The fingers and claws of* Deinonychus *were especially long and strong.*

Asia

● **Hundreds of different kinds** of dinosaurs have been discovered on the continent of Asia.

● **Remains of *Titanosaurus***, the huge plant-eating sauropod, were uncovered near Umrer, in India.

● **It lived** about 70 mya, and was similar in shape to its cousin of the same time, *Saltasaurus*, from South America.

● ***Titanosaurus* was about** 12 m long and weighed 10–15 tonnes.

● **Fossils of the sauropod** *Barapasaurus* were found in India and described and named in 1975.

● ***Barapasaurus* was 14 m long** and probably weighed more than 10 tonnes.

● **It is one of the first** sauropods known from anywhere in the world, living around 190–180 mya.

● **Fossils of *Dravidosaurus***, once thought to belong to the stegosaur group, were found near Tiruchirapalli in southern India. Further studies suggest they are actually from a type of sea reptile.

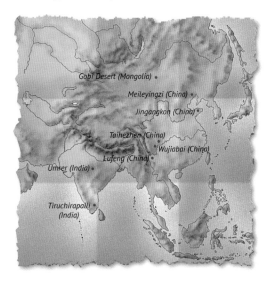

Gobi Desert (Mongolia) •

Meileyingzi (China) •

Jingangkou (China) •

Taihezhen (China) •

Wujiabai (China) •

Lufeng (China) •

Umrer (India) •

Tiruchirapalli • (India)

▶ *Dinosaur fossil finds span the vast continent of Asia.*

DID YOU KNOW?

In Asia, most of the dinosaur fossils that have been found so far have been located in the Gobi Desert in Central Asia, and in present-day China. Some were also found in present-day India.

Coelophysis

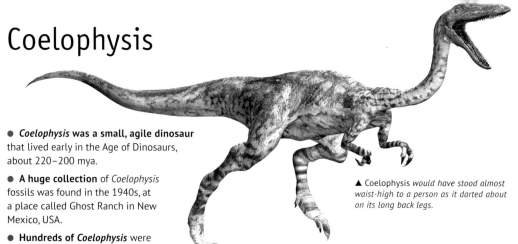

● *Coelophysis* **was a small, agile dinosaur** that lived early in the Age of Dinosaurs, about 220–200 mya.

● **A huge collection** of *Coelophysis* fossils was found in the 1940s, at a place called Ghost Ranch in New Mexico, USA.

● **Hundreds of** *Coelophysis* were preserved together at Ghost Ranch – possibly a herd that drowned in a flood.

● *Coelophysis* **was almost 3 m** in total length. Its slim, lightweight build meant that it probably weighed only 15–25 kg.

● *Coelophysis* **belonged** to the group of mostly meat-eating dinosaurs known as theropods.

● **It probably ate** small animals such as insects, worms and lizards.

▲ Coelophysis *would have stood almost waist-high to a person as it darted about on its long back legs.*

● **Long, powerful back legs** allowed *Coelophysis* to run very fast.

● **The front limbs** were like arms, each with a hand bearing three large, strong, sharp-clawed fingers to grab prey, and one small, non-functional finger.

● **The bird-like skull** was filled with small, sharp teeth.

● *Coelophysis* **means** 'hollow form'. It was so-named because some of its bones were hollow, like the bones of birds, making it lightly built.

Dinosaur fossil hunters

● **Many dinosaurs** were found in the USA in the 1870s–90s by Othniel Charles Marsh and Edward Drinker Cope.

● **Marsh and Cope** were great rivals, each one trying to find bigger, better and more dinosaur fossils than the other.

● **Between 1877 and 1897**, Cope and Marsh found and described about 130 new kinds of dinosaurs.

● **Joseph Tyrrell** discovered fossils of *Albertosaurus* in 1884, in what became a very famous dinosaur region, the Red Deer River area of Alberta, Canada.

● **Lawrence Lambe** found many North American dinosaur fossils, such as *Centrosaurus* in 1904.

● **German fossil experts** Werner Janensch and Edwin Hennig led expeditions to east Africa in 1908–12, and discovered *Giraffatitan* and *Kentrosaurus*.

● **From 1933**, Yang Zhong-jiang (also called CC Young) led many fossil hunting expeditions in China.

● **José Bonaparte** from Argentina has found many fossils in that region, including *Carnotaurus* in 1985.

● **Paul Sereno** from the University of Chicago has discovered and named huge dinosaurs and crocodiles from South America and North Africa.

Othniel Charles Marsh
(1831–99)

Edward Drinker Cope
(1840–97)

◀ Othniel Charles Marsh and Edward Drinker Cope had a rivalry between them that came to be known as the 'Bone Wars'. Allegedly, this began when Marsh pointed out a mistake that Cope had made with the reconstruction of a plesiosaur skeleton. Cope never forgave him, but the rift led to the discovery of almost 140 new dinosaur species.

Estimating size

● **The biggest dinosaurs** were the sauropods such as *Giraffatitan*, *Brachiosaurus* and *Argentinosaurus* – but working out how heavy they were when they were alive is very difficult.

● **Giraffatitan is known** from many remains, including almost complete skeletons, so its length is measured accurately – 22 m.

● **A dinosaur's weight** can be estimated from a model of its skeleton, which is 'fleshed out' with clay.

● **The clay represents** muscles, guts and skin, which are based on those of similar reptiles, such as crocodiles, for comparison.

● **Alternatively**, this can be done using a virtual model on a computer. Results have estimated weights of between 20 and 40 tonnes for *Giraffatitan*.

● **The size of the clay model** is estimated by immersing it in water to find its volume.

● **The volume of the model** is scaled up to find the volume of the real dinosaur when it was alive.

● **The sauropod *Apatosaurus*** is now well known from about 12 skeletons, which between them have almost every bone in its body.

● **Experts have 'fleshed out'** the skeleton of *Apatosaurus* by different amounts, so estimates of its weight vary from 15 tonnes to more than 40 tonnes.

● **The length of *Apatosaurus*** is known accurately to have been 21 m in total.

▼ *African* Giraffatitan *had very long front legs, like its North American cousin* Brachiosaurus.

Long neck allowed head to browse widely

DID YOU KNOW?

The weights and volumes of reptiles alive today are used to calculate the probable weight of a dinosaur when it was alive.

Heterodontosaurus

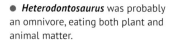
● **Heterodontosaurus lived** about 200–195 mya, at the beginning of the Jurassic Period.

● **A very small dinosaur** at only one metre in length (about as long as a large dog), Heterodontosaurus would have stood knee-high to a human.

● **Probably standing partly upright** on its longer back legs, Heterodontosaurus would have been a fast runner.

● **Fossils of Heterodontosaurus** come from Lesotho in southern Africa and Cape Province in South Africa.

● **Most dinosaurs had teeth** of only one shape in their jaws, but Heterodontosaurus had three types of teeth.

● **The front teeth** were small, sharp and found only in the upper jaw. They bit against the horny, beak-like lower front of the mouth.

● **The four middle teeth** of Heterodontosaurus were long and curved, similar to the tusks of a wild boar, and may have been used for fighting rivals or in self-defence.

● **The back teeth** were long and had sharp tops, or cusps, for chewing.

● **Heterodontosaurus** was probably an omnivore, eating both plant and animal matter.

▼ *Small and slim,* Heterodontosaurus *looked similar to meat-eaters such as* Compsognathus.

Speed

● **The fastest dinosaurs** had long, slim, muscular legs and small, lightweight bodies.

● **Ostrich dinosaurs** were probably the speediest, perhaps attaining the same top speed as today's ostrich – 70 km/h.

● **The main leg muscles** of the ostrich dinosaur Struthiomimus were in its hips and thighs.

● **The hip and leg design** of ostrich dinosaurs meant they could swing their limbs to and fro quickly, like those of a modern racehorse.

● **Large, powerful, plant-eating dinosaurs,** such as the duckbill Edmontosaurus, may have pounded along on their huge back legs at 40 km/h.

● **Plant-eaters** such as Iguanodon and Muttaburrasaurus may have trotted along at 10–12 km/h for many hours.

● **Some experts** once suggested that the great meat-eater Tyrannosaurus may have been able to run at 50 km/h.

● **Other experts think** Tyrannosaurus was a relatively slow runner at 20 km/h.

● **The slowest dinosaurs** were giant sauropods such as Brachiosaurus, which probably plodded at 4–6 km/h (about human walking speed).

● **The fastest land animal today,** the cheetah, would beat any dinosaur with its maximum burst of speed of more than 100 km/h.

◀ *In 2007, computer predictions based on data taken from fossils suggested that the top speed of* Tyrannosaurus *may have been about 28 km/h.*

Allosaurus

● **A big meat-eater**, *Allosaurus* was almost the same size as *Tyrannosaurus*.

● **It lived** about 155–150 mya, during the Late Jurassic Period.

● *Allosaurus* **was 11–12 m** in total length and its weight is variously estimated between 1.5 and 4 tonnes.

● **The head** was almost one metre in length, but its skull was light, with large gaps, or 'windows', that would have been covered by muscle and skin.

● **Not only could** *Allosaurus* open its jaws in a huge gape, it could also flex them so that the whole mouth became wider, for an even bigger bite.

● **Most** *Allosaurus* **fossils** come from the states in the American Midwest, especially Utah, Colorado and Wyoming.

● *Allosaurus* **may have hunted** giant sauropod dinosaurs such as *Diplodocus*, *Camarasaurus* and *Brachiosaurus*.

◄ *Allosaurus almost rivalled Tyrannosaurus in size, but lived 90 million years earlier.*

DID YOU KNOW?

The remains of 60 Allosaurus were found in the Cleveland-Lloyd Dinosaur Quarry, Utah, USA.

● **Fossils similar to** *Allosaurus* were identified in Europe and Africa, and a smaller 'dwarf' version was found in Australia.

Armour

● **Many kinds of dinosaurs** had protective 'armour'.

● **Some armour** took the form of bony plates, or osteoderms, embedded in the skin.

● **A dinosaur with armour** might weigh twice as much as a same-sized dinosaur without armour.

● **Armoured dinosaurs** are divided into two main groups – the ankylosaurs and the nodosaurs.

● **The large sauropod** *Saltasaurus*, unusual for its group, had a kind of armour in the form of hundreds of small, bony lumps packed together in the skin of its back.

● **On its back**, *Saltasaurus* also had about 50 larger pieces of bone, each one the size of a human hand.

● *Saltasaurus* **is named** after the Salta region of Argentina, where its fossils were found. Its fossils have also been found in Uruguay, South America.

● *Saltasaurus* **was 12 m long** and weighed about 6–8 tonnes.

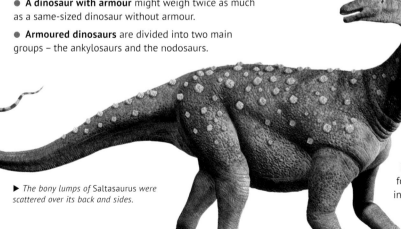

▶ *The bony lumps of* Saltasaurus *were scattered over its back and sides.*

Carnotaurus

● **The big, powerful, meat-eating** *Carnotaurus* belongs to the theropod dinosaur group. It lived about 75–70 mya.

● *Carnotaurus* **fossils** come mainly from the Chubut region of Argentina, South America.

● **A medium-sized dinosaur,** *Carnotaurus* was about 8–9 m in total length and weighed over one tonne.

● **The skull was relatively tall** from top to bottom and short from front to back, compared to other meat-eaters such as *Allosaurus* and *Tyrannosaurus*. This gave *Carnotaurus* a snub-snouted appearance.

● **The name** *Carnotaurus* means 'meat-eating bull', referring partly to its bull-like face.

● *Carnotaurus* **had** two cone-shaped bony crests, or 'horns', one above each eye.

● **Rows of extra-large scales,** like small lumps, ran along *Carnotaurus* from head to tail.

● **Like** *Tyrannosaurus*, *Carnotaurus* had small front limbs that could not reach its mouth and may have had no use.

● *Carnotaurus* **probably ate** plant-eating dinosaurs such as *Chubutisaurus*, although its teeth and jaws were not especially big or strong.

◀ *The first, and so far only, fossil remains of* Carnotaurus *were discovered in 1984 and the dinosaur was named in 1985. It had small pebble-like scales embedded in its skin.*

Ankylosaurs

● **Ankylosaurs had** a protective armour of bony plates.

● **Unlike the armoured nodosaurs,** ankylosaurs had a large lump of bone at the end of their tail, which they used as a hammer or club.

◀ *The tail club of* Euoplocephalus *was made from pieces of bone that had fused (stuck) together.*

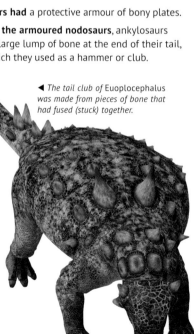

● **One of the best known ankylosaurs,** from the preserved remains of about 40 individuals, is *Euoplocephalus*.

● **The hefty** *Euoplocephalus* was about 6 m long and weighed 2 tonnes or more.

● **It lived** about 76–75 mya in Alberta, Canada, Montana, USA and other places.

● *Euoplocephalus* **had bony shields** on its head and body, and even had bony eyelids. Blunt spikes ran along its back.

● **Specimens of** *Euoplocephalus* are usually found singly, so it probably didn't live in herds.

● **The ankylosaur** *Pinacosaurus* had bony nodules like chainmail armour in its skin, and rows of blunt spikes from neck to tail.

● **Ankylosaurs had small,** weak teeth, and probably ate soft, low-growing ferns and horsetails.

Herbivores

● **Hundreds of kinds of dinosaurs** were herbivores, or plant-eaters. As time passed, the plants available for them to eat evolved, and new dinosaurs became adapted to them.

● **Early in the Age of Dinosaurs**, during the Triassic Period, the main plants for dinosaurs to eat were conifer trees, ginkgoes, cycads, ferns, horsetails and club mosses.

● **A few cycads** are still found today. They resemble palm trees, with umbrella-like crowns of long green fronds on top of tall, unbranched, trunk-like stems.

● **In the Triassic Period**, only prosauropod dinosaurs were big enough or had necks long enough to reach tall cycad fronds or ginkgo leaves.

● **In the Jurassic Period**, tall conifers such as redwoods and araucarias or 'monkey puzzle' trees became common.

● **The huge, long-necked sauropods** of the Jurassic Period may have been able to reach high into tall conifer trees to rake off their needles.

● **In the Middle Cretaceous Period**, a new type of plant food appeared – the flowering plants.

● **By the end of the Cretaceous Period** there were many flowering trees and shrubs, such as magnolias, maples and walnuts.

● **These new plants meant** that many new kinds of animals, including new herbivorous dinosaurs, evolved to eat them.

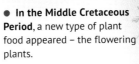

▶ *During the warm, damp Jurassic Period, plants grew in most areas, covering land that previously had been barren. Massive plant-eaters such as* Barosaurus *thrived on the fronds, needles and leaves of towering tree ferns, ginkgoes and conifers.*

Barosaurus *was 26 m long and weighed 25–30 tonnes*

DID YOU KNOW?

To maintain their huge bodies, sauropods probably had to eat for 20 hours a day.

Triceratops

● **Many fossil remains** of *Triceratops* have been found. It is one of the most-studied and best known dinosaurs, and lived at the very end of the Age of Dinosaurs, 68–66 mya.

● *Triceratops* **was the largest** of the plant-eating ceratopsians, or 'horn-faced' dinosaurs.

● **Fossils of more than** 100 *Triceratops* have been discovered in North America, though no truly complete skeletons.

● *Triceratops* **was about 9 m long** and weighed up to 10 tonnes – as big as the largest elephants of today.

● **As well as a short nose horn** and two one-metre eyebrow horns, *Triceratops* also had a wide, sweeping frill that covered its neck like a curved plate.

● **The neck frill** may have been an anchor for the dinosaur's powerful chewing muscles.

● **Acting as a shield**, the bony neck frill may have protected *Triceratops* as it faced predators head-on.

● **The neck frill** may also have been brightly coloured to impress rivals or enemies – or even potential mates.

● **The beak-like front** of *Triceratops*' mouth was toothless, but it had sharp teeth for chewing in its cheeks.

▶ *The beak, head and neck frill of* Triceratops *made up almost a quarter of its length.*

Earliest dinosaurs

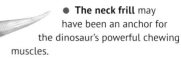

DID YOU KNOW?

Eoraptor and Herrerasaurus hunted small animals such as lizards, insects and lizard-like reptiles.

● **The first dinosaurs** had appeared by about 230 mya, in the Middle Triassic Period.

● **These dinosaurs** were small-to-medium meat-eaters with sharp teeth and claws. They ran quickly on their two longer, stronger back legs.

● **Fossils of** *Herrerasaurus* date from 230 mya and were found near San Juan in Argentina, South America.

● *Herrerasaurus* **was about** 3–5 m in total length, and probably weighed some 200–250 kg.

● **Perhaps slightly earlier**, about 231 mya, and in the same place as *Herrerasaurus*, there lived a similar-shaped dinosaur named *Eoraptor*, which was only 1–1.5 m long and weighed 10 kg.

● **The name** *Eoraptor* means 'dawn plunderer' or 'early thief'.

● *Staurikosaurus* was a meat-eater similar to *Herrerasaurus*. It is known to have lived around 225 mya, in present-day Brazil, South America.

● *Procompsognathus* was another early meat-eater. It lived 210 mya in the Late Triassic Period in Germany.

● *Pisanosaurus* lived in Argentina in the Late Triassic Period, and was only one metre long. It may have been a plant-eater.

▼ *The very early meat-eater* Herrerasaurus *dates to about 230 mya. The discovery of an almost complete skeleton in 1988 allowed a good reconstruction.*

Smallest dinosaurs

● **One of the smallest** dinosaurs was *Compsognathus*, which lived during the Late Jurassic Period, 155–150 mya.

● **Its fossils** come from Europe, especially southern Germany and southeastern France.

● *Compsognathus* **was probably** just over one metre in length and may have weighed less than 3 kg.

● **It had small, sharp, curved teeth** and it probably darted through the undergrowth after insects, spiders, worms and similar small prey.

● **Discovered in 2004** in China, *Mei* was just 50 cm long.

● **It is not only one** of the smallest dinosaurs ever found, it also has the shortest dinosaur name of just three letters.

● *Mei* **was fossilized** in a bird-like position with its head bent to one side under its front limb or 'arm', just like a bird tucks its head under its wing when asleep.

● **The smallest fossil dinosaur specimens** found to date are of *Mussaurus*, which means 'mouse reptile'.

● **These fossils** were of babies, just 20 cm long, newly hatched from eggs.

● **The babies** would have grown into adults measuring 3 m in length.

● **Two other small dinosaurs** that have been found were the 60-cm-long *Caenagnathasia* and the 40-cm-long *Parvicursor*.

◀ *The tiny dinosaur* Mei. *Its full name,* Mei long, *means 'soundly sleeping dragon'.*

Fruitadens

● *Fruitadens* **is named** not after a fruit-eating diet, but the place where its fossils were dug up, Fruita in Colorado, USA.

● **Living about 150–145 mya**, in the Late Jurassic Period, *Fruitadens* was one of the last of the small dinosaur group known as heterodontosaurs.

● **Fossil parts** of about four or possibly five individuals are known, together representing jaws, backbones and some front and rear limb bones.

● **These fossils were collected** from the 1970s but only assembled and described in 2010.

● **Like other heterodontosaurs**, *Fruitadens* had two longer teeth called canines, one on either side near the front of the lower jaw.

● *Fruitadens* **was very small** and lightly built, less than 80 cm long and weighing less than one kilogram.

● **It had long but well-muscled legs** and probably relied on speed and agility for survival.

● *Fruitadens* **would dart on its back legs** into the undergrowth or among rocks to escape from predators.

● *Fruitadens* **was probably an omnivore**, eating any small items such as leaves, seeds, tubers, insects, eggs and worms.

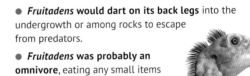

◀ Fruitadens *was one of the smallest of all known non-bird dinosaurs.*

Africa

- **The first major discoveries** of dinosaur fossils in Africa were made in 1907, at Tendaguru, in present-day Tanzania.

- **These included** *Giraffatitan*, *Dicraeosaurus*, and the stegosaur-like *Kentrosaurus*.

- **Remains of *Cetiosaurus*** have been found in Morocco, north Africa.

- ***Nigersaurus***, a 9-m, 10-tonne plant-eater, is known from fossils found in Niger. It had huge numbers of teeth, more than 500 at any one time.

- **Fossils of *Spinosaurus***, the largest meat-eating dinosaur, come from Morocco and Egypt.

- **The sail-backed *Ouranosaurus*** is known from remains found in Niger.

- **Many sauropod fossils** have been uncovered at African sites, including *Tornieri* from Tanzania, and *Vulcanodon* in Zimbabwe.

- **During the 1908–12** fossil-hunting expedition to Tendaguru, more than 250 tonnes of fossil bones and rocks from dinosaurs such as *Giraffatitan* were carried 65 km to the nearest port, for transport to Germany.

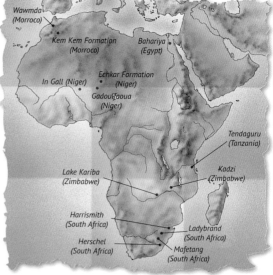

Wawmda (Morroco)
Kem Kem Formation (Morroco)
Bahariya (Egypt)
In Gall (Niger)
Echkar Formation (Niger)
Gadoufaoua (Niger)
Tendaguru (Tanzania)
Lake Kariba (Zimbabwe)
Kadzi (Zimbabwe)
Harrismith (South Africa)
Ladybrand (South Africa)
Herschel (South Africa)
Mafetang (South Africa)

▲ *In Africa, as elsewhere, fossils are easier to find in places with bare, rocky soils, such as the Sahara region in the north.*

- **Remains of *Massospondylus***, a plant-eating prosauropod, have been extracted from several sites in southern Africa.

- **Fossils named as *Gyposaurus*** have been found in Orange Free State, South Africa.

Mamenchisaurus

▲ *The joints between the fossil bones of Mamenchisaurus' neck show that it was not very flexible.*

- **At up to 15 m**, *Mamenchisaurus* had one of the longest necks of any dinosaur. The neck had up to 19 vertebrae, or neckbones – more than almost any other dinosaur.

- **The remains of *Mamenchisaurus*** were found in China and the dinosaur is named after the place where its fossils were discovered – Mamen Stream.

- **Other sauropod dinosaurs** found in the same region include *Euhelopus* and *Omeisaurus*.

- ***Mamenchisaurus* may have stretched** out its neck to crop leaves, or – less likely – may have lived in swamps and eaten water plants.

- **A massive plant-eating dinosaur**, *Mamenchisaurus* was similar in appearance to *Diplodocus*.

- **It lived during** the late Jurassic Period, from 160–145 mya.

- **This huge dinosaur** measured about 30 m from nose to tail. Its weight has been estimated at 20–35 tonnes.

Herds

● **When fossils of many individuals** of the same dinosaur type are found together, there are various possible causes.

● **One reason is because** their bodies were swept to the same place by a flood, although they may have originally been living in different places.

● **The dinosaurs may have died** in the same place if they had lived there as a group or herd.

● **There is much evidence** that various dinosaur types lived in groups or herds, examples being *Diplodocus*, *Triceratops* and *Iguanodon*.

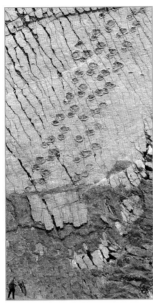

▲ *Dinosaur footprints were sometimes filled with sand or pebbles, which later hardened into rock, preserving them. A mixed-age herd would have left similar footprints of different sizes.*

● **Many fossil footprints** found together heading the same way also suggest that some dinosaurs lived in herds.

● **Some fossil groups** include dinosaurs of different ages, from babies through to youngsters and adults.

● **Footprints of a plant-eating dinosaur** have been found with the prints of a meat-eater to one side of them – perhaps evidence of a hunter pursuing its victim.

● **Prints all pointing** in the same direction indicate a herd travelling together to the same place.

● **Sometimes larger footprints** are found to the sides of smaller ones, possibly indicating that adults guarded their young between them.

● **Many jumbled prints** in what was once mud suggests a group of dinosaurs came to drink at a riverbank or lakeside.

Spinosaurus

● **No other meat-eating dinosaur**, or any other land-based carnivore found so far, is as big as *Spinosaurus*.

● **This immense predator** has been known for over 100 years, but new finds in the 1990s and 2000s showed that it was the new record-holder.

● **The original *Spinosaurus* fossils** came from Egypt in 1912. They were named in 1915 by German palaeontologist Ernst von Stromer.

● **However, those fossils**, kept in Munich Museum, Germany, were destroyed in 1944 by a World War II bombing raid.

● **In 1996**, 1998, 2000, 2002 and 2005, more fossils in North Africa were uncovered and identified as *Spinosaurus*.

● **This giant was probably** more than 14 m long and weighed over 9 tonnes, perhaps as much as 15 tonnes.

● **It had tall rods** of bone along its back called neural spines, that probably held up a sail-like area of skin, or perhaps a hump of flesh.

● ***Spinosaurus* and other finds** led to a new group of huge hunting dinosaurs being identified, the spinosaurs, which also included *Giganotosaurus*, *Carcharodontosaurus*, *Baryonyx*, *Oxalaia* and *Suchomimus*.

◄ *The skull and jaws of* Spinosaurus *were long and low, similar in shape to a crocodile and alligator and also to the dinosaur* Baryonyx.

Reconstructions

● **No complete fossilized dinosaur**, with its skin, muscles, guts and other soft body parts, has ever been found.

● **Most dinosaurs are reconstructed** from the fossils of their teeth, bones, horns and claws.

● **The vast majority** are known from only a few fossil parts, such as several fragments of bones.

● **Fossil parts** of other, similar dinosaurs are often used in reconstructions to 'fill in' missing bones, teeth, and even missing heads, limbs or tails.

● **Soft body parts** from modern reptiles, such as lizards, are used as a guide for the reconstruction of a dinosaur's muscles and guts.

● **On rare occasions**, remains are found of a dinosaur body that dried out rapidly so that quite a few parts were preserved as mummified fossils.

● **One of the best known** of the best-preserved dinosaur fossils is of *Brachylophosaurus*, a 9-m hadrosaur (duckbill) from about 75 mya.

▲ *This fossil skeleton of an ankylosaur,* Euoplocephalus, *has been restored with soft parts inside, then muscles and finally the skin covering with scales and horns.*

● **Nicknamed 'Elvis'**, this amazing fossil was discovered in 1994 by fossil hunter Nate Murphy in Montana, USA.

● **In 2000 Murphy** found an even better *Brachylophosaurus*, which was called 'Leonardo'.

Dinosaur National Monument

● **Dinosaur National Monument** is a protected area in the southwest of America, spanning the border between the states of Colorado and Utah.

● **It was one of the first sites** in the world to be given special protection for having valuable fossils, in 1915.

● **Dinosaur National Monument today** covers more than 85,000 hectares.

▼ *A field worker carefully excavates fossil bones on a sloping rock layer at Dinosaur National Monument.*

● **The rocks** at Dinosaur National Monument were originally the banks and bed of a river, where animal bodies were washed during floods, and preserved.

● **The area contains** not only the fossil-rich Dinosaur Quarry, but also surrounding beautiful areas of the Uinta Mountains and the Yampa and Green Rivers.

● **Today's harsh climate** at the Dinosaur National Monument area means many rocks are bare and wear away, or erode, to reveal thousands of fossils.

● **Remains of more than 20 kinds** of dinosaurs and similar creatures have been found here, including the meat-eaters *Allosaurus* and *Ceratosaurus*.

● **There are also fossils** of the 'ABCD' plant-eating sauropods *Apatosaurus*, *Barosaurus*, *Camarasaurus* and *Diplodocus*, and plate-backed *Stegosaurus*.

● **Dinosaur National Monument** receives up to half a million visitors each year.

● **At Dinosaur Wall** in the Quarry Visitor Center, people can see jumbled fossil bones and other remains sticking out of the rocks.

Male and female

- **In dinosaur fossils**, the shapes of the hip bones and head crests can indicate if the creatures were male or female.

- **Head crest fossils** of different sizes and proportions belonging to the hadrosaur (duckbilled dinosaur) *Lambeosaurus* have been found.

- **Some *Lambeosaurus*** had short, rounded main crests with small, spike-like spurs pointing up and back.

- **Other *Lambeosaurus*** had a large, angular main crest with a large spur pointing up and back.

- **The head crest differences** in *Lambeosaurus* fossils may indicate that males and females looked different.

- **Remains of the hadrosaur** *Corythosaurus* show two main sizes of head crest, perhaps one belonging to females and the other to males.

- **New studies** in the variations of head crests led to about ten different species of these dinosaurs being reclassified as just two species of *Corythosaurus*.

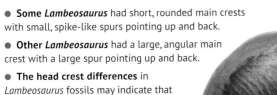

◀ *Male and female* Lambeosaurus *may have had different-shaped head crests, with this individual being male. The crests may also have become relatively larger compared to body size as the dinosaurs grew.*

Deinonychus

- ***Deinonychus* is one of** the best known raptors.

- **It thrived** in the Middle Cretaceous Period, about 115–105 mya.

- **Fossils of *Deinonychus*** come from the American Midwest, mainly from Montana and Wyoming.

- ***Deinonychus* was about 3–3.5 m long** from nose to tail and weighed 60–70 kg, about the same as an adult human.

- **When remains of *Deinonychus*** were dug up and studied in the 1960s, they exploded the myth that dinosaurs were slow, small-brained and stupid.

- **Powerful, speedy and agile,** *Deinonychus* may have hunted in packs, like today's lions and wolves.

- **It had large hands** with three powerful fingers, each tipped with a dangerous sharp claw.

◀ *There is no direct fossil evidence for feathers in* Deinonychus, *but remains of many other raptor-type dinosaurs show feathers of various kinds, not for flight, but perhaps for insulation or display.*

- ***Deinonychus* also had** the massive, scythe-like claw, typical of the raptor group, on each second toe.

- **The tail was stiff** and could not be swished.

- ***Deinonychus* and other similar dromaeosaurs,** such as *Velociraptor*, were the basis for the cunning and terrifying raptors of the *Jurassic Park* films.

Stegosaurs

● **Plant-eating dinosaurs** that mostly lived around 160–140 mya, stegosaurs are named after the best known of their group, *Stegosaurus*.

● **They are often called** 'plated dinosaurs', from the large, flat plates or slabs of bone on their backs.

● **Stegosaurs probably** first appeared in eastern Asia, then spread to other continents, especially North America and Africa.

● *Kentrosaurus* **was** a 5-m-long stegosaur and weighed an estimated one tonne. Its name means 'spiky reptile'. It lived about 155–150 mya in East Africa.

● **Most stegosaurs lacked teeth** at the front of the mouth, but had horny beaks, like those of birds, for snipping off leaves. They chewed food with small, ridged cheek teeth.

▶ *The back plates of Kentrosaurus were taller and narrower than those of Stegosaurus.*

DID YOU KNOW?

In 2006, fossils of *Stegosaurus* were identified in Portugal, which is the first evidence that this dinosaur lived in Europe.

Noses

● **Dinosaurs breathed** through their mouths and/or noses, like many other creatures today.

● **Fossil dinosaur skulls** show that there were two nose openings, called nares, in the bone.

● **The nasal openings**, or nares, led to nasal chambers inside the skull, where the smell organs were located.

● **Some meat-eaters**, especially carnosaurs such as *Allosaurus* and *Tyrannosaurus*, had very large nasal chambers and probably had an excellent sense of smell.

● **In most dinosaurs**, the nasal openings were at the front of the snout, just above the upper jaw.

● **In some dinosaurs**, especially sauropods such as *Mamenchisaurus* and *Brachiosaurus*, the nasal openings were higher on the skull, between the eyes.

● **Fossils show** that air passages led backwards from the nasal chambers into the head for breathing.

● **The nasal openings** led to external openings, or nostrils, in the skin.

● **New evidence from modern animals** suggests that a dinosaur's nostrils would have been lower down than the nares, towards the front of the snout.

Nares

DID YOU KNOW?

In hadrosaurs, the nasal passages inside the bony head crests were more than one metre long.

▶ *The nares (nasal openings) at the snout tip of Tyrannosaurus were especially large.*

Nests

● **There are hundreds** of discoveries of fossil dinosaur eggs and nests, found with the parent dinosaurs.

● **Eggs and nests** of the plant-eater *Protoceratops*, an early kind of horned dinosaur, were found in 2011.

● **Some of the nests** once thought to be of *Protoceratops* are now believed to belong to *Oviraptor*.

● **Many of these nests** were found in a small area, showing that these dinosaurs bred in colonies.

● **The nests were shallow**, bowl-shaped pits about one metre across, scraped in the earth.

● **The eggs were probably covered** with earth and incubated by the heat of the sun.

● **New nests had been made** on top of old ones, showing that the colony was used year after year.

● **Nests and eggs** of the plant-eater *Orodromeus* have been found in Montana, USA.

● **In each nest**, about 20 *Orodromeus* eggs were neatly arranged in a spiral, starting with one in the centre and working outwards.

▼ *Various clues from fossil evidence show that the hadrosaur* Maiasaura *may have brought food back to its newly hatched young in the nest. Whether one parent or both did is not known.*

DID YOU KNOW?
Some preserved nests of Maiasaura babies contain traces of fossil buds and leaves – perhaps food brought to them by a parent.

Eggs

● **Fossil finds since the 1970s** show that some dinosaurs may have looked after their young.

● **Fossils of the small** parrot-beaked dinosaur *Psittacosaurus* suggest one adult may have guided and guarded many young.

● **These fossils were probably preserved** when the adult and young sheltered in a cave that collapsed on them all.

● **Many fossils** of adult *Maiasaura* have been found, together with its nests, eggs and hatchlings (newly hatched young).

● **Fossils of *Maiasaura*** come mainly from Montana, USA, and are about 75 million years old. The main fossil area is nicknamed 'Egg Mountain'.

● **There are remains** of more than 100 *Maiasaura* specimens of different ages.

● **The teeth of *Maiasaura*** babies found in the nest are slightly worn, suggesting that they had eaten food.

● **The leg bones and joints** of the *Maiasaura* babies were not quite fully formed, showing that they were not yet able to move about to gather their own food.

● **Evidence from the *Maiasaura*** nesting sites shows the nests were about 7 m apart, which would just allow room for a 9-m adult. Each nest had up to 40 eggs laid in spiral pattern.

DID YOU KNOW?
The first fossilized dinosaur eggs to be scientifically described were found in Mongolia in the 1920s by a US-led team of palaeontologists.

● **The name *Maiasaura*** means 'good mother reptile' and was given in 1979 by US palaeontologists John 'Jack' Horner and Robert Makela.

▼ *A cast of a baby* Maiasaura *duckbill dinosaur, among the fossil remains of a nest site. These fossils were discovered in Montana, USA.*

Diplodocus

- **A huge plant-eating sauropod,** *Diplodocus* lived during the Late Jurassic Period, about 155–145 mya.
- **The first discovery** of *Diplodocus* fossils was in 1877, near Canyon City, Colorado, USA.
- **The main fossils** were found in the USA, in Colorado, Utah and Wyoming.
- **At an incredible 27 m** or more in length, *Diplodocus* is one of the longest dinosaurs known. Some species may have reached 33 m.

- ***Diplodocus* probably** swung its tiny head on its enormous neck to reach fronds and foliage in the trees.
- **Its teeth were slim rods** that formed a comb-like fringe around the front of its mouth.
- ***Diplodocus* may have used** its teeth to strip leaves from twigs and swallow them without chewing.
- **Its nostrils** were once thought to be positioned almost above its eyes. Recent evidence shows they were probably lower down, halfway between the eyes and snout tip.

▼ Diplodocus *was long but light for a sauropod, weighing about 10–25 tonnes.*

Dinosaur names 2

- **More than 150 types** of dinosaur have been named after the people who first discovered their fossils, dug them up, or reconstructed the dinosaur.
- **The large duckbill (hadrosaur)** *Lambeosaurus* was named after Canadian fossil expert Lawrence Lambe.
- **Lambe worked mainly** during the early 1900s, and named one of his finds *Stephanosaurus*.
- **In the 1920s,** *Stephanosaurus* was renamed, along with *Didanodon*, as *Lambeosaurus*, in honour of Lambe's work.
- **The full name** of the 'heavy claw' meat-eater *Baryonyx* is *Baryonyx walkeri*, after Bill Walker, the discoverer of its massive claw.
- **Part-time fossil hunter** Bill Walker found the 30-cm claw in a clay pit quarry in Surrey, England, in 1983.
- **Some dinosaur names** are quite technical, such as *Diplodocus*, which means 'double beam'. It was named for its tail bones, which have two long projections like a pair of skis.

◄ The first fossil find of Baryonyx was its huge thumb claw.

DID YOU KNOW?

One of the shortest dinosaur names is Kol, a tiny meat-eater known from only one fossil foot.

- **The 4-m-long plant-eater** *Othnielia* was named after 19th-century fossil hunter Othniel Charles Marsh.
- ***Parksosaurus*,** a 2.5-m-long plant-eater, was named in honour of Canadian dinosaur expert William Parks.

Colours

- **No one knows for certain** what colours most dinosaurs were.

- **Some fossil specimens** of dinosaur skin show patterns or shading, but all are stone coloured, as fossils are living things that have turned to stone.

- **However recent detailed fossil finds** have allowed the study of microscopic details of structures called melanosomes in dinosaur feathers, that give clues to colours.

- **The feathered dinosaur** *Sinosauropteryx* probably had white and reddish ginger feathers.

- **According to some experts**, certain dinosaurs may have been bright yellow, red or blue, and possibly striped or patched, like some lizards and snakes today.

- **Some dinosaurs** may have been brightly coloured in order to frighten off predators or to intimidate rivals at breeding time.

- **Colours may** have also attracted potential mates.

◄ The 2-m-long Dilong *had hair-like feathers, whose tiny structures in well-preserved specimens give some clues to colours. However, for the vast majority of reconstructions from fossils, the colours are intelligent guesswork.*

- **Tall 'sails'** on the backs of the plant-eater *Ouranosaurus* and the meat-eater *Spinosaurus* may have been for visual display, as well as for temperature control.

- **The large, bony back plates** on stegosaurs may have been used for colourful displays to rivals and mates.

- **The large neck frills** of dinosaurs such as *Triceratops* may have been colourful and used for display.

- **Some dinosaurs may have** been similar in colour to crocodiles – dull greens and browns, to help camouflage them among trees, rocks and earth.

Ornitholestes

DID YOU KNOW?
According to some experts, Ornitholestes *may have had a slight ridge or crest on its nose. Other experts disagree.*

- ***Ornitholestes*** was a smallish meat-eater from the theropod dinosaur group.

- **The name** *Ornitholestes* means 'bird robber' – experts who studied its fossils in the early 1900s imagined it chasing and killing the earliest birds.

- **The home of** *Ornitholestes* was actually in present-day Wyoming in the USA – a continent away from the earliest birds in Europe.

- **Only one specimen** of *Ornitholestes* has been found. Parts of a hand at another site have been assigned to a different dinosaur.

- ***Ornitholestes*** was about 2 m long from nose to tail and probably weighed about 12–15 kg.

- **The teeth were small** and well-spaced, but also slim and sharp, and very well suited to grabbing small animals for food.

- ***Ornitholestes*** had strong arms and hands with powerful fingers and long claws – ideal for grabbing baby dinosaurs newly hatched from their eggs.

▲ Ornitholestes *relied on speed and its good senses of sight and smell for survival.*

Duckbills

Tall, hollow head crest probably amplified sounds

Possible inflatable bag of skin on snout and forehead

▶ Hadrosaurs such as Corythosarus are often shown feeding on water plants with their wide, duck-like beaked mouths.

Long, relatively narrow tail with a muscular base to swish it from side to side

Wide, beak-like front to mouth

Powerful rear legs for rapid walking and trotting

● **The common name** for the hadrosaur group of dinosaurs is 'duckbills'.

● **Hadrosaurs were big plant-eaters** that walked mainly on their two large, powerful rear legs.

● **They were one of** the last main dinosaur groups to appear on Earth, less than 100 mya.

● **Hadrosaurs were named** after *Hadrosaurus*, the first dinosaur of the group to be discovered as fossils.

● **These fossils were found** in 1858 in New Jersey, USA.

● **Most hadrosaurs** had wide mouths that were flattened and toothless at the front, like a duck's beak.

● **Large numbers** of cheek teeth filled the back of the hadrosaur's mouth, arranged in rows called batteries. They were ideal for chewing tough plant food.

● **Some hadrosaurs** had tall, elaborate crests or projections of bone on their heads, notably *Corythosaurus, Saurolophus* and *Parasaurolophus*.

● **Hadrosaurs that lacked bony crests** and had low, smooth heads included *Anatosaurus, Bactrosaurus, Kritosaurus* and *Edmontosaurus*.

● **The name *Hadrosaurus*** means 'big reptile'.

DID YOU KNOW?

Edmontosaurus may have had a loose bag of skin on its nose that it blew up like a balloon to make a honking or trumpeting noise – perhaps as a breeding call.

Utahraptor

● **The finding of *Utahraptor*** fossils dates back to 1975 near Moab, Utah, USA, but these caused little excitement.

● **More fossils from the** early 1990s were added to the discovery and dated to about 130–125 million years ago, the Early Cretaceous Period.

● **By 1993** enough remains had been identified to name this new medium-sized meat-eater *Utahraptor*.

● **It was one of the biggest members** of the raptor or dromaeosaur group, far larger than *Velociraptor* and *Deinonychus*.

● ***Utahraptor* measured** about 7 m long and weighed up to 420 kg.

● **Like other raptors**, it was fast and powerful, with a fearsome curved claw on each foot.

◀ The main fossils of Utahraptor were excavated following the discovery of its huge foot claw in a quarry in Utah, USA.

● **One of these claws** was more than 22 cm long. It could swing on its flexible toe in a slashing or slicing movement to wound prey.

● **Preserved feathers** have not been found with *Utahraptor* remains, but since many of its close relatives had them, it may have possessed feathers, too.

● **The full name is *Utahraptor ostrommaysorum***, partly in honour of the US palaeontologist John Ostrom whose work on *Deinonychus* did so much to change people's opinions of dinosaurs.

Warm or cold blood?

● **If dinosaurs were cold-blooded**, like reptiles today, they would have been slow or inactive in cold conditions.

● **If dinosaurs were warm-blooded**, like birds and mammals today, they would have been able to stay warm and active in cold conditions.

● **Experts once believed** that all dinosaurs were cold-blooded, but today there is much disagreement.

● **Some evidence** for warm-bloodedness comes from the structure of fossil bones.

● **The structure** of some dinosaur bones is more like that of warm-blooded creatures than of reptiles.

● **Some small meat-eating dinosaurs** very probably evolved into birds. As birds are warm-blooded, these dinosaurs may have been warm-blooded too.

● **If some dinosaurs were warm-blooded**, they would probably have needed to eat at least ten times more food than if they were cold-blooded, to 'burn' food energy to make heat.

● **In a 'snapshot' count** of dinosaur fossils, the number of predators compared to prey is more like the comparisons seen in mammals than in reptiles.

● **Many small meat-eaters** are now known to have had feathers. One reason could be as insulation, to keep in body heat if the dinosaur was warm-blooded.

◀ Crocodiles, which were around even in the very earliest dinosaur period (the Triassic), are cold-blooded.

Eustreptospondylus

● *Eustreptospondylus* **was a large meat-eater** that lived in present-day Oxfordshire and Buckinghamshire, in England. It lived about 165–160 mya.

● **In the 1870s**, a fairly complete skeleton of a young *Eustreptospondylus* was found near Oxford, but was named as *Megalosaurus*, the only other big meat-eater known from the region.

● **In 1964**, British fossil expert Alick Walker showed that the Oxford dinosaur was not *Megalosaurus*, and gave it a new name, *Eustreptospondylus*.

● **A full-grown** *Eustreptospondylus* measured about 6 m in length and is estimated to have weighed over 400 kg, although the Oxford specimen was only part-grown.

● **In its enormous mouth**, *Eustreptospondylus* had a great number of small, sharp teeth.

● *Eustreptospondylus* may have hunted sauropods such as *Cetiosaurus* and stegosaurs, dinosaurs that roamed the region at the time.

▶ The fossils of Eustreptospondylus were found with those of sea creatures, suggesting it may have hunted along the seashore.

DID YOU KNOW?

Eustreptospondylus means 'well-curved backbone'. This is due to the arrangement of its spine as seen in its fossils.

Pachycephalosaurs

● **Pachycephalosaurs were one of** the last dinosaur groups to appear. Most lived 80–66 mya.

● **They are named after** one of the best known members of the group, *Pachycephalosaurus*.

● ***Pachycephalosaurus* means 'thick-headed reptile'**, due to the domed and hugely thickened bone on the top of its skull – like a cyclist's crash helmet.

● **About 4.5 m long** from nose to tail, *Pachycephalosaurus* lived in the American Midwest.

● ***Stegoceras***, also from the American Midwest, was about 2 m long with a body the size of a goat.

● ***Homalocephale*, about 2 m long**, lived in Asia 80 mya. It had a flatter skull, but some experts think it was a young *Prenocephale*.

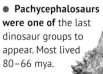

◄ *Typical of its group,* Pachycephalosaurus *had a thickened layer of bone on the top of its head.*

● **Pachycephalosaurs may have defended** themselves by lowering their heads and charging at their enemies.

● **At breeding time**, the males may have tried to butt each other, but how and where is not clear.

DID YOU KNOW?

Pachycephalosaurs are often known as the 'bone-heads', 'dome-heads', or 'helmet-heads'.

Baryonyx

● ***Baryonyx* was a large meat-eating dinosaur** that lived about 130 mya.

● **The first fossil find** of *Baryonyx* was its huge thumb claw, discovered in Surrey, England, in 1983.

● **The total length** of *Baryonyx* was 9–10 m.

● ***Baryonyx* had a slim build** and a long, narrow tail, and probably weighed less than 2 tonnes.

● **The snout was unusual** for a meat-eating dinosaur because it was very long and narrow – similar to today's slim-snouted crocodiles.

● **The teeth were long** and slim, especially at the front of the mouth.

● **The general similarities** between *Baryonyx* and a crocodile suggest that *Baryonyx* may have been a fish-eater.

● **It may have lurked** in swamps or close to rivers, darting its head forward on its long, flexible neck to snatch fish.

● **The massive thumb claw**, which measured up to 35 cm in length, may have been used to hook fish or amphibians from the water.

● **The dinosaur was named** after this outsized feature – the name *Baryonyx* means 'heavy claw'.

◄ *Fossils of* Baryonyx *were found with the remains of fish scales, suggesting this dinosaur was a semi-aquatic fish catcher.*

DID YOU KNOW?

The fossil skeleton of Baryonyx had over two-thirds of its parts, which is an unusually complete find, allowing experts to find out many details of its lifestyle.

Archosaurs

- **Archosaurs were a large group** of reptiles that included the dinosaurs as one of their subgroups.

- **Other archosaur subgroups** included flying pterosaurs, crocodiles, and birds – since birds evolved from dinosaurs.

- **Pseudosuchians are living crocodilians**, as were the lesser-known reptile group, the ornithosuchians, which were closely related to them but are now all extinct.

- **A dinosaur-like ornithosuchian** was *Ornithosuchus*, which gave its name to this group.

- **Four-metre-long** *Ornithosuchus* could stand almost upright and was probably a powerful predator.

- ***Ornithosuchus* fossils** have been found in Scotland.

- **Features in *Ornithosuchus'* backbone**, hips and feet indicate that it was not quite a dinosaur, but still an archosaur.

- **Some experts classify** *Archosaurus* from the Permian Period as one of the first archosaurs, while others disagree.

- ***Ornithosuchus* had a mix of features**, both non-dinosaur (hips and back plates) and dinosaur (legs and skull).

▶ *Crocodilians, like this hatchling, are living members of the great archosaur group of reptiles.*

Footprints

DID YOU KNOW?

In 2009, sauropod footprints 1.7 m across were found in the Jura region of France.

- **Fossilized dinosaur footprints** have been found all over the world.

- **Some dinosaurs left footprints** when they walked on the soft mud or sand of riverbanks. Then the mud baked hard in the sun, and was gradually filled and covered by more sand or mud, which eventually turned into rock, helping to preserve the footprints as fossils.

- **Some footprints were made** when dinosaur feet left impressions in soft mud or sand that was then covered by volcanic ash, which set hard.

- **Many footprints** have been found together in lines, called 'trackways'. These suggest that some dinosaurs lived in groups, or used the same routes regularly.

- **The distance between** same-sized footprints indicates whether a dinosaur was walking, trotting or running.

- **Footprints of big meat-eaters** such as *Tyrannosaurus* show three toes with claws, on a forward-facing foot.

- **In big plant-eaters**, such as *Iguanodon*, each footprint shows three separate toes, but less or no claw impressions, and the feet point slightly inwards.

- **In giant plant-eating sauropods**, each footprint is rounded and has indentations of nail-like 'hooves'.

- **Some sauropod footprints** are more than one metre across.

▼ *Fossilized footprints are called trace fossils because they are signs or prints made by dinosaurs, or other creatures, rather than actual body parts.*

Teeth

● **Some of the most common** fossil remains are of dinosaur teeth – the hardest parts of their bodies.

● **Dinosaur teeth** come in a huge range of sizes and shapes – daggers, knives, shears, pegs, combs, rakes, file-like rasps, crushing batteries and vices.

● **In some dinosaurs**, up to three-quarters of a tooth was fixed into the jaw bone, so only one-quarter showed.

● **The teeth of plant-eaters** such as *Iguanodon* had angled tops that rubbed past each other in a grinding motion.

● **Some duckbill dinosaurs** (hadrosaurs) had more than 1000 teeth, all at the back of the mouth.

▲ Tyrannosaurus *had 50-plus 'banana' teeth. They were long and strong for tearing flesh and crushing bone.*

● **Some of the largest teeth** of any dinosaur belonged to 9-m-long *Daspletosaurus*, a tyrannosaur-like meat-eater. They measured up to 18 cm in length.

◄ Edmontosaurus *had no front teeth, only a flattened 'duck-bill'.*

> **DID YOU KNOW?**
>
> Like modern reptiles, dinosaurs probably grew new teeth to replace old, worn or broken ones.

Plateosaurus

● **The name** *Plateosaurus* means 'flat reptile', and the first kinds appeared around 215 mya.

● **Groups of** *Plateosaurus* have been found at various European sites, totalling more than 100 individuals.

● *Plateosaurus* **had jagged teeth** for chewing plants.

● **Its flexible, clawed fingers** may have been used to pull branches of food to its mouth.

● *Plateosaurus* **could bend** its fingers 'backwards', allowing it to walk on its hands and fingers, in the same posture as its feet and toes.

● **The thumbs** had large, sharp claws, perhaps used to jab and stab enemies.

● **Fossil experts** once thought that *Plateosaurus* dragged its tail as it walked.

● **Experts today think** that *Plateosaurus* carried its tail off the ground to balance its head, neck and the front part of its body.

> **DID YOU KNOW?**
>
> Plateosaurus was one of the earliest dinosaurs to be officially named, in 1837, before the term 'dinosaur' had even been invented.

▶ Plateosaurus *may have been able to reach leaves 2–3 m above the ground.*

Growth

● **In very well-preserved fossils**, sometimes fine details can be seen as lines, rings and other marks relating to how the dinosaur or other animal grew through the seasons and years.

● **The spacing of the marks** may show slow or limited growth due to food shortage, disease or severe climate conditions. Marks farther apart indicate faster growth, for example, with plentiful food.

● **More than 60 dinosaur bones** have been studied in this way to assess growth speed at different ages.

● **The bones included** *Tyrannosaurus* and its smaller cousins *Albertosaurus*, at up to 2 tonnes, and *Daspletosaurus* at 2–3 tonnes.

● **Results show all three kinds** of dinosaurs grew especially fast in adolescence.

▲ *A young* Tyrannosaurus *had slightly different proportions to the adult shown here, with a shorter, rounder snout and slimmer limbs.*

● ***Albertosaurus* and *Daspletosaurus*** had growth spurts at around 11–15 years of age, when they put on an estimated 0.3–0.5 kg of weight every day.

● ***Tyrannosaurus* gained weight** between 14 and 18 years old. During its peak growth spurt, it put on 2 kg daily.

● **This growth surge meant** that a fully grown adult *Tyrannosaurus* was two to three times heavier than *Albertosaurus* and *Daspletosaurus*.

● ***Tyrannosaurus* was fully grown** by the age of about 20 years.

Oviraptor

● ***Oviraptor* was an unusual meat-eater** from the theropod dinosaur group. It lived during the Late Cretaceous Period, about 75 mya.

● **Its fossils were found** in the Omnogov region of the Gobi Desert in Central Asia.

● **From beak to tail**, *Oviraptor* was about 2 m long.

● **It was named 'egg thief'** because its fossils were found lying among the broken eggs of what was thought to be the dinosaur *Protoceratops*.

● **They were probably** the eggs of *Oviraptor* itself, the adult brooding or protecting them.

● ***Oviraptor* had no teeth**. Instead, it had a strong, curved beak, like that of a parrot or eagle.

● **On its forehead**, *Oviraptor* had a tall, rounded piece of bone, like a crest or helmet, sticking up in front of its eyes.

● ***Oviraptor's* head crest** resembled that of today's flightless bird, the cassowary.

● ***Oviraptor* may have eaten eggs**, or cracked open shellfish with its powerful beak.

▼ Oviraptor's *unusual features included its parrot-like beak. It may have been covered in filament-like feathers.*

DID YOU KNOW?

Oviraptor had two bony spikes inside its mouth that it may have used to crack eggs when it closed its jaws.

Anchisaurus

- *Anchisaurus* **was** an early sauropod-like dinosaur.
- **Although officially named** as a dinosaur in 1885, *Anchisaurus* had in fact been discovered over 70 years earlier.
- *Anchisaurus* **was very small** and slim compared to other sauropods, with a body roughly the size of a large dog.

◄ Anchisaurus *was about 2.2 m long. Its name means 'near lizard'.*

- **Fossils of** *Anchisaurus* date from the Early Jurassic Period, 200–190 mya.
- **The remains of** *Anchisaurus* were found in Connecticut and Massachusetts, eastern USA, and in southern Africa.
- **With its small, serrated teeth**, *Anchisaurus* probably bit off the soft leaves of low-growing plants.
- **To reach leaves** on higher branches, *Anchisaurus* may have been able to rear up on its back legs.
- *Anchisaurus* **had a large**, curved claw on each thumb.
- **The thumb claws** may have been used as hooks to pull leafy branches towards the mouth, or as weapons for lashing out at enemies and inflicting wounds.

DID YOU KNOW?

Remains of Anchisaurus or a similar plant-eater were the first fossils of a dinosaur to be discovered in North America in 1818.

Feathered dinosaurs

- **Fossils found** since the mid-1990s show that some dinosaurs may have been covered with feathers or fur.
- *Sinosauropteryx* **was a small**, one-metre-long meat-eater that lived 125–120 mya in China.
- **Fossils of** *Sinosauropteryx* show that parts of its body were covered not with the usual reptile scales, but with feathers instead.
- **The overall shape** of *Sinosauropteryx* shows that, despite it being covered in feathers, it could not fly.
- **The feathers may have been** for camouflage, for visual display, or to keep it warm – suggesting it was warm-blooded.
- **Fossils of** *Avimimus* come from China and Mongolia, and date from about 75–70 mya.
- **The fossil arm bones** have small ridges that are the same size and shape as the ridges on birds' wing bones, where feathers attach.
- **The 1.5-m-long** *Avimimus* had a mouth shaped like a bird's beak for pecking at food.

- **Most scientists today** believe that birds are descended from a group of small meat-eating dinosaurs called maniraptorans, such as *Troodon*.
- **If this is so,** the modern way of classifying or grouping animals, called cladistics, means that birds are a subgroup of dinosaurs, not a separate group.
- **It also means** that dinosaurs are alive today – in the form of birds.

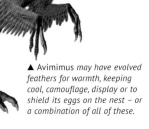

▲ Avimimus *may have evolved feathers for warmth, keeping cool, camouflage, display or to shield its eggs on the nest – or a combination of all of these.*

Giganotosaurus

● **In 1994** there was great news that the remains of a meat-eating dinosaur even bigger than *Tyrannosaurus* had been found in Patagonia, in the south of Argentina.

● **The new find** was named as *Giganotosaurus*, 'giant southern lizard'.

● **The length of *Giganotosaurus*** was estimated at up to 13 m, and the weight between 8 and 10 tonnes.

● **The skull was at first said to be** 1.8 m in length, although this was then reduced to 1.6 m. It is still one of the most massive skulls of any dinosaur.

● **The remains of *Giganotosaurus*** were first noticed by Rubén Carolini, a local vehicle mechanic who went fossil-hunting in his spare time.

● **Its full name is *Giganotosaurus carolinii*,** in honour of its discoverer.

● **Carolini went on to become** Director of the Villa El Chocón Municipal Museum, which celebrates his enormous find.

● **The main *Giganotosaurus* find** was an exceptional specimen, almost three-quarters complete.

● ***Giganotosaurus* lived** around 100–95 mya.

● **Not far away**, the fossils of the colossal plant-eater *Argentinosaurus* were located, which lived around the same time – perhaps a victim of *Giganotosaurus*?

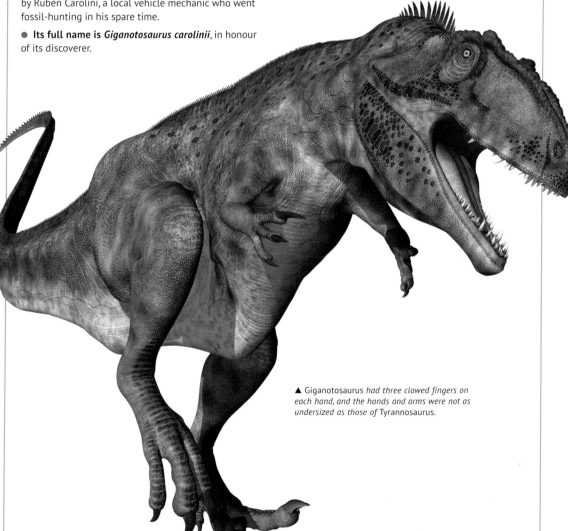

▲ Giganotosaurus *had three clawed fingers on each hand, and the hands and arms were not as undersized as those of* Tyrannosaurus.

Skin

● **Several fossils of dinosaur skin** have been found, revealing that many dinosaurs had scales like today's reptiles.

● **As in crocodiles**, dinosaur scales were embedded in the thick, tough hide, rather than lying on top of the skin and overlapping, as in snakes.

● **When the first fossils** of dinosaur skin were found in the mid-1800s, scientists thought they were from giant prehistoric crocodiles.

● **Fossil skin** of the horned dinosaur *Chasmosaurus* reveals that larger bumps or lumps, called tubercles, were scattered among the normal-sized scales.

DID YOU KNOW?

Many dinosaur scales were roughly six-sided, which made them both strong and flexible.

● **Fossil skin** of the duckbilled hadrosaur *Edmontosaurus* has also been found.

● *Edmontosaurus* **was covered** in thousands of small scales, like little pebbles, with larger lumps or tubercles spaced among them.

● **Various specimens** of fossil skin show that the scales of *Iguanodon*-type dinosaurs were larger than those of same-sized, similar duckbill dinosaurs.

● **Scaly skin** protected a dinosaur against the teeth and claws of enemies, accidental scrapes, and the bites of pests such as mosquitoes and fleas.

◀ *Scelidosaurus was covered from head to tail with hard scutes (bony plates in the skin) and nodules. These would have helped to protect it from meat-eating dinosaurs.*

Camarasaurus

DID YOU KNOW?

Detailed fossil studies show that one Camarasaurus replaced its teeth every 8–9 weeks, and another reached adulthood at 20 years of age and died aged 26.

● *Camarasaurus* was a giant plant-eating sauropod that lived during the Late Jurassic Period, about 155–150 mya.

● **It is one of the best known** of all big dinosaurs, because so many almost-complete fossil skeletons have been found.

● **Famous American fossil hunter** Edward Drinker Cope gave *Camarasaurus* its name in 1877.

● **The name means** 'chambered reptile', because its backbones, or vertebrae, had large, scoop-shaped spaces in them, making them lighter.

● *Camarasaurus* was up to 21 m long and had a very bulky, powerful body and legs.

▶ *Compared to other sauropods, Camarasaurus had a short neck and tail.*

● **North America** was home to *Camarasaurus*, with similar fossils from Europe and Africa given different names.

● **A large, short-snouted head,** similar to that of *Brachiosaurus*, characterized *Camarasaurus*.

● **A fossil skeleton** of a young *Camarasaurus* was uncovered in the 1920s, and had nearly every bone in its body lying in the correct position, as they were when the dinosaur was alive – an amazingly rare find.

Yutyrannus

- **Named in 2012,** *Yutyrannus* or 'feathered tyrant' is a large predator dinosaur in the same group as the great *Tyrannosaurus*.

- **However, it lived** almost 60 million years earlier than *Tyrannosaurus*, about 125 mya, in what is now northwest China.

- ***Yutyrannus* was almost 9 m long** and could have weighed more than 1.5 tonnes.

- **It is the biggest dinosaur** so far that has feathers preserved with its fossil bones and teeth.

- **The feathers were slim,** flexible filaments, some more than 15 cm long.

- **Different specimens** of *Yutyrannus* have feathers on different parts of the body, so taking them all together, the filaments could have covered most of the dinosaur.

- **The skull of the largest** *Yutyrannus* specimen is almost one metre long.

- **It also has a small 'horn'** above each eye, like several other tyrannosaur-group dinosaurs.

- **Like its relatives,** *Yutyrannus* was a powerful predator with a huge mouth and many sharp teeth.

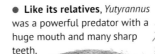

▲ Yutyrannus *lived in a region that was quite cool 125 mya, so its hair-like or plume-like feathers may have helped to control its body temperature.*

Age and lifespan

- **Detailed studies of the growth lines** and rings in very well-preserved fossils reveal how long dinosaurs and other prehistoric creatures lived.

- **Analysis of *Tyrannosaurus* bones** showed that by 20 years of age, and weighing around 5 tonnes, they almost stopped growing during adulthood.

- **The oldest and biggest specimen** of *Tyrannosaurus*, nicknamed 'Sue', died at 28 years of age.

- **Other estimates of dinosaur growth** rates and ages come from comparisons with today's birds, mammals and reptiles.

- **Some reptiles today** continue to grow throughout their lives, although their growth rate slows with age.

- **Birds today** reach adult size in one or two years, then do not grow any more.

- **Like many animals today,** a dinosaur's growth rate probably depended largely on its food supply, the temperature, disease and other factors.

▶ *Crocodiles frequently exceed 50 years of age, and some may reach 100, while alligators have been recorded at 50–60 years old.*

- **Small meat-eating dinosaurs** such as *Compsognathus* may have lived to be only five to eight years old.

- **A giant sauropod probably lived** to be 50 years old, or even more than 100 years old.

- **During its lifetime,** a big sauropod such as *Brachiosaurus* would have increased its weight 2000 times (compared to 20 times in a human).

DID YOU KNOW?

The longest-lived land animals today are reptiles – the giant tortoises and other tortoise species. There are several recorded ages of 150–200 years, with a few claims for over 250 years.

Pack hunters

● **Dinosaurs were reptiles**, but no reptiles today hunt in packs in which members co-operate with each other.

● **Certain types of crocodiles** and alligators come together to feed where prey is abundant, but they do not co-ordinate their attacks.

▼ *Small predatory dinosaurs such as* Troodon *may have gathered in groups to chase prey or scavenge.*

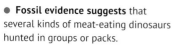

● **Fossil evidence suggests** that several kinds of meat-eating dinosaurs hunted in groups or packs.

● **Sometimes the fossils** of several individuals of the same type of dinosaur have been found in one place, suggesting the dinosaurs were pack animals.

● **The fossil bones** of some plant-eating dinosaurs have been found with many tooth marks on them, apparently made by different-sized predators, which may have hunted in packs.

● **Tyrannosaurus** may have been a pack hunter.

● **At several North American sites**, the remains of several *Deinonychus* were found near the fossils of a much larger plant-eater named *Tenontosaurus*.

● **One Deinonychus** probably would not have attacked a full-grown *Tenontosaurus*, but a group of three or four might have done so.

Ceratopsians

● **Ceratopsians were large plant-eaters** that appeared less than 120 mya.

● **Ceratopsian fossils** come from Europe, North America and Asia.

● **Ceratopsian means 'horn-face'**, after the long horns on the dinosaurs' snouts, eyebrows or foreheads.

● **Most ceratopsians** had a neck shield or frill that swept sideways and up from the back of the head to cover the upper neck and shoulders.

● **Well known ceratopsians** include *Triceratops*, *Styracosaurus*, *Centrosaurus*, *Pentaceratops*, *Anchiceratops*, *Chasmosaurus* and *Torosaurus*.

● **The neck frills** of some ceratopsians, such as that of *Chasmosaurus*, had large gaps or 'windows' in the bone.

● **The windows in the neck frill** were covered in thick, scaly skin.

● **Ceratopsians had no teeth** in the fronts of their hooked, beak-like mouths.

● **Using rows** of powerful cheek teeth, ceratopsians sheared off their plant food.

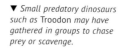

DID YOU KNOW?

Torosaurus had one of the longest skulls of any land animal, at about 2.6 m from the front of the snout to the rear of the neck frill.

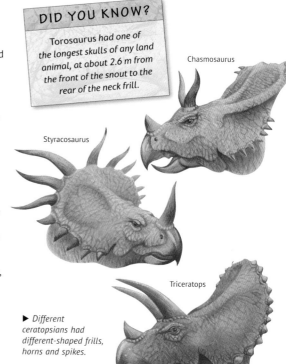

Chasmosaurus

Styracosaurus

Triceratops

▶ *Different ceratopsians had different-shaped frills, horns and spikes.*

Caudipteryx

- **The discovery of *Caudipteryx* fossils** in 1997 in Liaoning Province, China, increased the debate about the relationship between dinosaurs and birds.

- **The detailed fossils show** *Caudipteryx* was not much larger than a chicken and had a very bird-like shape and proportions.

- **They also revealed feathers** like a modern bird's, each with a shaft or quill and side vanes, on its front limbs and tail.

- **Some of these feathers** were up to 20 cm long.

- **There were also simple,** fluffy feathers on the body of *Caudipteryx*.

- **The fossils of *Caudipteryx*** come from 125 mya during the Early Cretaceous Period.

- **There are several views** about the grouping of *Caudipteryx*. Some experts say it was a small meat-eating dinosaur in the same group as *Oviraptor*, related to the raptors.

- **Another opinion** is that it is a dinosaur-like bird, rather than a bird-like dinosaur.

- **The front limbs and build** of *Caudipteryx* meant it could not fly.

- ***Caudipteryx* could have come** from a group of birds that evolved flight, of which some kinds later became flightless again.

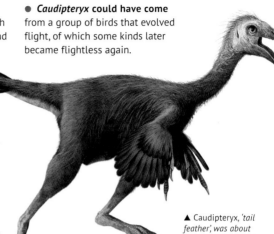

▲ Caudipteryx, 'tail feather', was about one metre long and weighed 5–8 kg. At the end of the tail the long quilled feathers spread out like a fan.

Protoceratops

- ***Protoceratops* was a kind** of horned dinosaur or ceratopsian, living some 77–70 mya.

- **It has some features** of its ancestors, and also some of the later ceratopsians, such as a neck frill or shield.

- **However the nose horn** of *Protoceratops* was hardly developed, unlike other ceratopsians.

▼ One fossil find shows how Protoceratops *(left)* may have battled with the meat-eater Velociraptor *(right)*.

> ### DID YOU KNOW?
> People in ancient Asia who found Protoceratops fossils may have started the legend of the mythical griffin – a winged, lion-sized beast with four legs and an eagle-like beak that made its nest on the ground.

- **The neck frill was not solid** but had gaps or 'windows' probably to save weight, which in life would be filled in with skin.

- ***Protoceratops* was about the size of a pig**, around 1.8 m long and weighing 150 kg.

- **Lots of fossils** found near each other suggest *Protoceratops* lived and travelled in herds.

- **Remains of *Protoceratops*** come from east Asia, especially Mongolia.

- **They were first dug out** in 1922 by a group of American palaeontologists and adventurers who were hoping to find fossils of early humans or 'ape-men'.

- **One find of dinosaur nests and eggs** – the first ever to be identified – was said to have been laid by *Protoceratops*.

- **However later studies showed** they belonged to the beaked theropod *Oviraptor*.

Coprolites

- **Coprolites are the fossilized droppings**, or dung, of animals from long ago, such as dinosaurs. Like other fossils, they have become solid rock.

- **Thousands of dinosaur coprolites** have been found at fossil sites across the world.

- **Cracking or cutting** open coprolites may reveal what the dinosaur had eaten.

- **Coprolites produced** by large meat-eaters such as *Tyrannosaurus* contain bone from their prey.

- **The microscopic structure** of the bones found in coprolites shows the age of the prey when it was eaten. Most victims were very young or old, as these were the easiest creatures for a predator to kill.

- **Coprolites produced** by small meat-eaters such as *Compsognathus* may contain the hard bits of insects, such as the legs and wing cases of beetles.

- **Huge piles** of coprolites found in Montana, USA, were probably produced by the large plant-eater *Maiasaura*.

- *Maiasaura* **coprolites** contain the remains of cones, buds and the needle-like leaves of conifer trees, showing that these dinosaurs had a diet of tough plant matter.

◀ *Fossilized dinosaur dung may provide clues as to the kind of food eaten by dinosaurs.*

Eyes

- **No fossils have been found** of dinosaur eyes because they were made of soft tissue that soon rotted away after death, or were eaten by scavengers.

- **The main clues** to dinosaur eyes come from the bowl-like hollows, or orbits, in the skull where the eyes were located.

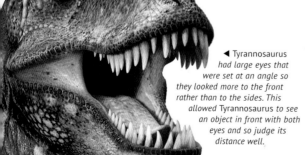

◀ *Tyrannosaurus had large eyes that were set at an angle so they looked more to the front rather than to the sides. This allowed Tyrannosaurus to see an object in front with both eyes and so judge its distance well.*

- **The orbits** in fossil skulls show that dinosaur eyes were similar to those of reptiles today.

- **The 6-m-long sauropod** *Vulcanodon* had tiny eyes relative to the size of its head.

- **Small-eyed dinosaurs** probably only had good vision in the daytime.

- **The eyes of many** plant-eating dinosaurs, such as *Vulcanodon*, were on the sides of their heads, giving them all-round vision.

- **The small meat-eater** *Troodon* had relatively large eyes, and it could probably see well, even in dim light.

- *Troodon's* **eyes** were on the front of its face and pointed forwards, allowing it to see detail and judge distance.

- **Dinosaurs that had large bulges**, called optic lobes, in their brains – detectable by the shapes of their skulls – could probably see very well, perhaps even at night.

Scelidosaurus

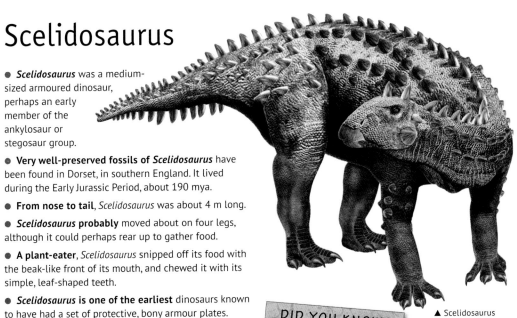

- **Scelidosaurus** was a medium-sized armoured dinosaur, perhaps an early member of the ankylosaur or stegosaur group.

- **Very well-preserved fossils of Scelidosaurus** have been found in Dorset, in southern England. It lived during the Early Jurassic Period, about 190 mya.

- **From nose to tail**, Scelidosaurus was about 4 m long.

- **Scelidosaurus probably** moved about on four legs, although it could perhaps rear up to gather food.

- **A plant-eater**, Scelidosaurus snipped off its food with the beak-like front of its mouth, and chewed it with its simple, leaf-shaped teeth.

- **Scelidosaurus is one of the earliest** dinosaurs known to have had a set of protective, bony armour plates.

- **A row of bony plates**, or scutes, stuck up from Scelidosaurus' neck, back and tail. It also had rows of conical bony plates along its flanks, resembling limpets on a rock.

DID YOU KNOW?

Scelidosaurus was described and named in 1859 and 1861 by Richard Owen, who also invented the name 'dinosaur'.

▲ Scelidosaurus was a forerunner of bigger, more heavily armoured dinosaur types, with bony plates called scutes.

Australia

- **In the past 50 years**, some of the most exciting discoveries of dinosaur fossils have come from Australia.

- **Remains of the large plant-eater** Muttaburrasaurus were found near Muttaburra, Queensland.

- **Muttaburrasaurus** was about 8 m long and similar in some ways to the well known plant-eater Iguanodon.

- **Fossils of Rhoetosaurus**, a giant plant-eater, were found in 1924 in southern Queensland.

- **The sauropod Rhoetosaurus** was about 15 m long and lived about 180–160 mya.

- **Near Winton, Queensland**, more than 3300 footprints show where about 130 dinosaurs once passed by.

- **One of the major fossil sites** in Australia is Dinosaur Cove, on the coast near Melbourne, Victoria.

- **Fossil-rich rocks** at Dinosaur Cove are part of the Otway-Strzelecki mountain ranges, and are 120–110 million years old.

- **Remains found** at Dinosaur Cove include Leaellynasaura, a smaller version of the huge meat-eater Allosaurus, and the 3-m, 120-kg plant-eater Atlascopcosaurus.

DID YOU KNOW?

Dinosaur Cove is difficult to reach, and many of the fossils are in hard rocks in the middle of sheer cliffs with pounding waves far beneath.

▼ Many exciting fossils have been found in Australia over the past 50 years – most of these are found nowhere else in the world.

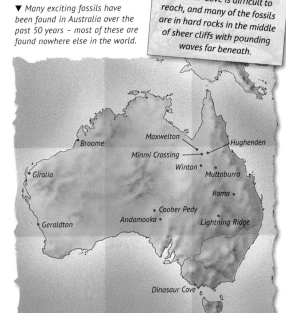

Broome

Maxwelton

Hughenden

Minmi Crossing

Winton

Muttaburra

Giralia

Roma

Coober Pedy

Andamooka

Lightning Ridge

Geraldton

Dinosaur Cove

Sauropods

● **Sauropods were the biggest dinosaurs**. They lived mainly during the Jurassic Period, around 201–145 mya.

● **These huge plant-eaters** had tiny heads, very long necks and tails, huge, bulging bodies. They also had massive legs, similar to those of an elephant, but much bigger.

● **Sauropods included** the well known *Mamenchisaurus*, *Cetiosaurus*, *Diplodocus*, *Brachiosaurus* and *Apatosaurus*.

● *Rebbachisaurus* **fossils** were found in Morocco, Tunisia and Algeria. It lived 100 mya.

● *Cetiosaurus* **was about** 15 m long and weighed 10–20 tonnes.

● **The first fossils** of *Cetiosaurus* were found in Oxfordshire, England, in the 1830s.

● **It was the first sauropod** to be given an official name. This was in 1841 – one year before the term 'dinosaur' was invented.

● *Cetiosaurus*, or 'whale reptile', was so-named because British fossil expert Richard Owen thought that its giant backbones came from a prehistoric whale.

> **DID YOU KNOW?**
>
> The name 'sauropod' means 'lizard/reptile foot'. It was given in 1878 by US fossil-hunter and dinosaur expert Othniel Charles Marsh, after the discovery of the famous Diplodocus.

◄ *Sauropods such as* Apatosaurus *could perhaps browse for food in tree tops.*

Feet

● **Dinosaur feet differed**, depending on the animal's body design, weight and lifestyle.

● **A typical dinosaur's front feet** had metacarpal bones in the lower wrist or upper hand, and two or three phalanges (bones) in each digit (finger or toe), tipped by claws.

● **The rear feet** of a typical dinosaur had metatarsal (instead of metacarpal) bones in the lower ankle.

● **Some dinosaurs** had five toes per foot, like most other reptiles (and most birds and mammals).

● **Sauropods probably had feet** with rounded bases supported by a wedge of fibrous, cushion-like tissue.

● **Most sauropods had claws** on their first two or three toes, and smaller, blunter 'hooves' on the other two toes.

● **Ostrich dinosaurs** such as *Gallimimus* had very long feet and long, slim toes for running fast.

● **Many fast-running dinosaurs** had fewer toes, to reduce weight – *Gallimimus* had three toes per back foot.

● **The ornithopod**, or 'bird feet' dinosaur group, includes *Iguanodon*, duckbilled dinosaurs, *Heterodontosaurus* and many other plant-eaters.

▶ *A* Tyrannosaurus *had three clawed toes per foot.*

▶ *The living ostrich has two toes per foot, the inner one – the first or big toe – being larger and claw-tipped.*

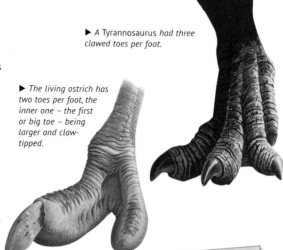

> **DID YOU KNOW?**
>
> The dinosaur group that includes all the meat-eaters, both large and small, is named the theropods, or 'beast feet'.

Prenocephale

- *Prenocephale* **was one** of the last of the 'bone-heads' or pachycephalosaur dinosaurs, and indeed one of the last of all dinosaurs, living around 70 mya or less.

- **It was quite small**, around 1.8 to 2.5 m long and between 80 and 140 kg in weight.

- **The size of** *Prenocephale* is vague because it is estimated, since limited amounts of its fossils have been found, in East Asia.

- **However there are enough** *Prenocephale* remains to show it was similar in body shape to other, better-known bone-heads.

- *Prenocephale* **had a thickened**, egg-shaped upper skull, like a smooth dome.

- **Around the lower edges of the dome**, like the brim of a hat stretching down to the front of the snout, were a row of small lumps, bumps and spikes.

- **The eyes of** *Prenocephale* were large and faced partly forwards to see in detail and judge distances.

- **The eating habits of** *Prenocephale*, and most pachycephalosaurs, are not clear. Most experts think they ate soft plant material, with perhaps small worms and bugs and eggs, but their teeth were small and not very strong.

- **Fossils of** *Prenocephale* were discovered during an expedition by Polish, Mongolian and Russian fossil experts to the Gobi Desert.

- **The name** *Prenocephale* was given in 1974 and means 'sloping head'.

◀ *A herd of* Prenocephale *scatter in panic as they are attacked by the giant carnivore* Tarbosaurus *(which may be the Asian form of* Tyrannosaurus*).*

Antarctic dinosaurs

- **The huge continent of Antarctica** has not always been ice-covered at the South Pole.

- **Through parts of prehistory**, Antarctica was joined to Australia, and the climate was much warmer, allowing forests with trees and bushes to grow.

- **This happened** during the Early Jurassic Period, 201–174 mya, and again in the Early Cretaceous Period, 145–100 mya.

- **At this time**, insects, worms, reptiles such as dinosaurs and crocodiles and flying pterosaurs, mammals and many other creatures lived in Australia, and fossils of some have been found on Antarctica.

- **Finding fossils** on Antarctica is very difficult, with intense cold, bitter winds, blizzards, and rocks covered with ice and snow for most of the year.

- **The first dinosaur fossils** found on Antarctica were dug out in 1986 on James Ross Island, at the tip of the Antarctic Peninsula, south of South America.

- **The dinosaur**, of the ankylosaur or armoured dinosaur group, was named *Antarctopelta*, meaning 'Antarctic shield'.

- *Antarctopelta* **was about 4 m long**, weighed up to one tonne, and lived about 70 mya.

- **The first discovery** of a meat-eating dinosaur on Antarctica was *Cryolophosaurus*, in 1991.

- *Cryolophosaurus* **lived** during the Early Jurassic Period, some 190 mya. It was about 6 m long and weighed up to half a tonne.

- **The name** *Cryolophosaurus* means 'frozen crest lizard' because this dinosaur had a bony crest that rose up between its eyes and had a comb-like tip.

▶ Cryolophosaurus *fossils were found in the same region as those of sauropod dinosaurs, pterosaurs and therapsids (mammal-like reptiles) the size of rats.*

Dilophosaurus

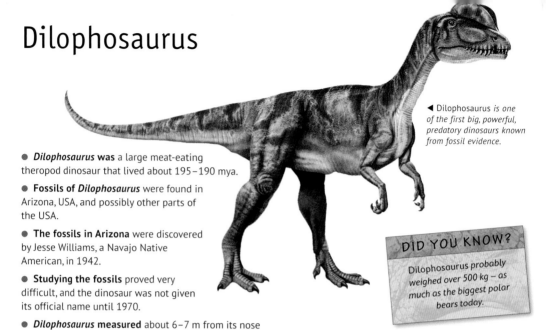

◄ *Dilophosaurus is one of the first big, powerful, predatory dinosaurs known from fossil evidence.*

● ***Dilophosaurus* was** a large meat-eating theropod dinosaur that lived about 195–190 mya.

● **Fossils of *Dilophosaurus*** were found in Arizona, USA, and possibly other parts of the USA.

● **The fossils in Arizona** were discovered by Jesse Williams, a Navajo Native American, in 1942.

● **Studying the fossils** proved very difficult, and the dinosaur was not given its official name until 1970.

● ***Dilophosaurus* measured** about 6–7 m from its nose to the end of its very long tail.

● **The name *Dilophosaurus*** means 'two ridged reptile', from the two thin, rounded, bony crests on its head, each shaped like half a dinner plate.

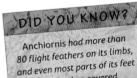

DID YOU KNOW?

Dilophosaurus probably weighed over 500 kg – as much as the biggest polar bears today.

● **The crests were too thin** and fragile to be used as weapons for head-butting.

● **Brightly coloured skin** may have covered the head crests, as a visual display to rivals or enemies.

Anchiornis

DID YOU KNOW?

Anchiornis had more than 80 flight feathers on its limbs, and even most parts of its feet were feather-covered.

● ***Anchiornis*, or 'near bird'**, was a tiny dinosaur that lived 160–150 mya. Its fossils were found in Liaoning in China, and were named in 2009.

● **A member of the troodontid group**, *Anchiornis* was almost completely covered in feathers.

● ***Anchiornis* was only 40 cm long** and probably weighed less than 0.2 kg. Its head, four legs, body and tail were all covered in feathers.

● **The leg and tail-end feathers** had central quills with vanes branching off, similar to a modern bird's flight feathers.

● **The head, body and upper tail** had plume-like or downy feathers that were soft and flexible.

● ***Anchiornis* fossils were so detailed** that scientists could see tiny parts called melanosomes, which make the coloured substances, or pigments, for the feathers.

● **The shapes, sizes and positions** of melanosomes were compared with those of modern birds, to show the colours and patterns of *Anchiornis*' feathers.

● ***Anchiornis* had a brown head crown**, a dark face with brown patches, and legs with rows of blackish-grey and white feathers, giving a striped effect.

● **Perhaps *Anchiornis* glided** from tree to tree and also used its feather patterns for display, such as to frighten rivals from its territory, or attract a mate.

▶ *The colours of Anchiornis in life are known from the microscopic details of its feathers – except for the tail, which was not preserved.*

Psittacosaurus

- **Psittacosaurus was a plant-eater**, and an early relative of the group known as ceratopsians, or 'horn-faced' dinosaurs.

- **Appearing in the Middle Cretaceous Period**, different species of *Psittacosaurus* lived from 125 to 100 mya.

- **Psittacosaurus was named** in 1923 from fossils found in Mongolia, Central Asia. Fossils have been found at various sites across Asia, including Russia, China and Thailand.

- **The rear legs** of *Psittacosaurus* were longer and stronger than its front legs.

- **This suggests** that the dinosaur may have reared up to run fast on its rear legs, rather than running on all four legs.

- **Psittacosaurus** measured about 2 m long, weighed around 20 kg and had four toes on each foot.

- **The name Psittacosaurus** means 'parrot reptile', after the dinosaur's beak-shaped mouth, like that of a parrot.

- **Inside its cheeks**, *Psittacosaurus* had many sharp teeth capable of cutting and slicing through tough plant material.

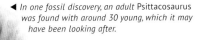

◀ In one fossil discovery, an adult Psittacosaurus was found with around 30 young, which it may have been looking after.

DID YOU KNOW?

Fossil evidence shows that when newly hatched from their eggs, baby Psittacosaurus were hardly longer than a human hand.

Beaks

- **Several kinds of dinosaurs** had a toothless, beak-shaped front to their mouths.

- **Beaked dinosaurs** included ceratopsians (horn-faces) such as *Triceratops*, ornithopods such as *Iguanodon* and the hadrosaurs (duckbills), stegosaurs, ankylosaurs (armoured dinosaurs) and fast-running ostrich dinosaurs.

- **Most beaked dinosaurs** had chopping or chewing teeth near the backs of their mouths, in their cheeks, but ostrich dinosaurs had no teeth.

- **A dinosaur's beak** was made up of the upper (maxilla) and the lower (dentary or mandible) jaw bones.

- **The bones at the front** of a dinosaur's jaw would have been covered with horn, which formed the outer shape of the beak.

- **Dinosaurs almost certainly used** their beaks for pecking, snipping, tearing and slicing their food.

- **They may also have used** their beaks to peck fiercely at any attackers.

DID YOU KNOW?

Some of the largest beaks in relation to body size belonged to Oviraptor and Psittacosaurus.

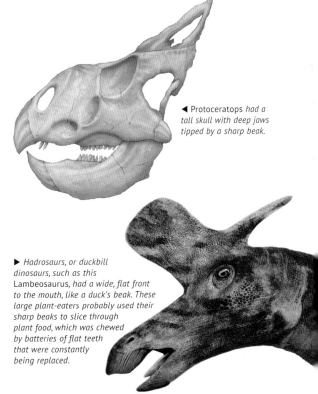

◀ Protoceratops had a tall skull with deep jaws tipped by a sharp beak.

▶ Hadrosaurs, or duckbill dinosaurs, such as this Lambeosaurus, had a wide, flat front to the mouth, like a duck's beak. These large plant-eaters probably used their sharp beaks to slice through plant food, which was chewed by batteries of flat teeth that were constantly being replaced.

Massospondylus

● **Massospondylus was a medium-sized** plant-eater belonging to the group known as the prosauropods.

● **Africa and perhaps North America** were home to Massospondylus, about 200–185 mya.

● **In total**, Massospondylus was about 4.5 m long, with almost half of this length being its tail.

● **The rear legs** of Massospondylus were bigger and stronger than its front legs, so it may have reared up to reach food high up.

● **The name Massospondylus** means 'huge backbone'.

● **Fossils of over 80 Massospondylus** have been found, making it one of the best-studied dinosaurs.

● **The front teeth** of Massospondylus were large and strong with ridged edges.

● **The cheek teeth** were too small and weak to chew large amounts of food, so perhaps food was mashed in the dinosaur's stomach.

● **In the 1980s**, some scientists suggested that Massospondylus was a meat-eater, partly due to its ridged front teeth, but this idea is now outdated.

● **Massospondylus had a tiny head** compared to its body, so it must have spent hours each day gathering enough food to survive.

◀ Massospondylus probably spent most of its time eating to fuel its bulky body.

Stomach stones

● **Some dinosaur fossils** are found with smooth, rounded stones, like seashore pebbles, jumbled up among or near them.

● **Smooth pebbles occur** with dinosaur fossils far more than would be expected by chance alone.

● **These stones** are mainly found with or near the remains of large plant-eating dinosaurs, especially prosauropods such as Massospondylus, Plateosaurus and Riojasaurus, sauropods such as Brachiosaurus and Diplodocus, the parrot-beaked Psittacosaurus and the stegosaurs.

KEY

1 Gullet	6 Lung
2 Crop	7 Gizzard (stomach)
3 Windpipe	8 Small intestine
4 Heart	9 Large intestine
5 Liver	10 Kidney

▶ Gastroliths as small as a pea and as large as a football have been found.

● **Some plant-eating dinosaurs** may have used smooth stones to help process their food.

● **The smooth pebbles** associated with dinosaur remains are known as gastroliths.

● **Gastroliths were stones** that a dinosaur deliberately swallowed.

● **In the stomach**, gastroliths acted as 'millstones', crushing and churning food, and breaking it down into a soft pulp for better digestion.

● **As gastroliths churned** and rubbed inside a dinosaur's guts, they became very rounded, smoothed and polished.

● **Gastroliths may be the reason** why many big plant-eaters, especially sauropods, had no chewing teeth – the mashing was done inside the guts.

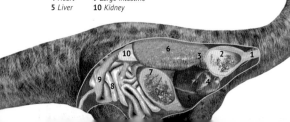

◀ Sauropods, like Barosaurus, swallowed stones that ground up their food in a part of the digestive system called the gizzard. This meant that no feeding time was wasted in chewing.

Migration

- **Today, almost no land reptiles** go on regular, long-distance journeys, called migrations.

- **Over the past 30 years,** some scientists have suggested that certain dinosaurs regularly migrated.

- **Evidence for migrating dinosaurs** comes from the positions of the continents at the time. In certain regions, cool winters would have prevented the growth of enough plants for dinosaurs to eat.

▼ Fossils of Pachyrhinosaurus *have been found in parts of Alaska that were inside the Arctic Circle at the end of the Cretaceous Period. It is possible they migrated here from farther south.*

- **Fossil evidence** suggests that some plants stopped growing during very hot or dry times, so some dinosaurs would have migrated to find food.

- **The footprints or tracks** of many dinosaurs travelling in herds is possible evidence that some dinosaurs migrated.

- **Dinosaurs that may have migrated** include *Pachyrhinosaurus*, sauropods such as *Diplodocus* and *Camarasaurus*, and ornithopods such as *Iguanodon* and *Muttaburrasaurus*.

- **One huge fossil site** in Alberta, Canada, contains the fossils of about 1000 *Pachyrhinosaurus* – perhaps a migrating herd that got caught in a flood.

- **In North America,** huge herds of horned dinosaurs may have migrated north for the brief sub-Arctic summer.

- **In 2012, teeth from** *Camarasaurus* suggested they migrated perhaps 300 km each way to avoid the dry season.

China

- **For centuries,** dinosaur fossils in China were identified as belonging to creatures from folklore such as dragons.

- **The first fossils** studied scientifically in China were uncovered in the 1930s.

- **Since the 1980s,** dinosaur discoveries in almost every province of China have amazed scientists around the globe.

- **A few exciting dinosaur finds** in China have been fakes, such as part of a bird skeleton that was joined to the part-skeleton of a dinosaur along a natural-looking crack in the rock.

- **Some better-known Chinese finds** include *Mamenchisaurus, Psittacosaurus, Tuojiangosaurus* and *Avimimus*.

- **Remains of the prosauropod** *Lufengosaurus* were uncovered in China's southern province of Yunnan, in 1941.

- **China's** *Lufengosaurus* lived during the Early Jurassic Period, and measured about 6–7 m in length.

- **Many recently found fossils** in China are of feathered dinosaurs such as *Caudipteryx, Sinosauropteryx* and *Microraptor*.

▼ *Recent fossil finds in China are causing scientists to change many long-held ideas.*

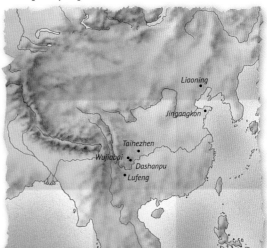

Liaoning

Jingangkon

Taihezhen

Wujiabai

Dashanpu

Lufeng

South America

● **Many of the most important** discoveries of dinosaur fossils in the last 30 years were made in South America.

● **Dinosaur fossils** have been found from the north to the south of the continent, many in the countries of Brazil and Argentina.

● **Most dinosaur fossils** in South America have been found on the high grassland, scrub and semi-desert of southern Brazil and Argentina.

● **Some of the earliest known dinosaurs**, such as *Herrerasaurus* and *Eoraptor*, lived more than 225 mya in Argentina.

▶ Saltasaurus *is named after the region in Argentina where its fossils were discovered – Salta Province.*

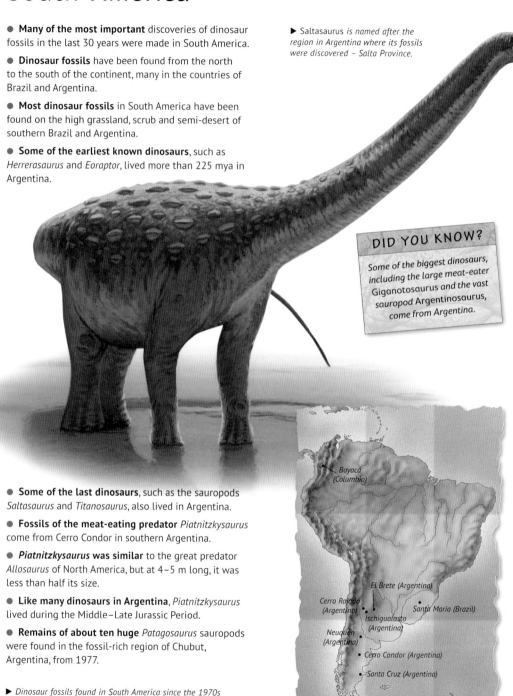

DID YOU KNOW?

Some of the biggest dinosaurs, including the large meat-eater Giganotosaurus and the vast sauropod Argentinosaurus, come from Argentina.

● **Some of the last dinosaurs**, such as the sauropods *Saltasaurus* and *Titanosaurus*, also lived in Argentina.

● **Fossils of the meat-eating predator** *Piatnitzkysaurus* come from Cerro Condor in southern Argentina.

● ***Piatnitzkysaurus* was similar** to the great predator *Allosaurus* of North America, but at 4–5 m long, it was less than half its size.

● **Like many dinosaurs in Argentina**, *Piatnitzkysaurus* lived during the Middle–Late Jurassic Period.

● **Remains of about ten huge** *Patagosaurus* sauropods were found in the fossil-rich region of Chubut, Argentina, from 1977.

Boyacá (Columbia)

El Brete (Argentina)

Cerro Rajado (Argentina)

Santa Maria (Brazil)

Ischigualasto (Argentina)

Neuquén (Argentina)

Cerro Condor (Argentina)

Santa Cruz (Argentina)

▶ *Dinosaur fossils found in South America since the 1970s reveal unique kinds of meat-eaters, among the biggest predatory dinosaurs, some of the earliest members of the dinosaur group, and possibly the largest of all dinosaurs,* Argentinosaurus.

Tuojiangosaurus

- **Tuojiangosaurus was part** of the stegosaur group. It lived during the Late Jurassic Period, about 170–155 mya.

- **The first nearly complete** dinosaur skeleton to be found in China was of a *Tuojiangosaurus*, and fossil skeletons are on display in several Chinese museums.

- **The name** *Tuojiangosaurus* means 'Tuo River reptile'.

- **Tuojiangosaurus was 7 m long** from nose to tail and probably weighed about 3–4 tonnes.

- **Like other stegosaurs,** *Tuojiangosaurus* had tall plates of bone on its back.

- **The back plates** were roughly triangular and probably stood upright in two rows that ran from the neck to the middle of the tail.

- **Tuojiangosaurus plucked** low-growing plants with its beak-shaped mouth, and partly chewed them with its ridged cheek teeth.

> **DID YOU KNOW?**
> The spiked tail of many stegosaurs, probably used in defence, has become known as a 'thagomizer' – a term invented in the 1980s by American cartoonist Gary Larson.

▲ Tuojiangosaurus *had four long V-shaped spikes on its tail that it swung at enemies in self-defence.*

Head crests

- **Many dinosaurs had lumps,** plates, ridges or other shapes of bone on their heads, called head crests.

- **Head crests** may have been covered with brightly coloured skin for visual display.

- **Meat-eaters with head crests** included *Carnotaurus* and *Dilophosaurus*.

- **The dinosaurs with the largest** and most complicated head crests were the hadrosaurs.

- **The largest head crest** was probably a long, hollow, tubular shape of bone belonging to the hadrosaur *Parasaurolophus*.

- **The head crests of hadrosaurs** may have been involved in making sounds.

- **Some years ago,** the hadrosaur *Tsintaosaurus* was thought to have a very unusual head crest – a hollow tube sticking straight up between the eyes, like a unicorn's horn.

- **The so-called head crest** of *Tsintaosaurus* was then thought to be from another hadrosaur, *Tanius*.

- **Then another** *Tsintaosaurus* **specimen** was found with a similar crest, but more paddle-shaped, so this dinosaur is again regarded as being crested.

> **DID YOU KNOW?**
> The head crests of some large Parasaurolophus, perhaps full-grown males, reached an incredible 1.8 m in length.

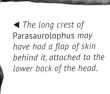

◄ *The long crest of Parasaurolophus may have had a flap of skin behind it, attached to the lower back of the head.*

Sails

- **Long, bony extensions**, like rods or spines, stuck up from the backs of some dinosaurs.

- **These extensions** may have held up a large area of skin, commonly called a back sail.

- **Dinosaurs with back sails** included the meat-eater *Spinosaurus* and the plant-eater *Ouranosaurus*.

- *Spinosaurus* and *Ouranosaurus* both lived over 100 mya.

- **Fossils of *Spinosaurus*** and *Ouranosaurus* were found in North Africa.

- **The skin on a back sail** may have been brightly coloured, or may even have changed colour, like the skin of a chameleon lizard today.

- **Colours and patterns** could be used to startle enemies, deter rivals, and impress mates at breeding time.

- **A back sail** may have helped to control body temperature. Standing sideways to the sun, it would absorb the sun's heat and allow the dinosaur to warm up quickly.

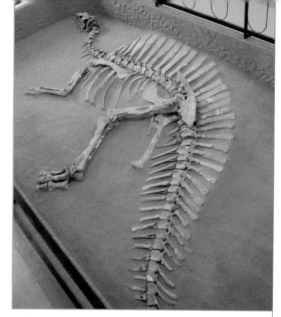

▲ *Apart from its back sail,* Ouranosaurus *was similar to its close cousin, the plant-eater* Iguanodon.

- **Standing in the shade**, a back sail would lose warmth and help the dinosaur to avoid overheating.

North America

- **North America** is the continent where most dinosaur fossils have been found.

- **Most of these fossils** come from the West, which includes the US states of Montana, Wyoming, Utah, Colorado and Arizona, and Alberta in Canada.

- **Several fossil-rich sites** in North America are now national parks.

- **The US Dinosaur National Monument**, on the border of Utah and Colorado, was established in 1915.

- **The Cleveland-Lloyd Dinosaur Quarry** in Utah contains fossils of stegosaurs, ankylosaurs, sauropods and meat-eaters such as *Allosaurus*.

- **Along the Red Deer River** in Alberta, a large area containing thousands of dinosaur fossils has been designated the Dinosaur Provincial Park.

- **Fossils found in Alberta** include those of the meat-eater *Albertosaurus*, armoured *Euoplocephalus* and the duckbill *Lambeosaurus*.

- **The Dinosaur Provincial Park** in Alberta is a United Nations World Heritage Site – an area of outstanding natural importance.

Colville (Alaska)

Peace River (Canada)

Drumheller (Canada)

Choteau (USA)

Billings (USA)

Cleveland–Lloyd Dinosaur Quarry

Moreno Hills (USA)

Dinosaur Provincial Park (Canada)

Hell Creek (USA)

Lance Creek (USA)

Como Ridge (USA)

Dinosaur Nat. Monument (USA)

San Juan River (USA)

Ghost Ranch (USA)

Coahuila State (Mexico)

Bay of Fundy (Canada)

Mt Tom (USA)

Haddonfield (USA)

Garden Park (USA)

Paluxy River (USA)

- **A huge, 20-m-long plant-eater** was named *Alamosaurus* from the Ojo Alamo rock formations, now known as Kirtland Shales, in New Mexico, USA.

- ***Coelophysis* was discovered** in New Mexico, USA, in 1881. In the 1940s, another expedition found dozens of skeletons at a single site.

Iguanodon

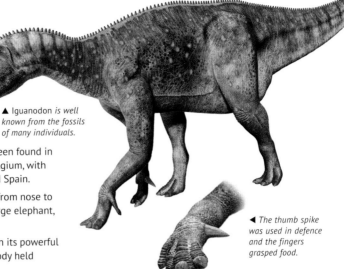

▲ Iguanodon *is well known from the fossils of many individuals.*

- **Part of the ornithopod group,** *Iguanodon* was a large plant-eating dinosaur.

- **It lived** during the Early to Middle Cretaceous Period, 130–125 mya.

- **Numerous fossils** of *Iguanodon* have been found in several countries in Europe, especially Belgium, with similar fossils from England, Germany and Spain.

- *Iguanodon* **measured** about 10–11 m from nose to tail. It probably weighed the same as a large elephant, around 4–5 tonnes.

- *Iguanodon* **probably walked** and ran on its powerful back legs for much of the time, with its body held horizontal.

◄ *The thumb spike was used in defence and the fingers grasped food.*

DID YOU KNOW?

Iguanodon was one of the very first dinosaurs to be given an official scientific name in 1825.

- **A cone-shaped spike** on the thumb may have been used as a weapon for jabbing at rivals or enemies.

- **The three central fingers** on the hands had hoof-like claws for occasional four-legged walking.

- **The fifth, or little finger,** was able to bend across the hand for grasping objects, and was perhaps used to pull plants towards the mouth.

Hibernation

DID YOU KNOW?

Leaellynasaura means 'Leaellyn's lizard/reptile', named after Leaellyn Rich, the young daughter of the palaeontolgists who discovered its fossils.

- **Dinosaurs may have** gone into an inactive state called torpor or 'hibernation' during cold periods, as many reptiles do today.

- **The plant-eater** *Leaellynasaura,* found at Dinosaur Cove, Australia, may have become torpid due to the yearly cycle of seasons there.

- **Dinosaur Cove** was nearer the South Pole when dinosaurs lived there, 110–105 mya. At this time, the climate was relatively warm, with no ice at the North or South Poles.

- **Dinosaurs living** at Dinosaur Cove would have had to cope with periods of darkness in winter. They may have become torpid to survive the cold.

- **The eye and brain shapes** of *Leaellynasaura* suggest it had good eyesight, which would have helped it to see in the winter darkness, or in dim forests.

- **Dinosaur fossils** have been found in the Arctic region near the North Pole.

- **Arctic dinosaurs** either became torpid in winter, or migrated south to warmer regions.

◄ *Leaellynasaura may have slept through the cold season, perhaps protected in a burrow. This 3-m dinosaur had a longer tail, in proportion to size, than almost any other dinosaur.*

Sounds

● **Few reptiles today** make complicated sounds, except for simple hisses, grunts, coughs and roars.

● **Fossils suggest** that dinosaurs made a variety of sounds in several different ways.

● **The bony, hollow head crests** of duckbills (hadrosaurs) may have been used for making sounds.

● **The head crests** of some hadrosaurs contained tubes called respiratory airways, which were used for breathing.

● **Air blown forcefully** through a hadrosaur's head crest passages could have made the whole crest vibrate.

● **A vibrating head crest** may have made a loud sound like a honk, roar or bellow – similar to an elephant trumpeting with its trunk.

● **Fossil skulls** of some hadrosaurs, such as *Edmontosaurus* and *Kritosaurus*, suggest that there was a loose flap of skin, like a floppy bag, between the nostrils and the eyes.

● ***Kritosaurus* may have inflated** its loose nasal flap of skin like a balloon to make a honking or bellowing sound, as some seals do today.

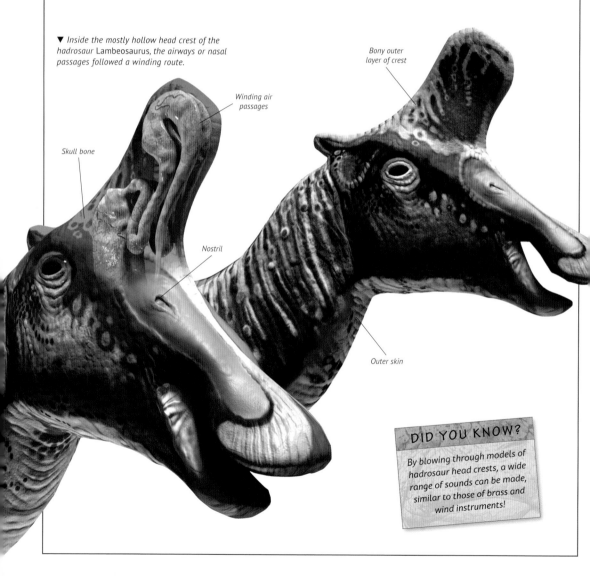

▼ *Inside the mostly hollow head crest of the hadrosaur* Lambeosaurus, *the airways or nasal passages followed a winding route.*

Bony outer layer of crest

Winding air passages

Skull bone

Nostril

Outer skin

DID YOU KNOW?

By blowing through models of hadrosaur head crests, a wide range of sounds can be made, similar to those of brass and wind instruments!

Nodosaurs

- **Nodosaurs were a subgroup** of armoured dinosaurs in the main ankylosaur group.

- **The nodosaur subgroup** included *Edmontonia*, *Sauropelta*, *Polacanthus* and *Nodosaurus*.

- **Nodosaurs were slow-moving**, heavy-bodied plant-eaters with thick, heavy nodules, lumps and plates of bone in their skin for protection.

- **Most nodosaurs lived** during the Late Jurassic and Cretaceous Periods, 160–66 mya.

- *Edmontonia* **lived** in North America during the Late Cretaceous Period, 75–66 mya.

- **It was about 7 m long**, but its bony armour made it very heavy for its size, at 4–5 tonnes.

- **Along its neck**, back and tail *Edmontonia* had rows of flat and spiky plates.

▶ Edmontonia, *one of the last dinosaurs, was covered in many sharp lumps and spikes of bone that gave it some protection from its enemies.*

- **The nodosaur** *Polacanthus* was about 5 m long and lived 130–120 mya.

- **Fossils of** *Polacanthus* come from the Isle of Wight, England, and perhaps from North America, in South Dakota, USA.

Inventing the dinosaur

- **When fossils of dinosaurs** were first studied by scientists in the 1820s, they were thought to be from huge lizards, rhinoceroses or even whales.

- **The first dinosaur** to be officially named in 1824 was *Megalosaurus*, by Englishman William Buckland.

- **Fossils of dinosaurs** were found and studied in 1822 by Gideon Mantell, a doctor in Sussex, southern England.

- **In 1825**, Mantell named the creature *Iguanodon*, because its teeth were very similar in shape to, but larger than, the teeth of the iguana lizard.

- **In the late 1830s**, British scientist Richard Owen realized that some fossils did not belong to lizards, but to an as yet unnamed group of reptiles.

- **In 1841–42**, Richard Owen invented a new name for the group of giant prehistoric reptiles – Dinosauria.

- **The name 'dinosaur'** means 'terrible lizard/reptile'.

- **Life-sized models** of several dinosaurs were made by British sculptor Waterhouse Hawkins in 1852–54.

- **Hawkins' models** were displayed at the Crystal Palace Exhibition in London, and caused a public sensation.

DID YOU KNOW?

The three main dinosaurs of the newly named Dinosauria in the 1840s were Iguanodon, Megalosaurus and Hylaeosaurus.

▼ Megalosaurus *was the first dinosaur to be given an official scientific name, even though the term 'dinosaur' had not yet been invented.*

Brains

- **There is a broad link** between the size of an animal's brain compared to the size of its body, and the level of intelligence it shows.

- **Some fossil dinosaur skulls** have preserved the hollow where the brain once was, revealing its approximate size and shape.

- **In some cases**, a lump of rock formed inside a fossil skull, taking on the size and shape of the brain.

- **The tiny brain** of *Stegosaurus* weighed about 70–80 g, while the whole dinosaur weighed perhaps 4 tonnes.

- **The brain** of *Stegosaurus* was only 1/50,000th of the weight of its whole body (in a human it is 1/50th).

- *Brachiosaurus'* **brain** was perhaps only 1/100,000th of the weight of its whole body.

- **The brain of the small meat-eater** *Troodon* was about 1/100th the weight of its body, which means that *Troodon* was probably one of the most intelligent dinosaurs.

- **The brain-body size comparison** for most dinosaurs is much the same as that of living reptiles.

- **Small- and medium-sized** meat-eaters such as *Troodon* may have been as 'intelligent' as parrots or rats.

- **It was once thought** that *Stegosaurus* had a 'second brain' in the base of its tail. Now this lump is thought to have been a nerve junction.

◀ Camarasaurus *had one of the smallest brains for its body size of any dinosaur – about the size of a human fist.*

◀ *Small meat-eaters such as* Troodon *had the biggest brains for their body size, and probably showed the most intelligence.*

Therizinosaurs

- **For years**, finds of huge fossil claws puzzled experts as to which creatures they came from.

- **In the mid 1990s** more finds made the picture clearer. They came from a previously unknown group of dinosaurs, related to meat-eaters, but plant-eaters themselves.

- **The new group was named in 1997** as the therizinosaurs, 'scythe lizards' or 'reaper lizards', after their massively long claws.

▼ Therizinosaurus *was one of the last of its group, living about 70 mya in what is now Mongolia, Central Asia. Its first fossils were found in the 1940s but remained a mystery for almost half a century.*

- **Another name used less often** is segnosaurs, meaning 'slow lizards'.

- **Therizinosaurs belonged** to the dinosaur group known as theropods, in which all the other kinds were meat-eaters, from tiny raptors to giants like *Tyrannosaurus* and *Spinosaurus*.

- **But the skulls and teeth** of therizinosaurs show they were probably plant-eaters.

- **Most therizinosaurs stood** on their back legs, had wide hips, feathers and were large.

- **Some were enormous** – *Therizinosaurus* itself stood 5 m tall, was 10 m long, and weighed 5 tonnes.

- **Most therizinosaur fossils** come from the Middle and Late Cretaceous Period, 130–66 mya, and are found in East Asia, with some from North America.

- *Alxasaurus* **was one of** the smaller therizinosaurs, about 2.2 m tall and 3.5 m long.

- **Its discovery in the 1990s** helped to establish the group, and show it was a subgroup of the theropods, whose close relatives were the raptors and oviraptors – themselves very bird-like.

Microraptor

● *Microraptor* is one of the smallest and most feathered dinosaurs ever found.

● It probably weighed less than one kilogram and was only 80–90 cm long.

● Its fossils are 125–120 million years old and come from the Liaoning area of northeast China.

● Finds so far are of more than 250 specimens, making *Microraptor* one of the most common creatures at that time.

● *Microraptor* was probably a raptor, in the dromaeosaur group.

● It was also 'four-winged' – it had feathers on its arms and legs.

● These feathers were up to 20 cm long on the arms, 15 cm on the legs, and well designed for flight.

● There were also simpler, plume-like feathers on the tail.

DID YOU KNOW?

Detailed fossil remains of several Microraptor contain tiny bones and other parts from mammals, birds, lizards and even fish, many smaller than thumb-sized, which were probably their last meals.

◀ Microraptor *was the first known 'four-winged dinosaur', receiving its official name in 2000.*

● It is not clear whether *Microraptor* was an extremely good glider, swooping down skilfully from trees, or whether it could truly fly in a controlled, sustained way, like a bird.

● The feathers meant *Microraptor* would have had problems walking and running on the ground, so it probably lived in trees.

Latirhinus

● *Latirhinus* is one of the most recently discovered hadrosaurs, named in 2012.

● Its fossils are from the Late Cretaceous Period, 80–70 mya, when many kinds of hadrosaurs were evolving.

● The remains of *Latirhinus* were dug from the Cerro del Pueblo Formation in Coahuila, Northern Mexico.

● These rocks have also yielded fossils of other hadrosaurs, horned dinosaurs (ceratopsians), pterosaurs and turtles.

● *Latirhinus* is one of the most southern of all hadrosaurs, most of which came from northern lands.

● One of its main features was its extra-large nose or snout, making up almost half of the head's length.

● The name *Latirhinus* means 'wide or broad nose'.

● This very large nose could have had a flap of loose skin that was blown up like a balloon, to make sounds or for visual display.

● From similar hadrosaurs, the size of *Latirhinus* was about 9 m long and 3 tonnes in weight.

▼ Latirhinus *may have used its nose flap to make honking sounds or to inflate like a balloon and attract mates at breeding time.*

1000 **WILD ANIMAL** FACTS

Monkeys

● **Monkeys are primates** – mammals that are mainly adapted for living in the trees. They have long arms and legs and flexible fingers for gripping branches.

● **Unlike their fellow primates** the apes, most monkeys have tails.

● **Monkeys from Africa and Asia** are called Old World monkeys. They include baboons, langurs and macaques.

● **Old World monkeys** have close-set nostrils and hard pads on their bottoms to help them sleep comfortably sitting up.

● **The tail** of an Old World monkey does not grasp branches, like that of a New World monkey (a monkey from the rainforests of Central and South America).

▶ *A male mandrill threatens a rival by showing off his long, sharp canine teeth.*

● **Japanese macaques** live in the mountains, where it gets very cold. They grow thick coats, and sit in pools of hot water that bubble up from volcanic springs to keep warm.

● **The proboscis monkey** gets it name from the huge nose of the male (proboscis is another word for nose), which probably helps it to attract females.

● **Baboons are large** African monkeys. They spend most of their time on the ground. They are strong and agile enough to catch other monkeys, birds and small antelope.

● **Colobus monkeys** have long back legs that help them to leap great distances between trees. The tail of the black and white colobus helps it to steer and change direction.

● **Male mandrills** have bright red and blue faces, and females prefer males with brighter colours. Mandrills are the heaviest monkeys in the world, weighing up to 55 kg.

Skates and rays

● **Skates and rays belong** to a group of over 650 species of fish. It includes stingrays, electric rays, manta rays, eagle rays, sawfish and guitarfish.

● **Most skates and rays** have flat, almost diamond-shaped bodies, with pectoral fins elongated into broad wings. Guitarfish and sawfish have longer, more shark-like bodies.

● **The gills and mouths** of skates and rays are on the undersides of their bodies.

● **They have no bones.** Like sharks, they are cartilaginous fish – their skeleton is made of rubbery cartilage instead.

● **Skates and rays live** mostly on the ocean floor, feeding on shellfish.

● **Manta rays live near** the surface and feed on plankton.

● **Stingrays get their name** from their whip-like tail with its poisonous barbs.

● **The Atlantic manta ray** is the biggest ray, often more than 7 m wide and 6 m in length.

● **Electric rays are tropical rays** that are able to give off a powerful electric charge to defend themselves against attackers.

▶ *Stingrays use their poisonous barbs for defence. The blue-spotted stingray lies on the sea bed but can whip its tail over its body to plunge its toxin into an attacker.*

DID YOU KNOW?

The black torpedo ray can give a 220 volt shock – as much as a household electric socket.

Coastal fish

● **At the coast** the sea is shallow and sunlight can reach the sea bed. Many ocean plants and seaweeds live here, making the coast an ideal habitat for fish.

● **Young fish often live** in coastal areas. They hide from predators among the plants and seaweeds.

● **Common stargazer fish** bury themselves in sand. Their eyes are on the top of their heads so they can see prey and predators above them. They have sharp venomous spines behind their gills, which they use to defend themselves.

◄ There are about 50 species of stargazer fish and they typically grow to about 75 cm long. They live in the Atlantic, Pacific and Indian Oceans and are most common in warm coastal waters.

● **Sand eels are long,** thin fish that live in sandy bays in northern Europe. They are preyed upon by puffins, which dive into the sea to catch them.

● **Wolf fish live in shallow water** and around deep sea corals in the North Atlantic Ocean. They have large teeth for cracking open shelled animals.

● **Capelin fish swim** to shallow water when it is time to lay their eggs. Each female lays up to 60,000 eggs in coastal sand.

● **When it is time to mate,** oyster toadfish make such loud grunting noises that they can be heard by people living nearby.

● **Unlike many fish,** oysterfish are able to survive in the heavily polluted waters of some coastal areas.

● **East Atlantic red gurnards** use the stiff spines on their fins to feel their way along the sea bed as they hunt for crustaceans, such as shrimps and crabs.

● **Some coastal fish,** such as summer flounder, migrate between the sea and estuaries (where rivers meet the sea). They prefer to spend warmer months inshore, and migrate offshore for the winter and to spawn.

Lizards

● **Lizards make up a large,** successful group of reptiles of about 5500 species. They live in many parts of the world and in a variety of habitats. They are mostly small animals with four legs and a long tail.

● **Lizards move in many ways** – running, scampering and slithering. Some can glide between trees. Unlike mammals, their limbs stick out sideways rather than downwards.

● **Most lizards lay eggs,** although a few give birth to their young. Unlike birds or mammals, a mother lizard does not nurture (look after) her young.

● **Some lizards** are able to shed their tails when they are chased. The predator is left holding onto a wriggling tail while the lizard escapes. The lizard usually grows a new tail.

● **A lizard has five clawed** toes on each foot. Web-footed geckoes have webbed feet so they can run across sand dunes without sinking.

● **The basilisk lizard** is also known as the Jesus Christ lizard because it can walk on water.

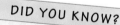

DID YOU KNOW?

Most lizards live just a few years but a blue iguana called Godzilla died in 2004 – aged 59.

● **When threatened,** a chuckwalla runs into a rock crevice and expands its body with air until it is so tightly wedged that predators can't pull it out.

● **Lizards can live** in deserts because they only need a small amount of water to survive.

● **The amphisbaenians** are very closely related to lizards, but they do not have legs. They are also known as 'worm lizards'. They burrow through soil looking for worms and insects.

▼ Thorny devils are spiny lizards that can survive in the extreme habitat of the Australian desert. They only eat ants – feasting on up to 2500 in one meal.

Birds of prey

● **There are about 280 species** of birds of prey. The group includes kestrels, falcons, goshawks, buzzards and vultures.

● **Most birds of prey** are hunters. They feed on other birds, fish and small mammals, catching their prey in their claws.

● **Most birds of prey** are strong fliers, with sharp eyes, powerful talons (claws) and a hooked bill.

● **Birds of prey** are active during the day, unlike owls, which hunt at night.

● **Eagles are the most powerful** birds of prey. Female harpy eagles from the Amazon rainforest are strong enough to snatch monkeys and sloths from the treetops.

● **The bald eagle** is the symbol of the USA. It is named after the white feathers on its head – an old meaning of the word 'bald' is 'white'.

● **There are two** kinds of hawks. Accipiters, such as the goshawk, catch their prey by lying in wait on perches. Buteos, like the kestrel, hover in the air. Buzzards are buteo hawks.

DID YOU KNOW?

The peregrine falcon can reach speeds of 350 km/h when stooping (diving) on prey.

● **The Everglade kite** has an unusual diet – it feeds only on water snails. This kite's thin, hooked bill reaches inside the snail's shell to pull out its body without even breaking the shell.

● **In the Middle Ages**, merlins and falcons were trained to fly from a falconer's wrist to catch birds and other animals.

◀ *The powerful, hooked bill of a golden eagle is used to tear food into pieces small enough for the bird to swallow.*

Frogs and toads

● **Frogs and toads** are amphibians – creatures that live both on land and in the water.

● **There are about 3900** species of frog and toad. Most live near water, but some live in trees and others live underground.

● **Frogs usually have smooth skins** and long back legs for jumping. They tend to live in or near water. Toads are usually bigger, with a thicker, warty skin. They prefer to live on land.

● **Frogs and toads** are carnivores, catching fast-moving insects by darting out their long, sticky tongues.

● **Frogs and toads begin life** as fish-like tadpoles, hatching in the water from huge clutches of eggs called spawn.

● **After 7–10 weeks**, tadpoles grow legs and lungs and develop into frogs, ready to leave the water.

● **In midwife toads**, the male looks after the eggs. He winds strings of eggs around his back legs and carries them about until they hatch.

● **The Goliath frog** of West Africa is the largest frog – over 86 cm in length. The biggest toad is the cane toad of Queensland, Australia – one weighed 2.6 kg and measured more than 25 cm in length.

● **The colourful poison-arrow frogs** found in Central American rainforests are named because native peoples tip arrows with poison from glands in the frogs' skin.

DID YOU KNOW?

A male Darwin's frog swallows his eggs and keeps them in his throat until they hatch – and pop out of his mouth.

▲ *The warty bumps on a toad's skin produce poison to deter predators.*

Bats

● **Bats** are the only flying mammals. Their wings are made of leathery skin stretched between four long finger bones on each hand. Fast-flying bats can reach speeds of almost 100 km/h.

● **Most bats sleep** during the day, hanging upside down in caves and other dark places. They emerge at night to hunt for insects.

● **Bats find things** in the dark by giving out a series of high-pitched clicks. They can locate prey from the echoes (sounds that bounce back to them) of the clicks. This is called echolocation.

● **Bats are not blind** – their eyesight is as good as that of most humans.

● **There are more than 1100 species of bat**, living on all continents except Antarctica. One in every four mammal species is a bat!

● **Kitti's hog-nosed bat** is probably the world's smallest mammal. Its body is only about 2.5 cm in length and it is so small that it could sit on the tip of your finger.

◄ *The huge ears of this big-eared bat help it to catch the sounds reflected from its surroundings.*

● **Many tropical flowers** rely on fruit bats to spread their pollen.

● **Frog-eating bats** can tell edible frogs from poisonous ones by the frogs' mating calls.

● **The vampire bats** of tropical Latin America feed on blood, sucking it from animals such as cattle and horses. Each bat drinks about two tablespoonfuls of blood each night.

● **False vampire bats** are bats that do not suck on blood, but feed on other creatures such as smaller bats and rats. The greater false vampire bat of Southeast Asia is one of the biggest of all bats.

Senses

● **In order to survive**, an animal needs to know what is happening in the world around it. It uses its senses to get this information.

● **The five main senses** are sight, hearing, smell, touch and taste. The senses gather information about the animal's situation. The animal's brain then sends out instructions that cause the animal to react in a certain way, such as running from danger. Even simple animals without brains have senses and are able to react to a change in their environment.

● **Some animals**, such as sharks, are able to sense the electricity given off by another animal's muscles.

● **Insects are not able** to see the colour red.

● **Blood-sucking mosquitoes** can detect carbon dioxide – the gas that humans breathe out – which guides them to their victims.

● **Some whales** may 'feel' the Earth's weak magnetic force, which humans would detect using a compass. This magnetic sense may help them to find their way on their migrations, through the wide and featureless ocean.

● **Dung beetles look up** at the stars to help them walk in a straight line when they are rolling balls of dung back to their dens.

● **Falcons are birds of prey** with great eyesight. They can see a mouse up to 1.5 km away.

● **Spiders' legs are covered** with little hairs that can smell and taste. Similarly, butterflies can taste with their feet.

● **Fish have a line** of special sense cells that run along their bodies, called a lateral line. It senses movement in the water, warning fish if a predator is nearby.

◄ *A monarch butterfly has two large compound eyes, each made up of thousands of tiny lenses. It tastes and smells through holes found all over its body, but especially on its super-sensitive antennae.*

Lions

- **Lions are one of the biggest** cats, weighing up to 230 kg. The males may be 3 m in length.

- **They live** mainly in Africa but about 300–350 Asiatic lions live in the Gir Forest in northwest India.

- **Lions usually live** in grassland or scrub, in large family groups called prides. A typical pride contains 12 related females and their cubs, and up to five adult males. The males protect the pride and the females do the hunting.

- **Female lions** are called lionesses. They hunt prey such as gazelle and zebra and even animals as big as buffalo.

- **Lionesses catch their prey** by stealth, stalking to within 30 m of their victims and then dashing forwards to make the kill.

- **They often hunt** at dusk or dawn, and have very good night vision.

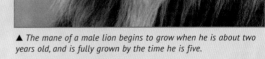

▲ *The mane of a male lion begins to grow when he is about two years old, and is fully grown by the time he is five.*

- **Lions usually rest** for about 20 hours a day, and walk no farther than 10 km or so a day.

- **A male lion's** huge, shaggy mane makes him look bigger and stronger, and protects him when fighting.

- **Male lion cubs** leave the pride when they are two years old, and have to fight an older male to join another pride.

▼ *Like all cats, lions are supreme predators. Their forward-facing eyes help them to spy and focus on prey far away, even when the light is fading.*

DID YOU KNOW?

A male lion is able to drag a 300 kg zebra along the ground – it would take at least six men to do this.

Gulls and waders

● **Gulls are big seabirds** that live on coasts all around the world, nesting on cliffs, islands or beaches.

● **They are related** to skuas and terns. Terns are smaller, more graceful birds than gulls, and have forked tails.

● **The great black-backed gull** is a fierce predator, feeding on a wide variety of prey, from fish to rabbits.

● **Herring gull chicks** peck at the red spot on their parents' bills to make them regurgitate (cough up) food for them to eat.

● **The ivory gull** is the only gull with completely white feathers. It lives mainly on Arctic coasts and islands.

● **The pied avocet** uses its pointed, upturned bill to sweep through water or mud in search of food.

● **A ringed plover** will lead predators away from its nest by pretending to have an injured wing.

● **Female phalaropes** are more brightly coloured than the males. They leave the camouflaged males to take care of their eggs and rear the young.

● **The woodcock** is an unusual wader because it lives in woodland instead of along the shoreline. Its mottled brown feathers provide good camouflage.

● **In the breeding season**, groups of male ruffs gather at 'leks', places where they show off their remarkable head and neck feathers. This helps them to attract females.

▼ *A gull chick's speckled feathers make it well camouflaged, helping it to hide from predators.*

Beetles

● **At least 300,000** species of beetle have been identified and they live on land all over Earth. Unlike other insects, adult beetles have elytra – a pair of thick, hard, front wings that form an armour-like casing over the body.

● **The Goliath beetle** of Africa is the heaviest flying insect, at over 100 g. It can grow to 15 cm in length.

● **Dung beetles** roll away the dung of grazing animals so they can lay their eggs on it. Fresh dung from one elephant may contain 7000 beetles.

● **A click beetle** can jump 30 cm into the air to escape, startle predators or to right itself. It is named after the loud sound it makes when it jumps.

● **The bombardier beetle** mixes a cocktail of chemicals inside its body to make a boiling hot spray, which it then squirts from the end of its abdomen.

DID YOU KNOW?
The Arctic beetle feeds on rotting wood and can survive in temperatures below −60°C.

● **The bloody-nosed beetle** wards off predators by giving off a bright-red liquid from its mouth.

● **Great diving beetles** live underwater in ponds and lakes. They breathe from air bubbles that they collect from the surface and store under their elytra.

● **Stag beetles'** huge jaws look like a stag's antlers. Males use them in fights to win females. Each male tries to lift his rival into the air and smash him to the ground.

● **Fireflies produce a special pattern** of flashing lights to signal mates. They make the light by mixing chemicals inside their abdomens to cause a reaction that releases light energy.

◄ *The male stag beetle has much bigger jaws than the female. It uses them to frighten away rival males and predators.*

Slow-moving sharks

● **All sharks** are closely related to skates and rays, and have skeletons made of bone-like cartilage.

● **While many fast sharks** have torpedo-shaped bodies, others are slow movers that stay near the sea bed.

● **Carpet sharks** often have highly patterned skin and flattened bodies. There are many types, but they commonly swim near the sea floor as they look for animals, such as crabs, to eat.

● **Sharks either lay eggs** or give birth to live young. Shark eggs are protected by rubbery cases called mermaid's purses.

● **Spotted wobbegongs** are carpet sharks that are so well camouflaged they can lie in wait for an unsuspecting animal to come close – and then launch an attack.

DID YOU KNOW?

The largest carpet sharks – and the largest fish in the world – are whale sharks, which swim slowly at the sea's surface. A whale shark can grow to 14 m or more.

● **Bamboo sharks** have strong fins that they can use to 'walk' on the sea bed or clamber along rocks and coral reefs.

▶ Whale sharks are most commonly seen in warm coastal waters, especially around coral reefs. They can make incredible migrations and one individual was found to have swum 13,000 km in just over three years.

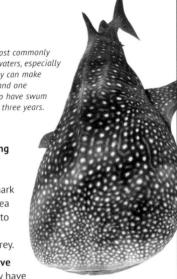

● **A sawshark's long saw-shaped** snout is lined with sharp teeth. As the sawshark cruises along the sea bed it uses its saw to swipe through the sand and feel for prey.

● **Sharks don't have scales**. Instead they have denticles, which are made of enamel (like teeth) and are rough to the touch.

● **Whale sharks** do not hunt large animals. They use their gills to collect plankton (small animals and plants that float in the sea).

Large rodents

● **Beavers are large rodents** with flat, paddle-like tails. They live in northern America and northern Eurasia.

● **Incredibly strong front teeth** allow beavers to chop down quite large trees. They gnaw around the tree in a ring until it finally crashes down.

● **Beavers build dams** across streams using tree branches laid onto a base of mud and stones. Families of beavers often work together on a dam.

▼ Beavers play an important role in developing watery habitats for other animals. They slow a river's flow, help to keep the water clean, and create wetland areas where birds and amphibians can thrive.

● **A beaver's cutting teeth** are strengthened with iron so they are strong enough to chew wood.

● **Porcupines are large rodents** that have hard hairs called quills on their backs. These can be up to 35 cm in length and have sharp tips. If the quills stick into an attacker's skin, they cause serious wounds.

● **The world's largest rodent** is the capybara. It weighs up to 75 kg but is a good swimmer in the rivers of Central and South America.

● **North American porcupines** climb trees so they can feed on bark and the needles (leaves) of conifers.

● **The mara** is a large rodent that looks like a cross between a hare and an antelope. Maras live in South America and they mate for life, which is unusual in the rodent family.

● **The fur of a chinchilla** is thick and velvety soft. Up to 60 hairs can grow from a single follicle (the part of the skin where one hair would normally grow).

● **Chinchillas have been hunted** for their fur, which means they are in danger of becoming extinct in the wild.

Otters

- **Otters are small hunting mammals** that are related to weasels. They are one of 58 species of mustelid, the animal group that also includes stoats, skunks and badgers.

- **They usually live** in burrows in riverbanks.

- **Otters are brilliant swimmers**, and can reach speeds of up to 10 km/h. They can close off their nostrils and ears, allowing them to remain underwater for up to five minutes.

- **They are very lively creatures**, and can often be seen playing on riverbanks and sliding down into the water.

- **These mammals hunt fish**, usually at night, but they also eat crayfish and crabs, clams and frogs.

- **Otters can use their paws** to play with objects such as stones and shellfish.

◄ *The hairs in an otter's fur coat are packed together densely to keep out the cold water and trap warm air close to the body. Just one square centimetre contains 70,000 hairs.*

- **Otters detect their prey** by sight or touch. They use their long whiskers to detect the vibrations and ripples in the water made by swimming animals.

- **Sea otters** eat shellfish. They will balance a rock on their stomach while floating on their back, and crack the shellfish by banging it on the rock.

- **To survive in cold water**, a sea otter needs a high-energy diet of at least 100 g of fish per hour.

- **The giant otter** of Brazil's Amazon river is very rare. It grows up to 1.8 m from its nose to the tip of its tail.

Jellyfish

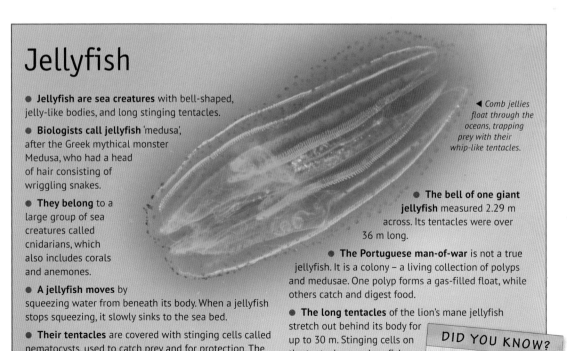

- **Jellyfish are sea creatures** with bell-shaped, jelly-like bodies, and long stinging tentacles.

- **Biologists call jellyfish** 'medusa', after the Greek mythical monster Medusa, who had a head of hair consisting of wriggling snakes.

- **They belong** to a large group of sea creatures called cnidarians, which also includes corals and anemones.

- **A jellyfish moves** by squeezing water from beneath its body. When a jellyfish stops squeezing, it slowly sinks to the sea bed.

- **Their tentacles** are covered with stinging cells called nematocysts, used to catch prey and for protection. The cells explode on contact, driving poisonous threads into the victim.

- **Jellyfish vary in size** from a few millimetres to over 2 m.

◄ *Comb jellies float through the oceans, trapping prey with their whip-like tentacles.*

- **The bell of one giant jellyfish** measured 2.29 m across. Its tentacles were over 36 m long.

- **The Portuguese man-of-war** is not a true jellyfish. It is a colony – a living collection of polyps and medusae. One polyp forms a gas-filled float, while others catch and digest food.

- **The long tentacles** of the lion's mane jellyfish stretch out behind its body for up to 30 m. Stinging cells on the tentacles paralyze fish, plankton or other jellyfish while the lion's mane jellyfish feeds.

DID YOU KNOW?

The poison of the Australian box jellyfish can kill a human in less than five minutes.

Penguins

● **There are 17 different species** of penguins, and all of them live in the Southern Hermisphere.

● **Eight species** live in or around the Antarctic – the coldest, driest and windiest place on Earth. The eight species are: Adélie, Chinstrap, Emperor, Gentoo, King, Macaroni, Rockhopper and Royal.

● **Nine species** live some distance from the icy South Pole. These are: Erect-crested, Fairy, Fjordland, Galápagos, Jackass, Magellanic, Peruvian, Snares and Yellow-eyed.

● **The smallest penguin species** is the fairy penguin, at just 40 cm in height.

● **Penguins cannot fly** but are superb swimmers, using their flippers to 'fly' underwater and their tails and feet for steering and braking.

● **Penguins spend three quarters** of their lives in the cooler parts of the southern oceans.

● **Penguin feathers** are waterproofed with oil and fat so they can survive in temperatures as low as –60°C.

DID YOU KNOW?

Some penguins dig burrows to nest in. A burrow is a safe place to lay an egg.

● **They can leap high** out of the water to land on an ice bank, but on land penguins waddle clumsily or toboggan along on their bellies. They only come on to land or sea ice in order to breed. Most penguins nest in huge colonies called rookeries.

● **Adélie penguins waddle** up to 100 km across ice every year to reach their breeding ground.

◄ *Chinstrap penguins live near the Antarctic, breeding in huge colonies along coasts. Parents regurgitate (vomit) food for their chicks to eat, until the chicks lose their fluffy feathers and can hunt for themselves.*

Termites

● **They look alike**, but termites and ants are not closely related. Termites have no 'waist'. Their antennae are beaded and short. They live mainly in hot places.

● **The number** of males and females in a termite colony is roughly equal. All colonies have a male called the king and a queen who lays the eggs. The king and queen can live for up to 70 years.

● **Termite colonies** have soldiers with well-developed jaws to guard the colony and workers to do all the work. All termite workers and soldiers are wingless and blind because they live underground.

● **Termite nests** are mounds built like cities with many chambers – including a garden used for growing fungus. Many are air-conditioned with special chimneys.

● **Some termites** develop wings in the breeding season. These fly away from the nest to mate and start new colonies of their own.

● **The Australian compass termite** builds tall nest mounds that face north-south, which helps to control the temperature inside. In the morning and evening, the sun warms the wide surface but at midday, the narrow side does not absorb very much of the hot sun.

● **Tree termites** build round nests on tree branches high above the ground. Mud barriers above the nest help to funnel rain away from the nest.

● **A termite queen** can grow up to 15 cm in length and is nothing more than an egg-producing machine. She can lay up to 30,000 eggs in a day.

● **Termites feed on plant material**, especially wood, and can cause serious damage to wooden buildings in the tropics.

● **Nasute termites** defend their nest by squirting a poisonous glue out of their long, nozzle-like snouts.

▼ *Soldier termites have large jaws to help defend their nest.*

Crocodiles and alligators

● **Crocodiles, alligators, caimans and gharials** are large reptiles that make up the group known as crocodilians. There are 13 species of crocodile, two alligators, six caimans and two gharials.

● **Crocodilian species** lived alongside the dinosaurs 200 million years ago.

● **Crocodilians are hunters** that eat a lot of fish, although larger species may eat animals as large as zebras.

● **A crocodilian's body temperature** is the same as its surroundings. They usually bask in the sunshine in the morning, then seek shade or go for a swim to cool off.

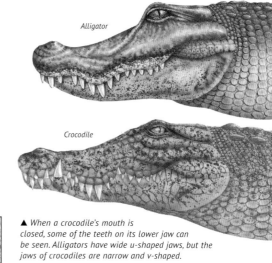

Alligator

Crocodile

▲ *When a crocodile's mouth is closed, some of the teeth on its lower jaw can be seen. Alligators have wide u-shaped jaws, but the jaws of crocodiles are narrow and v-shaped.*

▲ *Despite its great size, a saltwater crocodile can easily haul its body out of the water. It can raise its body above its legs and even chase its prey on land.*

● **The biggest crocodilians** are saltwater crocodiles and Nile crocodiles, which can grow to 7 m in length.

● **Gharials have thin, pointed snouts**. They are named for the pot-shaped bump on males' snouts (ghara means 'pot' in Hindi). They are on the verge of extinction.

● **Crocodiles have thinner snouts** than alligators, and a fourth tooth on the lower jaw, which is visible when the mouth is shut.

● **When her eggs hatch**, a mother Nile crocodile picks up her babies in her mouth and carries them to the water.

● **Alligators are found** both in the Florida Everglades in the United States and in the Yangtze River in China.

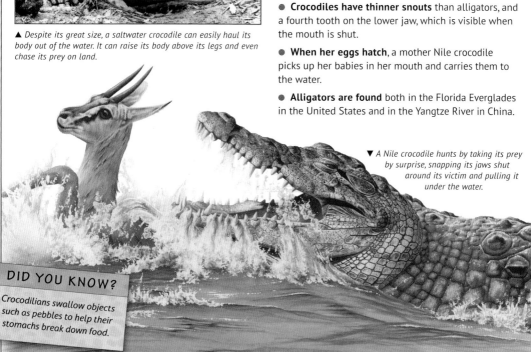

▼ *A Nile crocodile hunts by taking its prey by surprise, snapping its jaws shut around its victim and pulling it under the water.*

DID YOU KNOW?

Crocodilians swallow objects such as pebbles to help their stomachs break down food.

Wolves

● **The largest of all wild dogs**, wolves hunt in packs to track down animals bigger than themselves, such as moose, caribou (reindeer) and musk oxen.

● **A wolf pack** may have 7–20 wolves, led by the eldest male and female.

● **A wolf pack's territory** may be 1000 sq km or more. Wolves can travel vast distances when hunting.

● **Wolves once lived** throughout Europe and North America. Now they are rare in Europe and are found only in Asia and remote areas of North America.

● **Wolves are the ancestors** of all domestic dogs.

● **Like all dogs**, wolves walk on their toes and have strong claws that do not retract. They are agile and graceful, and can jump distances of up to 4.5 m.

● **Their very sensitive hearing** means that wolves can detect sounds up to 3 km away.

● **Wolves howl** to keep in touch with other pack members, before hunting, and to warn rival packs away.

● **Wolf packs** have a distinct hierarchy, reinforced by body language. High-ranking wolves stand tall with ears and tail pointing up. Low-ranking wolves crouch, hold their tail down and flatten their ears against their heads.

● **In cold areas of North America**, Northern Europe and Northern Asia, wolves often have pale coats, which camouflage them against the snow and ice.

▲ *Wolves are more likely to form packs in winter. If two packs meet, violent fights can occur.*

Bees and wasps

● **Bees and wasps** are narrow-waisted insects with four transparent wings. They usually have hairy bodies.

● **There are over** 20,000 species of bee. Many, such as leaf-cutter bees, live alone but over 500 species, such as honeybees, live in colonies.

▼ *Wasps build hexagonal cells in their nests. Each cell contains an egg or a growing grub. The adults take care of the brood.*

● **Worker bees collect nectar** and pollen from flowers.

● **Wasps do not make honey** but adults feed on sweet food, such as fruit, plant sap and nectar.

● **Female ichneumon wasps** lay their eggs inside caterpillars and other insect grubs. When the eggs hatch, the young wasps have a supply of living food to help them grow and develop.

● **Spider-hunting wasps** attack and paralyze spiders with their venom.

● **The tarantula hawk wasp** lays its eggs in tarantula spiders and grows to 8 cm. It has a painful sting.

● **Sawflies are close relatives** of bees and wasps with striped abdomens. They don't sting, but they do attack crops, especially fruit, so they are regarded as pests.

● **Some bumblebees** live in colonies, like honeybees. They make nests using grass and usually build them at ground level, or in the soil.

● **Fig wasps lay their eggs** inside figs, which have tiny flowers inside. As they travel between fig trees, the female pollinates the flowers so the fig seeds can grow.

Mongooses and meerkats

● **The mongoose family** includes mongooses, meerkats, and about 66 species of civets, genets and linsangs.

● **Civets and genets** look like cats, with long bodies, short legs and pointed ears. Mongooses and meerkats have long bodies, short legs and rounded ears.

● **The small-spotted genet** hunts rodents, reptiles, insects and birds at night, using its senses of sight, hearing and smell.

● **The Asian binturong** has coarse fur, ear tufts and a grasping (prehensile) tail, which it uses when climbing.

● **Meerkats live in family groups** in burrows or under rocks. They sit up on their back legs to watch for prey or danger.

● **The diet** of a meerkat is wide, and includes insects, arachnids, small mammals, reptiles, birds and plants.

● **The Egyptian mongoose** was sacred to the ancient Egyptians. Paintings of mongooses have been found on tombs and temples that are nearly 5000 years old.

▶ *Meerkats make loud calls to warn each other of danger and band together to drive off predators.*

● **Most mongooses** live on their own and usually come out at night. Some species, such as the banded mongoose, live in groups and come out during the day.

● **The fossa** is rare, and lives only on the island of Madagascar off the southeast coast of Africa.

● **The fossa** hunts lemurs and other mammals, as well as birds and reptiles.

Parrots and cockatoos

▼ *Scarlet macaws live in the Amazon rainforest of South America.*

● **There are 330 or so parrot species** divided into three main groups – true parrots, cockatoos and lories. Typical parrots and parakeets have broad, fleshy tongues with spoon-shaped tips. Cockatoos have narrow, stubby tongues. Lories and lorikeets have brush-tipped tongues for feeding on pollen and nectar.

● **Typical parrots** are brightly coloured. Flocks live in tropical forests, feeding on fruits, nuts and seeds.

● **Parrots have two toes pointing forwards** and two backwards, so they can grip branches and hold food.

● **Cockatoos are the only** parrots with feathery head crests. They raise and lower their head crests when they are excited, frightened or angry.

● **The budgerigar** is a small parakeet from central Australia. It is very popular as a pet.

● **The hanging parrots** of Southeast Asia get their name because they sleep upside down like bats.

● **The kea of New Zealand** is a parrot that eats meat as well as fruit. It was once wrongly thought to kill sheep.

● **Parrots are well known** for their mimicry of human voices. Some have a repertoire of 300 words or more.

● **The kakapo of New Zealand** is a rare, nocturnal, ground-dwelling parrot. It is the heaviest of all parrots – too heavy to fly. In the breeding season, the males' loud booming calls can be heard up to one kilometre away.

DID YOU KNOW?

Parrots often pair for life, and they can live long lives – up to 80 years in some species.

Flightless birds

▶ The emu of Australia is the world's second largest bird, growing up to 1.7 m tall and weighing up to 45 kg.

Bony crest

◀ The cassowary lives in the forests of tropical Australia and New Guinea. It has a crest that it uses like a crash helmet as it charges through the undergrowth.

◀ Ostriches have soft downy plumage, but their head, neck and legs are almost bare.

Two toes with very sharp toenails

● **Some birds** are so good at swimming or running that they do not need to fly. Flightless birds include large species such as ostriches, emus and rheas, as well as penguins and a few unusual birds that live on islands, such as kiwis.

● **The collective name** for flightless birds is ratites, from the Latin *ratis* meaning 'raft'. Unlike flying birds, ratites have flat, raft-like breastbones that cannot support the muscles needed for flight.

● **The ostrich** is the biggest living bird, up to 2.75 m in height and weighing over 150 kg. It also lays the largest egg of any bird – almost as big as a football.

● **To escape a lion**, the ostrich can hurtle over the African savannah grasslands at speeds of 70 km/h – as fast as a racehorse. Even when the ostrich tires, its strong legs can still deliver a massive kick.

● **Ostriches have only two toes** on each foot – unlike the rhea of South America which has three, and most other birds, which have four. The inner toe has a formidable claw for slashing enemies.

● **Rheas are probably** related to ostriches and emus but they live on the grasslands of South America. These flightless birds all have a similar lifestyle and are able to run fast across grasslands.

● **The rare kakapo parrot** of New Zealand lost the power of flight over time because it had no natural predators – until Europeans introduced dogs and cats to New Zealand.

● **The Galápagos cormorant** uses its small wings to help it balance on the rocky islands of its home.

● **The kiwi of New Zealand** is no bigger than a chicken. It has fur-like feathers and is the only bird with nostrils located at the tip of its bill, which it uses to sniff out worms and grubs.

◀ The nocturnal kiwi's good sense of smell helps it to find worms, insects and spiders in the ground at night.

Dogs and foxes

● **The dog family** is a large group of four-legged, long-nosed, meat-eating animals. It includes dogs, wolves, foxes, jackals and coyotes.

● **Every kind of dog** has long, pointed canine teeth for piercing and tearing its prey. Canine means 'dog'.

● **When hunting**, dogs rely mainly on their good sense of smell and acute hearing.

● **African wild dogs** live in packs of 10–20 members. They hunt as a team, which enables them to bring down prey much larger than themselves such as antelope or wildebeest.

▶ *The red fox is a common member of the dog family, found all over Europe, Asia, North America and Australia.*

● **Strong endurance runners**, African wild dogs are able to chase their prey for 5 km or more at speeds of up to 60 km/h. Their sturdy claws grip the ground firmly as they run.

● **The fennec fox** of Africa and the kit fox of North America both have big ears to help them hear their prey at night and keep cool by day.

● **The Arctic fox** grows a white coat in winter, which camouflages it against the winter snow. In summer, when the snow melts, it grows a brown coat instead.

● **Foxes are cunning** hunters. They prowl at night, alone or in pairs. Their typical prey includes small mammals such as rats, mice and rabbits.

● **The red fox** has adapted to the growth of towns and cities, and may often be seen at night raiding surburban rubbish bins and dumps.

● **The jackals** of Africa look similar to wolves, but they hunt alone for small prey and only meet in packs to grab the leftovers from the kill of a lion.

Poisonous invertebrates

● **Invertebrates use poisons to kill** or paralyze their prey or to defend themselves from their own predators.

● **Invertebrates such as spiders**, wasps and scorpions produce poisons inside their bodies.

● **Insects such as** caterpillars, grasshoppers and beetles often get their poisons from the plants they eat.

● **Most poisonous insects** are brightly coloured – including many caterpillars, wasps and cardinal beetles – to warn off potential enemies.

● **The stings** of bees and wasps are at the back of their bodies. Bumblebees and wasps can sting repeatedly. A honeybee can only sting once because its sting has a barbed tip which sticks in its victim so some of its organs are pulled out when the bee flies off.

● **Velvet ants** are not really ants at all, but wingless wasps with such a nasty sting that they are known as 'cow killers'.

● **Ladybirds** make nasty chemicals in their knees.

● **When attacked**, swallowtail caterpillars whip out a smelly forked gland from a pocket behind their head and hit their attacker with it.

● **Centipedes inject poison** into their prey with their claws. Giant centipedes can kill animals as big as mice.

● **Scorpions have sharp stings** at the end of their tails, linked to sacs of poison. They can control how much poison they inject. Large scorpions use their poison mainly for defence, and use their big pincers for killing prey.

▶ *The giant tropical centipede grows over 30 cm in length. Pain from its bite lasts several days.*

Emperor penguins

- **The emperor penguin** is the biggest swimming bird, at up to 1.2 m tall and weighing over 40 kg. This is twice the weight of any flying bird.

- **They can dive briefly** to depths of 250 m or more, and can hold their breath for up to 22 minutes while they dive in search of fish, krill and squid. They are able to cope with less oxygen than other diving birds, and are able to store it in their body.

- **These birds spend** their whole lives in the Antarctic and the surrounding seas.

- **Emperors are able** to survive winter on the world's coldest land, where there is a permanent blanket of snow and ice.

- **Males look after** the eggs for 100–120 days while the female returns to the sea to feed. The male doesn't eat during this time and endures temperatures as low as −50°C and freezing winds.

▶ *Penguin chicks may look different from adult birds to help parents recognize their own chicks, or to encourage adults to be gentler with them.*

DID YOU KNOW?

The male emperor penguin keeps the female's egg warm on his feet until it hatches.

- **When a chick hatches** from its egg it can feed on fatty 'milk' that its father makes in its throat.

- **When females return** from their trip to the sea they regurgitate food for the growing chicks to eat. Adult emperor penguins can go on trips of 1000 km to get food and return to their mate and chick.

- **Penguin chicks** have soft, grey, fluffy feathers. They cannot swim until their adult plumage of black and white feathers grows in. It is so cold that if a chick is left alone on the Antarctic ice it will die within two minutes. Only one in five chicks survives its first year of life.

- **The main predators** of emperor penguins are orcas, leopard seals and giant petrels, which snatch chicks from the ice.

Iguanas

DID YOU KNOW?

Female iguanas often develop orange spots after mating. The spots deter males from pestering the females!

- **Iguanas are large lizards** that live mainly around the Pacific and in the Americas.

- **Unlike other lizards**, larger iguanas are plant eaters. Most eat flowers, fruit and leaves.

- **The common iguana** lives high up in trees, but lays its eggs in a hole in the ground.

- **When disturbed**, common iguanas will jump from heights of 10 m or so, from their homes in the branches of trees into the water below. They then swim quickly away from danger.

- **The rhinoceros iguana** of the West Indies gets its name from the pointed scales on its snout.

- **The marine iguana** of the Galápagos Islands is the only lizard that spends much of its life in the sea.

- **Marine iguanas gather** together in large groups to sleep at night, which helps them to save energy and keep warm.

- **When in the water**, a marine iguana may dive for 15 minutes or more, pushing itself along with its tail.

- **Although marine iguanas** are not able to breathe underwater, their heart rate slows to allow them to use less oxygen when diving. These iguanas have an unusual diet: they feed on the seaweed growing on underwater rocks.

◀ *Iguanas are often colourful, and many species even change their skin colour. A green iguana is larger than most lizards in this group, growing up to one metre long. Their green skin provides excellent camouflage in trees.*

Crabs and lobsters

- **Crabs and lobsters** are in a group of creatures called crustaceans, named for the crusty coatings on their bodies.

- **Hermit crabs** protect the soft parts of their bodies by living inside the empty shells of sea snails.

- **Crabs and lobsters** are decapods – they have ten legs. The first pair are often strong pincers, which they use to tear food.

▼ Hermit crabs have to swap their adopted shells for larger ones as they grow.

- **For spotting prey**, crabs and lobsters have two pairs of antennae on their heads as well as a pair of eyes on stalks.

- **One of a lobster's claws** usually has blunt knobs for crushing victims. The other has sharp teeth for cutting.

- **Male fiddler crabs** have one giant pincer which they wave to attract a mate.

- **The world's largest land crustacean** is the coconut crab. Its legspan measures up to one metre, which helps it climb coconut trees to feed or escape predators. They are also known as robber crabs, because they steal food whenever they can.

- **The largest crab** is the Japanese spider crab, with a legspan of over 4 m.

- **Spiny lobsters** migrate hundreds of kilometres, clinging to each others' tails in a long line.

- **The largest lobster** ever caught was off the coast of Nova Scotia, Canada, in 1977. It was 1 m long and weighed just over 20 kg – that's the size of a 4-year-old child!

Weasels and their relatives

- **Weasels are one** of 67 species in the mustelid family, which also includes stoats, skunks and badgers.

- **Although small**, weasels or polecats are fierce hunters, able to kill prey much larger than themselves.

- **The European common weasel** (also called the stoat or ermine) turns from brown to white in winter for camouflage against snow. The tip of its tail stays black.

- **Mink feed** on a great range of animals, including crabs, fish, small mammals and birds. Their partly webbed feet enable them to hunt underwater.

- **Large paws** and sharp claws make graceful martens good climbers. Their long, bushy tails help them balance.

- **A wolverine** can kill animals as big as caribou. Its powerful jaws can break through thick bones.

- **If threatened**, skunks spray a foul-smelling liquid at their predators. The smell lasts for days.

▶ All weasels kill even if they are not hungry. They store food in underground burrows for times when it is less available.

- **The European badger** lives in groups of 12 or more in an underground burrow (sett). Badgers feed on small animals, and fruits, roots, bulbs and nuts.

- **The African ratel**, or honey badger, uses its powerful claws to break open bees' nests to reach the honey inside. The animal's thick, loose, rubbery skin helps to protect it from stings, and from other predators.

- **Otters usually live** in burrows in riverbanks. They hunt fish, usually at night, but they also eat crayfish and crabs, clams and frogs. These brilliant swimmers can close off their nostrils and ears to remain underwater for up to five minutes, and can reach speeds of up to 10 km/h.

Reproduction

- **The way that an animal** makes its young is called reproduction.

- **Some small animals**, such as coral polyps, can reproduce simply by growing an exact copy of themselves.

Strong shell has pores (tiny holes) to allow air to pass through

- **Many animals** need a mate to reproduce. In order to attract a mate they enact certain behaviours, known as courtship.

- **Male frogs** croak loudly to attract mates when it is time to breed, and many birds sing to each other.

- **Male birds of paradise** perform incredible dances and show off their feathers to females. Females are fussy about which male they will mate with.

- **Male walruses** are much larger than females. They need to be huge to survive the battles they have with one another in order to win the right to reproduce.

- **Most insects**, amphibians, reptiles, snakes and birds lay eggs that contain their developing young.

Yolk sac contains food

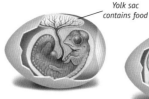
Egg white supplies proteins, water and vitamins

Egg tooth

◄ All birds lay eggs and their chicks grow inside. When it is time to hatch, the chick taps away at the shell with an egg tooth on the tip of its beak to break it open.

- **The young** then continue to develop inside the egg, outside of their parents' bodies. The egg also contains food for the growing animal.

- **Some parents produce thousands** – even millions – of eggs which they abandon. Only a tiny number of the eggs are likely to grow into adults.

- **Most mammals** keep their young inside their bodies while they grow. They invest so much time and energy into their young that mammals usually have far fewer young than other animals.

Snakes

- **Snakes are long**, thin reptiles with scaly bodies and no legs. There are about 2700 different species of snake, living all over the world, except Antarctica.

- **The tiny thread snake** is only 11 cm in length but the giant reticulated python grows up to 10 m in length.

- **All snakes are meat eaters**, and swallow prey whole.

- **Egg-eating snakes** swallow eggs whole, then use the sharp, downward-pointing spines on their backbone to crack the shell. When the snake has swallowed the contents of the egg, it coughs up the shell.

- **Some snakes kill their prey** by squeezing (constricting) it to death. Other snakes use poison.

- **About 700 snake species** are poisonous. Snake poison is called venom and is injected into prey or predators through a snake's hollow teeth, called fangs.

- **About six times a year**, snakes shed their outer layer of skin. This is called moulting, and it allows the snake to grow. A new skin grows under the old one.

▲ The poisonous common krait is one of the deadliest snakes of Pakistan, India and Sri Lanka.

- **Most snakes lay eggs** in damp, warm places and leave them to hatch by themselves. A few female snakes, such as pythons, coil around their eggs to protect them from predators or bad weather while the young develop inside.

- **A few snakes**, such as boas, rattlesnakes, adders and most sea snakes, give birth to live young.

- **Sea snakes** can dive to depths of 100 m to feed on fish. They have tails like oars to push them through water. The most poisonous snake in the world is the black-headed sea snake.

Elephants

- **There are two main kinds** of elephant – the African elephant and the Asian elephant. The animals usually live for about 70 years.

- **African elephants** are the largest land animals, with some males growing to 4 m in height.

- **Asian elephants** are smaller, and have smaller ears. They also have one 'finger' on the tips of their trunks while African elephants have two.

- **Elephants are very intelligent**, with the biggest brain of all land animals. They have good memories.

- **They make a wide range of low rumbling sounds** that carry for long distances. We can only hear about one third of the sounds that elephants make.

- **Female elephants** (cows) live with their calves and young males (bulls) in herds. Older bulls are solitary animals.

- **When males are ready to mate**, they are said to be in 'musth'. This is a dangerous time, as the males become aggressive towards one another.

- **During musth**, glands between the males' eyes and ears produce an oozing substance, warning other males that they are in a fighting mood.

- **In dry areas**, herds may travel vast distances to find food. The bigger elephants protect the little ones between their legs.

> **DID YOU KNOW?**
> Elephants use their highly mobile trunks like snorkels when crossing deep rivers.

▲ Bull elephants push against each other, wrestling with trunks and tusks to establish dominance. Serious injury is rare, as elephants back down when they know they have lost the fight.

▼ A herd of African elephants is headed by a female called the matriarch who is often the oldest and largest in the herd. She leads the way during a journey.

Camels

● **Camels are the biggest desert mammals** and they have adapted to live in extremely dry conditions.

● **Dromedary camels** have one hump and live mainly in the Sahara Desert and the Middle East. Bactrian camels live in central Asia and have two humps.

● **A camel's hump** is made of fat, but its body can break the fat down into food and water when these are scarce.

● **Camels can go for many days** or even months without water. But when water is available, they can drink over 200 litres in a day.

● **Camels sweat** very little, to save liquid. Instead, their body temperature rises by as much as 6°C when it is hot.

● **Their feet** have two joined toes to stop them sinking into soft sand or soft snow.

● **A camel's nostrils** can close up completely to block out sand.

DID YOU KNOW?

Camels have by far the worst-smelling breath in the entire animal kingdom!

● **A double row** of eyelashes protect a camel's eyes from sand and sun.

● **A camel's stomach is huge**, with three different sections. Like cows, camels are ruminants – they partially digest food, then bring it back into their mouths for further chewing – known as 'chewing the cud'.

▼ *The dromedary camel has been the 'ship of the desert', transporting people and baggage for thousands of years.*

Nutrition

● **Nutrition is the term** for what animals eat and how they get their food.

● **Plants can make** their own food using sunlight, carbon dioxide and water. Animals, however, must eat in order to get energy.

● **Carnivores eat other animals**. Usually they have to hunt, catch and kill those animals, so most carnivores are predators too.

● **A scavenger** is an animal that eats any food it finds. Some scavengers eat the carrion (dead bodies) of other animals. These animals, such as vultures, are called carrion-feeders.

● **A herbivore is an animal** that eat plants, such as a hippopotamus or a hare. Herbivores often have large stomachs and long guts because plant material is difficult to digest.

● **Omnivores are animals** that eat a range of foods, including plants and animals. For example, humans, pigs and brown bears are omnivores.

● **Carnivores need sharp** slicing teeth for cutting meat while herbivores need big, broad teeth for grinding tough plants.

● **Birds have a gizzard** – an organ for grinding up food as it passes through the body. Some birds have stones or grit in the stomach to mash it into smaller pieces.

● **Merriam's kangaroo rats** live in deserts and never need to drink. They get all the water they need from the seeds they eat.

● **While some animals**, such as sharks and crocodiles, may survive for many weeks without a meal, others – such as shrews – must eat every few hours.

◄ *Grizzly bears that live near salmon rivers grow bigger and stronger than other brown bears. Their fishy diet is packed with muscle-building protein.*

Gamebirds

● **Many gamebirds** were hunted by humans for food or sport, which is how they got their name.

● **These birds** spend most of their time strutting about on the ground looking for seeds. They fly only in emergencies.

● **There are 250 species** of gamebird. These include pheasants, grouse, partridges, quails and peafowl.

● **Most of the 48 different species** of pheasant originated in China and central Asia.

● **Many hen (female) gamebirds** have dull brown plumage that helps them to hide in their woodland and moorland homes.

● **Many cock (male) gamebirds** have very stiking, colourful plumage to attract the attention of mates.

● **During the breeding season**, gamebird cocks strut and puff up their plumage to attract a mate. They also draw attention to themselves by cackling, whistling and screaming.

● **Pheasant cocks** often fight each other violently to win a particular mating area.

● **The jungle fowl** of Southeast Asia is the wild ancestor of the domestic chicken.

● **Sandgrouse live** in the desert and male birds fly many kilometres to find water. They store water in their belly feathers and carry it back to their chicks.

◀ *In winter, the California quail gathers in flocks of between 200 and 300 birds.*

Dolphins

● **Dolphins** are sea creatures that belong to the same family as whales – the cetaceans.

● **They are mammals**, not fish, because they are warm-blooded, and feed their young on milk.

● **Dolphins usually live** in groups of 20–100 animals.

● **There are two kinds** of dolphin – marine dolphins (32 species) and river dolphins (five species).

● **The Yangtze river dolphin** has probably been driven to extinction by harmful fishing methods, dams across rivers and pollution of river water.

● **Dolphins look after** each other. Often, they will support an injured companion on the surface.

▼ *Dolphins are among the most intelligent of animals, along with humans and chimpanzees.*

● **They communicate** with high-pitched clicks called phonations. Some dolphin clicks are higher than any other animal noise – so high that humans are not able to hear them.

● **Dolphins use sound** to find things and can identify different objects even when blindfolded.

● **They can be trained** to jump through hoops, toss balls, and even 'walk' backwards through the water on their tails.

● **Bottle-nosed dolphins** get their name from their short beaks (which also make them look like they are smiling). They are friendly and often swim near boats.

Pouched mammals

● **Marsupials are a group of mammals** that include kangaroos, koalas and wombats. Marsupial babies are born before they are ready to survive in the outside world, and live for a while protected in a pouch on their mother's belly.

● **Kangaroos are big Australian marsupials** that hop around on their hind legs.

● **A kangaroo's tail** can be over 1.5 m in length. Kangaroos use their tails for balance when hopping, and for support when sitting.

● **Red kangaroos** can reach speeds of 55 km/h over short distances. They can leap 9 m forwards in a single bound, and jump over fences that are up to 3 m in height.

● **A baby koala** spends six months in its mother's pouch and another six months riding on her back.

▼ *Baby kangaroos spend 6–8 months in their mother's pouch.*

● **Koalas spend** 18 hours a day sleeping. The spend the rest of their time eating – they diet consists entirely of the leaves of eucalyptus trees.

● **Other Australian marsupials** include the wombat, several kinds of wallaby (which look like small kangaroos) and bandicoots (which look like rats).

● **The sugar glider** is a tiny, mouse-like marsupial that can glide for distances of more than 50 m between trees.

● **The Tasmanian devil** is a small, fierce Australian marsupial. It eats meat and has strong jaws and teeth to crush the bones of its prey.

▲ *A newborn koala weighs less than 0.5 g. It cannot feed on leaves until it is 5 months old and does not climb out of the pouch until it is 6 months old.*

DID YOU KNOW?

After a female echidna lays her single egg, she keeps it in a pouch on her body until it hatches.

▶ *Wombats spend most of their time in burrows, usually only emerging to chomp on grasses, roots and tough bark with their sharp teeth.*

Eels

- **Eels are long,** slimy fish that look like snakes. Most eels do not have scales and there are about 700 species living all over the world.

- **Baby eels** are called elvers.

- **True eels** all develop from leaf-shaped larvae that drift on the surface of the oceans. Some species migrate back to rivers to breed.

- **Every autumn,** some European common eels migrate over 7000 km, from the Baltic Sea in Europe to the Sargasso Sea near the West Indies to lay their eggs.

- **Migrating eels** are thought to find their way partly by detecting weak electric currents created by the movement of the water.

- **When European eels** hatch in the Sargasso Sea they are carried northeast by the ocean current, developing as they go into tiny transparent eels called glass eels.

▲ *Eels look rather like snakes but their fins identify them as fish.*

- **Moray eels** are huge and live in tropical waters, hunting fish, squid and cuttlefish.

- **Gulper eels** can live more than 7500 m down in the Atlantic Ocean. Their mouths are huge to help them catch food in the dark, deep water.

- **The electric eels** of South America can produce an electric shock of over 500 volts – enough to stun a person or kill a small fish.

- **Garden eels** live in colonies on the sea bed, poking out from holes in the sand to catch food drifting by. Their colonies look like gardens of strange plants.

Wild equids

- **Horses, ponies, zebras and asses** all belong to the same animal family – the equids.

- **The African wild ass** is the ancestor of the domestic donkey. Donkeys are very strong for their size and are used in some countries for carrying heavy loads.

- **Like horses,** zebras and asses have a single toe on each foot. The horse family's nearest relatives are rhinos and tapirs, which also take their weight on a long, central toe.

- **Zebras are noisy,** inquisitive African mammals. They live in family groups of between two and 20 members. People have never managed to tame zebras.

- **There are three species** of zebra – common, mountain and Grevy's. Each has a distinct general pattern of stripes. Within each species, no two individual animals have exactly the same pattern of stripes.

- **Zebras bite** or kick rival zebras during the mating season. They also kick out at predators, such as lions.

- **Wild asses** live on the deserts and scrublands of central Asia, the Middle East and North Africa. They can go for long periods without drinking.

- **The largest wild ass,** the kiang, develops a layer of fat for winter. This keeps it warm and provides a food store.

- **The female African wild ass** gives birth to a single foal. She lives in a troop with other females and their young.

- **Mules are the offspring** of a male donkey and a female horse. They are strong and can carry very heavy loads.

◀ *Zebras are speedy striped equids. They can run at speeds of up to 65 km/h to escape danger.*

What are mammals?

- **Mammals are animals** with furry bodies, a backbone for support and a unique habit of suckling their young on milk from the mother's teats.

- **All mammals** are warm-blooded – they regulate their body temperature and can stay active in the cold.

- **Fur and fat** protect mammals from the cold. When they do get cold, they curl up, seek shelter or shiver.

- **Every type of mammal** except monotremes give birth to live young. Monotremes are mammals that lay eggs instead of giving birth to their young. These strange mammals all live in, or near, Australia.

- **Most mammals** are placental – their young are nourished inside the mother's womb through an organ called the placenta until they are fully developed.

- **Marsupial mammals are not** placental. Their young are born at an early stage in their development, and are nourished on milk instead of through a placenta.

- **The period of time** from mating to birth is called pregnancy or gestation. In mammals this varies from 12 days for some opossums to 22 months for elephants.

- **About one quarter** of all mammal species are bats.

- **Mammals vary in size** from the finger-sized Etruscan shrew to the blue whale, at 30 m in length.

- **One of the first mammals** was a tiny shrew-like creature called *Megazostrodon* that lived alongside the dinosaurs about 200 million years ago.

▼ *Black bears are placental mammals. Females give birth to cubs in January or February and suckle them for 6–8 months.*

Ocean fish

- **Nearly 75 percent** of all fish live in the seas and oceans, rather than in freshwater.

- **The biggest, fastest-swimming fish**, such as swordfish and marlin, live near the surface of the open ocean, far from land.

- **These fish often migrate** vast distances in order to spawn (lay their eggs) or find food.

- **The swordfish** can swim at up to 80 km/h. It uses its long spike to slash or stab squid.

- **The bluefin tuna** can grow to as long as 3 m and weigh more than 500 kg. It is also a fast swimmer – one crossed the Atlantic in 199 days.

- **The Antarctic cod** manages to survive in the freezing oceans around the Antarctic by having a chemical antifreeze in its blood.

- **Deep-sea angler fish** have 'fishing rods' growing out of the top of their heads that glow in the dark. They feed on fish that are attracted to these glowing lights.

- **Barracudas are fearsome predators** that hunt in packs. They have torpedo-shaped bodies to help them swim fast and sharp, dagger-like teeth to kill their prey.

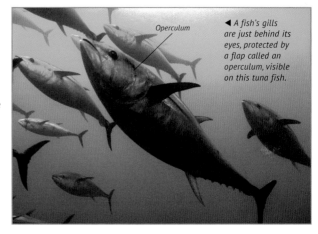

Operculum

◄ *A fish's gills are just behind its eyes, protected by a flap called an operculum, visible on this tuna fish.*

- **The ocean sunfish** is the heaviest and broadest bony fish in the world. It reaches a maximum length of up to 3 m and a maximum height of 4 m. A female sunfish can lay up to 300 million eggs at a time.

- **Porcupine fish** defend themselves by swallowing a lot of water so that their bodies inflate like balloons. Spines on the fish's skin then stick out, making it impossible for a potential predator to swallow such a prickly mouthful.

Grasshoppers and crickets

● **The 20,000 species** of grasshoppers, crickets and katydids are most common in warm parts of the world.

● **Most grasshoppers and katydids** feed on plants but many crickets sometimes eat other animals as well as plants.

● **Powerful back legs** allow grasshoppers and crickets to jump huge distances.

● **Some grasshoppers** can cover up to one metre in a single leap. This helps them to escape from predators.

● **Grasshoppers sing** by rubbing their hind legs across their closed forewings. Crickets sing by rubbing rough patches on their wings together.

● **Grasshoppers have ears** on the side of the abdomen, while crickets have ears on the knees of their front legs.

● **Crickets chirrup faster** the warmer it is.

● **If you count** the number of chirrups a snowy tree cricket gives in 15 seconds, then add 40, you get the temperature in degrees Fahrenheit.

● **Locusts are grasshoppers** that sometimes form vast swarms that can include millions of individuals. They can devastate huge areas of crops when they land to feed.

● **Katydids are named** for their song, which sounds like 'katy-did, katy-did'. Their ears are on their front legs, like crickets.

DID YOU KNOW?

Wetas are giant, flightless tree crickets from New Zealand that are as heavy as three mice. They can live for up to five years.

◀ *Most grasshoppers are smaller than 8 cm long and are camouflaged to hide among plants. They have much shorter antennae than crickets.*

Leopards

● **Leopards live** in Africa, the Middle East and central and southern Asia. They survive in a variety of habitats, from grassland and forests to deserts and mountains.

● **Most leopards** have rosette-shaped spots. The black leopard, or 'black panther', has a dark coat so the spots are hard to see.

● **They live** on their own and usually hunt at night. Leopards lie in wait for their prey or stalk until they are close enough to make the final attack.

● **Leopards hunt** a great range of prey, such as monkeys, snakes, birds, fish and chickens.

● **They are good climbers** – their strong, sharp claws help them to grip tree branches when climbing.

● **Female leopards** usually give birth to two or three cubs. The cubs stay with their mother until they are at least 18 months old.

● **If a mother leopard** senses danger, she picks each of her cubs up by the scruff of its neck and carries them in her mouth one by one to a place of safety.

● **The snow leopard** is not closely related to the leopard and cannot roar like the other big cats.

▲ *A leopard will drag large prey into a tree to prevent other animals from stealing it.*

● **The snow leopard** lives in the Himalayan Mountains. It has large paws to help it walk on the snow and its long tail is useful for balance on steep, slippery slopes.

● **There are only** between 3500 and 7000 snow leopards left. They are threatened by people farming and hunting in the mountains. Snow leopards are still hunted for their thick fur and for their bones, which are used in some traditional medicines.

Corals and anemones

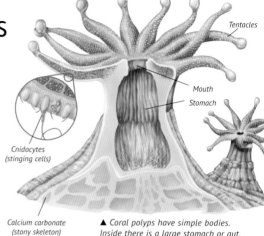

Tentacles

Mouth

Stomach

Cnidocytes
(stinging cells)

Calcium carbonate
(stony skeleton)

▲ Coral polyps have simple bodies.
Inside there is a large stomach or gut.
A tough, rock-like skeleton grows outside.

● **Sea anemones** are tiny, meat-eating animals that look a bit like flowers. They cling to rocks and catch tiny prey with their tentacles.

● **Coral reefs are long ridges**, and other shapes, made from billions of tiny, sea-anemone-like animals called polyps and their skeletons.

● **Coral polyps** live all their lives in just one place, either fixed to a rock or to dead polyps.

● **When coral polyps die**, their limestone skeletons build up one on top of the other to become a coral reef.

● **They are the undersea equivalent** of rainforests, teeming with fish and other sea life.

● **Coral is easily damaged**, and the polyps are very sensitive to environmental change. Dead coral turns white and is described as 'bleached'.

● **Fringing reefs** stretch from the seashore, while barrier reefs form long underwater walls a little way offshore.

● **The Great Barrier Reef** off northeastern Australia is just over 2000 km long. It is the only non-human animal activity visible from space (up to 200 km up).

● **Coral atolls** are ring-shaped islands that formed from fringing reefs around old volcanoes (which have long since sunk beneath the waves).

● **Coral reefs** take thousands or millions of years to form. The Great Barrier Reef started to grow about two million years ago but individual periods of coral reef growth have probably lasted for between 5000 and 15,000 years.

Flatfish

▼ The eyes of a flatfish are both on one side of its head.

● **There are about 500 species of flatfish.** They have no swim bladders, so they can lie on the sea bed without floating.

● **All flatfish** start life as normal-shaped fish, but as they grow older, one eye slides around the head to join the other. The pattern of scales changes so that one side becomes the top, the other the bottom.

● **The upper side** of a flatfish is usually camouflaged to help it blend in with the sea floor.

● **Plaice lie on the sea bed** on their left side, while turbot lie on their right side.

● **The world's largest flatfish** is the halibut, which grows to over 2 m in length. Unlike other flatfish, it catches fish in open water instead of lying in wait on the sea bed.

● **Peacock flounders** have bright blue rings, which are like the blue feather 'eyes' of a peacock.

● **Most flatfish live in the sea**, but a few species can live in freshwater. The European flounder often migrates up rivers to feed.

● **The eggs of flatfish** contain oil droplets, which enable them to float at or near the surface of the sea.

● **Plaice feed** mainly on worms and other small sea creatures, using their sensitive skin to find their food mainly by touch.

● **If they are placed on a board** of black and white squares, some flatfish can change their colours to match the background.

Butterflies

● **Butterflies are insects** with four large wings that feed either on the nectar of flowers or on fruit.

● **The body shape** of a butterfly completely changes between the larval stage and adulthood.

● **Butterfly larvae** are called caterpillars. When they are ready to develop into adults, the caterpillars form a pupa, inside a chrysalis.

● **Many butterflies** are brightly coloured and fly by day. They have slim bodies and club-shaped antennae.

● **The biggest butterfly** is the female Queen Alexandra's birdwing of New Guinea, with 28-cm-wide wings. The smallest is the Western pygmy blue.

▲ *Like many butterflies, the small copper has become more rare in the last century. It prefers warm, dry habitats, especially wastelands, grasslands and heaths.*

● **Peacock butterflies** have eye-like markings on their wings, which may startle predators and divert their attention away from the butterfly's real eyes.

● **Leaf butterflies look** exactly like a dry, brown leaf when they hold their wings shut. The Indian leaf butterfly even has lines on its wings that look like the veins on a real leaf.

● **Monarch butterflies** are such strong fliers that they migrate between North and Central America, covering distances of thousands of kilometres. A few have even crossed the Atlantic Ocean.

● **Most female butterflies** live for only a few weeks, so they have to mate and lay eggs quickly. Most males court them with elaborate flying displays.

● **Every butterfly's caterpillar** has its own chosen food plants – different from the flowers the adult feeds on.

▲ *Many butterflies spread their wings but green hairstreaks rest with their wings closed, showing the green metallic undersides. They usually feed on nectar from shrubs such as bramble.*

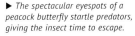

▶ *The spectacular eyespots of a peacock butterfly startle predators, giving the insect time to escape.*

Octopuses and squid

● **Octopuses, squid**, cuttlefish and nautiluses belong to a family of molluscs called cephalopods, which all live in the sea.

● **Octopuses and squid** seize their prey, such as fish, with long arms that are covered in strong suckers.

● **The most intelligent invertebrates**, octopuses and squid have both long- and short-term memories. They can remember solutions to problems, and then go on to solve similar problems.

● **All octopuses have two very large eyes**, and a beak-like mouth.

● **When threatened**, squid and octopuses produce a cloud of black or brown ink to confuse predators.

● **Squid have an internal shell** called a pen in the middle of their body. Cuttlefish also have one too – the cuttlebone.

● **The smallest octopus** is 2.5 cm across. The biggest measures 6 m from tentacle tip to tentacle tip.

● **A squid** has eight arms and two tentacles and swims by forcing a jet of water out of its body.

▲ *A squid has a streamlined shape for swimming fast through the water.*

● **Nautiluses** are the only cephalopods with external shells. They can have as many as 90 arms but no suckers. Animals that looked similar to today's nautiluses swam in the world's oceans 500 million years ago.

> **DID YOU KNOW?**
>
> *The 20-cm-long blue-ringed octopus' poison is so deadly that it kills more people than are killed in shark attacks.*

Strange invertebrates

● **A millipede** doesn't have a million legs, but may have as many as 330. A centipede doesn't have a hundred legs – only about 30.

● **Some sea slugs** feed on jellyfish, then use the stinging cells from the jellyfish for their own defence.

● **Giant clams** have rows of eyes along the edges of their shells, and grow up to 1.4 m across.

● **Some barnacles** glue themselves to the skin of whales and hitch a ride around the oceans.

● **Unlike most animals**, sponges do not have a symmetrical body and have no clearly distinct parts.

● **Billions of microscopic dust mites** live in our beds, carpets and chairs, feasting on flakes of old skin.

● **Some spiders** are camouflaged so they look like ants, wasps or even bird droppings!

● **Giant crabs**, giant tube worms and clams live around deep-sea vents in the ocean floor. They eat animals that feed on minerals in the water that pours from the vents.

● **Some female scorpions** carry their young on their backs until they are strong enough to survive independently.

● **Octopuses can change colour** for camouflage but also as their moods change. If frightened, they turn white!

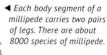

◄ *Each body segment of a millipede carries two pairs of legs. There are about 8000 species of millipede.*

Giraffes

● **Giraffes are the tallest mammals**, growing to more than 5 m in height. This allows them to reach and eat the leaves, twigs and fruit at the very tops of trees.

● **A giraffe's legs** are almost 2 m in length. Its neck may be over 2 m long, but it only has seven bones – the same number as a human's.

● **Giraffes live** in Africa, south of the Sahara, in bush country.

● **A giraffe's tongue** is so tough that it can wrap it around the thorns of thorn trees to grab twigs to eat.

● **When drinking**, a giraffe has to spread its forelegs wide or kneel down to reach the water. This position makes it very vulnerable to attack by lions.

● **When giraffes walk**, they move the two legs on one side of their body, and then the two on the other side.

● **Giraffes can run very fast** on their incredibly long legs, and can actually gallop as fast as a racehorse.

● **A giraffe's coat** has patches of brown on cream, and every giraffe's pattern is unique. The reticulated giraffes of East Africa have triangular patches, but the South African Cape giraffes have blotchy markings.

● **During breeding time**, rival males rub their necks together and swing them from side to side. This is known as necking.

● **When newborn**, a baby giraffe is very wobbly on its legs and cannot stand up for at least half an hour.

▼ *Giraffes are the world's tallest animals, but they are five times lighter than elephants.*

Albatrosses, shearwaters and petrels

● **The wandering albatross** has the biggest wingspan of any bird – 3.5 m across.

● **Albatrosses** have been known to live for up to 80 years.

● **A wandering albatross** can reach speeds of almost 90 km/h. It glides without flapping its wings, and can cover thousands of kilometres in a day.

● **Most birds lay** more than one egg at a time, but albatrosses lay only one egg each year.

● **Of the 21 species** of albatross, 19 are threatened with extinction. They are being killed by longlining – a type of fishing that accidentally pulls the birds underwater so they drown.

● **A wandering albatross** chick spends nearly 10 months in its nest before it grows all its adult feathers.

● **Giant petrels** of Antarctica use their powerful, hooked bills for feeding on dead animals and killing prey, such as penguins and albatrosses.

● **Short-tailed shearwaters** breed on islands near Tasmania but for the rest of the year the adults fly about 32,000 km, around the whole of the Pacific Ocean.

● **The storm petrel** is the smallest European seabird. It flutters above the waves, picking up fish and plankton from the surface.

● **Diving petrels** dive into the sea and use their short wings to 'fly' underwater in search of fish and other prey.

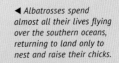

◀ *Albatrosses spend almost all their lives flying over the southern oceans, returning to land only to nest and raise their chicks.*

Whales

● **Whales, dolphins and porpoises** are large mammals called cetaceans that live mostly in the seas and oceans. Dolphins and porpoises are small whales.

● **Like all mammals,** whales have lungs, so they have to come to the surface to breathe every 10 minutes or so, although they can stay underwater for up to 40 minutes. A sperm whale can hold its breath for two hours.

● **Whales breathe** through blowholes on top of their heads. When a whale breathes out, it spouts out exhaled air that turns into water vapour. When it breathes in, it sucks in about 2000 litres of air within about 2 seconds.

● **Like land mammals,** whales nurse their babies with their own milk. Whale milk is rich, so babies grow very fast. Blue whale babies are over 7 m in length and weigh around 1800 kg when they are born, and gain an extra 100 kg or so a day for about seven months.

● **Toothed whales** have teeth and prey on large fish and seals. The six groups of toothed whale are sperm whales, beaked whales, belugas and narwhals, dolphins, porpoises, and river dolphins.

● **Baleen whales,** such as the blue and humpback, have a comb of thin plates called baleen in place of teeth. They feed by straining small, shrimp-like creatures called krill through their baleen. There are five baleen whale groups, including right whales, grey whales and rorquals. Rorquals have grooves on their throats and include humpback, minke and blue whales.

● **The blue whale** is the largest creature that has ever lived. Blue whales grow to be over 30 m in length and weigh more than 150 tonnes. In summer, they eat over 4 tonnes of krill every day – around four million krill.

● **Whales keep in touch** with each other using sounds called phonations. Large baleen whales make sounds which are too low for humans to hear, but they can be heard by other whales at least 80 km away.

● **Most baleen whales** live alone or in small groups, but toothed whales often swim together in groups called pods, or schools.

▼ *A humpback whale leaps out of the water, crashing back down again in a shower of spray. This 'breaching' may be a way of stunning or panicking shoals of fish, or a form of communication with other humpbacks.*

What are birds?

- **There are currently more than 9000** different bird species.

- **Birds are the only** animals that have feathers.

- **Wrens** have 1000 feathers, while swans have 20,000.

- **Birds have three** main kinds of feather: flight feathers on the wings and tail, body feathers to cover the body and fluffy down feathers for warmth.

- **A bird's wings** are made of flight feathers joined to their arm bones.

- **Flight feathers** are made of strands called barbs, which hook together. If the hooks come apart, they can be repaired easily, like doing up a zip.

- **Instead of teeth**, birds have a hard beak or bill. The size and shape of a bird's bill depends mainly on what it eats and where it finds its food.

- **Birds lay eggs** instead of giving birth to babies. The chicks that hatch out of the eggs may be independent (such as ducks, geese and chickens) or helpless (such as sparrows and starlings).

- **Like mammals**, birds are warm-blooded – they keep their bodies at the same warm temperature all the time.

- **Nearly half** of the world's birds go on special journeys called migrations to find food, water or nesting places, or to avoid bad weather. The Arctic tern is the champion bird migrant, flying from one end of the world to the other and back again every year.

▶ *Most birds, such as this bald eagle, flap their wings to fly. Even birds that spend much of their time gliding flap their wings to take off and land.*

Seahorses and pipefish

- **Most seahorses** and their relatives – pipefish, flute mouths, shrimp fish and snipe fish – live in the sea.

- **Seahorses have heads like horses** and gripping tails like monkeys, to hold onto corals and plants.

- **The small, transparent fin** on its back pushes the seahorse through the water, beating as fast as 20 or 35 times a second! It steers with fins on the sides of its head.

- **Seahorses** suck up shrimps in their long hollow jaws. A young sea horse can eat 3000 shrimps a day.

- **They have armoured outer skeletons that** support and protect their internal organs. They do not have ribs, but they do have a bony internal skeleton.

- **Female seahorses** lay their eggs in a pouch on the front of the male's body. The male carries the eggs until the young emerge through a hole in the top of the pouch.

- **Leafy seadragons** are closely related to seahorses. Their bodies are covered in leaf-like flaps, which camouflage them against the seaweeds.

- **A seahorse** can change colour to match its habitat and keep out of sight of predators.

- **The pipefish** has a long, straight body, with tiny fins and the same sort of body armour as a seahorse. Most pipefish swim horizontally, but some swim vertically.

- **Like seahorses**, male pipefish carry the eggs until they hatch.

▶ *A seahorse uses its prehensile (gripping) tail to hold onto coral.*

Cobras and vipers

● **About 300 species of snake** are able to kill people.

● **Cobras' venom** (poison) is stored in short, fixed fangs, while vipers' fangs are so long that they are usually folded away.

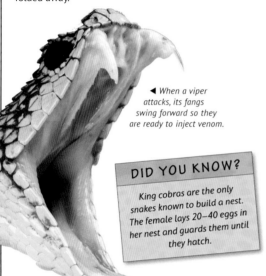

◄ *When a viper attacks, its fangs swing forward so they are ready to inject venom.*

DID YOU KNOW?

King cobras are the only snakes known to build a nest. The female lays 20–40 eggs in her nest and guards them until they hatch.

● **A cobra's venom** affects its prey's nervous system, paralyzing muscles and stopping the heart and lungs from working.

● **The king cobra** is the world's largest poisonous snake, growing to over 5 m in length.

● **Snake charmers** use the spectacled cobra, playing to it so that it follows the pipe as if about to strike – but the fangs of the snakes they use are removed to make them harmless.

● **A spitting cobra** squirts venom into its attacker's eyes, accurate at a distance of 2 m or more. The venom is not deadly, but it blinds the victim and is very painful.

● **A viper's venom kills** its victims by making their blood clot. Viper venom has been used to treat haemophiliacs (people whose blood does not clot well).

● **The largest viper** is the bushmaster, which lives in the forests of Central and South America and grows up to 3.6 metres in length.

● **Pit vipers** of the Americas have heat-sensitive pits on the sides of their heads. They can track their warm-blooded prey such as mice in total darkness.

Horses and ponies

● **Horses are four-legged,** hooved animals, now bred mainly for human use.

● **Adult males** are called stallions, females are called mares and babies are called foals.

● **Przewalski's horse** looks similar to the horses that roamed Europe and northern Asia until a few thousand years ago. Today, they survive mainly in zoos.

● **The mustangs** (wild horses) of the USA are descended from tame horses.

● **Tame horses** are of three main kinds – light horses for riding (such as Morgans and Arabs), heavy horses for pulling ploughs and wagons (such as Percherons and Shire horses), and ponies (such as Shetlands).

● **Ponies are small horses,** between 10 and 15 hands high (a 'hand' is 10 cm). They are often used to teach children how to ride.

● **Lipizzaners** are beautiful white horses. Many are trained to jump and dance at the Spanish Riding School in Vienna.

● **The Shire horse** is the largest horse, growing up to 2 m in height and weighing over one tonne.

● **Quarter horses** are agile, athletic horses with calm temperaments. They are used by cowhands for cutting out (sorting cows from the herd). They got their name from running quarter-mile (402-m) races.

● **A horse** has all its permanent teeth by the age of five or six. This includes 12 molars (grinding teeth) and six incisors (cutting teeth). A horse can be aged accurately by its teeth up to the age of ten.

▼ *Semi-wild white horses roam the marshlands of the Camargue, in southern France. Camargue horses are hardy, and are able to survive on a tough diet of marsh reeds.*

Seals, sea lions and walruses

● **Seals, sea lions and walruses** are sea mammals that mainly live in water and are agile swimmers, but which waddle awkwardly when they emerge onto land.

● **Most seals** eat fish, squid and shellfish. Crabeater seals eat mainly shrimp-like krill, not crabs.

● **Both seals and sea lions** have ears, but only sea lions (which include fur seals) have ear flaps.

● **Only sea lions** can move their back flippers under their body when travelling about on land.

● **When seals come ashore** to breed, they live for weeks in vast colonies called rookeries.

● **Walruses are bigger** and bulkier than seals, and they have massive tusks and face whiskers.

● **They use their tusks** to haul themselves out of the water and to break breathing holes into ice from below.

● **There are freshwater seals** in Lake Baikal in Russia.

> **DID YOU KNOW?**
>
> The 4-m-long leopard seal of Antarctica feeds on penguins and even other seals.

● **Elephant seals** are named after the huge swollen noses of the males, which look like elephant trunks. The males use their noses like loudspeakers to roar at rivals in the breeding season. Male elephant seals are up to ten times heavier than females.

▶ *All seals and sea lions have fur. Only the walrus lacks a furry coat.*

Moths

● **With butterflies**, moths make up the Lepidoptera ('scaly wings') group. There are about 170,000 species of Lepidoptera – about 10 percent are butterflies, the rest are moths.

● **The young (larvae)** of moths are called caterpillars. When they are ready to develop into adults they form a pupa, protected by a case called a chrysalis, or a cocoon made from silk. Finally the adult crawls out, dries off and flies away.

● **At rest**, moths spread their wings or fold them flat, while butterflies hold their wings upright. Moths have thread-like or feathery antennae (feelers), while butterfly antennae have clubs on the end.

● **Many moths fly** at dusk or at night. By day, they rest in trees, where they are hard for predators to spot. However, there are also many brightly coloured day-flying moths.

● **Tiger moths** give out high-pitched clicks to warn that they taste bad and so escape being eaten.

● **The biggest moths** are the giant Atlas moth and the Giant Agrippa moth, with wingspans of up to 30 cm.

● **The hornet clearwing moth** looks like a hornet, so birds leave it alone, even though it cannot sting.

● **Hawk moths migrate** long distances. The oleander hawk moth flies from Africa to northern Europe in summer.

● **The caterpillars** of small moths live in seeds, fruit, stems and leaves, eating them from the inside. Big moths' caterpillars feed on leaves from the outside, chewing chunks out of them.

● **When threatened**, the caterpillar of the puss moth rears up, thrusts its whip-like tail forward and squirts a jet of formic acid from its head end.

▶ *The Morgan's sphinx moth is particularly well-known because it is the only insect able to reach the nectar in Darwin's orchids – flowers with very long nectar tubes. The moth's proboscis (mouthpart) is about 30 cm long.*

Eggs and nests

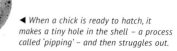

- **All birds reproduce** by laying hard-shelled eggs.

- **Birds that lay eggs** in the open usually lay camouflaged eggs.

- **Birds that nest in holes** or burrows, such as owls or kingfishers, usually lay white eggs.

- **Most birds build nests** to lay their eggs in – usually bowl-shaped and made from twigs, grass and leaves.

- **The Australian mallee fowl** builds the biggest nest – a mound of soil 5 m across, with chambers filled with rotting vegetation to keep eggs warm.

- **Weaverbirds** of Africa and Asia are very sociable. Some work together to weave huge, hanging nests with scores of chambers, each with its own entrance.

- **Flamingos nest** on lakes, building mud nests that look like upturned sandcastles poking out of the water. They lay one or two eggs on top.

◄ *When a chick is ready to hatch, it makes a tiny hole in the shell – a process called 'pipping' – and then struggles out.*

- **Ovenbirds of Central and South America** get their name because their nests look like the clay ovens made by local people. Some ovenbird nests can be 3 m in height.

- **The edible nest swiftlet** builds its nest out of its own saliva, which hardens like cement. People collect these nests to make 'bird's nest soup', considered to be a delicacy.

> **DID YOU KNOW?**
>
> Grey partridges lay the largest clutches (set of eggs laid at one time) – up to 16 eggs.

Jaguars

▲ *A jaguar's territory is always near water. Its spotted coat provides camouflage among vegetation, allowing it to creep up on prey without being seen.*

- **The jaguar is the largest** South American cat and grows up to 2.6 m in length, including the tail.

- **It has a heavier build** than the leopard, with a broader head, strong legs and powerful paws. It has black marks inside each rosette, unlike the leopard.

- **Jaguars swim and climb well**, often lying in wait for prey on tree branches. They also stalk prey on the ground, waiting until they are close before pouncing.

- **They catch animals** such as peccaries, deer, monkeys, tapirs, birds, turtles, caiman, frogs and fish.

- **Jaguars usually live** on their own but stay with a mate for a few weeks during the breeding season.

- **Female jaguars** give birth to a litter of up to four young in a den among rocks or in a hole.

- **The females** defend their young fiercely from predators.

- **Jaguar cubs** are blind at birth but open their eyes after about two weeks.

- **Young jaguars** stay with their mother for about two years while they learn how to survive on their own.

- **The jaguar cannot roar**, although it is grouped with the big cats, which can roar.

Great apes

● **Apes are our closest relatives** in the animal world. The great apes are gorillas, chimpanzees, orang-utans and bonobos. Humans are sometimes called the fifth great ape.

● **Like humans**, great apes have long arms, and fingers and toes for gripping. They are clever and can use sticks and stones as tools.

● **Gorillas are the biggest** of all the great apes, weighing up to 225 kg and standing as tall as 2 m. But they are gentle herbivores and eat leaves and shoots.

● **Mountain gorillas** live in Central Africa in Uganda and on the borders of Uganda, Rwanda and the Democratic Republic of Congo. There are only about 700 of them left.

● **When danger** threatens a gorilla troop, the leading adult male stands upright, pounds his hands against his chest, and bellows loudly.

● **Chimpanzees** live in the forests of western and eastern Africa. They are noisier and fight more often than the other great apes.

● **Chimpanzees** are very clever and use tools more than any other animal apart from humans – they use leaves as sponges to soak up water to drink, and they crack nuts with stones.

● **Chimpanzees communicate** with each other by means of a huge range of different grunts and screams. They also communicate through facial expressions and hand gestures, just as humans do. Experiments have shown chimpanzees can learn to respond to many words.

▲ *Male gorillas are up to twice the size of females. Dominant males defend and control family groups of females and their young.*

● **Between 20,000 and 30,000** orang-utans remain in the forests of Borneo and Sumatra. These highly intelligent great apes could be extinct in as little as five or ten years if their habitat continues to be destroyed at the same rate.

● **Bonobos look similar** to chimpanzees but are slimmer, with longer legs, smaller heads and black faces. Unlike the male-dominated chimpanzee groups, bonobo groups are led by females and are more peaceful. Bonobos also spend more time in the trees than chimpanzees.

▶ *As bonobos groom each other's fur it helps them to relax and strengthens friendships.*

Rhinos and hippos

● **Rhinoceroses** are big, tough-skinned animals of Africa and southern Asia.

● **African black and white** rhinos and the smaller Sumatran rhino have two horns in the middle of their heads. Indian and Javan rhinos have just one.

● **Javan and Sumatran rhinos** are almost extinct and the other three types of rhinos are increasingly threatened by habitat destruction and the demand for their horns. Rhino horn is used to make traditional medicines in eastern Asia.

● *Baluchitherium* lived 20 million years ago and was a type of rhino. At over 5 m tall, it was much bigger than any elephant.

● **Hippopotamuses** are big, grey, pig-like creatures that live in Africa. They have the biggest mouth of any land animal.

● **When a hippo yawns** its mouth gapes wide enough to swallow a sheep whole, but they only eat grass.

▶ *Black rhino numbers have plummeted from about 65,000 in 1970 to only about 3600 today. Some gamekeepers cut off the animals' horns, to make them less of a target for poachers.*

● **Hippos spend their days** wallowing in rivers and swamps, and only come out at night to feed.

● **A hippo's eyes**, ears and nose are all on the top of its head, and so remain above the water when the rest of its body is completely submerged.

● **The word 'hippopotamus'** comes from the ancient Greek words for horse (hippo) and river (potamos).

DID YOU KNOW?

The African white rhinoceros' front horn can grow to an incredible 1.5 m in length.

Freshwater fish

● **Freshwater fish live** in rivers, lakes and ponds throughout the world. Some fish spend part of their lifecycle in fresh water and part of it in the sea.

● **Although far more fish live** in the ocean, nearly half of all known species are found in fresh water.

● **Elephantnose fish live in murky rivers** of West and Central Africa. They can sense electricity made by other animals' muscles and use this skill to find food and mates, and find their way around in dark water.

● **An electric eel is not a true eel,** but a type of knifefish. It can make large amounts of electricity – enough to stun or even kill a human.

● **The red-bellied piranha fish** has a reputation as a fearless predator that can hunt in a group and kill large animals. However, it mostly feeds on insects and small fish.

● **Longnose gars grow** to 1.8 m and hide among river plants so they can ambush other fish that come close.

● **When an arapaima fish** cannot get enough oxygen it swims to the surface of a river and takes a big gulp of air through its mouth. These predators grow to 4 m long.

● **Mexican tetras are small fish** that are either orange and live in rivers and creeks, or white and live in caves. Cave-dwelling tetras are blind.

● **Tigerfish are fast-moving predators** that can swallow fish that are half their size.

● **A freshwater butterfly fish** can leap out of a river to grab insects. Although one of these fish only measures about 10 cm it can leap up to one metre, using its large pectoral fins to glide over the water's surface.

◀ *Red piranhas are about 30 cm long and are equipped with strong jaws and extremely sharp teeth that can slice through flesh. These fish live in rivers throughout much of South America.*

Deer and antelope

- **Deer and antelope** are four-legged, hooved animals.

- **Along with cows, hippos and pigs**, they belong to the group called artiodactyls – animals with an even number of toes on each foot.

▼ *The place where male fallow deer display their size and strength is called a lek. Males on a lek fight each other at mating time, and one male may fight up to ten times a day. Females visit leks to choose the best mates.*

- **Deer and antelope** chew the cud like cows and camels – they chew food again, after first partially digesting it in a special stomach.

- **Deer have branching antlers** of bone on their heads, which drop off and grow again each year.

- **Most deer species** live in the woods and grasslands of mild regions such as northern Europe and North America.

- **Male deer** are called stags or bucks, females are called does or hinds and babies are fawns or calves.

- **The moose or elk** grows antlers more than 2 m in width.

- **Usually only stags** have antlers. The only female deer to have antlers are caribou (reindeer).

- **Most antelope species** live in herds in Africa. Many are fast and graceful, including the impala and Thompson's gazelle.

- **The horns** on an antelope's head last for its entire lifetime.

Turtles and tortoises

◄ *Sea turtles have strong flippers to push themselves through the water, and they have streamlined shells.*

- **Turtles and tortoises** are hard-shelled reptiles. With terrapins, they make up a group called the chelonians.

- **There are about 300 species** of chelonian, living in warm places all over the world. They all lay their eggs on land, even those that live in rivers or the sea.

- **The shield** on the back of a chelonian is called a carapace. Its flat belly armour is called a plastron.

- **Most turtles and tortoises** have no teeth. Instead, their jaws have sharp edges that they use for eating plants and tiny animals.

- **North American snapping turtles** are the only chelonians that can be dangerous to people.

- **Giant tortoises** can weigh as much as three men, grow up to 1.3 m in length, and may live for over 200 years.

- **The pancake tortoise's flat shell** allows it to squeeze under rocks to avoid predators and the hot sun in Africa.

- **The giant leatherback** is the largest turtle, growing up to 2 m in length. It is also the only soft-shelled sea turtle.

- **Green turtles swim** about 2250 km from their feeding grounds off the coast of Brazil to their nesting beaches on Ascension Island in the south Atlantic Ocean.

Pelicans and cormorants

● **Pelicans and cormorants** have webs of skin between all four of their toes. So do their relatives, the gannets and frigatebirds.

● **Pelicans and their relatives** all feed on fish. Most of them live at sea and are strong fliers.

● **The Australian pelican** has the longest bill of any bird. It can be up to 47 cm in length. The yellow or pink throat pouch becomes a scarlet red colour during courtship. Baby Australian pelicans may climb into their parents' pouches to feed on food their parents have regurgitated (coughed up).

● **The great white pelican** usually fishes in groups, forming a circle that moves forwards to force fish into the centre.

◀ Brown pelicans hunt by diving into the water from heights of 3–10 m above the surface. As they enter the water, they open their bills to trap fish in their throat pouches.

◀ Great white pelicans have a characteristic blue bill with a red stripe. They have huge wings and a wingspan of up to 3.6 m.

● **Pelicans scoop** up fish in their enormous throat pouches. A pelican's pouch expands to hold more food than its stomach.

● **A cormorant's feathers** soak up water easily, helping the bird to dive underwater to catch fish.

● **The magnificent frigatebird** is named after the pirate ships called frigates because it steals food from other birds, like pirates steal from other ships. These birds are excellent fliers, twisting and turning to catch food in mid-air.

● **To attract a mate**, a male frigatebird puffs out his red throat pouch like a balloon. Frigatebirds build a flimsy stick nest and the female lays one egg, which both parents incubate until it hatches. The chick can fly when it is 4–5 months old.

● **Blue-footed boobies** are related to gannets. Their name comes from the Spanish word bobo, meaning 'clown'. These birds show off their blue feet to impress a mate. They also use their feet to keep their eggs warm, which are laid on bare rock.

▲ A large and striking waterbird, the cormorant has a primitive appearance, with its long neck making it appear almost reptilian. It is often seen standing with its wings held out to dry.

DID YOU KNOW?
Great white pelicans nest in colonies near water, forming groups of between 1000 and 30,000 pairs.

Woodpeckers and toucans

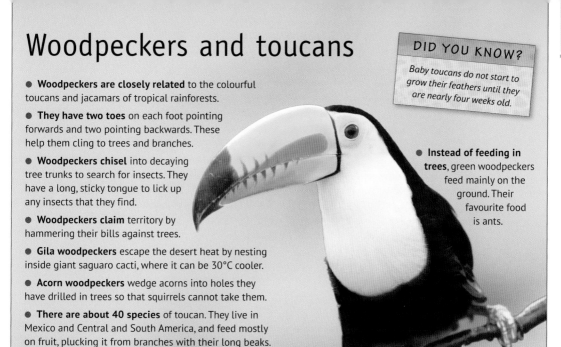

- **Woodpeckers are closely related** to the colourful toucans and jacamars of tropical rainforests.

- **They have two toes** on each foot pointing forwards and two pointing backwards. These help them cling to trees and branches.

- **Woodpeckers chisel** into decaying tree trunks to search for insects. They have a long, sticky tongue to lick up any insects that they find.

- **Woodpeckers claim** territory by hammering their bills against trees.

- **Gila woodpeckers** escape the desert heat by nesting inside giant saguaro cacti, where it can be 30°C cooler.

- **Acorn woodpeckers** wedge acorns into holes they have drilled in trees so that squirrels cannot take them.

- **There are about 40 species** of toucan. They live in Mexico and Central and South America, and feed mostly on fruit, plucking it from branches with their long beaks.

- **A toucan's bill** is not as heavy as it looks. Inside it is full of air spaces, supported by a honeycomb of criss-crossing bones.

- **Instead of feeding in trees**, green woodpeckers feed mainly on the ground. Their favourite food is ants.

▲ *Toucan bills are longer than their bodies. Why the bills are so big is still unknown.*

What are invertebrates?

- **Invertebrates are animals** without backbones or any bones inside their bodies. They are cold-blooded and include insects, spiders, crabs, jellyfish and squid.

- **At least 99 percent of all** animal species are invertebrates. They are divided into over 30 groups, and probably include over five million species.

- **Invertebrates are usually** smaller than vertebrates (animals with backbones). Some forms are microscopic.

- **The biggest invertebrates** are the 16-m-long giant squid and the even larger colossal squid.

- **In 2007**, scientists discovered a claw from a giant sea scorpion, which lived between 460 and 255 million years ago. This massive invertebrate was 2.5 m in length.

- **The bodies of some invertebrates** are supported by an external skeleton. This skeleton cannot grow so it must be shed (moulted) to allow the animal to grow.

- **There are at least one million** different kinds of insects and they are common all over the world.

- **Insects have six legs** and a body divided into three parts – the head, thorax and abdomen.

▶ *Scorpions have poisonous stings at the ends of their tails, which they use to defend themselves or kill prey.*

- **They do not have lungs**, instead breathing through spiracles (holes in their sides), linked to their body through tubes called tracheae.

- **The world's longest insect** is the giant stick insect of Indonesia, which can grow more than 50 cm in length.

Rabbits, hares and pikas

● **Rabbits, hares and pikas** all belong to a group of mammals called lagomorphs, which means 'hare-shaped'.

● **Lagomorphs have long**, soft fur – even their feet are furry. They have big ears and their eyes are high on the sides of their head, giving them a wide field of vision.

● **Hares live above ground** and escape enemies through sheer speed. Rabbits live in burrows underground.

● **Baby hares** are born above ground, covered in fur and with their eyes open. Rabbits are born hairless and blind in burrows.

● **Rabbits and hares** have very long back legs to help them run away from danger. Some large hares can reach speeds of 80 km/h.

▶ *Mountain hares turn white in winter for camouflage against the snow.*

● **The incisors** (front teeth) of lagomorphs grow continuously throughout their lives but are worn down by tough plant food.

● **The black-tailed jackrabbit** lives in the desert. Its huge, thin ears act like radiators to get rid of body heat and cool the animal.

● **Pikas are lively**, agile mammals that are active during the day. They live high in the mountains or below the ground in deserts.

● **During the summer and autumn**, pikas build haystacks of plant material to last them through the winter. They do not hibernate.

Ducks, geese and swans

● **Ducks, geese and swans** are known as waterfowl, and they all live on or near water. There are about 150 species and each group makes a different sound – ducks quack, geese honk and swans hiss.

● **Waterfowl can float for hours** and have webbed feet for paddling along. On water they are graceful, but on land they waddle awkwardly, since their legs are set far back under their body for swimming.

● **Ducks have** shorter necks and wings, and flatter bills than swans. Males are called drakes, females are called ducks, and babies are called ducklings.

● **Diving ducks** (such as the pochard, tufted duck and the scoter) dive for food such as roots, shellfish and insects on the riverbed.

● **Dabbling ducks** (such as the mallard, widgeon, gadwall and teal) dabble – they sift water through their beaks for food.

● **Some dabblers** feed at the surface. Others up-end – sticking their heads into the water to sift out water weeds and snails from muddy water.

● **Swans** are the largest waterfowl. They have long, elegant necks and pure white plumage – apart from the black-neck swan of South America and the Australian black swan.

● **Baby swans** are called cygnets and are mottled grey.

● **Most waterfowl** feed in water but geese feed on land, pulling up grass and other plants using their strong bills.

● **Baby geese** are called goslings.

◀ *Teals are the smallest British surface-feeding ducks and they often live together in groups that range in size from 20 to several hundred.*

Reef fish

- **Many colourful fish species** live in the warm seas around coral reefs.

- **Some butterfly fish** have a false eye near the tail to confuse predators, and can even swim backwards to complete the deception.

- **Male triggerfish** can increase their colour to attract females at mating time.

- **Cuckoo wrasse** are all born female, but big females change sex when they are between 7 and 13 years old.

- **The cheeklined Maori wrasse** changes colour to mimic harmless plant-eating fish, such as damselfish.

- **The Hawaiian reef fish** Humuhumunukunukuapua'a is a type of triggerfish, and makes pig-like snorting sounds if threatened.

- **Larger fish** such as groupers are cleaned by small fish that nibble away any pests and dead skin on them.

- **The sabre-toothed blenny** looks similar to a cleaner fish, so it can swim up close to fish and attack them.

- **The Great Barrier Reef** is home to a huge variety of living things, including more than 1500 species of fish.

▼ *Parrotfish have beak-like teeth to bite off lumps of coral.*

DID YOU KNOW?

Some coral sharks are not aggressive, and divers can feed them by hand.

Ants

- **Ants are a vast group** of insects related to bees and wasps. Most ants have a tiny waist, long, jointed antennae and are wingless.

- **They are the main insects** in tropical forests, living in colonies of anything from 20 to millions of individuals.

- **Ant colonies** are mostly female. One or more queens lay the eggs, which are fertilized by males called drones. Female ants do all the work in the colony, including defending the nest and caring for the eggs.

- **Ants that protect** the nest are called soldiers. They have bigger jaws, for fighting, than other ants.

- **Wood ants squirt acid** from their abdomen to kill their enemies.

- **Army ants march** in huge swarms, eating small creatures they meet.

- **Groups of army ants** cut any large prey they catch into pieces, which they carry back to the nest. Army ants can carry 50 times their own weight.

- **Ants known as slavemakers** raid the nests of other ants and steal their young to raise as slaves.

- **Honeypot ants** have special workers that store sugary liquid in their abdomens. In a drought, they release the sugary food to other workers in the nest.

- **Tropical weaver ants** use silk produced in the jaws of their own grubs to sew leaves together and make a nest.

▶ *Leafcutter ants feed on fungus, which they grow in underground farms. They cut leaves and carry them back to the farm, where they are used to grow the fungus.*

Swifts and hummingbirds

● **Swifts and hummingbirds** have tiny feet and legs, spending most of their time on the wing. They only use their feet to perch when breeding or roosting.

● **Swifts glue their nests together** with sticky saliva from special salivary glands.

● **Their short**, gaping bills allow swifts to catch insects while flying.

● **Swifts may fly** through the night, and even sleep on the wing. European swifts will fly all the way to Africa and back without stopping.

● **The fragile nest** of the crested tree swift is only about 2.5 cm across and has a single egg that is glued inside with saliva. The parents will take it in turns to incubate the egg.

● **Great dusky swifts** nest and roost behind waterfalls, and have to fly through the water to get in and out.

● **Hummingbirds are tiny**, bright, tropical birds that sip nectar from flowers. There are around 340 species.

● **They are the most amazing** aerial acrobats, hovering and twisting in front of flowers.

● **The bee hummingbird** is the world's smallest bird – including its long bill, it measures just 5 cm.

▲ *Hummingbirds' bills let them reach right inside tube-shaped flowers to feed on sugary nectar.*

> **DID YOU KNOW?**
>
> When hovering, horned sungem hummingbirds beat their wings 90 times per second.

Lemurs and lorises

● **Lemurs and lorises** belong to a group of mammals called primates, along with monkeys, apes and humans. They have smaller brains and a better sense of smell than their primate relatives.

● **Lemurs live only** on the islands of Madagascar and Comoros, off the east coast of Africa.

● **Most are active at night** and live in trees, but the ring-tailed lemur lives on the ground and is active during the day.

● **Most lemurs** eat fruit, leaves and insects but some eat only bamboo or nectar.

● **The largest primate** on Madagascar is the indri. This large lemur also has a very loud song that can be heard more than 2 km away. Indris sing to tell other indris to keep out of their area of forest.

● **In the mating season**, ring-tailed lemurs have stink fights for females, rubbing their wrists and tails in stink glands under their arms and rear – then waving them at rivals to drive them off.

● **Lorises and pottos** are furry, big-eyed primates of the forests of Asia and Africa. All are brilliant climbers.

▶ *Ring-tailed lemurs forage for fruit on the ground, but also eat leaves, flowers, and the bark and sap of trees.*

● **Bushbabies are the acrobats** of the loris family. Their name comes from the fact that their cries sound like a human baby crying.

● **Bushbabies** are nocturnal animals. Their big eyes help them see in the dark.

● **Tarsiers of Southeast Asia** are small, huge-eyed primates. They have very long fingers and can turn their heads halfway round to look backwards.

Pythons and boas

● **The six biggest snake species** in the world are all boas and pythons. These are the anaconda, boa constrictor, Indian python, reticulated python, African rock python and Amethystine, or scrub python.

● **Pythons and boas** are constricting snakes. They wind their coils tightly around their victims until they die from suffocation or shock.

● **Constrictors usually swallow** victims whole, then spend days digesting them. Their special jaws allow their mouths to open very wide. A large meal can be seen as a lump moving down the body.

● **Pythons live in Asia**, Indonesia and Africa. Boas and anacondas are the big constrictors of South America.

● **Boas lie in wait** for their victims. Like all snakes, they can go for weeks without food.

● **Tree boas** are good climbers. The emerald tree boa hangs from branches to seize birds in its teeth. It uses pits along its lips to sense the heat given off by its prey.

● **The markings of boa constrictors** give them excellent camouflage in a variety of habitats, from deserts to forests.

● **Boas have tiny remnants** of back legs, called spurs, which males use to tickle females during mating.

● **Anacondas spend time** in swampy ground or shallow water, lying in wait for their victims to approach for a drink. They are the heaviest snakes, weighing up to 227 kg.

● **When frightened**, the royal python coils itself into a tight ball. It is sometimes called the ball python.

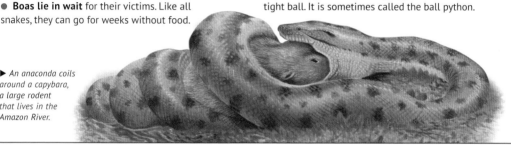

▶ *An anaconda coils around a capybara, a large rodent that lives in the Amazon River.*

Bivalves

● **Cockles and mussels** belong to a group of molluscs called bivalves, which includes oysters, clams, scallops and razorshells.

● **Bivalve means** 'having two halves', and all of these creatures have two halves to their shells, joined by a hinge.

● **Most bivalves feed** by using a tube called a siphon to draw water over their gills. Food particles are trapped in the sticky, hairy gills and sent to the mouth.

● **Cockles burrow in sand** and mud on the seashore. Mussels cling to rocks and breakwaters between the high and low tide marks.

● **Oysters and some other molluscs** line their shells with a hard, shiny, silvery white substance called nacre.

● **When a lump of grit** gets into an oyster shell, it is gradually covered in a ball of nacre, making a pearl.

● **The best pearls** come from the Pinctada pearl oysters, in the Pacific Ocean. The world's biggest pearl was 24 cm across and weighed 6.4 kg. It came from a giant clam.

● **Scallops can swim away** from danger by opening and shutting their shells rapidly to pump out water. However, most bivalves escape danger by shutting themselves up inside their shells.

● **Razor clams** live in deep, vertical burrows in sandy sediments.

● **Shipworms are bivalves** that use their shells to drill into wood, including the wood of ships, and live on the sawdust that they generate.

▶ *A cockle secures itself to the sea bed and removes food from the water as currents pass over it. Most cockles have very thick, ridged shells that can cope with the strong buffeting action of waves at a shore.*

Snails and slugs

- **Snails and slugs** are small, slimy, soft-bodied creatures.

- **They belong** to a huge group of animals called molluscs. Squid and oysters are also molluscs.

- **Snails and slugs** are gastropods, a group that also includes whelks and winkles.

- **Gastropod means** 'stomach foot', because these animals seem to slide along on their stomachs.

- **Gastropods have a special tongue** called a radula, which is covered with thousands of tiny, hook-shaped teeth. They use this to scratch and scrape away at their food.

- **Most land snails and slugs** ooze a trail of sticky slime, which helps them move along the ground.

- **Garden snails** are often hermaphrodites, which means they have both male and female sex organs.

- **The great grey slugs** of western Europe court by circling each other for over an hour on a branch, then launching themselves into the air to hang together from a long trail of mucus.

- **Among the largest gastropods** are the tropical tritons, the shells of which reach 45 cm in length. Conches are another big kind of gastropod.

▼ Giant African snails can measure up to 20 cm in length and weigh more than 800 g. They eat plants, fruits (such as bananas) and dead animals.

> **DID YOU KNOW?**
>
> Some cone snails in the Pacific and Indian oceans have teeth that can inject a poison that can actually kill people.

Moles and hedgehogs

- **Moles and hedgehogs** are in a group of mammals called insectivores, named because they eat insects.

- **Insectivores include** 350 different kinds of tenrecs, golden moles, hedgehogs, moonrats, shrews, moles and solenodons.

- **Most insectivores** are solitary and come out at night. They have long snouts and a good sense of smell.

- **Hedgehogs are protected** by a coat of spiny quills, which are actually modified hairs. These animals can roll up into a ball to hide their soft underparts.

- **At birth**, a baby hedgehog's spines are beneath its skin so they don't harm the mother during the birth process. The spines break through the skin by the time they are three days old.

- **Hedgehogs in colder** places hibernate (go into a deep sleep) over winter. This helps them survive the cold months, when their insect food is not available.

- **Water shrews** dive underwater to catch fish, small frogs and small water creatures.

- **Some shrews** have a poisonous bite. The American short-tailed shrew produces enough poison to kill 200 mice.

- **Moles spend most** of their lives underground, relying on touch and smell to find worms and beetles.

- **The molehills** on the surface are heaps of soil that moles have dug out of their tunnels. The nest is underneath a large, more permanent molehill called a fortress.

◀ If alarmed, a hedgehog raises its spines so it looks bigger and more dangerous.

Lesser apes

● **Gibbons are known** as lesser apes because they are smaller and lighter than the great apes, such as gorillas and chimpanzees.

● **Like the great apes**, gibbons do not have a tail.

● **Gibbons live high up** in the trees and hardly ever come down to the ground. They use their long arms to swing quietly from branch to branch at speeds of up to 56 km/h. This way of moving is called 'brachiation'.

● **Special wrist bones** allow gibbons to turn their bodies as they swing through the trees while keeping a tight grip on the branches.

● **There are 11 different species** of gibbon, which all live in the forests of Asia.

● **Siamangs are the biggest gibbons**, weighing up to 14 kg. They sing to tell other gibbons where they live. Their throat pouches swell with air as they sing, making their calls very loud.

● **They feed mainly on fruit**, but gibbons also eat leaves, shoots, buds, flowers and occasionally insects and eggs.

▶ *Gibbons spend their lives in trees and have long arms and strong shoulders to support their weight as they swing.*

● **Gibbons are the only apes** to live in pairs and stay with the same partner for life. The young do not leave their parents until they are six or seven years old.

● **They are the only apes** that do not build nests. Instead, gibbons sleep sitting up on the branches, resting on their tough sitting pads.

● **Male and female hoolock gibbons** have different coloured fur. Adult males are blackish-brown, while adult females are yellowish-brown. Newborn hoolock gibbons have fur that is a greyish-white colour.

Fast-moving sharks

● **Most sharks are active**, agile swimmers that race through the oceans when they are pursuing their prey – usually other fish, turtles and mammals such as seals.

● **A fast shark's main weapons** are its large, sharp teeth. Although shark teeth are easily broken and lost there are many rows of teeth growing at a time, and new ones constantly move forwards to replace them.

● **The bendy skeleton** and powerful muscles of a fast shark allow it to move its body from side to side as it swims, propelling it through the water when it needs a burst of speed.

● **Most fast sharks** must keep swimming at all times, or sink. Whitetip reef sharks are able to rest on the seafloor by pumping water across their gills.

● **Most sharks** have good eyesight and an incredible sense of smell and taste. They can detect the electrical fields given off by other animals, and one part of blood in one million parts of water.

● **A young shark** is called a pup.

● **The fastest shark** is believed to be the shortfin mako, which can reach top speeds of 80 km/h or more.

● **Hammerheads** have a bizarre appearance. Their hammer-shaped heads help them to locate their prey more easily and to change direction quickly.

● **The tail of a thresher shark** is almost as long as its body. It uses its huge tail to thrash and wallop its prey, stunning it so it is easier to catch and eat.

● **Tiger sharks** are sometimes called 'bins with fins' – they bite and swallow almost anything they find.

▼ *Most fast-moving sharks look similar. The faint stripes on a tiger shark's flanks help to distinguish it from other species. The size and shape of teeth, snout, fins and tails are also used to identify fast sharks.*

Bears

- **There are eight species** of bear. Only two live south of the Equator – the spectacled bear of South America and the sun bear of Southeast Asia.

- **Although bears** are the largest meat-eating land animals, they also eat many other foods, including fruits, nuts and leaves.

- **The polar bear** is the largest land carnivore, but it is only the size of a guinea pig at birth. They are the only bears that have a diet consisting almost entirely of meat, feeding mainly on seals, which they catch when they come up for air at breathing holes in the Arctic ice. A swipe from a bear's massive paw and a bite at the back of the skull is enough to kill a seal.

◄ Polar bear cubs are born in the middle of winter in a snow den dug by their mother. They feed on their mother's milk and grow fast. By spring they are strong enough to leave the den with their mother.

- **Polar bears are under threat** from climate change. The world is warming up, melting the sea ice, which the bears rely on to hunt for seals.

- **Brown bears** sleep through the winter when food is scarce. At this time, they only breathe around four times per minute, and their heart rates slow to reduce the amount of energy they use.

- **The grizzly bear** is a type of brown bear with grizzled (grey) fur on its shoulders. Grizzlies from Alaska and Kodiak bears are the biggest brown bears.

▼ Brown bears fight each other over food, mates or places to live. They prefer to live on their own.

- **Giant pandas** live only in patches of bamboo forest in southwestern China. They are threatened by people cutting down the forests, and may also be killed illegally or caught in traps set for other animals. There are thought to be only about 1600 pandas left in the wild.

- **A giant panda's diet consists** mainly of bamboo. The digestive systems of these bears are bad at extracting the goodness from bamboo so they must eat up to 38 kg of it per day.

- **Thick, waterproof fur** keeps giant pandas warm in the snowy winter of their habitat.

▲ Giant panda cubs are about the size of hamsters when they are born, and don't open their eyes for 6–8 weeks. They are 3 months old before they start to walk.

DID YOU KNOW?

The sun bear of Southeast Asia is the smallest bear, and a very good climber.

Flies

- **Flies are one of the biggest groups** of insects, common nearly everywhere. There are more than 90,000 species.

- **Most flies** are agile, acrobatic fliers. They can hover, and fly backwards, sideways and upside down. Some can even take off and land while upside down.

- **Flies include** bluebottles, black flies, gnats, midges, horseflies, mosquitoes and tsetse flies.

- **The eyes of the stalk-eyed fly** are at the end of long stalks, much wider than its body. Males compete to see who has the longest eye stalks.

- **Flies suck up** their food – typically sap from rotting plants. Houseflies will often suck liquid from manure, while blowflies drink juices from rotting meat.

- **Some flies** have mouthparts that suck. Others have a pad that dissolves their food and soaks it up like a sponge.

- **The larvae** (young) of flies are called maggots, and they are tiny, white, wriggling and tube-shaped.

- **Flies mimic** (copy) other insects. There are wasp-flies, drone-flies, ant-flies, moth-flies and beetle-flies.

- **Many species** of fly are carriers of dangerous diseases. When a fly bites or makes contact, it can infect people with some of the germs it carries – especially the flies that suck blood. Mosquitoes spread malaria, and tsetse flies spread sleeping sickness.

> **DID YOU KNOW?**
> The buzzing of a fly is actually the sound of its wings beating. Midges beat their wings at a rate of 1000 times a second.

▶ *Horse flies are among the fastest flying insects, reaching maximum speeds of 39 km/h.*

Sparrows and starlings

- **About 60 percent** of all bird species are perching birds (the Passerines). Their feet have three toes pointing forwards and one backwards, to help them cling to a perch.

- **Perching birds** build small, neat, cup-shaped nests. They also sing – this means that their call is not a single sound, but a sequence of musical notes.

- **Songbirds such as thrushes,** nightingales and warblers, are perching birds with particularly attractive songs.

- **Usually only male songbirds** sing – mainly in the mating season, in order to warn off rivals and attract females.

- **House sparrows** are one of the most widespread birds. They have adapted well to living with people, nesting everywhere from farms to city centres.

- **There are more than** 100 species of starling.

- **The European starling** has brown-black feathers but many African starlings are brightly coloured.

- **The millions** of European starlings in North America are all descended from 100 that were set free in New York's Central Park in the 1890s.

- **Many perching birds,** including mynahs, are talented mimics. The lyre bird of southeastern Australia can imitate car sounds, such as sirens, and chainsaws, as well as other birds.

- **The red-billed quelea** of Africa is the world's most common bird. There are over 1.5 billion of them.

◀ *House sparrows are highly social, very vocal birds. They nest in colonies in buildings, trees and nest boxes.*

Spiders

● **Spiders are scurrying creatures** which, unlike insects, have eight legs not six, and bodies with two parts not three.

● **They belong to a group** of 70,000 creatures called arachnids, which also includes scorpions, mites, harvestmen and ticks.

● **The world's biggest spider** – the Goliath tarantula – is about the size of a dinner plate, and the smallest spider is only as big as a full stop.

● **Spiders are hunters** and most of them feed mainly on insects. Despite their name, bird-eating spiders rarely eat birds, preferring lizards and small rodents such as mice.

● **They have eight eyes**, but most spiders have poor eyesight and hunt by feeling vibrations with their legs.

● **About half of all spiders** catch their prey by weaving silken nets called webs. Some webs are simple tubes in holes. Others, called orb webs, are elaborate and round. Spiders' webs are sticky to trap insects.

▲ *A spider's main eyes, clearly visible on this huntsman spider, help it to find prey, while its smaller eyes pick up movements in its surroundings.*

▼ *Spiders wrap their prey in silk to stop it escaping.*

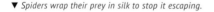

● **The Australian trapdoor** spider ambushes its prey from a burrow with a camouflaged entrance flap.

● **Most spiders** have a poisonous bite that they use to stun or kill their prey. Female spiders are usually bigger and more poisonous than male spiders. Tarantulas and sun spiders crush their victims with their powerful jaws.

● **The bites of black widow**, redback and funnelweb spiders are so poisonous they can kill humans. Only about 30 of the 35,000 different kinds of spider are dangerous to people.

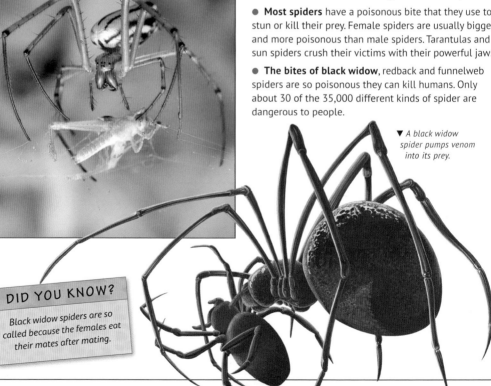

▼ *A black widow spider pumps venom into its prey.*

DID YOU KNOW?

Black widow spiders are so called because the females eat their mates after mating.

Small cats

- **Small cats** crouch down when they feed, whereas big cats lie down to feed.

- **At rest**, small cats bend their paws under their bodies and wrap their tails around themselves. Big cats place their paws in front of their bodies when they rest and stretch their tails out behind them.

- **The lynx** is a small cat that lives in cold northern lands. It has thick fur to keep it warm, wide feet to stop it sinking into the snow and long legs to help it travel through deep snow.

- **The European wildcat** looks similar to a striped pet cat, but has a bushy tail with a rounded tip and a larger head, with bigger eyes.

- **Most cats** don't like water but the fishing cat spends most of its life in and around rivers and streams. It has partly webbed front paws and feeds on fish.

▲ *The puma is the biggest North American cat, with a tail up to 78 cm in length.*

- **The puma**, or mountain lion, of the Americas lives in a range of habitats from mountains to swamps. Its sandy or grey-brown fur has no markings, but the kittens are spotted when they are born, for camouflage.

- **The caracal** is very good at catching birds, jumping up to knock low-flying birds right out of the air.

- **Male ocelots** stay with the females after mating and help look after the kittens by bringing food to the den.

- **The serval** of Africa uses its sensitive hearing to listen for the rustling sounds made by its prey, before making the final pounce.

- **Sand cats** stay in burrows during the heat of the day, emerging at night to hunt insects, lizards, birds and mice. Their furry feet give them a good grip on the sand.

What are reptiles and amphibians?

- **There are nearly 6000 species** of reptiles and they are divided into four groups: crocodiles and alligators, snakes and lizards, turtles and tortoises, and the tuatara.

- **Reptiles have scaly skin**, a bony skeleton with a backbone, and they either lay eggs with waterproof shells or give birth to live young.

- **Reptiles can live** in many different places on land, even in the driest deserts, but some live in freshwater or in the sea.

- **They are most common** in warm places because reptiles rely on their surroundings for warmth. This is called being 'cold-blooded'.

▶ *Lizards that live above the ground have large ear openings and large eyes.*

- **Reptiles move** between hot and cold places to control their body temperature. They bask in the sunshine to warm up and are usually less active at cooler times of year.

- **Amphibians are animals** that live on land and in water. They include frogs, toads, newts and salamanders.

- **Most reptiles lay their eggs** on land but most amphibians return to the water to mate and lay eggs.

- **Amphibians develop** from tadpoles or larvae into adults. This process is called metamorphosis.

- **Like reptiles**, amphibians are cold-blooded.

- **Reptiles were the first** large creatures to live entirely on land, about 340 million years ago.

Fleas and lice

● **Fleas and lice** are insects that live their lives as parasites.

● **Fleas feed on blood.** They live on the outside of an animal's body and use their piercing mouthparts to suck.

● **There are about** 2400 species of flea but they all look similar. Fleas are tiny, with flattened bodies and long legs that they use to leap. Fleas don't have wings.

● **Some fleas only live** on one type of animal, but others are more adaptable and can take blood from many types of host.

● **Flea eggs hatch** into tiny larvae that do not live on a host. They often live in birds' nests, animal burrows, or pets' bedding. When they turn into adults the fleas wait until they sense a host animal is nearby, then jump onto it.

● **Rat fleas** carried the bubonic plague – a terrible disease that caused the deaths of millions of people in Medieval Europe.

● **Lice are wingless** with flattened bodies.

● **The shape** of a louse's body is perfect for scampering through hair, feathers and fur. These animals use their clawed legs to grip onto their hosts – birds or mammals – so that they can feed on their blood. Human lice live on the head and glue their eggs to strands of hair. The eggs are white and shiny and are called nits.

● **Bird lice feed** on blood, but they also eat away at feathers and damage a bird's skin, making it more likely to get other infections.

◀ *Fleas are described as hematophagous, which means they live on a diet of blood. Their bodies are surprisingly tough, which is why they often survive scratching, squeezing and squashing by their host.*

DID YOU KNOW?

Fleas have little elastic pads at the base of their legs, which catapult them into the air.

Kingfishers and bee-eaters

● **Kingfishers belong** to a varied group of birds, which also includes rollers, hoopoes, bee-eaters and hornbills.

● **Many birds** in this group are brightly coloured, with large bills.

● **They nest in tunnels**, often in riverbanks but also in tree holes or termite nests.

● **Kingfishers perch** on branches over clear streams and rivers, or hover over still water, watching for signs of fish swimming below. When they spot their prey, they move with lightning speed.

● **The laughing kookaburra** is a giant kingfisher named for its loud call, which sounds like a person chuckling.

● **Rollers are named** for the male's rolling courtship flight. He flies high up in the air and then dives down, somersaulting through the air as he falls.

● **The hoopoe** is named for its call, which sounds like 'hoo-poo-poo'. It uses its long, curved bill to probe the ground for worms and insects.

● **Parent green wood hoopoes** have up to ten helpers that gather food and defend the nest. When the chicks mature, they help the adults that raised them.

● **Bee-eaters are brightly coloured** birds that catch and eat flying insects. A large proportion of their diet is made up of bees and wasps.

● **Bee-eaters hold bees** or other stinging insects in their bills and beat or rub them against a hard surface to get rid of the poison from the sting. Then they can safely swallow the insect.

▶ *The African pygmy kingfisher is one of the smallest kingfishers. It feeds mainly on insects and spiders, not on fish.*

Tigers

● **Tigers are the largest** of the big cats, with huge heads. The average male grows to over 2 m in length, plus a one-metre-long tail.

● **They live** in Asia, but are becoming rare as their forest homes are destroyed and poachers kill them. There are probably fewer than 5000 left in the wild.

● **Tigers prey on large animals** such as deer, buffalo, antelope and wild pigs. They hunt silently at night, stalking their prey, then making a sudden bound.

● **They find prey** by following scent trails. They also sniff out smaller animals such as lizards and even go fishing.

● **Although they are fast** and strong, tigers tire quickly, and may give up if they fail to catch their prey first time.

▲ *A female tiger rears her cubs in a den – usually a rock crevice, cave or a thicket of dense plants – with little or no help from the male.*

● **Usually, between two and four cubs** are born at a time. The cubs are playful, and totally dependent on their mother for 2–3 years.

● **Cats' eyes are famously sensitive** in the dark. A tiger can see objects more than 100 m away when humans can hardly peer 5 m in the dark.

▼ *Siberian tigers live in very cold, snowy places. Their thick, shaggy fur helps to keep them warm.*

▲ *A tiger's stripes provide good camouflage in long grass and under trees. Each tiger has its own unique pattern of stripes.*

● **A large adult tiger** can eat almost 30 kg of food in one session, enough to sustain it for a week or more, but it needs water daily.

● **Adult tigers** usually live alone, and mark out their territory by scratching trees and urinating on them. Males try to keep other males out of their territory. A male's territory often includes that of two or three females, but they only meet to mate.

DID YOU KNOW?

Tigers are good swimmers and often lie in rivers to cool off on hot days.

Vultures

- **Vultures are the biggest** birds of prey. They do not hunt, but feed on carrion (dead animals).

- **The palm-nut vulture** is the only plant-eating bird of prey and it feeds on palm oil nuts.

- **Many vultures are bald**, with no head feathers to get matted with blood when digging into dead animals.

- **Egyptian vultures** sometimes throw stones at ostrich eggs to break open the thick shells and feed on the contents.

- **The Californian condor** is very rare. All the wild birds were captured in the mid 1980s, but some have since been bred in captivity and returned to the wild.

- **Vultures spend hours** soaring, scanning the ground with their sharp eyes for food.

- **King vultures** have a strong sense of smell, which helps them to find animal remains in their dense tropical forest habitat.

- **The lammergeier** is known as the bearded vulture because it has a beard of black bristles on its chin.

- **Lammergeiers** fly to great heights and drop animal bones onto rocks to smash them open. Then they feed on the nourishing marrow inside the bones.

DID YOU KNOW?

The Andean condor is the largest vulture in the world and has a wingspan of over 3 m.

◀ *Vultures have broad wings, which they use to glide high on rising warm air currents, called thermals.*

Dugongs and manatees

- **Dugongs live** in the southwest Pacific Ocean. Two types of manatees live in the rivers of West Africa and the Amazon. The third lives in the Atlantic Ocean.

- **They are the only** completely aquatic mammals, and feed on plants, so they are sometimes known as 'sea cows'.

- **Paddle-shaped tails** allow manatees to move through the water.

- **Manatees** have only six neck bones, unlike all other mammals, which have seven neck bones.

- **They are sometimes** used to clear the weeds from tropical man-made reservoirs.

- **Manatee calves** stay with their mothers for up to 18 months, learning where to find the best feeding areas.

- **The dugong** feeds on seagrasses, sometimes digging up and eating the roots of smaller kinds.

- **Adult dugongs** have only a few peg-like teeth and use rough pads in their mouths to grind up food.

- **Unlike manatees**, the tail of the dugong is 'fluked', resembling that of whales and dolphins.

- **A dugong** may live for up to 70 years, but a female dugong will produce only five or six calves during her long lifetime.

▼ *Dugongs and manatees have to surface every few minutes to breathe.*

Chameleons

- **There are more than** 150 species of chameleon, most of which live on the island of Madagascar and in mainland Africa.

- **The smallest chameleon** could balance on your finger but the biggest, Oustalet's chameleon, is the size of a small cat.

- **A chameleon can look** forwards and backwards at the same time, as each of its amazing eyes can swivel in all directions independently of the other.

- **A chameleon's tongue** may be as long – or longer – than its body but is normally squashed up inside its mouth.

- **A chameleon shoots** out its tongue in a fraction of a second to trap its victim on a sticky pad at the tip.

- **The tongue is fired** out from a launching bone on the chameleon's lower jaw.

- **Most lizards can change colour,** but chameleons are experts, changing quickly to all sorts of colours.

- **Chameleons change** colour when they are angry or frightened, too cold or too hot, or sick. They sometimes change to match their surroundings.

- **The colour of a chameleon's** skin is controlled by pigment cells called chromatophores, which change colour as they change size.

- **Chameleons feed on insects** and spiders, hunting in trees by day.

◀ *Male panther chameleons are among the most colourful of all animals. Chameleons can wrap their tails around a branch, and their toes are a good shape for gripping tightly.*

Life cycles

- **The way that an animal** begins its life, grows, reproduces and dies is called its life cycle.

- **Vertebrates usually live** longer lives than invertebrates, some of which live for just one day as adults.

- **Animals grow** to maturity so that they can reproduce. Once they are adults, most animals don't get any bigger. Snakes, however, keep growing longer as they age.

- **An animal's body** is always repairing itself, so new cells are constantly growing to replace old or damaged ones. New blood is made inside bones.

- **When an elephant dies** the rest of its family appears to mourn, as they stand quietly around the dead body. Years later, they sometimes visit the spot where their relative died.

- **Most rodents live** for fewer than three years but naked mole rats have been known to live for 30 years. This makes them the longest-living rodents.

- **It is thought** that bowhead whales may live for up to 200 years.

- **Some male killer whales** and their mothers never separate, living their entire lives together.

- **Clown anemone fish** begin life as males but some of them change to become females. Similarly, parrotfish are females when they hatch from their eggs, but some turn into males.

- **An elephant's tusks** keep growing throughout its lifetime.

▶ *Parrotfish can change sex, body shape and even colour as they age. It is difficult to tell males and females apart, but mature males often have the most vibrant colours.*

Animals in danger

● **When an entire** animal species, or type, dies out completely it is said to be extinct. Animals that are at risk of becoming extinct are described as endangered, or threatened with extinction.

● **Animals that do not adapt**, or evolve, fast enough to suit a changing environment can become extinct.

● **A mass extinction event** (MEE) occurs when huge numbers of species die out at the same time. This happens when sudden changes on Earth take place, such as a dramatic drop in temperature.

● **There have been** five MEEs so far, but scientists think that the world might be going through another now – caused by humans.

● **Animals struggle** to survive when their habitats are damaged, if they cannot find food or fight disease, and when humans hunt them in large numbers.

● **Pollution may play** an important role in the extinction of amphibians. Since 1980 more than 120 species of amphibian have disappeared.

● **Mountain gorilla numbers** fell below 1000 after many years of being hunted by humans. They still face an uncertain future.

● **Spix's macaw** is probably extinct in the wild. None of these birds have been seen since 2000.

● **The Javan rhinoceros** is probably the rarest mammal in the world – there are fewer than 70 left alive in the wild, and none in zoos.

● **Kakapos are large** flightless parrots that have been saved from extinction. There are fewer than 130 birds left and they are guarded from predators on four New Zealand islands.

◀ *The dodo was a large flightless bird on the island of Mauritius. It probably became extinct in the 1670s because dogs and pigs, which sailors had brought to the island, raided the birds' ground nests and ate the eggs.*

Starfish and sea urchins

● **Starfish are not fish**, but belong to a group of sea creatures called echinoderms, meaning 'spiny skinned'.

● **Sea urchins** and sea cucumbers are also echinoderms.

● **Starfish have star-shaped bodies**. They feed mostly on shellfish, prising them open with their arms. The starfish pushes its stomach out of its mouth and into its victim where it sucks out its flesh.

● **Starfish have up to 2000 tube feet**, which are like small balloons full of seawater. They are used for moving, as well as to take in food and oxygen from the seawater.

● **If a starfish sheds one of its arms** to escape a predator, or if one of its arms is crushed or bitten off, a new arm grows to take its place.

● **Sea urchins** are ball-shaped creatures. Their shell is covered with bristling spines, which can be poisonous.

● **A sea urchin's spines** are used for protection. Urchins also have sucker-like feet for moving.

● **Their mouths** are just holes with five teeth, located on the underside of the sea urchins' bodies.

● **Sea cucumbers** have leathery skin and a covering of chalky plates called spicules.

● **When threatened**, a sea cucumber expels pieces of its gut as a decoy and swims away. It grows a new one later.

▼ *Most starfish have five arms, but some have as many as 50.*

Dragonflies

- **Dragonflies are big hunting insects** with four large transparent wings and long, slender bodies that may be shimmering reds, greens or blues.

- **Dragonflies have 30,000 lenses** in each of their compound eyes, and the sharpest vision of any insect.

- **A dragonfly's huge eyes** allow it to detect movement easily and spot prey, such as midges, mosquitoes or moths, from up to 12 m away.

- **As it swoops** in on its prey, a dragonfly pulls its legs forwards like a basket to scoop up its victim.

- **Dragonflies often mate in mid-air**, and the male may then stay hanging onto the female until she lays her eggs.

- **Dragonfly eggs** are laid in water or in the stem of a water plant, and hatch in 2–3 weeks.

- **Newly hatched dragonflies** are called nymphs and look like fatter, wingless adults.

- **Dragonfly nymphs** are ferocious hunters, often feeding on young fish and tadpoles.

- **The nymphs** grow and moult over many years before climbing onto a reed or rock to emerge as an adult.

▶ *Blue dasher dragonflies are also called blue pirates. Females are rarely as blue as the males, which only turn blue as they mature. These dragonflies live in North America.*

Owls

- **Owls feed on live animals** and most of them hunt their prey at night. They roost in trees during the day, so many owls have mottled brown feathers for camouflage.

- **There are two big families of owl** – barn owls and typical owls. Barn owls have a heart-shaped disc of feathers on the face, relatively small eyes and long, slim legs. Typical owls have enormous eyes set in a circular disc on the face and very large ears.

- **There are 135** typical owl species.

- **There are 12 species** of barn owl. The most widespread is the common barn owl, found everywhere but Antarctica.

- **Small owls** eat mostly insects. Bigger owls eat mice and shrews. Eagle owls can catch young deer.

- **In the country**, the tawny owl's diet is 90 percent small mammals, but many now live in towns where their diet is mainly small birds such as sparrows and starlings.

- **Owls can hear sounds** that are ten times softer than those humans can hear. They hunt in darkness by picking up the sounds made by their prey.

- **Most bird's eyes** look out to the sides, but owls' look straight forward like those of humans. This is probably why the owl has been a symbol of wisdom since ancient times.

- **The flight feathers** on an owl's wings muffle the sound of its wingbeats so that it can swoop silently onto its prey.

- **The white feathers** of snowy owls provide good camouflage in the snow- and ice-covered wastes of the Arctic. These owls can swoop down on their prey, taking it by surprise.

▲ *Owls swallow their prey whole, coughing up indigestible parts of their meal as pellets.*

Hornbills

● **Hornbills have** a horn-like casque (helmet-like structure) on top of their bills. This may amplify their calls, making them louder.

● **The two uppermost neck bones** are joined or fused, and the neck has very strong muscles, so the bird can move its huge bill very accurately to feed on small food items such as seeds and buds.

● **The hornbill's amazing bill** is covered in keratin (a tough, lightweight material) and has many uses, from feeding and preening to pecking enemies.

● **The beak and casque** are not quite as heavy as they look, being partly honeycomb-like, with air spaces inside.

● **The female** uses her bill to mix chewed food and droppings into a paste. She uses this paste for a strange purpose – to wall off the entrance to her nest hole, trapping herself inside. Only a narrow slit is left, through which the male passes food and she ejects droppings.

▶ *The hornbill's nesting strategy means the eggs stay hidden and protected from predators until they hatch.*

DID YOU KNOW?

Papuan hornbills have been known to eat crabs, the honeycomb of bees, and soil.

● **Sealed inside** her nest hole for more than one month, the female incubates her two or three eggs and then looks after the chicks once they have hatched.

● **Despite their large size**, hornbills fly strongly on their long, powerful wings, with noisy, whooshing wingbeats.

● **A hornbill's eyes** face partly forwards and can see along the tapering bill to its tip, which allows these birds to peck and pick up food with great precision.

● **Helmeted hornbills** perform incredible aerial jousts, colliding with each other in mid-air. These contests often take place near fig trees, so the birds may be competing for ripe figs – their favourite food.

Egg-laying mammals

● **Some mammals lay eggs** instead of giving birth to their young. These strange mammals are called monotremes and they all live in, or near, Australia.

● **Duck-billed platypuses** have a broad, flat, beaklike mouth and webbed feet. They live in eastern Australia and Tasmania.

● **After a baby platypus** has hatched from its egg, it sucks on its mother's fur and drinks the milk that oozes out of her skin.

● **Platypuses dig burrows** in riverbanks and are excellent swimmers. Their dense fur is warm and waterproof and they feed on small creatures that they find at the bottom of rivers, streams, and lakes.

● **Most monotremes** are nocturnal, which means they are most active between dusk and dawn.

● **Monotremes are one** of only two groups of venomous mammal—the other group is a type of shrew.

● **Male platypuses** have a horned spur on each ankle. Each spur is hollow and filled with venom that causes terrible pain. It is used during self defence, and is powerful enough to kill a dog.

● **There are four species** of echidna, also known as spiny anteaters. Their bodies are covered with spines and their snouts are long and toothless.

● **A female echidna** lays a single egg and puts it in a pouch on her belly. After 10 days, the egg hatches and the baby echidna feeds on its mother's milk.

● **Echidnas feed on small animals** such as worms, ants, and termites, but they can survive for weeks without food.

◀ *Echidnas have small eyes and rely on a long snout and superb sense of smell to find food. They also use their slender snout rather like a snorkel when they swim across rivers or ponds.*

What is a fish?

● **Fish are mostly slim**, streamlined animals that live in water. Many are covered in tiny shiny plates called scales.

● **There are over 25,000 species** of fish. They vary in size from the pygmy goby, at 8 mm long, to the 12-m-long whale shark.

● **Fish are cold-blooded**: their temperature is controlled by their surroundings.

● **They breathe through gills** – rows of feathery brushes inside their heads.

● **There are three main groups** of fish. Most have bony skeletons and a backbone. Salmon are bony fish.

● **Around 800 species**, including sharks and rays, have skeletons made of cartilage.

● **Jawless fish** (about 70 species), including hagfish and lampreys, have snake-like bodies and sucking mouths.

● **Fish have fins**, not limbs. Most have a pectoral fin behind each gill and two pelvic fins below to the rear, a dorsal fin on top of their body, an anal fin beneath, and a caudal (tail) fin.

▲ *Many fish live in large groups called shoals.*

● **Most bony fish** control their floating depth by letting gas in and out of a special organ called a swim bladder.

● **Some fish** communicate by making sounds with their swim bladder.

Worms

● **Worms are long**, soft-bodied, tube-shaped animals without legs. Annelids are worms such as the earthworm, the bodies of which are divided into segments.

● **There are 15,000 species** of annelid. Most live underground in tunnels, or in the sea.

● **The world's largest earthworm** is the giant earthworm of South Africa, which can grow to as long as 4 m.

● **Earthworms spend their lives** burrowing through soil. Soil goes in the mouth end, passes through the gut and comes out at the tail end.

● **An earthworm** is both male and female (called a hermaphrodite), and after two earthworms mate, both develop eggs.

● **Over half** of annelid species are marine bristleworms, such as ragworms and lugworms. They are named because they are covered in bristles, which they use to paddle over the sea bed or dig into mud.

● **The sea mouse** is a bristleworm with furry hairs.

● **Flatworms look like ribbons** or as though an annelid worm has been ironed flat.

● **Of the thousands of flatworm species**, many live as parasites on or in other animals. Some live in the soil or in fresh or salt water.

● **Leeches are segmented worms** that often feed on blood. They produce a substance that keeps blood from clotting so that they can go on feeding.

▼ *Earthworms are most active at night, when there are fewer predators around. They are an important source of food for many vertebrates.*

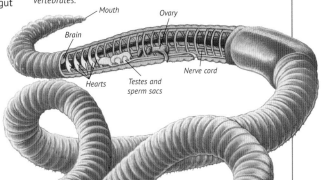

Mouth

Ovary

Brain

Nerve cord

Hearts

Testes and sperm sacs

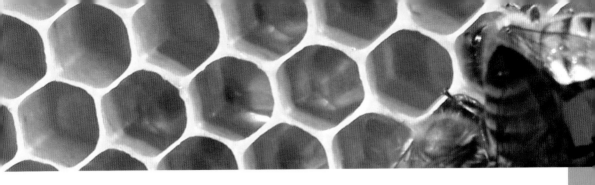

1000 **INSECT** FACTS

Classification

● **Experts have divided** all living things on Earth into different groups and given them special names. Each group shares certain features.

● **All living creatures** are classified into five major kingdoms – animals, plants, fungi, monerans (such as bacteria) and protists.

● **These kingdoms** are further divided into phyla (singular phylum). There are around 20 phyla in the animal kingdom. The phylum Arthropoda is the largest in the animal kingdom and includes insects, spiders, crabs and centipedes.

● **The different phyla** are split into smaller groups called classes. Birds, mammals, reptiles and insects all belong to different classes.

● **Insects belong to** the class Insecta. Spiders and scorpions belong to the class Arachnida.

● **There are** different orders within each class. For example, ants, bees and wasps belong to the order Hymenoptera within the class Insecta. All hymenopterans have wings and many can sting.

● **The study of insects** is known as entymology. Entomologists have divided all the insects discovered so far into 32 orders.

● **Orders are** further sub-divided into families. Lions, tigers and pet cats belong to the family Felidae. Similarly, all ants belong to the family Formicidae.

● **Families are even further** divided into genus and species. Only animals that belong to the same species can mate together to reproduce fertile offspring.

● **Scientists called taxonomists** give scientific names to living things. These names are in Latin and include the genus and species name.

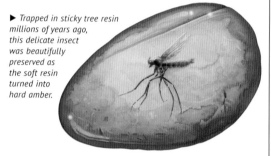

▶ *Trapped in sticky tree resin millions of years ago, this delicate insect was beautifully preserved as the soft resin turned into hard amber.*

Insect fact file

● **Insects are small** six-legged animals that generally have one or two pairs of wings.

● **There are between** one and eight million species of insects, compared to just one human species.

● **Insects are successful survivors** for different reasons, such as their powerful exoskeletons, their ability to fly and their minute size.

● **Insects are** the largest food source for other animals.

● **Some insects** can fly for long distances. Certain butterflies migrate thousands of kilometres to avoid bad weather.

DID YOU KNOW?

Scientists discovered the fossils of a dragonfly that lived 300 mya (million years ago). It had a wingspan as big as a seagull.

● **Cockroaches have been** living on Earth for around 300 million years. Today's cockroaches look very similar to those living hundreds of millions of years ago.

● **Fairyflies are the smallest** insects in the world. They are only 0.2 mm – that is the size of a full stop.

● **People have domesticated** silkworms for so long that these insects do not exist in the wild anymore.

● **Insects are cold-blooded** animals, so their growth and development depends upon how hot or cold the weather is.

● **Scientists have developed 'insect robots'** that copy the agility of real insects. These robots are used to explore dangerous areas, such as minefields and the surface of other planets. Robots are not nearly as agile as real insects, but mimic the way they move.

▼ *Together, moths and butterflies, such as this swallowtail butterfly, make up one of the largest groups of insects. There are ten times more moths than butterflies.*

Record-breaking insects

● **Mayflies have the shortest lives**. As nymphs, they spend two to three years at the bottom of lakes and streams. When they emerge on dry land as adults, they live for an average of one or two days.

● **Locusts are the most destructive insects**. The desert locust is the most damaging of them all. Although they are only 4.5–6 cm long, they can eat their body weight in food every day. One tonne of locusts, a fraction of a swarm, can eat the same amount of food in one day as around 2500 people.

● **The calling song** of the African cicada measures at 106.7 decibels (as loud as a road drill), making it the loudest insect. The male cicada produces loud buzzing sounds by vibrating drumlike membranes on its abdomen.

● **Female Malaysian stick insects** lay eggs measuring 1.3 cm – larger than a peanut! Insects, such as cockroaches, lay egg cases that are larger than this, but they contain about 200 individual eggs.

● **The highest insect jump** measured was 70 cm by the froghopper. When it jumps, the froghopper accelerates at 4000 m/sec and overcomes a G-force of more than 414 times its own body weight.

▶ *The giant weta, a type of cricket, can weigh up to 70 g – as much as a small bird!*

● **Weighing up to 33 g**, a rhinoceros cockroach is 500 times bigger than a domestic pest cockroach. This species lives in burrows.

● **With a wingspan** of 30 cm, the atlas moth is the biggest recorded moth. It is often be mistaken for a bird.

● **The Mother-of-Pearl** moth caterpillar can travel at 40 cm/sec, the equivalent of 1.6 km/h. It is the only creature that deliberately rolls away when attacked.

● **The larva** of the North American Polyphemus moth eats an amount equal to 86,000 times its own birthweight in the first 56 days of its life. For a human, this is the equivalent of an average baby eating 273 tonnes of food.

● **The giant mydas fly** lives in South America and females are larger than males. The largest specimen found had a wingspan of 11.7 cm and a body length of 5.8 cm.

Insects and people

● **Insects have always** been of great importance to human civilizations. People rear insects such as silkworms and honeybees to obtain important materials from them, such as silk, honey and wax.

● **Archaeologists have** discovered prehistoric cave paintings that show scenes of honey collection and the extraction of honey from beehives.

● **Japanese Samurai warriors** painted intricate butterfly patterns on weapons and flags to symbolize nobility.

● **Cicadas and crickets** have been captured and reared by humans for the beautiful sound they can produce.

● **Many insects**, such as mosquitoes, lice and bedbugs, feed on human blood.

● **Some people eat insects**, such as cicadas, ants and water bugs, and consider them to be delicacies. Witchetty grubs eaten in Australia are moth caterpillars.

● **Deadly diseases** such as the bubonic plague and malaria are transmitted to humans by insects such as fleas and flies, and cause millions of deaths.

● **Doctors used to insert** maggots into wounds to eat away the dead flesh and keep the wound clean.

● **Some insects are pests** and can cause serious damage by destroying crops and fields. However, many insects feed on agricultural pests and help farmers.

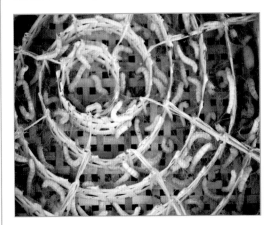

◀ *Silkworms are bred at silk factories, so the yellow-white silk cocoons can be easily collected.*

Forensic entomology

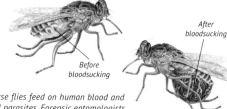

- **Insects can help detectives** and other experts to solve crimes. There is a special science in which scientists study the insects found on dead bodies. This is called forensic entomology.

- **A lot of changes** take place in the body once a person dies. The corpse becomes host to a variety of diferent insects.

- **Blowflies are the very first** insects that normally infest a corpse. They lay eggs that hatch into maggots. Other insects soon find their way to the corpse, in search of these maggots and flies.

- **Forensic experts** can estimate the time of death by studying these insects. They study the life cycle of the flies and determine the time of death. For instance, if maggots are found on a corpse, they know that death occurred a few days previously. This would give the flies enough time to lay eggs and then the eggs to hatch into maggots.

- **The cause of death** can also be detected by studying the insects on the corpse. Sometimes, experts spot maggots and eggs on cuts and wounds in the skin that may have been fatal.

▶ *Tsetse flies feed on human blood and spread parasites. Forensic entomologists can use their presence at the scene of a crime to discover vital information.*

- **Sometimes, the body is moved** from the crime scene. This can disturb the life cycle and growth of the insects on the corpse. Forensic experts can detect this change in growth and find out if the body has been moved.

- **Most insects** that live on corpses usually live in the local area. However, if the body contains insects that do not normally live in that location, the detective knows that the crime was committed elsewhere.

- **If someone takes illegal drugs**, their body undergoes many changes. These can affect the insects living on the body and help provide important clues about the death.

- **Flies, beetles and gnats** are some of the most common insects found on corpses. Small spiders and worms can also be spotted on dead bodies.

- **Forensic entomology** is not new. In the 1300s, the Chinese studied insects to find clues about crimes.

Anatomy

- **The segmented body of an insect** is divided into three parts: head, thorax (middle section) and abdomen (rear section).

- **All insects have six legs** that are joined to the thorax. Many also have one or two pairs of wings, also joined to the thorax.

- **Insects have an exoskeleton**, which is a strong outer skeleton. It protects the insect's muscles and delicate organs.

- **Two antennae** on the head are used to sense smell, touch and sound.

- **The head** also contains mouthparts that are adapted to different feeding methods, such as chewing, biting, stabbing and sucking.

- **The digestive and reproductive** systems of insects are in the abdomen.

- **Insect blood** does not move through lots of tubes. Instead it is pumped through the whole body. It is greenish-yellow in colour rather than red.

- **Special openings** on the side of the body (spiracles) are used for breathing.

- **Insects have a tiny brain**, which is just a collection of nerve cells bundled together. The brain sends signals to control the body.

▶ *An insect has three main parts to its body – the thorax, abdomen and head. Some insects, such as this honeybee, also have wings.*

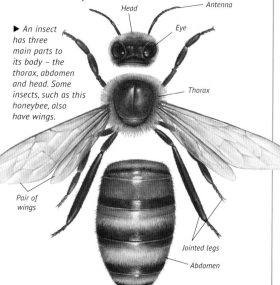

Head

Antenna

Eye

Thorax

Pair of wings

Jointed legs

Abdomen

Moulting

- **An insect's hard exoskeleton** does not stretch so it needs to be shed, or moulted, as the insect grows. All insects moult during the early stages of life.

- **To moult**, insects puff up their body, either by swallowing a lot of air or water, or by using blood pressure. The old exoskeleton splits and the insect pushes out from inside.

- **This exposes a soft new exoskeleton**, which quickly hardens to form a protective case.

- **The new exoskeleton** becomes darker as it hardens.

- **It forms around** the insect's inflated body so it is bigger than the old one, providing growing room for the insect.

◀ *A young adult dragonfly emerges during its moult. After resting, it will pump blood into its short wings to spread them out to their full adult size.*

- **Insects normally** moult five to ten times in a lifetime, depending on their species.

- **A silverfish** can moult up to 60 times in a lifetime.

- **The larval stage** between moults is known as an instar.

- **Moulting takes a long time** and the insect is vulnerable to predator attacks during this period. Therefore, most insects moult in hidden places.

> **DID YOU KNOW?**
>
> A caterpillar grows about 2000 times bigger than its size at the time of hatching.

Communication

- **Insects use various methods** to communicate with members of the same species, as well as with other animals. They 'tell' each other about new food sources and even communicate their likes (in the case of mating partners) or dislikes (in the case of enemies).

- **Insects normally use** their sense of touch to communicate with each other.

- **Ants release pheromones** (special chemical scents) in order to communicate with other ants.

- **Some insects** use distinct colours to let other animals know they are dangerous. Other insects may have designs on their bodies that warn predators away.

- **Some cockroaches** and butterflies have huge, eyelike motifs on their thorax or wings, which scare predators.

- **Certain beetles** emit strong-smelling substances from their bodies. This is to warn predators to avoid eating them. Most of the time, these strong-smelling bugs taste bad as well.

- **Strange colours** and special scents are not always used to warn enemies. Insects also use displays of colour to attract mates.

- **Insects were** the first animals to use sound as a means of communication. Bees use buzzing sounds to warn about danger, indicate the presence of food and convey a variety of other information.

- **The rate** at which fireflies blink light is important for successful mating. If a female blinks back too fast, she is thought to be unattractive and if her response is too slow, she is assumed to be uninterested in the male.

▶ *Red and black colours, like those on this postman butterfly, are common among poisonous insects. Predators soon learn to avoid eating these poisonous butterflies.*

> **DID YOU KNOW?**
>
> Worker honeybees perform a special 'bee dance' to inform other workers about the source and direction of flower nectar. In 1923, Dr Karl von Frisch decoded the bee language and won the Nobel prize.

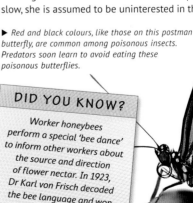

Pollinators

● **Insects play a major role** in the pollination of flowers. In fact, there are many plants that depend on insects for pollination.

● **Plants developed flowers** in order to attract the insects they need to carry their pollen to other flowers.

● **Insects visit flowers** for pollen and nectar. They are less likely to visit flowers that do not produce sweet nectar. Bees rarely visit roses for this reason.

● **Plants adapt** their appearance to make them appear attractive to insects. The insects' reward is sugary nectar.

● **Some flowers** have strong lines and marks on their petals that can only be seen by insects and are not visible to humans. They lead to the centre of the flower where the pollen and nectar are situated.

● **Some flowers smell sweet**. This is to attract insects to come close to them. Butterflies and other nectar-sucking insects help in pollinating these flowers by carrying pollen grains on their hairy bodies.

● **Not all flowers** smell nice. Some, such as arum flowers, smell like dead and decaying matter. This attracts flies and other insects that lay eggs in rotting matter.

▲ *The partnership between insects and flowering plants has helped both groups to survive in increased numbers.*

● **Brightly coloured** flowers attract a lot of insects. Butterflies are most attracted to red and purple flowers, while moths usually like pink or white flowers.

● **Some species** of plant change the colour of their flower after an insect has pollinated it. The new colour discourages other insects from visiting the flower.

● **Some plants resemble** female insects. Male insects are attracted to these flowers and when they try to mate, the flower is pollinated.

● **Bees and butterflies** are the most common pollinators. Beetles also help in pollination, but are less effective.

Camouflage and mimicry

● **Insects use certain defence strategies**, such as camouflage and mimicry, to protect themselves from predators. Killer insects sometimes use the same strategies to catch their prey.

● **Certain insects cleverly hide** themselves by blending in with their surroundings. This is known as camouflage.

● **Some harmless insects mimic** (imitate) harmful insects in appearance and behaviour. This fools predators into leaving them alone.

● **Hoverflies have** yellow-and-black stripes on their bodies, which makes them resemble stinging insects called wasps or hornets. Predators avoid the harmless hoverflies, assuming them to be wasps or hornets.

● **The larvae of some butterflies** resemble bird droppings, or even soil.

● **Stick insects and praying mantids** appear to be the twigs and leaves of plants. Predators often miss out on a possible meal because these insects blend into their environment very well. Even the pupae of some butterflies look like twigs.

Hornet moth

Hornet

◀ *The hornet moth is a mimic of a type of wasp known as a hornet that has a painful sting.*

● **Monarch butterflies** are bitter-tasting and poisonous, so birds do not eat them. Viceroy butterflies have orange and black wings similar to those of monarch butterflies. Birds avoid viceroy butterflies because they think that they are poisonous as well.

● **Some moths imitate** dangerous wasps and bees in behaviour and sound. Their buzz startles predators, which leave them alone.

● **Adults and caterpillars** of some moths and butterflies have large eyelike spots to scare away predatory birds.

● **The hornet moth** has transparent wings and a yellow-and-black striped body, making it look like a large wasp called a hornet. Predators, avoid hornet moths because they look as if they might sting.

Defence

- **Insects use** other strategies as well as camouflage and mimicry to protect themselves from predators.

- **Some caterpillars** and larvae have special glands that secrete poison when they are attacked. Predatory birds soon learn to avoid them.

- **Stick insects and weevils** sometimes 'play dead' when attacked. They keep very still and the attacker leaves them alone because most predators do not eat dead prey.

- **Ants, bees and wasps** can deliver painful stings to an attacker. These insects pump in venom and cause pain and irritation.

- **Some butterflies**, such as the monarch butterfly, are poisonous and cause the attacking bird to vomit if eaten.

- **Certain insects are able to** shed their limbs if an attacker grabs them. This phenomenon is known as autotomy.

- **The bombardier beetle** has special glands at the end of its abdomen, which can spray boiling hot poisonous fluids at an attacker.

- **Stink glands** found in some bugs release repelling smells that predators cannot tolerate.

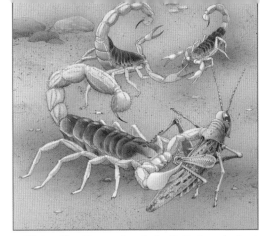

▲ This katydid could escape from the formidable claws of a desert scorpion by shedding a leg and flying away.

- **Some moths, grasshoppers and mantids** suddenly show the bright colours on their hind wings to startle a predator. These are called flash colours.

DID YOU KNOW?

When alarmed, ants raise their abdomen. This sends a signal to other ants in the colony, and all the other ants raise their abdomens too.

Stings

- **Insects that belong** to the order Hymenoptera, such as ants, bees and wasps, are the best-known stinging insects.

- **A stinging insect** has special organs that produce venom (poison) and a sharp stinger or mouthparts to inject venom into the victim.

- **A wasp or ant sting** has evolved from an egg-laying tube. The insects do not lay eggs, but use the tube to pump venom into victims.

- **The venom** can have a paralyzing effect on the prey. If larger animals are stung, the venom can damage tissue and cause pain. Hornet venom is the most potent.

- **Some insects**, such as mosquitoes, do not sting. They puncture the skin's surface with a sharp feeding tube and suck up blood. Their bite creates an itchy bump. Mosquitoes and other biting insects can spread diseases to humans.

- **Insects sting** for two purposes – to catch prey and to defend themselves from predators.

- **Honeybees sting only once** and die soon after. Their jagged sting remains stuck in their victim's skin, which tears out the honeybee's insides when it flies away.

- **Wasps sting** their victims many times over because their stings are smooth and can be pulled out of the victims and used again.

▶ Ants can sting and bite. They inject formic acid into their victim when they sting.

▶ A honeybee's jagged sting is a modified egg-laying tool, so only female bees can sting.

Habitats

- **Insects have adapted** to survive in almost every habitat on Earth, including some with extreme climates.

- **Entomologists** have discovered species of insect that live on volcanic lava and others that survive in cold polar regions.

- **Most insects live** in tropical regions where the warm year-round temperatures most suit their growth and development.

- **The vast majority of insects** live on land – in soil or decomposing plant matter, under rocks, in trees, on flowers or leaves.

- **Some insects can live** in the fresh water of ponds, lakes, streams, rivers, and even muddy pools, small waterholes and salty lakes.

▲ *A hornet's nest can be as large as a basketball and is constructed in a hollow tree, under roof eaves, porches and outbuildings.*

- **Some insect species** can live deep underwater, while others need to come to the surface to breathe air.

- **Many insects lay their eggs** in water and their larvae feed underwater, breathing with gills. These insects climb out to live on land when they become adults.

- **Some insects**, such as the larvae of house flies, live on rotting material, including leftover food.

- **Others, such as lice and fleas**, are parasites, which means they live on another organism such as humans or other mammals.

DID YOU KNOW?

Around 97 percent of the insect world lives on the land or in freshwater. Very few insects can survive in the sea.

1 Elm beetle

2 Elm beetle larva

3 Mealybug

4 Furniture beetle

5 Woodworm (Furniture beetle larva)

6 Flower bug

7 Shield bug

8 Lace bug

9 Capsid bug

10 Fruit fly

▼ *Temperate woodlands are home to a rich variety of insects because of the range of food and shelter available. The numbers and species of insect living in woodlands vary with the seasons and the types of tree.*

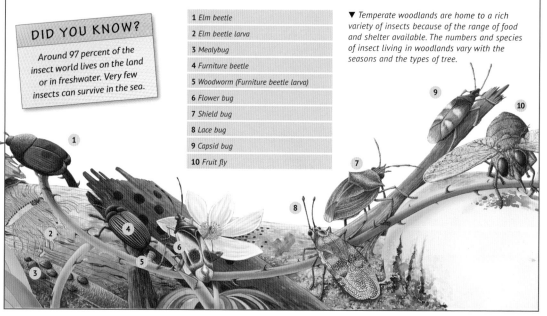

Migration

- **Insects migrate** across great distances in search of suitable living and breeding conditions. They often migrate when the weather gets colder or hotter or when food becomes scarce.

- **Migrating insects** may land in certain places and lay a large number of eggs before moving on.

- **Insects migrate in two ways**, which are known as homeostatic and dynamic migration.

- **Homeostatic migration** is when insects pass through a defined path and also return the same way.

- **In dynamic migration**, insects depend upon the wind or tides to decide their path of movement.

▶ Every autumn, huge numbers of monarch butterflies fly from cold northern areas of North America to the warmth of Florida, California and Mexico. In spring, new generations of monarchs make the long return journey north again.

- **Monarch butterflies** are known to migrate across continents and can cover distances of over 3000 km.

- **Butterflies may travel** in huge groups of millions of butterflies. Most of the older butterflies cannot withstand the journey and die on the way.

- **Pilots have spotted** migrating butterflies at altitudes of 1200 m.

- **Locusts migrate** across farmlands in large swarms in search of greener pastures.

- **Army ants** do not build permanent nests because they constantly migrate in search of food.

DID YOU KNOW?

Migrating butterflies such as the painted lady do not return to their home ground, but the next generation does.

◀ Migrating locusts have broader backs and longer wings to help them fly fast and for long distances. A swarm of locusts may fly as much as 3200 km in a year.

Flight

- **Insects fly to escape from danger**, to find suitable mates, to hunt for food or to find a new place to lay their eggs. Some fly very long distances in search of food, while others cross continents when they migrate.

- **The wing** helps to distinguish between insect groups. In fact, the orders to which most insects belong are named after their wings. The order names usually end with 'ptera', which stands for wings.

- **Most insects** have evolved two pairs of wings, which enable them to fly. The earliest insects had wings that helped them glide through the air. These evolved into sturdier wings that could flap up and down.

◀ Like many flying insects, the larvae stage of the dragonfly is spent without wings. As adults, however, they are skilled and speedy fliers and catch prey with ease.

- **Not all insects** can fly. Some insects, such as female vapourer moths, have lost their wings during the course of evolution.

- **The size** of the wing does not determine how good the insect is at flying. Some insects, such as dobsonflies, have large wings but are poor fliers.

- **Insect wings** are membrane-like structures. They have veins and nerves running across them through which blood and oxygen are circulated. The wing's edge is usually sturdier than the rest of the wing, helping it cut through the air during flight.

- **The wings** are attached to the insect's thorax by strong muscles, which help the insect to flap its wings.

- **In insects** such as beetles, the front pair of wings is hard and protects the more delicate hind wings.

- **A dragonfly** flaps its wings as though it were writing the number eight in the air. This movement helps to create air currents near the wings that balance the dragonfly while flying.

- **Some of the fastest** and highest insect fliers belong to the order Lepidoptera – butterflies and moths.

Ants

● **One of the most successful insects** on Earth, there are more than 9000 different species of ant.

● **Ants belong** to an order of insects known as Hymenoptera. Bees and wasps also belong to this group.

● **Entomologists believe** that ants evolved from wasps millions of years ago.

● **These social insects** live in huge colonies, consisting of the queen ant, thousands of female workers and a few male ants.

● **In ant colonies,** the worker ants divide themselves into groups that perform various tasks. Some are cleaners, some take care of the young while others gather food or defend the nest.

● **Worker ants** take care of the eggs. At night, they carry them into deep nest tunnels to protect them from the cold. In the morning, workers carry the eggs back to the surface to warm them.

● **When ants find food**, they leave a chemical trail of pheromones so that other ants can find their way from the nest to the food.

● **Rare trap-jaw ants** are found in Costa Rica. They have large jaws, which are used to trap and stab the enemy.

● **An ant can lift a weight** that is 20 to 50 times more than its own body weight.

◀ *The biggest worker ants are soldiers. They protect the nest from predators.*

Ant nests

● **Ants live in nests** that are built by the worker ants. These nests are known as formicariums.

● **Ant nests** are usually built on the ground. They can be either underground or above the soil. Some species of ant support their nests by building them against man-made structures, such as telephone poles.

● **Ant nests that are built** above the ground are in the form of mounds of soil, twigs and leaves.

● **Some ant mounds** can be as tall as one metre. These ant nests are many metres wide.

● **Some ant species** build simple nests with only a few chambers and corridors, while others' build nests with separate chambers for the queen, the eggs and the young.

● **Worker ants** control the temperature inside the nest and ensure there is proper ventilation in the chambers.

● **Some ant species** grow 'fungus gardens' inside their nests to provide food for their young. Special cells inside the nest store food material for the fungus.

● **Certain ants** build nests in trees. These are not confined to one tree. The ants connect different trees with the help of underground tunnels and corridors.

● **Leafcutter ants** make the largest ant nests. Some leafcutter nests contain millions of ants.

● **Ants sometimes make use** of old, empty wasp nests. They also live in tree galls, dead wood and tree stumps.

● **The pagoda tree ant** builds its nest with wood pulp and saliva. These ants pile small scraps of tree bark on top of each other making a tall structure that looks like an oriental pagoda.

◀ *Ants can build large and complex nests with many chambers housing the winged males (1), larvae (2), eggs (3) and the queen (4).*

Army ant

- **Not all ants** live in anthills. Army ants are nomadic insects. They carry their eggs and young ones along with them while travelling and set up temporary camps.

- **Army ants constantly migrate** in search of food. They march at night and stop to camp in the morning.

- **Nomadic in nature**, army ants do not build permanent nests. However, they do stay in one place for two or three weeks, while the queen produces thousands of eggs.

- **The nests** are called bivouacs and are built by a mass of army ants surrounding the queen at the centre. The ants cling onto each other to form the walls and the chambers.

- **While the queen is laying eggs**, the workers forage for food.

- **When the eggs** begin to hatch, the colony starts to swarm. The workers carry the queen and her larvae through the forest.

- **When the larvae pupate**, the ants stop swarming and build a new bivouac. The pupae become workers and the queen lays more eggs.

- **Army ants are huge eaters**. They march in swarms of up to one million ants and eat 50,000 insects a day!

- **They eat insects, birds and small animals**. Army ants have even been known to eat the body of a dead horse.

- **Army ants can attack** and enslave ants living in other colonies.

- **They have not evolved**, or changed, much in the last 100 million years.

- **Army ants have been known** to march into people's homes in their search for food.

▼ The army ants of tropical America march in columns, just like real soldiers. To cross gaps, some of the ants form bridges with their bodies, allowing the rest of the army to swarm over the living bridge. The worker ants also link up to form chains that surround the queen and young.

DID YOU KNOW?

A queen army ant can lay up to four million eggs in one month.

Weaver ant

- **Weaver ants** build their colonies in the top of trees, using live green leaves.

- **Weaver ant larvae** secrete a sticky silklike substance. Adult ants use the young larvae like glue sticks.

- **A team of worker ants** holds two leaves together, while a single worker holds a larva in its mouthparts and uses the silky secretion to stick the leaves together.

- **A colony can contain** about 150 weaver nests in 20 different trees. The queen ant's nest is built in the centre of the colony and is made with extra silk.

- **The larger worker (soldier) ants** fiercely protect their nest, while the smaller workers take care of various chores inside the nest.

- **Weaver ants are carnivores** and feed on body fluids from small, soft-bodied insects. Some species also feed on honeydew.

- **For 2000 years,** the Chinese have used weaver ants to control pest infestations in their crop fields.

- **Weaver ants do not sting** but they can inflict painful bites if provoked. When they bite, weaver ants squirt formic acid into the wound, causing even more pain.

- **Some caterpillars** and spiders camouflage themselves as weaver ants and attack weaver ant nests.

◀ *Weaver ants join leaves together to make their nests.*

Leafcutter ant

- **Leafcutter ants** cut out bits of leaves from plants and carry them back to their underground nest.

- **These ants cannot digest leaves.** Leafcutter ants feed on a fungus that is specially grown by them.

- **The cut leaf pieces** are used to fertilize special fungus farms that are grown inside the ant nest. There can be numerous fungus farms growing in a single nest.

- **Leafcutter ants** are normally found in tropical rainforests.

- **A queen leafcutter ant** can produce about 15 million offspring during her lifetime.

- **Leafcutter ants divide** themselves into workers and soldiers. The biggest ants are soldiers, which protect the nest.

- **Small worker ants** take care of the young and manage the nest, while bigger worker ants go out and cut pieces of leaves for the fungus farms.

- **In some species** of leafcutter ant, tiny workers ride on the pieces of snipped leaves. They protect the larger workers from flies that try to lay their eggs on them.

- **In some cultures, leafcutter ants are eaten.** They are a rich source of protein.

- **Leafcutter ants do not sting,** but they can bite.

▼ *Leafcutter ants carry cut pieces of leaf back to their nest. Each leaf fragment can take two or three minutes to cut and is often many times the size of the ant.*

Bees

- **There are approximately 20,000** species of bee. Many bees live alone but over 500 species are called 'social bees' and live in colonies.

- **Although bees look like wasps,** they have more hair and a thicker, more robust body. Unlike wasps, they have specialised organs to carry pollen.

- **Bees are small** in size, ranging from 2–4 cm in length. They have a sting to protect themselves.

- **Bees feed on pollen and nectar** collected from flowers. Hairs on their body collect the pollen. Pollen contains protein and nectar provides energy.

- **Social bees secrete wax** to build their nests. A honeybee colony may contain 3000 to 40,000 bees depending on the species, the season and the locality. Each colony consists of one queen bee, female workers and male drones.

- **Males do not** have stings. Their only function is to mate with the queen and they die soon after. The queen then lays 600–700 eggs every day.

- **A normal worker's lifespan** ranges from five to six weeks, but a queen can live for up to five years.

- **Bees perform a dance** to tell other bees where food can be found.

- **Bees have two kinds** of mouthparts. The first kind, found in honeybees, is adapted for sucking. The other kind is adapted for biting. This is found in carpenter bees.

- **Bees' antennae** are their organs of touch and smell. They use their antennae to detect flower fragrances and find nectar.

- **When a bee stings**, it injects venom into the victim's body. As the bee moves away, the jagged sting remains in the victim, which pulls out the bee's internal organs, killing it.

▼ *Honeybee workers crowd around their queen. The workers lick and stroke their queen to pick up powerful scents called pheromones, which pass on information about the queen and tell the workers how to behave.*

Bee nests

● **Social bees** (species that live together in colonies) make complex nests, consisting of a number of cells, often built in flat sheets called combs.

● **Honeybees are the only species** that make honeycombs. These are formed of hexagonal cells made from wax, which is produced by the worker bees.

● **Honeycombs are divided** into three main sections. The upper section is used for storing honey and the middle section for storing pollen. The lower section is used to house the eggs and young.

● **The hexagonal shape** of honeycomb cells allows the maximum amount of honey to be stored and uses the least amount of wax.

● **Social bees use their nests** to raise their eggs, larvae and pupae, collectively called their brood. Some also use their nests to store honey for winter.

● **To maintain an optimum temperature** of 35°C in the hive, bees flutter their wings and use water as a coolant.

▲ *A honeybee hive has cells for storing pollen (1), honey (2), developing larvae (3) and eggs (4).*

● **A bumblebee queen** builds her nest in a hole in the ground.

● **Stingless bees build** saclike combs, made from a mixture of resin and wax. The combs are held together with a sticky substance in hollow trees or cracks in rocks. While building the nest, stingless bees hang the cells horizontally.

Bee behaviour

● **Bees can rarely distinguish** sweet and bitter tastes but can identify sour and salty tastes. Bees use their front legs, antennae and proboscis for tasting.

● **Bees have no sense of hearing**, but they can sense vibrations through their sensitive hairs.

● **Bees do not sleep**, although they may remain motionless.

● **Social bees** follow a hierarchical structure. They live in large colonies of queens, males and workers. The queen's cell is structurally different from the worker cells. Males do not help in the organization and other activities of the colony.

● **When a colony** becomes overcrowded, some bees fly to a different location. This is called swarming. It is a part of the annual life cycle of the bee colony.

● **A division of labour** exists among social bees. The queen bee lays eggs and male bees fertilize the queen bee. Worker bees perform various tasks, such as cleaning the cells, keeping the young warm and guarding them, feeding larvae, producing wax and collecting food for the colony.

● **The queen bee** secretes pheromones, which tell worker bees that she is alive and well and also inhibit the development of worker bees into queens.

● **Once she lays eggs**, the fertilized eggs become female worker bees and the unfertilized eggs become male bees.

● **Wild bees nest underground** or in tree holes, caves or under houses. Honeybees also live in hives constructed by people.

◀ *This bee's long, pink, ridged glossa (tongue) laps up nectar from deep in the flower. Bees are well equipped to eat both solids and liquids, and to use wax to make cells for the honeycomb.*

Honeybee

● **Honeybees are social insects**. They live in large colonies and are the most popular species of bees.

● **The biggest producers of honey** are honeybees. This is why they are the species most domesticated by humans.

● **Some well known species** of honeybee are Italian bees, Carniolan (Slovenian) bees, Caucasian bees, German black bees and Africanized honeybees.

● **In a honeybee colony**, different groups of bees carry out different tasks. A colony is made up of a queen bee, female workers and male drones.

● **Queen bees** are responsible for laying eggs that develop into drones and worker bees.

● **Workers have a sharp sting**, pollen baskets, wax secreting glands and a honey sac for collecting honey. The wax is used to build sheets of cells called combs.

● **Worker bees build** the nest as well as collect pollen and nectar for food. They are also responsible for maintaining the nursery temperature at 35°C, which is ideal for hatching the eggs and rearing the larvae.

▲ *Honeybees have hairs on their body to help them collect pollen.*

● **Drones do not have a sting.** Their sole function is to mate with the queen. They die after mating. During winter, they are driven out of the beehive by the workers.

● **Honeybees** have an amazing mode of communication among themselves – dancing. Dr Karl Von Frisch won the Nobel Prize for deciphering the bee dance.

● **Honeybees are susceptible** to various diseases and attacks by parasites. Parasite and virus attacks may cause paralysis in bees.

▼ *Stored honey keeps worker honeybees and their developing young alive during the long cold winters in temperate areas when other bee colonies die out.*

Honey

● **Honeybees collect** flower nectar and other plant secretions, and turn it into honey. It is then altered chemically into different types of sugar and stored in the comb cells.

● **The honey in a honeycomb** includes matured nectar, pollen, bee saliva and wax granules.

● **Honey mainly contains** water, sugars and minerals, as well as traces of calcium, phosphorous, magnesium, iron, silica and vitamin C.

● **Honey is thought** to be the only food that provides everything an animal needs to survive.

● **An alternative to sugar, honey** is a natural, unrefined sweetener.

● **Every 100 g of honey** provides 319 kilocalories of energy.

● **The colour and flavour** of honey depends upon the climate and the flowers from which the nectar has been collected.

● **Honey extracted** from wild beehives can be dangerous if the nectar is obtained from poisonous flowers.

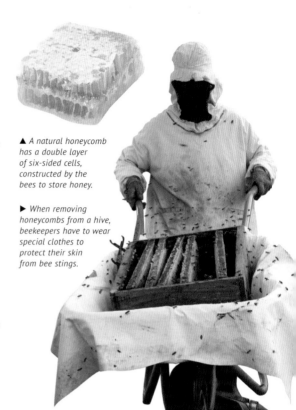

▲ *A natural honeycomb has a double layer of six-sided cells, constructed by the bees to store honey.*

▶ *When removing honeycombs from a hive, beekeepers have to wear special clothes to protect their skin from bee stings.*

Bumblebee

● **These large, hairy bees** have a black body with yellow or orange stripes. They are most common in temperate regions.

● **Bumblebees** are less aggressive than other bees.

● **They live** in small colonies of around 50–600 bees.

● **These bees help** to pollinate plants, such as red clover. Their long tongue enables them to reach deep inside flowers.

● **They build** their nests on the ground in rocky holes, grassy hollows or deserted rodent nests. The chambers are spherical with only one entrance. The cells inside are capsule shaped.

● **The queen secretes** wax from her abdominal glands into cups inside the nest, and then lays her eggs.

● **Only bumblebee queens survive** winter. The rest of the colony dies. The queen hibernates and comes out in spring to lay more eggs and start a new colony.

● **Bumblebees regulate** their body temperature with the help of their body hair.

◀ *Bumblebees collect pollen from flowers in pollen baskets (long, stiff bristles) on their back legs.*

Leafcutter bee

- **Leafcutter bees are named** after their habit of cutting pieces of leaf to make a protective casing for their eggs. They nest in the soil or hollow plant stems.

- **They have hair** on their abdomen, which helps them collect pollen.

- **Most leafcutter bees** are solitary in nature. Females construct individual nests independently.

- **Males are smaller** than females and have hairy faces.

- **The female bee** builds her nest from leaf pieces. Once a cell is ready, she stores pollen and honey inside, lays an egg and closes the cell with a disk of leaf. Then she repeats the sequence until the entire nest is complete.

- **Individual female leafcutter bees** do all the work. They select the nesting place, construct cells, lay the eggs and rear the larvae.

- **Leafcutter bees are docile** with a mild sting. They use the sting to defend themselves.

- **It is possible** for leafcutter bees to harm plants because of their habit of constructing nests with plant leaves.

▶ A female leafcutter bee snips off a piece of leaf with her sharp jaws. She will roll up the leaf fragment and carry it between her legs as she flies back to her nest.

- **Leafcutter bees help some plants**, such as alfalfa, with pollination. They do this by carrying the pollen from one plant to another.

- **The predators of leafcutter bees** include wasps, velvet ants and some species of blister beetle.

Carpenter bee

- **Carpenter bees** are named after their habit of drilling into wood to build nests.

- **Blue-black** or metallic in colour, carpenter bees resemble large bumblebees.

- **Carpenter bees are found** all over the world, especially in areas where woody plants flourish. They are common in forested regions of the tropics.

- **Solitary** in nature, carpenter bees do not live in colonies.

- **Male carpenter bees** have white-coloured faces or white markings and females have black-coloured faces.

- **Males** do not have a sting but they do guard the nest. The females have stings but are very docile and do not sting unless in danger.

- **Female carpenter bees** nest in their wooden tunnels. They prefer weathered, unpainted, bare wood. In these tunnels, carpenter bees drill holes, where they lay eggs in individual cells and store enough food for the larvae to grow. There is only a single entrance to each tunnel.

- **People take preventive measures**, such as spraying pesticides, to keep carpenter bees away from their homes and gardens.

◀ A carpenter bee is about 20–25 mm long. It is not as hairy as a bumblebee, with short hairs on its abdomen or sometimes no hair at all.

Cuckoo bee

● **Parasitic bees** are known as cuckoo bees. There are two types of parasitic bee – cleptoparasitic and social parasitic.

● **Cleptoparasitic bees invade** the nests of solitary bees, hide their own eggs in the brood chambers and close them up before the hosts can lay their own eggs. The host bee raises the cuckoo bee larvae as if they were their own.

● **Social parasitic bees** target the resident queen and kill her. Then they lay their own eggs in the host's cells, and force the workers to raise the young parasitic bees.

● **These bees do not forage** for food and cannot provide for their young because they do not have pollen baskets on their legs.

● **Some cuckoo bees** lay their eggs in the nests of bumblebees.

● **Cuckoo bee larvae** have huge jaws to kill the larvae of their host.

● **There are no workers** or queens among cuckoo bees. There are only males and females.

● **Males die** after mating in autumn.

● **After mating**, females hibernate all winter, emerging in spring to lay their eggs in the host's nest.

● **A female cuckoo bee has a thick cuticle**, which is the outermost layer of the skin. This helps to protect her from attacks by other bees when she tries to invade their nest.

▼ *Laying eggs in the nests of other bees may be a successful method of reproduction for cuckoo bees, but it does carry risks because they may be killed by the potential host bees.*

Mason bee

● **A solitary insect**, the mason bee works alone to build a nest and rear its young.

● **These bees** are found in many parts of the Northern Hemisphere, but are especially common in the forested regions of the western USA.

● **Mason bees** are generally smaller than honeybees. Males are smaller than females, but have longer antennae.

● **Unaggressive by nature**, these bees do not sting unless they are disturbed or mishandled.

● **They make their nests** from the chewed paste of plant fibre or mud. Several species build their nests in crevices or holes in wood.

● **Once the nests** are built, the bees mate in summer.

● **A nest** has 6–12 cells. Mason bees hibernate during winter and emerge from their nests during spring.

● **Farmers encourage** the presence of these bees because they pollinate crops and fruit plants.

● **In orchards**, drilled wood is placed to attract mason bees. They are important pollinators of apple and cherry trees, as well as blueberry and other fruit plants.

> **DID YOU KNOW?**
>
> Some mason bees nest inside empty snail shells. A large shell may contain up to 20 eggs.

◀ *Mason bees lay their eggs after filling the cells with enough pollen and honey for the larvae to feed on.*

Wasps

● **Along with bees and ants, wasps belong** to the order Hymenoptera. Like ants, they have a narrow 'waist' between the thorax and abdomen. All wasps have four wings.

● **Wasps live in all parts** of the world except for the polar regions.

● **Wasps are both solitary** and social insects. Social wasps live in huge colonies, while solitary wasps live alone. There are about 17,000 species of wasp, but only 1500 species are social.

● **Wasp nests** can be simple or complex. Some nests are just burrows in the ground. Others are built with mud and twigs and can have many cells and tunnels.

● **Not all wasps build nests**. Some lay their eggs in stems, leaves, fruits and flowers.

● **Adults feed** on nectar, fruit and plant sap, and the larvae feed on insects.

● **Many species** are parasitic. They live part of their lives as parasites inside other insects.

● **Large wasps are called hornets**. They are ferocious and have a painful sting.

● **Social hornets** form huge colonies, containing about 25,000 individuals.

● **Hornets build** the biggest nests, which can be 120 cm in length and 90 cm in circumference.

▲ *The small nest entrance is easy to defend from other insects and also helps the wasps to control the humidity and temperature inside the nest.*

● **Tarantula hawk wasps** can grow to 50 mm in length and can overpower spiders, including tarantulas, much bigger than themselves.

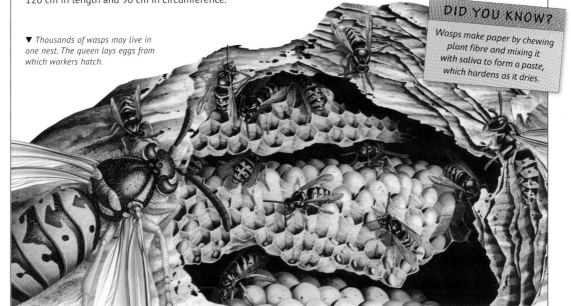

▼ *Thousands of wasps may live in one nest. The queen lays eggs from which workers hatch.*

DID YOU KNOW?

Wasps make paper by chewing plant fibre and mixing it with saliva to form a paste, which hardens as it dries.

Hornet

● **Hornets belong** to the order Hymenoptera and the Vespidae family. They have dark brown and yellow stripes all over their body.

● **These insects are known** for their ferocious nature and painful sting. They are huge, robust wasps and are social in nature.

● **Social hornets** form huge colonies that can contain about 25,000 individuals.

● **Hornets can build** their nest anywhere – at a height or even on the ground. They insulate their nests with layers of 'paper'.

● **Hornets chew plant fibre** and mix it with saliva to form a papery paste, which they use to build nests.

▶ *Apart from their larger size, hornets can be distinguished from smaller wasps by their deeper yellow colour.*

● **Hornet nests are** spherical, with an entrance at the bottom and are divided into many tiers inside. These tiers have hexagonal cells, in which the young are raised.

> **DID YOU KNOW?**
>
> Hornets are known to chase their tormentors. Hence the saying 'never stir a hornet's nest'.

● **Hornets can be** up to 30 cm in length.

● **Hornet colonies die** out in one year. No member of the colony survives the winter except the female hornets that have mated.

● **Abandoned hornet nests** provide shelter for other insects during the winter.

● **Some insects** have stripes, which resemble those of hornets. These ward off predators, which mistake harmless insects for hornets.

Gall wasp

▼ *Gall wasps are usually about 2–8 mm long. Their shiny abdomen is oval in shape and their wings have few veins.*

● **Gall wasps** are small parasitic insects that feed on plants.

● **These insects** are named after their habit of causing the formation of a tumour-like growth in plants, known as galls.

● **Galls are an abnormal growth** of plant tissues and leaves. Some of them look like greenish apples or berries on leaves.

● **When a female gall wasp injects** her eggs into a plant, galls are formed. When the eggs hatch, the larvae release chemicals, which causes the plant to cover them with soft tissues in the form of a gall.

● **Galls can be** either spongy or hollow inside.

● **A gall is like a nursery** for one or more species of gall wasp.

● **Gall wasp larvae** feed on the gall and pupate inside it. Adult gall wasps emerge from the gall either by boring a hole or by bursting through its surface.

● **Different types of galls**, such as leaf, flower, seed and stem galls, are caused by different species of gall wasp.

● **Fig wasps**, a species of gall wasp, cause the formation of seed galls inside wild figs and in the process, pollinates them. No other insect pollinates wild figs.

● **Gall wasps are very selective** about the plants on which they lay their eggs. For instance, some gall wasps lay their eggs on figs, while others prefer roses.

Paper wasp

● **Paper wasps are black or reddish-brown** in colour and have yellow stripes on their body.

● **Social insects**, paper wasps live in small colonies of 20 to 30. After the queen wasp mates, she builds a nest of six-sided cells with a material similar to papier mâché.

● **Paper wasps chew** plant fibre, which they mix with their saliva to build their nests.

● **Adult paper wasps** feed only on nectar while the young larvae feed on chewed insects.

▼ *This Costa Rican paper wasp is starting to build her nest under a leaf. She will use her antennae to measure the size of the cells.*

▶ *Wasps do not store food in their nest as the cells face downwards and are open at the bottom. The queen wasp glues her eggs inside the cells to stop them falling out.*

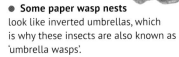

● **Some paper wasp nests** look like inverted umbrellas, which is why these insects are also known as 'umbrella wasps'.

● **A few queen paper wasps** build a nest together. The most powerful queen dominates and leads the colony, while the rest become workers.

● **The subordinate** queen wasps are called joiners. Sometimes, a joiner manages to overpower the reigning queen. She becomes the new queen while the original queen becomes a worker.

● **Unlike other wasps, bees and ants**, queen paper wasps closely resemble the worker wasps.

Parasitic wasps

● **These wasps lay their eggs** inside other wasps, spiders, bees, caterpillars and aphids.

● **Females inject** their eggs into the body of their host with the help of an ovipositor, or egg-laying tube. Once the eggs hatch, the larvae eat their host alive.

● **Parasitic wasps** can lay as many as 3000 eggs inside a host insect.

● **Some parasitic wasps**, such as chalcid and braconid wasps, are known for infesting moth and butterfly caterpillars. They are helpful to farmers because they can control pest caterpillars in crop fields.

● **Some tiny wasps** become parasites for insect eggs. The parasite's eggs multiply into many cells and almost 150 wasps of the same sex can hatch from only one egg.

● **A parasitic wasp can be infested** by a smaller parasitic wasp, which in turn can be infested by another wasp. This phenomenon is known as hyperparasitism.

● **Unlike social wasps and bees**, parasitic wasps do not sting.

● **Aphids that act** as hosts for parasitic wasps appear puffy and hard. They die once the wasp larvae are ready to pupate and are known as 'aphid mummies'.

▲ *Ichneumon wasps are mainly parasites of butterfly and moth larvae.*

◀ *The smallest insect, the fairyfly is an egg parasite wasp. A fairyfly measures only 0.2 mm in length.*

Velvet ant

- **Despite its name,** the velvet ant is a type of wasp.

- **Found in dry areas, velvet ants** are named after their hairy body, which is usually red, brown or black in colour.

- **When it is too hot** to venture outside, velvet ants burrow underground or climb into plants.

- **Males have wings** and cannot sting. Females do not have wings and can sting.

- **The sting of a velvet ant** is so powerful that this insect is nicknamed the 'cow killer'.

- **Females run quickly across** the ground like ants. They are often found busily searching for the burrows of solitary bees and wasps.

- **Velvet ants are parasites.** They lay eggs in the nests of bees and other wasps.

- **The larvae** emerge before the host's eggs get a chance to hatch. Then they eat the host's eggs.

- **Velvet ants** make a squeaky noise if they are attacked or captured.

◀ *Velvet ants are protected from stings by a tough outer skin and long body hair.*

Butterflies and moths

- **Butterflies and moths** are part of the Lepidoptera order, which means scaly wings. There may be 200 to 600 tiny scales on every square millimetre of wing.

- **Moths and butterflies** are ancient insects. Fossil records show that moths date back 140 million years and butterflies 40 million years.

- **Butterflies** usually have delicate and slender bodies. Moths tend to have more plump and robust bodies.

- **One feature** that butterflies and moths have in common is that they cannot survive extreme cold. Not one single moth or butterfly is found in Antarctica.

- **Both butterflies and moths** feed on nectar as well as on animal fluids.

- **Butterflies** usually fly by day while most moths are active after sunset.

- **Butterflies** and moths are important pollinators of plants.

◀ *Moths are more likely than butterflies to be active at night.*

▶ *Butterflies, such as this morpho butterfly, have two pairs of wings, which often have beautiful markings or are brightly coloured.*

- **While resting,** most butterflies fold their wings straight up above their backs. Most moths keep their wings spread flat or fold them like a tent over their body.

- **Most moth caterpillars** weave a structure around themselves for pupation. This is called a cocoon and is made of silk, leaves or soil. Most butterflies do not weave such cocoons.

- **Butterfly antennae** are plain stalks ending in a club (or a hook in the case of skipper butterflies). Moth antennae have many patterns, ranging from single strands to feathery branches, but they never end in a club.

DID YOU KNOW?

Many moths do not feed in their adult stage and so lack mouthparts. This is not the case for butterflies.

Butterfly lifestyle

- **Butterflies do not have a mouth** to eat food. Instead they have a long strawlike structure called a proboscis under their head to suck nectar.

- **There are four different stages** of development, or metamorphosis. First, the adult lays eggs on plants. Next, each egg hatches into a caterpillar. The caterpillar then develops into a pupa, or chrysalis. Finally, the pupa matures into a butterfly.

- **Caterpillars grow** 27,000 times bigger than their original size when they first emerge from the eggs.

- **Some male butterflies** have scent pockets on their wings, which give out pheromones. These chemicals attract mates.

- **The average lifespan of butterflies** is 20 to 40 days. Some species can survive up to ten months, while others last only three to four days.

- **Butterflies only consume liquid food**, such as flower nectar and liquids from rotten fruits or vines.

- **To protect themselves** from predators, such as birds, lizards, bats and spiders, butterflies use mimicry and camouflage.

- **After bees**, butterflies are the second-largest pollinators of crops.

- **Some butterflies** are destructive. Cabbage whites feed on cabbages and can destroy entire crops.

◄ *Butterflies drink nectar from flowers using their proboscis.*

Tortoiseshell butterfly

- **Large and brightly coloured**, tortoiseshells are found all over the world. They are one of the most common garden butterflies in the UK.

- **Tortoiseshells can also be found** in the dense hill forests of Asia and and northern USA.

- **Tortoiseshells have a long life** as adults, surviving for about ten months from one summer to the next.

- **Adults feed on fruit juices** or the nectar from flowers, such as daisy and aster.

- **Females are larger** than males.

- **After mating**, a female lays her eggs in batches on young nettle leaves. Each batch contains 60 to 100 eggs.

- **After ten days**, the eggs hatch and the caterpillars spin a web over the nettle's growing tip. Tortoiseshell caterpillars live in groups and feed on the nettle leaves.

- **The caterpillars** grow to about 2 cm in length within four weeks. They are poisonous.

- **Tortoiseshell butterfly pupae** are greyish-brown and have metallic spots.

▲ *The tortoiseshell's wings are mainly orange in colour with black spots. Black and blue patterns line the wing edges.*

Red admiral butterfly

● **Easy to recognize, the red admiral butterfly** is black in colour, with red bands and white markings on the upper and lower wings. Its wingspan is 4.5–7.6 cm.

● **Red admirals** are found in gardens, orchards and woodlands across Europe, North America and Asia.

● **Adults feed on** rotting fruits and flowers, and caterpillars feed on nettle plants.

● **The mottled brown undersides** of red admirals' wings provide excellent camouflage when they are resting on the ground or on tree trunks.

● **This species** is known for its migratory behaviour. Red admirals cannot survive cold winters, so they migrate to warmer places.

● **Females lay their eggs** on nettle leaves. After seven days, the caterpillars emerge and fold leaves around themselves to make a protective tent.

● **The caterpillars** are black to greenish-grey in colour and have a yellow line running along each side.

● **Adults may hibernate** in winter, storing enough fat in their body for survival.

● **The red admiral** has a very erratic, rapid flight. Unusually for a butterfly, it sometimes flies at night.

▼ *Named after their 'admirable' colours, red admirals feed on nectar, tree sap, rotting fruit and bird droppings.*

Bhutan glory butterfly

● **Bhutan glory butterflies** are found in Bhutan and north-eastern parts of Asia.

● **These butterflies** prefer to live in grass fields and undisturbed forests.

● **The wings** of Bhutan glory butterflies measure about 9–11 cm. They are black in colour.

● **Bhutan glory butterflies breed** twice a year from May to June and then August to October.

● **Very little** is known about the life-history of Bhutan glory butterflies.

● **Bhutan glory butterflies** protect themselves from predators by absorbing poison from the plants they feed on.

● **Experts believe** that these insects probably feed on the poisonous Indian birthwort plant.

● **These butterflies** fly at altitudes of 1700–3000 m in the mountains.

● **In the past Bhutan glory butterflies** were collected in large numbers. Now, their numbers have been greatly reduced and they are very rare.

● **Today, Bhutan glory butterflies** are listed as an endangered and protected species.

◄ *If disturbed, a Bhutan glory butterfly quickly opens and shuts it wings, exposing its bright orange markings. These sudden flashes of colour may confuse a predator and allow the butterfly time to escape.*

DID YOU KNOW?

When at rest, the Bhutan glory butterfly hides its colourful orange back wings with its front wings. This provides camouflage from predators.

Monarch butterfly

● **Monarch butterflies are found** all over the world, except in cold regions. They are bright orange and black in colour and have a wingspan ranging up to 10 cm.

● **These butterflies use** their body colour to frighten off enemies. The bright orange colour is considered a warning sign.

● **Monarchs are beneficial** for crops as they eat milkweed plants, which are weeds.

● **Monarch caterpillars** feed on the milkweed plants, retaining the sap in their bodies even when they mature into butterflies. Birds attempting to eat monarchs dislike the taste and spit them out.

● **The caterpillars are brightly coloured**, with bold black, white and yellow stripes.

● **Male monarch butterflies** have dark spots called scent scales on their hind wings. Females do not have scent scales.

● **A monarch butterfly** takes approximately one month to mature from an egg into an adult butterfly. Adult monarch butterflies feed on flower nectar and water.

● **Long-distance migratory insects**, monarch butterflies guide themselves during migration using the position of the Sun and the magnetic field of the Earth.

● **Habitat destruction** and changes caused by logging are constant threats to monarch butterflies. Spraying of pesticides for weed control kills milkweed plants. This endangers the habitat and food source of these butterflies.

▲ *Monarch butterflies travel up to 4000 km when they fly south for the winter.*

▼ *Monarch caterpillars eat milkweed plants, which are poisonous to predatory birds.*

DID YOU KNOW?

Monarch butterflies from northern USA and Canada migrate to the Sierra Madre Mountains, west of Mexico City, in the winter.

Painted lady butterfly

- **One of the best-known butterflies in the world**, painted ladies are black, brown and orange in colour. They have a wingspan of 4–5 cm.

- **The painted lady** is also known as the 'thistle butterfly' because its caterpillar commonly feeds on thistle plants.

- **Painted ladies** are mostly found in temperate regions across Asia, Europe and North America, especially around flowery meadows and fields.

- **Females lay their eggs** on plants. After three to five days, the eggs hatch into caterpillars.

- **The caterpillars**, or larvae, live in a silken nest, woven around the plant on which they feed.

- **Adults feed on nectar** from flowers such as aster, cosmos, ironweed and joe-pye weed.

- **An adult** painted lady lives for only two weeks.

- **Painted ladies are strong fliers** and long-distance migrants.

- **They fly in groups** containing thousands of individuals. The groups can cover hundreds of kilometres.

◄ *The painted lady butterfly can be distinguished from the tortoiseshell butterfly by the white marks on the black tips of its front wings.*

Birdwing butterfly

- **These butterflies** belong to the swallowtail group of butterflies, which have tails on their hind wings, like the wings of a swallow.

- **Males are brightly coloured** with yellow, pale-blue and green markings.

- **Females have cream** and chocolate-brown markings on their wings.

- **Predators avoid** birdwings because they are poisonous and taste bad. Birdwing caterpillars feed on pipevine plants and absorb poisons from them.

- **A birdwing butterfly** lives for about seven months. They are listed as an endangered species, so people are not allowed to hunt them.

- **Birdwings are found** in tropical areas. The best time to spot them is in the early morning when they collect nectar from flowers.

- **Female Queen Alexandra's birdwings** are the world's largest butterflies. They have a wingspan of up to 30 cm.

- **The golden and southern birdwing** are two cousins of the Queen Alexandra's birdwing.

▼ *The beautiful Rajah Brooke's birdwing soars high in the rainforest canopy from Malaysia to Sumatra and Borneo.*

▶ *Queen Alexandra's birdwing butterflies were named in honour of the wife of King Edward VII of England.*

Apollo butterfly

● **Apollo butterflies are mostly found** in mountains and hilly regions of Spain, central Europe, southern Scandinavia and Asia. Some Apollo butterflies live above an altitude of 4000 m and rarely descend to lower levels.

● **These butterflies are cream in colour** with red and yellow eyespots on their wings. They are frail-looking butterflies but are able to survive harsh weather conditions.

● **Habitat destruction** has made Apollo butterflies extremely rare. They are now an endangered species, protected by law in many countries.

● **The breeding season** of Apollo butterflies lasts from July to August. The female lays hundreds of eggs.

● **Female butterflies** lay round, white eggs either singly or in groups. The eggs usually hatch in August and September.

● **Apollo caterpillars** feed on stonecrop plants. They moult five times in their lifetime.

● **Attempts are being made** to save Apollo butterfly populations by managing their habitat, reducing insecticide use and carefully observing their behaviour.

▼ This mountain butterfly has a wingspan of 5–10 cm and a furry body to protect it from the cold. It survives the winter as a tiny caterpillar inside its egg.

Peacock butterfly

● **These brightly coloured butterflies** are named after their large, multi-coloured eyespots, which look like the 'eyes' on a peacock bird's feathers.

● **These butterflies inhabit** the mild regions of Europe and Asia.

● **Adults like orchards**, gardens and other places that have lots of flowers. They feed on the flower nectar of thistles, lavender and buddleia and also suck juices from overripe fruits.

● **Females have one brood** in a year. They lay up to 500 eggs and die soon after.

● **The caterpillars emerge** after one to two weeks and all live together in a communal web.

● **The caterpillars and adult butterflies** hibernate through winter and emerge in spring.

● **Fully grown caterpillars** are about 4 cm long. They have black-and-white spots and long, black dorsal spines.

● **The caterpillars feed** on nettle plants. They often live in groups.

● **The pupae** are greyish-brown or green, with metallic gold spots.

● **Peacocks have long lifespans** for lepidopterans – they can live for as long as one year.

◄ Females often lay their small, green eggs on nettles. Adults emerge from the pupae in July.

Viceroy butterfly

- **Viceroy butterflies** are mostly found in the USA, southern Canada and northern Mexico.

- **These butterflies have** black and orange patterns and white spots on their wings – resembling monarch butterflies.

- **They are found** in meadows, marshes, swamps and other wet areas with trees such as willow, aspen and poplar.

- **There are usually** two or three generations of viceroy butterflies born in each breeding season.

- **Viceroy butterflies** are known to mate in the afternoon. The female butterfly lays her eggs on the tips of poplar and willow leaves.

- **The eggs hatch** and the viceroy caterpillars feed on the leaves. They are voracious eaters and even eat their own shells. The caterpillars are white and olive brown.

- **Adult viceroy butterflies** feed on the liquids from decaying fungi, dung and other animal waste.

- **Predators often mistake** viceroy butterflies for monarch butterflies, and then avoid eating them because monarch butterflies taste bad.

▲ (1) *A Viceroy butterfly splits its chrysalis open by swallowing air, which makes its body expand. (2) It struggles free of its chrysalis. (3) The butterfly emerges and clings to the chrysalis. (4) It hangs from the chrysalis, pumping blood into its wing veins to stiffen and stretch them. (5) After about half an hour the wings are at their full size. Once the wings have dried the butterfly is able to fly.*

DID YOU KNOW?

Butterflies practise two kinds of mimicry – Batesian and Mullerian. In Batesian mimicry, a harmless species of butterfly mimics a toxic species. In Mullerian mimicry, two equally toxic species mimic each other for mutual benefit. Viceroy and monarch butterflies exhibit Batesian mimicry.

Moths

- **Moths make up about 90 percent** of the insects that belong to the order Lepidoptera, which also includes butterflies. All members of this order have scaly wings.

- **Moths feed on nectar** as well as other plant and animal juices. Some moths do not feed as adults because they do not have mouthparts.

- **In some species of moth**, the females do not have wings.

- **Most moths are only active** at night but there are some species of moth that remain active during the day.

- **Like butterflies**, some moths, such as hawk-moths, migrate long distances.

- **Some moths** have large spots on their wings. From a distance, these spots resemble the eyes of a fearsome animal and scare away potential predators.

- **Moths are masters** of mimicry and camouflage.

- **Certain moths** can be mistaken for bird droppings when they lie still on the ground. This helps them escape predatory birds.

- **The larvae of these moths** are destructive in nature and feed on different types of natural fabrics, such as wool, cotton, linen and even fur, feathers and hair.

- **Tiger moths produce** high-pitched clicks at night to warn bats that they taste bad. Bats soon learn to link the clicks with the awful taste and avoid eating these moths.

◀ *Unlike butterflies, which have clubbed antennae, some moths have feathery antennae.*

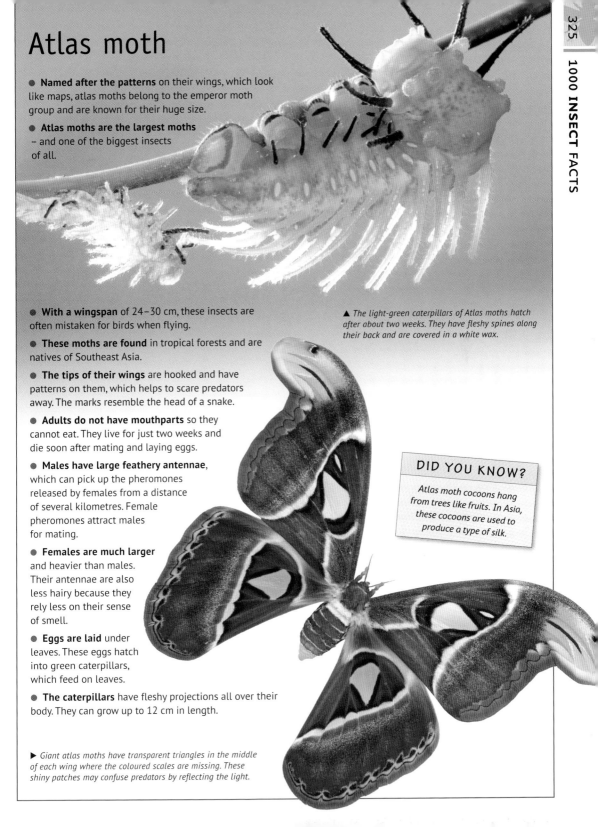

Atlas moth

● **Named after the patterns** on their wings, which look like maps, atlas moths belong to the emperor moth group and are known for their huge size.

● **Atlas moths are the largest moths** – and one of the biggest insects of all.

● **With a wingspan** of 24–30 cm, these insects are often mistaken for birds when flying.

▲ *The light-green caterpillars of Atlas moths hatch after about two weeks. They have fleshy spines along their back and are covered in a white wax.*

● **These moths are found** in tropical forests and are natives of Southeast Asia.

● **The tips of their wings** are hooked and have patterns on them, which helps to scare predators away. The marks resemble the head of a snake.

● **Adults do not have mouthparts** so they cannot eat. They live for just two weeks and die soon after mating and laying eggs.

● **Males have large feathery antennae**, which can pick up the pheromones released by females from a distance of several kilometres. Female pheromones attract males for mating.

DID YOU KNOW?

Atlas moth cocoons hang from trees like fruits. In Asia, these cocoons are used to produce a type of silk.

● **Females are much larger** and heavier than males. Their antennae are also less hairy because they rely less on their sense of smell.

● **Eggs are laid** under leaves. These eggs hatch into green caterpillars, which feed on leaves.

● **The caterpillars** have fleshy projections all over their body. They can grow up to 12 cm in length.

▶ *Giant atlas moths have transparent triangles in the middle of each wing where the coloured scales are missing. These shiny patches may confuse predators by reflecting the light.*

Death's head hawk-moth

● **Found in Africa, Asia and Europe**, death's head hawk-moths belong to the group of sphinx moths.

● **This moth** is named after a peculiar mark on its thorax that looks like a human skull.

● **Death's head hawk-moths** steal honey from bees' nests, so they are also known as 'bee robbers'.

● **At any point in its life** – as a caterpillar or adult – a death's head hawk-moth is capable of producing a loud squeaking sound to scare away its predators.

● **To make this squeaky sound**, the moth forces air out of its strong, thick, tube-shaped mouthpart.

● **Females lay single eggs** on a range of different plants, including potato and aubergine plants.

● **The caterpillars** are also known as hornworms because they have a horn on their tail end.

● **Before pupation**, the caterpillars make a deep cell in muddy soil, smoothing the walls with their head.

● **Death's head hawk-moths** find it difficult to survive harsh winters and migrate to warmer places in autumn.

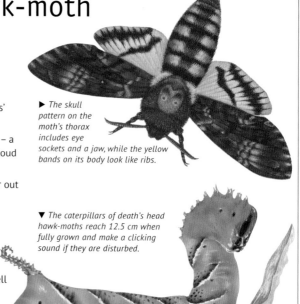

▶ *The skull pattern on the moth's thorax includes eye sockets and a jaw, while the yellow bands on its body look like ribs.*

▼ *The caterpillars of death's head hawk-moths reach 12.5 cm when fully grown and make a clicking sound if they are disturbed.*

Swallowtail moth

● **Swallowtail moths** belong to the family Geometridae of the order Lepidoptera.

● **These moths are** strikingly unusual and can be mistaken for butterflies. They have slender bodies, thin legs and a short proboscis.

● **Swallowtail moths can be colourful** and sometimes fly in the day.

● **These moths** are mainly found in tropical countries.

● **Brilliantly coloured species** are very large in size. Their colours are structural and do not contain pigments.

● **Some of the nocturnal species** have eyespots at the tip of their short pointed hind wings.

● **The eyespots** give an impression of a false head at the rear side of the moth, which protects it from predators. Therefore, during the day, the moths always rest on the upper side of leaves.

● **The size and marks** on the bodies differ in males and females.

● **Not much is known** about the life history of swallowtail moths.

DID YOU KNOW?

The swallowtail moth's name derives from a resemblance to swallowtail butterflies. Their hindwings have a tail similar to that of swallowtail butterflies.

▼ *This large swallowtail moth has broad wings, like a butterfly, but flies rapidly. In June and July it is widespread in Europe and parts of Asia, often flying around lights.*

Hummingbird hawk-moth

● **Found all over the world**, hummingbird hawk-moths belong to the hawk-moth group.

● **Unlike many other hawk-moths,** these moths fly during the day and can be spotted hovering over flowers in gardens and parks.

● **Hummingbird hawk-moths** are brown. They have black-and-white spots all over their body and their hind wings are orange.

● **These moths** have tufts of hair at the tip of their abdomen.

● **Like other butterflies and moths**, hummingbird hawk-moths have long, tubelike mouthparts that are coiled and tucked under their head. They use their long tongue to collect nectar from flowers.

● **The caterpillars pupate** in leaf litter (bits of dead leaves and bark on the ground) and weave a thick cocoon.

● **People often mistake** this moth for a hummingbird because it hovers over flowers and sucks nectar from them, like a hummingbird.

● **Hummingbird hawk-moths** hibernate in winter to survive the cold weather.

◄ *The broad body of the hummingbird hawk-moth shows that it is a powerful flier.*

Lobster moth

● **Lobster moths belong** to the group of moths known as prominent moths.

● **These moths** are commonly found in deciduous forests in Europe and Asia.

● **The wingspan** of lobster moths is about 5.5–7 cm.

● **Males** are often attracted towards the light, but females do not behave in the same way.

● **These moths** appear in two colour forms – one with light front wings and one with dark front wings.

● **Lobster moth caterpillars move** in a way that resembles the movements of ants.

● **The unusual shape** of lobster moth caterpillars often confuses their predators and scares them away.

● **As an act of defence,** the caterpillar curls back its large head and raises its legs in the air to startle small birds.

● **Lobster moth caterpillars** can also squirt formic acid over their predators.

● **The caterpillar** constructs a silken cocoon and pupates in it.

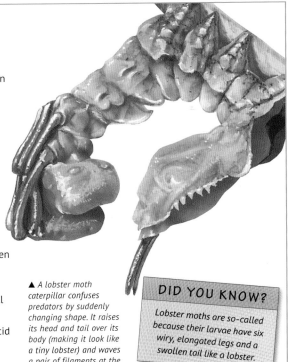

▲ *A lobster moth caterpillar confuses predators by suddenly changing shape. It raises its head and tail over its body (making it look like a tiny lobster) and waves a pair of filaments at the end of its abdomen.*

DID YOU KNOW?

Lobster moths are so-called because their larvae have six wiry, elongated legs and a swollen tail like a lobster.

Peppered moth

- **Delicate insects with long legs** and a slender body, peppered moths belong to the geometrid moth group.

- **The caterpillars** do not have any legs in the middle of their body. They hold onto branches with their first two pairs of fleshy limbs called prolegs and a clasper at their tail end.

- **Males have** feathery antennae, while females have hairlike antennae.

- **The antennae of males** are also longer than those of females.

- **Males are smaller** and more slender in comparison to the larger, heavier females.

▶ The dark-coloured peppered moth is less common today in industrial areas because it cannot camouflage in pollution-controlled areas.

- **The moths are nocturnal** and rest on lichen-covered trees during the day.

- **Peppered moth caterpillars** camouflage themselves by resembling a twig.

- **There are two varieties** of peppered moths – one is pale coloured, speckled with black-and-white marks and the other is brown and black in colour.

DID YOU KNOW?

Peppered moth caterpillars are known as inchworms because they move along as though they are measuring the ground.

▲ The pale-coloured peppered moth shows up well against dark backgrounds.

Moon moth

DID YOU KNOW?

Moon moths are also called 'lunar moths' because of marks on their wings that look like a new moon.

- **Moon moths belong** to the group known as emperor moths. They are found all over the world, but are mostly seen in tropical countries.

- **These moths** have a white body and maroon legs. Their wings are bright green. The colour of female moon moths is brighter than that of males.

- **Moon moths have a wingspan** of about 10–13 cm and their tail is almost 8 cm long.

- **The hind wings** of males are longer than those of the females. In overall size, male moon moths are much smaller than females.

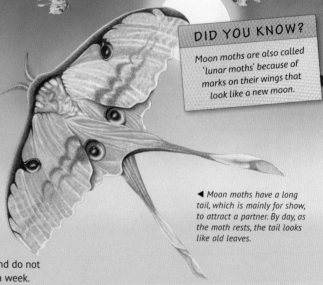

◀ Moon moths have a long tail, which is mainly for show, to attract a partner. By day, as the moth rests, the tail looks like old leaves.

- **Adult moon moths** have no mouthparts and do not eat anything. They do not live for more than a week.

- **Moon moths** make their cocoons in leaves. The silk of the cocoon does not shine and is brown in colour. This silk is not used commercially.

- **An adult female** lays about 250 eggs at a time, on walnut leaves. The eggs resemble seeds with grey specks on them.

- **Moon moths** grow only at the larval stage. If the larva grows into a small-sized moth, the moth does not grow further in size.

- **Moon moth caterpillars** are bright apple green in colour and are beautifully segmented, with some white hairs.

Horse fly

- **Horse flies** are strong-bodied flies with colourful patterns on their bodies.

- **There are about 25,000 species** of horse fly in the world.

- **Female horse flies suck and feed** on the blood of humans and animals. Some horse fly species get their names, such as deer flies or moose flies, depending on the animal they feed on.

- **Horse flies** have compound eyes, which are very prominent and occupy the entire surface of the head in the males.

- **Colourful patterns** on the compound eyes are caused by the refraction of light. There are no pigments present in the eyes and as a result, the colour is not retained when these insects die.

- **The mouthparts** of these insects consist of a short, powerful piercing organ capable of penetrating tough skin. If undisturbed, horse flies can suck blood from their host for as long as half an hour.

◀ *Horse flies are among the fastest flying insects, reaching maximum speeds of 39 km/h. Unlike most other flies, their flight can be silent, allowing females to sneak up on their prey.*

- **Female horse flies** bite animals to suck blood before they reproduce. However, male horse flies do not bite. They feed mainly on flower nectar and plant sap.

- **After mating,** females lay their eggs on plant and rock edges near water. The eggs are creamy white in colour.

- **Horse fly larvae feed** on soft-bodied insects and other small animals. They can become cannibalistic if there is a lack of food.

- **While biting** and sucking blood from animals, female horse flies can transmit diseases such as anthrax.

▶ *This horse is wearing a protective fly cover to prevent flies from biting it and possibly transmitting diseases.*

Crane fly

- **Crane flies** belong to the order Diptera and are closely related to mosquitoes.

- **Their legs** are weakly attached to their body and often break off.

- **Some of the larger species** of crane fly, such as phantom crane flies, have legs that are as long as 2.5 cm.

- **Crane flies** have extremely narrow wings. They have a thin body with long legs and resemble large mosquitoes. These insects cannot bite.

- **Crane flies are nocturnal insects** and remain inactive in the day.

- **Females lay their eggs** in moist soil. The eggs hatch into larvae, which are greyish to pale brown in colour.

▶ *Crane fly larvae eat the roots of grasses, including cereal crops such as wheat.*

◀ *The long, thin legs of a crane fly are usually twice the length of its body. These insects can also be recognized by the V-shaped groove on the top of their thorax.*

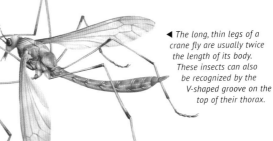

- **The larvae** of crane flies feed on dead and decaying matter. Some species also feed on small insects and others eat plant roots.

- **Crane fly larvae** are also known as leatherjackets because of their tough, brown skin. They are often used as fishing bait.

- **Farmers dislike** the larvae of these insects because they damage the roots and turf of grain fields and grass crops.

- **A rare species** of crane fly does not have wings. It is found in Hawaii.

Housefly

- **Houseflies** belong to the order Diptera and are one of the world's most common insects.

- **Like all flies**, houseflies have small projections below their front wings known as halteres, which help them to fly. Halteres are modified hind wings, which are used for landing and balancing.

- **Houseflies feed** on liquid food and do not bite animals and other insects. The mouthparts of a housefly are like a sponge, which absorbs liquid food.

- **Before eating**, houseflies often vomit some portion of their last feed on top of new food particles. This makes the new food material easier to digest.

- **Most of the time**, houseflies do not eat all the food and leave some particles behind. These remaining food particles can spread a variety of diseases.

- **Sticky pads** and sharp claws enable houseflies to walk upside down with ease. Fine hairs on the tip of a housefly's legs enable it to 'taste' liquids.

- **Houseflies** have compound eyes and 4000 individual lenses form each eye.

- **These insects** cannot see the colour red.

▶ Houseflies dribble saliva onto food. Powerful chemicals in the saliva break down the starch and other nutrients. They then dab up the liquid food with sponge-like mouthparts.

- **Females can** lay around 600 to 1000 eggs in a lifetime. However, most offspring do not survive to reproduce.

DID YOU KNOW?

Houseflies are known to spread 40 serious diseases. A single fly harbours as many as 33 million infectious organisms inside its intestines and 500 million on its body surface and legs.

Mosquito

- **Mosquitoes are the only flies** of the order Diptera that have scaly wings.

- **Most female mosquitoes** have to feed on the blood of other animals to reproduce. They need the protein extracted from blood for the development of their eggs.

- **These eggs** float on water and hatch to produce aquatic larvae known as wrigglers.

- **The larvae** cannot breathe underwater and 'hang' from the water's surface to take in air.

- **Mosquito larvae** pupate in water. The pupa is not completely immobile. It can change position according to the light and wind conditions in its environment.

- **Adult male mosquitoes** feed on nectar and other plant fluids. Only female mosquitoes feed on blood.

- **Male mosquitoes** cannot bite. Their mouthparts are modified for sucking only.

- **Mosquitoes have** infrared vision. They can sense the warmth of other insects and animals.

- **Dragonflies feed** on mosquitoes and are also known as mosquito hawks. Dragonfly nymphs also feed on mosquito larvae.

- **Mosquitoes are known** to spread many infectious diseases, such as yellow fever and dengue fever. The female anopheles mosquito spreads malaria.

◀ Mosquitoes have long mouthparts that they use to pierce skin (human or animal) and suck up blood.

Firefly

● **Fireflies are not flies** but a type of beetle. These insects are also known as lightning bugs.

● **These insects can grow** up to 2.5 cm in length and live for three to four months. Females live longer than males.

● **Fireflies have a special organ** under their stomach, which emits flashes of green or yellow light.

● **This light** is known as 'cold light'. The process of producing light is also known as bioluminescence. No other insect can produce light from their own bodies.

▼ *Each species of firefly has its own unique sequence of flashes to attract a mate of the same species. Some males flash in synchrony, which may help them to attract females more easily.*

▶ *A pair of fireflies mating on a leaf.*

● **Fireflies emit** only light energy. A normal light bulb emits only 10 percent of its energy as light. The remaining 90 percent is emitted as heat energy. Fireflies do not emit any heat energy.

● **Males and females** emit light to attract mates.

● **Fireflies are nocturnal** insects. They live on plants and trees during the day and are active at night.

● **Females and their larvae** are carnivorous and feed on snails, slugs and worms. Most males don't eat but some may feed on pollen and nectar.

● **Some females are wingless** and are also known as glow-worms.

Tiger beetle

● **Tiger beetles** are usually shiny metallic colours, such as green, brown, black and purple. They often have stripes like tigers.

● **The smallest tiger beetles** live in Borneo and measure up to 6 mm. The largest tiger beetles live in Africa and can reach up to 44 mm in length.

● **Tiger beetles are found** in sunny, sandy areas and are active during the day. However, there are some species that come out at night.

● **Tiger beetles are good fliers** and fly in a zigzag pattern if a predator approaches them. They are also very fast runners.

● **These insects are predatory.** Once they locate their prey, they pounce on it and use their jaws to tear it into pieces.

● **Tiger beetles** taste awful and predators avoid eating them.

● **Females lay their eggs** in burrows in the ground. The burrow can be almost 0.5 m deep.

● **The larvae** have a pair of powerful and large jaws, which are used to capture small insects.

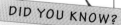

▶ *Tiger beetles are often very colourful, with distinct markings.*

● **Some species** of tiger beetles are endangered or nearing extinction. This is because of the lack of undisturbed sandy areas in which they can breed.

▼ *Tiger beetles have huge eyes. They use their massive biting jaws to catch and cut up their food.*

Goliath beetle

- **One of the largest** and heaviest insects in the world is the Goliath beetle. Males are as heavy as an apple.

- **Goliath beetles grow** up to 15 cm and weigh about 115 g.

- **Found in many colours**, most Goliath beetles have black-and-white markings on their wings.

- **Goliath beetles** used to be found only in Africa. Today, however, these insects can be found in almost all parts of the world.

- **Males** have a horn-shaped structure on their heads. They often fight each other with their horns.

- **Goliath beetles are good fliers.** They produce a low, helicopter-like whir while flying.

- **By feeding on** dead plant and animal tissues, Goliath beetles help to keep the environment clean.

▲ *When the Goliath beetle flies, the hard wing cases lift up to reveal the softer flying wings underneath.*

- **Scientists believe** that Goliath beetles, like some other insects, were much larger in prehistoric times. This may be because there was more oxygen in the air then.

- **A fossil** of the oldest Goliath beetle is almost 300 million years old.

◀ *Goliath beetles can be found in tropical forests in Africa, where they feed on tree sap and fruit.*

DID YOU KNOW?

The Goliath beetle is named after the Biblical giant, Goliath.

Diving beetle

● **Brown or black in colour,** diving beetles have an oval body. Their wings are shiny and look metallic green in the light.

● **These beetles** are found in ponds and other still water.

● **A diving beetle** has strong, hairy legs, which it uses like oars to push its body forwards when swimming.

● **Adult diving beetles** are up to 3.5 cm in length.

● **These insects** come to the surface to breathe. They store a supply of air under their wing covers.

● **Diving beetles often fly** around at night in search of new ponds.

● **The female** is much bigger than the male.

● **Females make small slits** in plant stems and lay their eggs inside.

● **The larvae float** on the water's surface and move to the shore to pupate.

● **Diving beetles are also known as** 'water tigers' because the larvae feed on other water insects.

◀ *Diving beetles feed on other water insects, small fish and tadpoles.*

Stag beetle

● **Although usually brown or black** in colour, some species of stag beetle are bright-green and red.

● **These beetles live** in damp wooded areas, especially near oak woodlands.

● **Stag beetles** have mandibles (jaws), which resemble the antlers of a stag.

● **Males have long, ferocious-looking jaws.** The jaws of females are not as long.

● **Males use their jaws** to attract females. They rarely use them to fight or defend themselves.

● **At dusk, males fly** in search of females to mate with. They fly in an irregular way and are often misguided by bright lights.

● **The larvae** feed on rotten wood and dead plants.

● **Larvae take a long time** to develop into mature adults because their food (rotting wood) is not nutritious.

● **Adults do not usually eat** anything because they have enough reserve energy stored as fat.

DID YOU KNOW?
Stag beetles are also known as 'pinching bugs' because they can nip with their jaws and draw blood from humans.

▼ *Stag beetles belong to the scarab beetle family, which contains more than 20,000 species.*

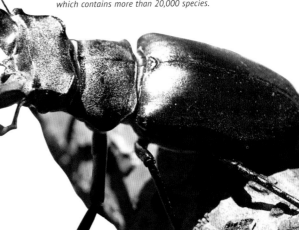

Rhinoceros beetle

- **Believed to be the strongest creatures** on Earth for their size, rhinoceros beetles can carry about 850 times their own weight.

- **These beetles can grow** up to 13 cm in length.

- **Rhinoceros beetles live** in tropical rainforests where the vegetation is thick and there is plenty of moisture in the atmosphere.

- **They are named after** the horns on their head, which look similar to rhinoceros horns.

- **Rhinoceros beetles** have between two and five horns.

- **Only males** have horns. The larger the horn is, the better their chances of winning a mate's attention.

- **They do not use** their horns for defence. Instead, the beetles use them to fight with other males for food and to attract females for mating.

- **The horns** are very strong and can pierce through an insect's exoskeleton.

- **Rhinoceros beetles are nocturnal**, with hunting and feeding taking place at night.

- **These beetles** help clear the jungle of dead plants. They feed on plant sap and rotten fruits that have fallen to the ground.

▼ *This rhinoceros beetle has three horns. The tough exoskeleton protects the beetle's body like a suit of armour.*

Ladybird

- **Ladybird beetles were dedicated** to the Virgin Mary. They were known as the 'beetle of Our Lady' during the medieval period because they often saved crops from damage by pests.

- **Ladybirds are found** in temperate and tropical regions all over the world.

- **These beetles** are one of the most beneficial insects because they feed on insect pests that damage crops.

- **To get rid of pests,** ladybirds are sometimes bred on a large scale and are then introduced into farms or greenhouses. However, some species are herbivorous and are considered to be pests themselves.

◄ *Brightly coloured beetles, ladybirds have round bodies and hard wing cases, called elytra.*

- **These insects are easily mistaken** for leaf beetles because of their similar colouring and spots.

- **When disturbed,** ladybirds secrete a foul-smelling fluid, which causes a stain.

- **Both adults and larvae** eat aphids, scale insects and other soft-bodied insects.

- **The larvae** do not have wings. They are metallic blue in colour with bright-yellow spots. Their bright colour warns birds not to eat them.

- **The halloween ladybird** is an orange-coloured beetle found in the USA during late October. It is named after Halloween, since it is often seen during this festival.

- **Adult ladybirds hibernate** in huge clusters in densely vegetated areas.

◄ *The number of spots on a ladybird differs from species to species. The two-spot ladybird is smaller than its seven-spotted cousin.*

True bugs

- **Belonging to the suborder Heteroptera** of the order Hemiptera, there are 55,000 different kinds of true bug.

- **These bugs** have two pairs of wings. The first pair is hard and protects the delicate membrane-like second pair of wings. The wing case only covers the top half of the hind wings.

- **Some true bugs** do not have wings, and the nymphs (young) of all true bugs are wingless.

- **True bugs have compound eyes** and their mouthparts are adapted for sucking and piercing.

- **Most true bugs** have beaks that are segmented into four or five parts.

- **True bugs undergo** incomplete metamorphosis. There is no pupal stage. The bugs grow into adults by moulting again and again.

- **They can survive** on land, in air, on the surface of water and even underwater.

- **True bugs feed** on plant and animal juices. There are some bugs, such as bedbugs, which are parasites. They live by sucking blood from other animals.

- **Carnivorous bugs** are predatory and help to control pests, while herbivorous bugs are a threat to crops.

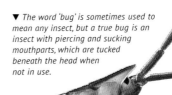

▼ *The word 'bug' is sometimes used to mean any insect, but a true bug is an insect with piercing and sucking mouthparts, which are tucked beneath the head when not in use.*

DID YOU KNOW?

In defence, some bugs give off a bad odour. This drives away predators.

Assassin bug

- **Assassin bugs** are either black or brown or bright red and black in colour.

- **Their wings** lie flat on their abdomen. They also have long legs, which are adapted for running.

- **Assassin bugs** are predatory. They grab their prey and 'assassinate' it by injecting venom. The venom paralyzes the prey and partially dissolves it. The bug then sucks up the liquid remains.

- **Their front legs have powerful muscles** for holding prey while sucking out the body fluid.

- **The bug's venom** is so powerful that caterpillars, which are much larger than assassin bugs, can be killed in seconds.

- **Assassin bugs** have a powerful curved beak, which is used for sucking the blood of insects, larger animals and even humans.

- **Males and females** are similar in appearance, but sometimes females do not have wings.

- **An assassin bug's bite** is quite painful and can transmit germs and diseases.

- **A species of assassin bug**, known as the masked assassin bug, camouflages itself by sticking dust and dirt to its body.

DID YOU KNOW?

The saliva of assassin bugs can cause temporary blindness in humans.

◀ *Assassin bugs give out a pungent smell, which, along with their poisonous bite, protects them from predators.*

Squash bug

● **Squash bugs are so named** because they are a threat to squash and other related plants. They can usually be found in colours ranging from brown to black.

● **Some squash bugs** have leaflike extensions on their hind legs. This makes them look like dead leaves, which helps with camouflage. These bugs are called leaf-footed bugs.

● **With their powerful beaks,** squash bugs can easily pierce and suck fluids from plants and insects.

● **Squash bugs have scent glands** that emit a pungent smell. However, the odour is not as strong as that of stink bugs.

● **Although most squash bugs** are carnivorous, a few feed on both plants and insects, and some are strictly vegetarian.

◄ *The squash bug of North America feeds on the juices of squash, pumpkin and other gourds. It does not have leaflike back legs.*

DID YOU KNOW?

A rice field affected by squash bugs can be smelt from a considerable distance.

● **While feeding,** the squash bug injects a toxic substance into the plant. As a result, the plant wilts and dies.

● **Squash bugs lay their eggs** in clusters on plants. The eggs are oval, flattish or elongated in shape.

● **The nymphs** that hatch from these eggs resemble black ants and moult four to five times before maturing into adults.

● **Farmers consider** squash bugs to be dangerous pests and adopt various measures to get rid of them.

Spittlebug

● **Different shades of yellow and brown,** spittlebugs have a triangular head, red eyes and spotted wings.

● **Also known as froghoppers,** spittlebugs have a froglike appearance. They are good jumpers but rarely fly, even though they have well-developed wings.

● **Adults have a large head** in comparison to their small body.

● **Females lay their eggs** in the stems of grasses and other plants.

● **These bugs are named** after the spitlike frothy mass secreted by the nymphs. This froth is sometimes known as cuckoo-spit.

● **The nymphs** are not easy to spot because they are often hidden in cuckoo-spit on leaves.

● **Cuckoo-spit helps** the nymphs to control their body temperature, preventing them from losing moisture and drying out.

◄▲ *Spittlebug nymphs produce 'cuckoo-spit' by giving off a sticky liquid and blowing it into a frothy mass of white bubbles.*

● **Some nymphs** build delicate tubes, 10–12 mm in length. They attach these tubes along the sides of twigs and live there after filling them with spittle.

● **Spittlebugs are considered** to be pests because they can destroy plants when feeding on the sap.

● **In Madagascar,** spittlebugs discharge a clear liquid instead of foam, which falls to the ground like rain.

Cicada

- **Cicadas belong** to the order Homoptera and are related to true bugs.

- **Most species of cicada** are found in deserts, grasslands and forests.

- **Cicadas have large**, colourful wings. They hold their wings in a slanting position over their abdomen, like a tent.

- **Males emit** sounds similar to that of a knife grinder, a railway whistle and fat spitting in an overheated pan.

- **To attract females**, males 'sing' using flexible drumlike membranes called timbals.

- **Female cicadas** do not produce any sound.

- **Birds feed on** cicadas and are attracted to large swarms.

- **Females lay their eggs** on plants and tree twigs. When the eggs hatch, the nymphs fall to the ground. They live underground for many years, feeding on the roots of plants. Later, they emerge from the ground, climb up trees and then moult into the adult form.

- **Adult cicadas only survive** a few weeks.

- **A species of cicada** known as the periodical cicada is found in America. It emerges from underground every 13 or 17 years. These insects are one of the longest-lived in the world.

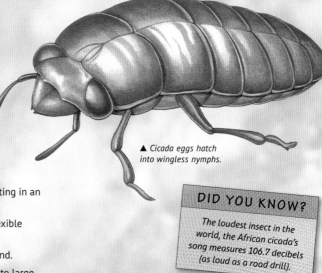
▲ *Cicada eggs hatch into wingless nymphs.*

DID YOU KNOW?

The loudest insect in the world, the African cicada's song measures 106.7 decibels (as loud as a road drill).

▲ *Cicadas are 2–5 cm in length and have large eyes at the front of their head.*

▼ *Cicadas have four pairs of membranous wings, although the front pair of wings is twice the length of the back pair.*

Aphid

● **Aphids are related** to cicadas. They can be green, red, brown or black in colour and are also called greenfly.

● **These bugs have** a large pear-shaped abdomen with two slender tubes called cornicles attached to it. The cornicles secrete wax.

● **Some aphids** grow wings at certain times of year. They are weak fliers, but can be blown great distances by the wind.

● **Many aphids** live underground and suck sap from roots.

● **Aphids use** their long, slender mouthparts to pierce a hole in the stems of plants. They then eat the liquid food that pours out.

● **Aphids cannot digest** all the plant sugar they eat, so they produce a sugary honeydew. This is clear and sweet, but turns black when a fungus grows on it.

● **Other insects**, especially ants, feed on the honeydew. Some ants keep a 'herd' of aphids to supply them with this sweet food.

● **Some aphids lay eggs** but others can reproduce without mating. These aphids give birth to their young, which are identical copies of their parents. This is called parthenogenesis.

● **Aphids breed** in huge numbers. A single aphid can produce up to 100 young at a time.

● **They can cause damage** to plants. Their saliva causes plant leaves to fold and curl.

◄ *Aphids produce a sugary substance that ants like to eat. In return, the ants protect the aphids from their predators, build shelters, take them to fresh pastures and even bring them into their ant nests during bad weather.*

Mealybug

● **Mealybugs are very small** insects up to 3 mm long. They are found in huge clusters on leaves, twigs and tree bark. These bugs are also called coccids.

● **Females do not** usually have wings, eyes or legs and remain immobile on plants. They are always covered in a white sticky coating of their own secretion. This protective coating looks like cornmeal.

● **Males usually** have one pair of delicate wings, well-developed legs and antennae, and no mouthparts.

● **Female mealybugs** never lay their eggs in the open. The eggs are attached to their bodies. However, some species of mealybugs can give birth to live young.

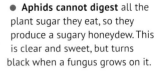

► *Mealybug nymphs do not usually move after their first moult. They stay in one place, joined to plants only by their sucking mouthparts.*

● **The flat**, oval larvae crawl about quite actively at first, but soon lose their legs and cover themselves with their mealy secretions.

● **A male mealybug's** hind wings are modified into tiny structures called halteres.

● **Mealybugs feed** on the sap extracted from plant tissues and are considered to be pests of citrus trees and greenhouse plants.

● **These bugs can harm plants** in many ways. Galls (growths) can form on plants, or their stems can become twisted and deformed.

● **Mealybugs produce** a sugary substance known as honeydew. Ants often visit these insects for this sweet-tasting secretion.

● **Beetles**, **lacewings** and caterpillars prey on mealybugs.

◄ *Female mealybugs secrete a mass of waxy threads as a protective covering. They are often wingless and legless, with reduced antennae.*

Lesser water boatman

● **Lesser water boatmen** are aquatic insects and are usually found in ponds and other freshwater bodies, such as canals and ditches.

● **These bugs have powerful**, hairy legs and are named after their habit of using their legs as oars to 'row' themselves through the water.

● **Most species** of lesser water boatman can fly. However, these insects usually cling to water plants or live at the bottom of ponds.

● **Lesser water boatmen** do not have gills and have to come to the water's surface to breathe.

● **Hairs on the body** trap air bubbles. This helps lesser water boatmen to stay under water for long periods.

● **Lesser water boatmen feed** on algae, plants and decaying animal matter.

● **Some males** rub their legs together to make squeaky sounds that attract females.

● **The female** lays her eggs under water. The young nymphs that hatch from the eggs resemble the adults (without wings), but they moult five times before they become winged adults.

● **In some countries**, lesser water boatmen are sold as bird food.

◄ *Lesser water boatmen are not buoyant enough to float, so when they stop swimming, they sink to the bottom. This is useful because they feed on the bottom of ponds, canals and ditches, using their shovel-like front legs to dig up food.*

Leafhopper

● **Related to cicadas**, leafhoppers have a distinct leaflike shape and colour and are easy to recognize.

● **Leafhoppers can survive** in almost any part of the world. They are terrestrial bugs and can be found in deserts as well as in marshy and moist places.

● **Strong fliers**, leafhoppers are also capable of jumping considerable distances.

● **If these insects** feed on plants, they can cause the leaves to curl and affect the plant's growth.

● **Leafhoppers** are considered pests because they damage food crops.

● **Leafhoppers search for mates** by making special mating calls.

● **Females lay their eggs** in slits made in plant stems. The eggs can remain dormant for a month. In some species, the eggs remain dormant for a year.

● **Like aphids**, leafhoppers produce honeydew from the excess plant sap that they feed on.

● **Leafhoppers** communicate with each other by producing low frequency sounds, which cannot be heard by humans.

▲ *Leafhoppers are common jumping insects that look like a narrow version of an adult spittlebug. They are tiny insects and measure only 2–15 mm long.*

● **Birds, reptiles and large insects**, such as wasps, are a threat to leafhoppers.

Backswimmer

● **Backswimmers spend almost** their entire life floating in an upsidedown position in ponds. They use their legs like oars.

● **These insects fly from one pond** to another in search of food.

● **While floating**, backswimmers identify direction with the help of light.

● **The underside** of backswimmers is dark in colour while the top of the body is light. The dark colour helps to hide the backswimmer from predators.

● **Backswimmers come to the water surface for air.** They carry a bubble of air under their belly, which helps them to stay underwater for a long time.

● **Backswimmers feed on other water insects**, worms and tadpoles.

● **Also known as water bees**, the backswimmer's bite is painful. It can even bite humans.

● **Backswimmers look very similar** to water boatmen. However, water boatmen float the right way up and feed mainly on plants. Backswimmers, in contrast, are predators.

▲ *Backswimmers are shaped like boats, with a keel along their back. As they swim on their backs, the keel points downwards, like the keel on a boat. The bubble of air held beneath the body makes the insect float to the surface if it stops swimming.*

● **When attacking**, backswimmers inject toxins into their prey. This has a chemical reaction, which kills the prey.

● **Some species of backswimmers** are known to hibernate. During winter, these insects are found moving under the surface of frozen water.

Giant water bug

● **Giant water bugs** are like snorkellers. They have flaplike back legs to help them swim fast and special breathing tubes that resemble a snorkel.

● **By lying still in the water**, giant water bugs camouflage themselves so that they look like dead leaves.

● **These insects can fly** but they can survive only for about 15 minutes if they are taken out of water.

DID YOU KNOW?

Female giant water bugs lay their eggs on the backs of the males. They secrete a waterproof glue to stick the eggs onto the male's back.

● **Giant water bugs hold their prey** with their claws and inject venom to paralyze it. Their mouthparts help them to pierce and suck fluid.

● **Giant water bugs store air** between their abdomen and their wings.

● **These bugs help to control** the mosquito population by feeding on mosquito larvae.

● **Males carry fertilized eggs on their backs** for about 10 days. They take care of the eggs until they hatch.

● **Giant water bugs are also known as 'toe biters'** because they may bite the toes of people wading.

● **In some Asian countries**, giant water bugs are considered a tasty snack.

◄ *Giant water bugs have large claws and a powerful bite. They are fierce hunters that feed on tadpoles, fish and other insects.*

Termites

- **Also known as white ants**, termites live in large colonies. However, termites and ants are not related.

- **These insects are thought** to have evolved from cockroach-like insects 250 million years ago.

- **Termites have straight antennae**, while ants have elbowed antennae.

- **They live mainly in hot tropical areas** such as Africa and Australia, but some also live in cooler places in America and Europe.

- **Termites belong** to the order Isoptera, meaning 'equal wings'. Termites have two pairs of large wings, which overlap each other on their back when at rest.

- **Leaving behind** a stublike wing base, termites often shed their wings. Winged termites are called alates. They hatch only once a year.

- **There are two main types of termite** – ground and wood. Ground termites nest in soil and wood termites nest in tree branches and wooden structures.

- **The mouthparts** of termites are ideally suited to chewing wood.

- **Termites have a very soft cuticle** (outer covering), which dries up easily. This is why they live in dark, warm, damp nests.

- **A termite queen** lays a small number of eggs at first but as a termite colony matures, she can lay as many as 36,000 eggs a day.

▼ *A termite queen can grow to such a size that she can no longer move.*

Termite behaviour

- **Termites are social insects** that live in well-organized colonies.

- **Large colonies** can be home to millions of termites.

- **There are different categories** of termite in a colony – the queen, king, workers and soldiers. Unlike ants, the workers and soldiers are both male and female, but they cannot reproduce.

- **Workers take care** of the eggs and the nest, as well as foraging for food and feeding the young.

- **Soldiers defend** the colony from predators. Their jaws are huge and used as weapons.

- **Termites communicate** with each other using chemical signals called pheromones.

- **Reproductive termites** and soldiers lick the nymphs, releasing a pheromone that stops the nymphs from developing into new reproductives or soldiers.

- **If the number** of termites decreases, fewer nymphs receive this pheromone, so reproductives and soldiers are again produced. This restores the balance of the colony.

- **Termite mounds can reach** up to 10 m in height.

- **The mounds** can have air-conditioning shafts built into them to control the temperature of the nest to within only one degree.

▶ *Termite mounds are highly complex constructions.*

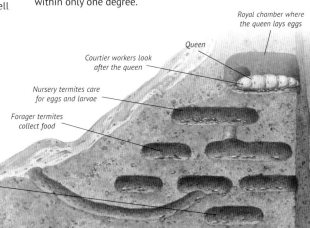

Royal chamber where the queen lays eggs

Queen

Courtier workers look after the queen

Nursery termites care for eggs and larvae

Forager termites collect food

Cleaner termites repair the nest and get rid of waste

Termite nests

● **Termites nest in humid conditions**, underground or in hollow tree stumps, shrub roots, cellar walls, window frames, wooden posts and even in books.

● **Nests provide termites with protection** from extreme weather conditions and enemies.

● **A large termite** nest is called a termitarium.

● **To build their nests**, termites collect dirt, clay particles and chewed wood, which they 'glue' together with saliva or excreta.

● **Workers build the nests**, which are damp, dark and sealed from the outside environment.

● **Compass termites** build their nests in long blade shapes. The wide sides face east and west to receive the warmth of the setting and rising sun. The hot, midday sun shines only on the mound's sharp ends, which face north and south.

● **Nests have many chambers**, called pockets, and a network of galleries that connect the horizontal layers of chambers.

● **The nest is ventilated** by holes in the nest walls. Some have air-conditioning systems that draw air into the chambers beneath the mound and release hot air through chimneys.

● **Nests can be completely underground**. However, some nests rise above the ground and are known as termite hills or mounds. These hills are a regular sight in tropical regions.

◄ *Termite nests have hard walls made of soil and termite saliva, and can be domelike or conical in shape.*

Cockroaches

- **There are about 4000 species** of cockroach. They belong to the order Blattodea.

- **Found almost everywhere** in the world, cockroaches are common in places where there is a lot of rubbish.

- **These insects** may be winged or wingless. Adults can measure 1–9 cm in length. They are nocturnal and prefer dark, damp places.

- **Their legs are adapted** for quick movement. They have flat, oval bodies that help them to squeeze into narrow cracks in walls and floors.

- **Most cockroach species** are omnivorous. Their main food is plant sap, dead animals and vegetable matter but they will even eat shoe polish, glue, soap and ink.

▲ Cockroaches are not dirty creatures. It is the bacteria they carry that makes them dangerous.

- **Females can lay** 30–40 eggs at a time and can reproduce four times in a year.

- **Each female stores** her eggs in a brownish egg case called an ootheca, which she either carries with her or hides.

- **Cockroaches work hard** to keep themselves clean in order to preserve a coating of wax and oils that prevents them from drying out.

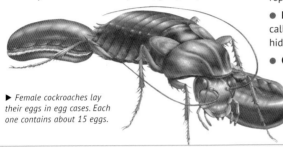

▶ Female cockroaches lay their eggs in egg cases. Each one contains about 15 eggs.

Oriental cockroach

- **Oriental cockroaches** are seasonal insects and can be most easily spotted during the spring and summer. They are found in damp basements, drains, leaky pipes and kitchen sinks.

- **These cockroaches** are dark brown or black in colour and so they are sometimes called 'black beetles'. Adults can grow up to 3.5 cm in length.

- **This cockroach** is sometimes called the 'shad roach' because its young appear in large numbers when shad (a type of fish) are swimming into fresh waters to breed.

- **Males have short wings** but females are wingless.

- **Females do have small wing stubs**. This is what makes them different from their own nymphs.

- **A female** can produce five to ten egg cases (oothecae) in her lifetime. Each egg case contains about ten eggs.

- **Young cockroach nymphs** hatch from the egg cases in six to eight weeks and mature in 6–12 months. Adult cockroaches can live for up to one year.

- **Oriental cockroaches** have cerci at the end of the abdomen. These are important sensory organs.

- **These cockroaches** can enter homes through sewer pipes, air ducts or any other opening.

- **Unlike other pest cockroaches**, oriental cockroaches do not have sticky pads on their feet and cannot climb slippery or smooth surfaces.

DID YOU KNOW?

Oriental cockroaches can survive for up to one month without food, as long as water is available. Adults have a lifespan of about one year.

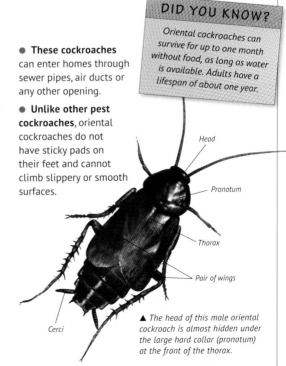

Head

Pronotum

Thorax

Pair of wings

Cerci

▲ The head of this male oriental cockroach is almost hidden under the large hard collar (pronotum) at the front of the thorax.

Madagascan hissing cockroach

● **Madagascan hissing cockroaches** are found on the island of Madagascar, off the south-east coast of Africa. They are large, wingless insects, famous for the loud hissing sound that they make. These hisses are loud enough for people to hear.

● **These cockroaches** are chocolate brown in colour, with dark orange marks on their abdomen. Adults can grow up to 10 cm in length.

● **A male cockroach** can distinguish between familiar males and strangers from the different hissing sounds that they make.

● **Males look different** from the females. They have a large, hornlike structure behind their heads and are more aggressive than the females. They also have hairy antennae, unlike the smooth antennae of the females.

● **These cockroaches** feed on dead animal matter, waste food or ripe fruits.

● **Females can produce** 30–60 eggs, which they store in an egg sac, either inside or outside their body. The eggs hatch into nymphs.

▲ Madagascan hissing cockroaches have spiky legs for grip and protection.

● **The nymphs** of these hissing cockroaches moult six times in a period of seven months before maturing into adults. While moulting, the skin of a cockroach splits down the middle of its back and the cockroach slowly wriggles out.

● **Newly moulted cockroaches** are whitish but their colour darkens within a few hours. Hissing cockroaches live for two to five years.

● **Madagascan hissing cockroaches** can be easily bred in homes and classrooms. For this reason, they are ideal for classroom study.

DID YOU KNOW?

Male hissing cockroaches are territorial. They fight among themselves by ramming and pushing with their horns and abdomens. Once the fight is over, the winner makes loud hissing sounds to declare victory.

◀ These hissing cockroaches make their distinctive noise by pushing air out of a pair of breathing holes in the side of their body.

Death's head cockroach

- **Large insects, death's head cockroaches** measure 5–8 cm in length. These cockroaches are mostly found in the Americas.

- **Death's head cockroaches** are named after the strange markings on their thorax. These markings look like skulls or vampires.

- **These insects** are also known as the palmetto bug or giant death's head cockroach.

- **Death's head cockroaches live mostly** in tropical forests or bat caves but sometimes they are also found in buildings.

- **These cockroaches** are brownish in colour with yellow and black marks on their body.

- **While adults are** beautifully coloured, the nymphs are dark in colour, although newly moulted nymphs are whitish.

▼ *Adult death's head cockroaches have yellow-and-black markings.*

- **The wings** are very long and cover their abdomen. The nymphs are wingless.

- **Females carry the eggs** inside their bodies and give birth to live young that hatch from the eggs.

- **Cockroaches are scavengers** and are active at night. Decaying plant and animal matter are their favourite food.

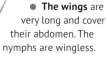

DID YOU KNOW?

Death's head cockroaches make good pets and are popular among cockroach lovers.

Crickets

- **Closely resembling grasshoppers**, crickets belong to the order Orthoptera. These insects are found almost everywhere.

- **Crickets have a flattened body**, long antennae and measure up to 5 cm.

- **Although crickets have wings**, some species do not fly and can only hop from one place to another.

- **Males make chirping sounds** to attract females and warn rival males to stay away.

- **They produce these sounds** by rubbing the bases of their specially modified forewings together.

- **Crickets are nocturnal insects** and have very good hearing and eyesight.

- **Their compound eyes** help crickets to see over distance and in many directions at the same time.

- **Crickets are omnivorous**, feeding on crops, flowers, vegetables, green plants, small animals and even each other.

- **Some species** are considered to be pests because they eat crops and lay their eggs on them.

▶ *Crickets begin life as an egg, which then hatches into a nymph that looks like a miniature adult without wings. Nymphs moult ten times as they develop into a winged adult.*

Cave cricket

● **Cave crickets are named** after their habit of living in caves and other dark and damp places.

● **Cave crickets** are also known as camel crickets because they have a hump on their back.

● **Very long hind legs** give cave crickets a spider-like appearance. Their strong hind legs make them good jumpers.

● **Cave crickets are brown** in colour and have long antennae. They do not have wings.

▼ The long, sensitive antennae of the cave cricket help it to find its way around in the dark. The long cerci at the end of the abdomen also have a sensory function.

● **These insects cannot chirp** or make sounds because they are wingless. Crickets normally produce a high-pitched sound by rubbing their wings together.

● **Cave crickets are omnivorous** and feed on decaying organic matter, plants and vegetables.

● **In the spring,** females lay their eggs in soil. The nymphs and adults spend the winter in sheltered areas.

● **Cave crickets** are sometimes troublesome in buildings and homes, especially in basements.

● **These insects** can damage articles stored in boxes, garages and laundry rooms.

◄ As well as in caves, these crickets are also found in wells, rotten logs, hollow trees and under damp leaves and stones.

Grasshopper

● **Often green or brown in colour**, grasshoppers have six legs, a pair of wings and compound eyes. Some species change colour throughout the year.

● **Found almost everywhere** except in the polar regions, grasshoppers prefer to live in green fields, meadows and forest areas.

● **There are three types** of grasshoppers – long-horned, short-horned and pygmy.

● **Grasshoppers have** shorter, straighter antennae than crickets.

▼ When a grasshopper jumps, it uses its powerful leg muscles to propel itself forwards.

● **During the mating season,** grasshoppers make loud noises to attract mates or scare away rivals. Unlike crickets, this noise is made by the legs rubbing against the wings.

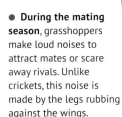

DID YOU KNOW?

When captured, grasshoppers spit a brown liquid to protect themselves from their predators. In some parts of the world, this brown liquid is known as tobacco juice.

● **After mating**, the female lays her eggs from her ovipositor in low-lying bushes or a hole in the soil. She covers the eggs with a hard shell called an eggpod.

● **Grasshoppers are herbivorous** and feed on a variety of plants, grasses and crops. They use their mandibles to chew food.

● **These insects** pose a serious threat to crops. A large group of grasshoppers can destroy an entire crop.

● **Flies, spiders, toads and reptiles** prey on grasshoppers and even eat their eggs.

● **In some parts of the world**, grasshoppers are considered a delicacy. They are ground into a meal, and sometimes fried or roasted.

Locust

- **Found worldwide**, except in cold regions, locusts are green or brown in colour. Their average length is less than 2.5 cm.

- **Locusts live in fields**, open woods or dry areas. They can fly for up to 20 hours, using reserves of fat stored in their body.

- **Locusts are normally** solitary insects. They live and feed like other members of the order Orthoptera.

- **They occasionally** form huge swarms, containing billions of insects, which can travel great distances and destroy crops.

- **A large swarm** can consume 3000 tonnes of green plants in a single day.

- **Females lay their eggs** – 20 at a time – in soil.

◀ *A locust can use its powerful leg muscles to jump a distance equivalent to ten times its own body length.*

- **Locusts breed very quickly** compared to other insects. Some well-known species are the desert locust, the red-legged locust and the Carolina locust.

- **A locust eats** its own weight in food every day. It feeds on crops, weeds, grass or other plants.

- **Young locusts live in crowded groups**, which causes swarming. This may be because the population has swelled due to good breeding conditions.

- **Overcrowding can also** be caused by droughts, which reduce the food supply, forcing nymphs to gather together.

- **Swarming locusts** look different to solitary locusts. When the crowded nymphs become adults, they are dark in colour with yellow spots. Their wings are long for flying great distances.

- **Locust swarms form clouds** several kilometres wide and thousands of metres tall. Swarms have been known to cross oceans.

- **Locusts are the most destructive** insects. The desert locust is the most damaging of all. One tonne of locusts, a fraction of a swarm, can eat the same amount of food in one day as around 2500 people.

Stick and leaf insects

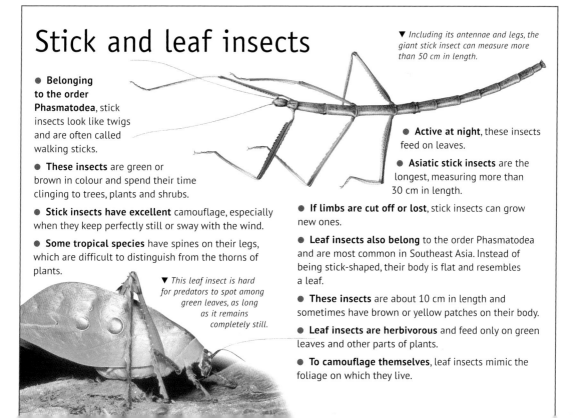

▼ *Including its antennae and legs, the giant stick insect can measure more than 50 cm in length.*

- **Belonging to the order Phasmatodea**, stick insects look like twigs and are often called walking sticks.

- **These insects** are green or brown in colour and spend their time clinging to trees, plants and shrubs.

- **Stick insects have excellent** camouflage, especially when they keep perfectly still or sway with the wind.

- **Some tropical species** have spines on their legs, which are difficult to distinguish from the thorns of plants.

▼ *This leaf insect is hard for predators to spot among green leaves, as long as it remains completely still.*

- **Active at night**, these insects feed on leaves.

- **Asiatic stick insects** are the longest, measuring more than 30 cm in length.

- **If limbs are cut off or lost**, stick insects can grow new ones.

- **Leaf insects also belong** to the order Phasmatodea and are most common in Southeast Asia. Instead of being stick-shaped, their body is flat and resembles a leaf.

- **These insects** are about 10 cm in length and sometimes have brown or yellow patches on their body.

- **Leaf insects are herbivorous** and feed only on green leaves and other parts of plants.

- **To camouflage themselves**, leaf insects mimic the foliage on which they live.

Dragonfly

● **These colourful insects** are named after their fierce jaws, which they use for catching prey.

● **Dragonflies can grow** up to 12 cm in length. They have a long, multi-coloured, slender body with two pairs of veined wings.

● **Larger dragonflies** are called hawkers, while smaller ones are called darters.

● **Adults live on land** but their nymphs, or naiads, live underwater.

● **The lifespan** of a dragonfly ranges from six months to more than seven years.

● **Male and female** dragonflies mate in flight. Once they have mated, the female lays her eggs in water or inside water plants.

● **A female lays** up to 100,000 eggs at a time. The eggs hatch into naiads, which feed on fish, tadpoles and other small aquatic animals.

● **Dragonflies are beneficial** to humans because they prey on pests such as mosquitoes and flies.

● **Experts have found** dragonfly fossils that are more than 300 million years old.

● **As far as we know**, the largest insect ever to live was a dragonfly called *Meganeura*. It had a wingspan of 75 cm.

▲ *A dragonfly has huge compound eyes, which cover its entire head.*

Damselfly

● **Damselflies belong** to the order Odonata and suborder Zygoptera. They have long, slender bodies and four long wings. They are weak fliers and timid predators.

● **These insects are beautiful**, slender cousins of dragonflies but are not as ferocious. They have compound eyes and excellent eyesight.

● **Damselflies are usually found** near water and their nymphs live in the water until they mature into adults.

● **Mosquitoes, midges, gnats** and small water insects are the preferred food of damselflies.

● **Damselfly nymphs** have external gills on the tip of their abdomen for breathing underwater. In dragonfly nymphs, these gills are internal.

● **Damselflies have** long legs, which they use to hold insects captured in flight. Their legs are not suited to walking.

● **Males and females** mate during flight or over shallow water. After mating, females deposit their eggs in and around water.

● **The lifespan** of a damselfly is around one year but it can live up to two years.

● **During winter**, damselflies hibernate to survive the cold weather.

▲ *Damselflies have large compound eyes that bulge out to the side of their head.*

Praying mantis

- **Closely related to cockroaches**, praying mantises belong to the order Mantodea.

- **Praying mantises** are so called because they hold their front legs together as if they are praying.

- **These insects can grow** up to 6.5 cm in length.

- **Usually green or brown in colour**, praying mantises are well camouflaged in their surroundings. One species, called the Asiatic rose mantis or orchid mantis, looks like flower petals.

- **They have triangular** heads that can turn in a full circle.

- **Camouflage protects** the mantis from predators such as lizards. It also helps the mantis stay hidden when stalking prey.

- **These insects** silently observe prey until it is in range, before grabbing it with their spiky forelegs.

- **Female mantises are larger** than males, and have been known to kill them after mating.

- **During autumn**, females lay their eggs inside an egg case (ootheca).

- **Females secrete** a sticky substance to attach their eggs to plant stems and tree twigs. Nymphs hatch from these eggs in spring or summer.

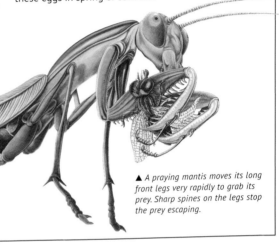

▲ *A praying mantis moves its long front legs very rapidly to grab its prey. Sharp spines on the legs stop the prey escaping.*

Antlion

- **These insects are named** after the larvae's habit of feeding on ants and other insects. Adults feed on pollen or nectar, or do not feed at all.

- **Antlions resemble dragonflies** – they both have a long, slender body and four delicate wings. However, unlike dragonflies, antlions are nocturnal.

- **These insects** are found in damp areas where vegetation is thick and near riverbeds.

- **Some antlion larvae** make pits in the sand by moving in circles and throwing sand outwards.

- **While making these pits**, the larvae leave behind 'doodles' on the sand. For this reason, antlions are also known as doodlebugs.

- **The larvae wait** inside their pit and feed on insects that fall in. When the prey tries to escape, the larvae throw sand at them, making them fall back into the pit.

◀ *The stout, clubbed antennae of adult antlions are very different from the short, thin antennae of dragonflies.*

- **Once the larvae** have sucked the body juices of their victim, the remains are thrown out of the pit. These larvae are voracious eaters and even eat adult antlions when food is scarce.

- **An antlion larvae** secretes silk and pupates inside a cocoon made of soil and silk.

- **Unlike the larvae** of other insects, and antlion larva secretes silk from the top of its abdomen instead of its mouth.

▼ *An antlion larva has captured an ant in its pit. The larva holds the ant with its pincer-like jaws.*

Mantisfly

- **Mantisflies are named** after their folded pair of front legs, which look like those of praying mantises. Although these insects look similar, they are not related.

- **These insects** are not common and are found in tropical regions.

- **Mantisflies**, along with lacewings and antlions, belong to the order Neuroptera.

- **Mantisflies lay** their rose-coloured eggs on slender plant stalks.

- **The mantisfly** has a complicated development cycle. It has two growth stages as a larva and two more stages as a pupa.

- **One species of mantisfly** has larvae that are a parasite of wolf spiders.

- **A single larva** enters the spider's sac and preys upon the egg or young.

- **The larva pierces the egg or spider** with its pointed mouthparts and feeds on its body fluids. The larva then pupates inside the spider's egg sac.

- **Unaware of the presence** of the parasite mantisfly, the parent spider watches over the cocoon.

- **Some mantisflies mimic** wasps and bees for protection.

- **Mantisflies** are predatory like praying mantises and have similar feeding habits.

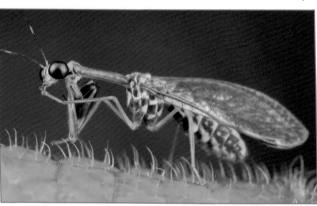

◀ *A mantisfly has huge folding front legs. The wings of a mantisfly are very different from those of a praying mantis.*

Lacewing

- **Delicate green or brown insects**, lacewings are named after their thin, translucent, lacelike wings.

- **These insects have long**, threadlike antennae and their eyes are bright yellow or brown in colour.

- **A lacewing lays** a large number of eggs at a time. The eggs are white in colour and are 'glued' to a twig or leaf. Green lacewings secrete a thin, white stalk for each egg.

- **The larvae** feed on small insects, such as aphids, so are also known as aphid lions.

- **Lacewing larvae** are sometimes reared commercially to get rid of pests.

- **With jawlike mouthparts**, the larvae suck the body fluids of their prey after injecting paralyzing venom.

- **Some lacewing larvae** camouflage themselves with debris, such as the skin and other remains of their prey.

- **Many species of adult lacewings** do not eat other insects. Instead, they feed on nectar and pollen.

- **Lacewings are not good fliers** because their wings are too weak to support their weight.

▶ *A lacewing has two similar pairs of wings, which are covered with a delicate network of veins.*

DID YOU KNOW?

Predators avoid lacewings because they give off a pungent, garlic-like odour when attacked.

Stonefly

● **Stoneflies are an ancient order** of insects that has been around for nearly 300 million years.

● **Stonefly nymphs** cling to stones in clear mountain streams or lakes. They are eaten by fish and are also used as fish bait.

● **Some stonefly nymphs** breathe through gills that are present near their legs. Others obtain oxygen through their body surface.

● **Adult stoneflies** are terrestrial, which means that they live on land. However, they never wander too far from water, spending their time crawling over stones. This is how they got their name.

● **Female stoneflies** deposit their eggs in deep water. To prevent the eggs from floating away, they stick them to rocks with a sticky secretion.

DID YOU KNOW?

Some male stoneflies attract females by drumming their abdomen against a hard surface. For this reason, these insects are popularly known as 'primitive drummers'.

● **A stonefly nymph** resembles an adult but does not have wings and its reproductive organs are not as well-developed. These nymphs grow into adult stoneflies and crawl out of the water.

● **Stonefly nymphs feed** on underwater plants, such as algae and lichens. Some species are carnivorous and feed on aquatic insects.

● **Adults may not** feed at all, although some eat algae and pollen.

● **Fish often attack** female stoneflies when they try to deposit their eggs in streams.

● **Stoneflies are sensitive** to water pollution. Experts use these insects to study the level of water purity.

◀ *The flattened body of a stonefly nymph helps to stop it being washed away as it clings to stones at the bottom of streams.*

Scorpionfly

● **Scorpionflies** are a small group of insects with dark spots on their two pairs of membranous wings. These primitive insects have been around for 250 million years.

● **The rear body part** of some males is curled upwards, similar to a scorpion's. Only males resemble scorpions.

● **Adult scorpionflies** have modified mouthparts. They have a long beak pointing downwards.

● **Scorpionflies feed** on dead as well as live insects. Some also feed on pollen, nectar and plants.

● **They are predators**, often stealing their food from spiders' webs. They catch their prey with their hind legs.

● **While mating**, a male scorpionfly secretes a sweet, sticky secretion, on which the female scorpionfly feeds.

● **The female** lays her eggs in wooden crevices and soil. The eggs hatch and the larvae live and pupate in loose soil or waste matter.

▶ *Male scorpionflies have a large sting on a long curved tail. It looks like the sting of a scorpion but is harmless.*

▲ *A distinctive feature of scorpionflies is their elongated head with a long 'beak', which ends in biting jaws.*

DID YOU KNOW?

During the mating season, a male scorpionfly offers the female a gift. This courtship gift can be a dead insect or a drop of his saliva.

● **Scorpionfly larvae feed** on dead and rotten plant and animal matter. Some larvae also feed on small insects.

● **Scorpionflies** are often considered helpful to humans because they keep the environment clean by feeding on dead insects.

Silverfish

● **Silverfish are primitive insects** that belong to the order Thysanura.

● **These insects** are soft-bodied and do not have wings. Silverfish have a longish body with three tail filaments.

● **Silver or brown** in colour, silverfish can move very swiftly.

● **Silverfish prefer to live in** places that are dark and very humid. They are mostly found in moist and warm places, such as kitchens and baths.

● **These insects generally feed** on flour, glue, paper, leftover food and even clothes. Silverfish can easily survive for months without any food.

● **Silverfish mate** in a unique manner. A male spins a silk thread and deposits his sperm on it. The female then comes near this thread, picks up the sperm and uses it to fertilize her eggs.

● **A female silverfish** can lay up to 100 eggs in her lifetime. After mating, she deposits clusters of her eggs in cracks or crevices.

● **Even after** maturing into adults, these insects continue to moult. They can live for two to eight years.

● **Generally harmless** to humans, silverfish can contaminate food.

● **Silverfish can destroy** books and are considered indoor pests.

▶ *Silverfish are named after the tiny, shiny scales that cover their carrot-shaped body. They belong to a group of insects called bristletails because their abdomen ends in a central tail, which is fringed with bristles.*

DID YOU KNOW?
Silverfish are able to squeeze their flattened bodies into the smallest of gaps.

Springtail

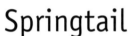

● **Springtails** belong to the order Collembola.

● **Wingless insects**, springtails measure 1–5 mm in length. Unlike most other insects, springtails do not have compound eyes.

● **These insects** have a springlike organ, known as a furcula, under their abdomen. It helps them to leap high into the air.

● **Springtails** do not have a respiratory system. They breathe through their cuticle (hard skin).

● **Even though springtails can jump**, they normally crawl from one place to another.

● **Springtails prefer** to live in soil and moist habitats. However, they can survive almost anywhere in the world including Antarctica and Arctic regions.

● **Decaying vegetable matter**, pollen, algae and other plants are the preferred food of springtails.

● **The lifespan** of a springtail is one year or less.

● **A female springtail** lays approximately 90–150 eggs in her lifetime.

DID YOU KNOW?
Springtails are also called snow fleas as they can survive in extreme cold. They are active even in freezing weather.

◀ *A springtail's forked tail is held under tension below the body. When released, it pings down and back, to fling the springtail away from danger.*

▼ *Springtails have to live in moist places because their bodies dry out easily. They are usually a grey or brown colour, sometimes with mottled colours for camouflage.*

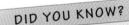

Lice

- **Lice are small, wingless insects**, measuring up to 11 mm in length. Two types of lice that frequently affect humans are the head louse and the body louse.

- **A louse's body** is flattened, which helps it to lie close to the skin. The head louse attaches itself to the hair or scalp, using the claws on its legs.

- **Human lice** belong to the order Phthiraptera and a subgroup called sucking lice.

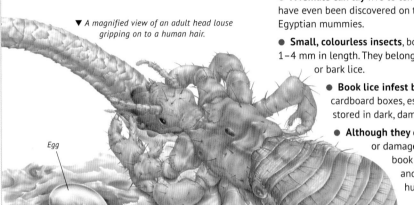

▼ *A magnified view of an adult head louse gripping on to a human hair.*

Egg

- **The head louse** is more common on clean hair.

- **Lice feed on human blood** and each feed takes a few minutes. They have three needle-like mouthparts, or stylets, which can pierce the skin.

- **Head lice are transmitted** by direct contact with an infested person or by using infested articles, such as headgear, combs, brushes or scarves.

- **A female can lay** five to ten eggs a day. Dead lice have even been discovered on the hair of ancient Egyptian mummies.

- **Small, colourless insects**, book lice measure 1–4 mm in length. They belong to the order Psocoptera, or bark lice.

- **Book lice infest books**, paper and cardboard boxes, especially those that are stored in dark, damp places.

- **Although they do not spread** diseases or damage household furnishings, book lice often damage books and papers. They do not bite humans or animals.

Earwig

- **Red-brown to black in colour**, earwigs belong to the order Dermaptera, meaning 'skin wings'. They measure 25–30 mm and are flat and slender. They have simple, biting mouthparts.

- **These insects** usually have membranous hind wings, which lie hidden under their leathery forewings. Some species of earwig are wingless.

- **When the hind wings** open, they are the same shape as a human ear.

- **Earwigs have a pair** of horned forceps, called cerci, at the tip of their abdomen. They look like pincers.

- **When alarmed**, earwigs curl the cerci over their body. Although the cerci give earwigs a fierce look and can inflict sharp bites, they are quite harmless to humans.

- **Males have longer**, more curved pincers than females.

- **Several species of earwig** release a foul-smelling liquid, which is produced in their abdominal glands. This helps to protect them from predators.

- **The female** lays 25 to 30 eggs underground. She incubates them and they hatch into nymphs, gradually developing into adults.

- **Earwigs feed on** algae, fungi, mosses, pollen, dead and live insects, spiders and mites. They damage flowers, vegetables and fruits by feeding on them.

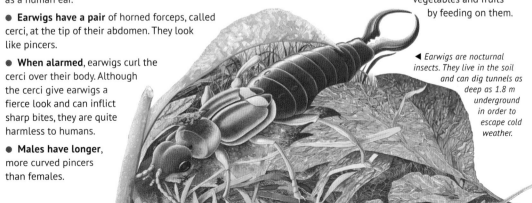

◄ *Earwigs are nocturnal insects. They live in the soil and can dig tunnels as deep as 1.8 m underground in order to escape cold weather.*

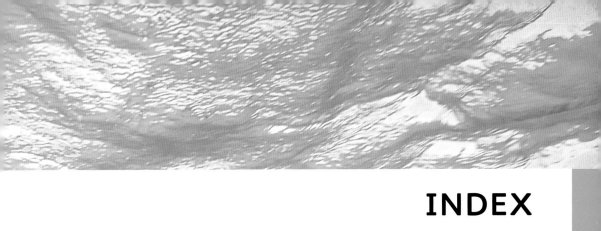

INDEX

Index

Acknowledgements

All artworks are from the Miles Kelly Artwork Bank.

The publishers would like to thank the following sources for the use of their photographs:

Cover: Shutterstock.com Front cover (tl) Ana Vasileva, (tr) Cathy Keifer, (cr) Kosarev Alexander, (c) Johannes Kornelius, (bc) XYZ, (cl, seashell) Yaroslava; Book spine Lukas Gojda; Back cover (tr) alslutsky, (cr) Rich Carey, (bc) Bob Orsillo, (bl) Anan Kaewkhammul

Alamy
104(br) Westend61 GmbH; 183(t) MasPix; 188(bl) Ronald Karpilo; 190(b) Stocktrek Images, Inc.

Depositphotos
260(br) daphot; 289(cl) Andaman

Dreamstime.com
111(b) Vladimir Seliverstov; 121(cr) Lawrence Wee

ESA
34(bl) ESA/Hubble & NASA

FLPA
173(tr) Steve Trewhella; 314(bl) Jef Meul/NIS; 325(t) Ingo Arndt/Minden Pictures; 332(b) Piotr Naskrecki/ Minden Pictures

Fotolia.com
10(bl) piccaya; 14(tr) Georgios Kollidas; 64–65(bg) Dmitry Pichugin; 72(c) Steve Estvanik; 91(cr) Michael Siller; 110(bl) QiangBa DanZhen; 114(bl) overthehill; 116(tl) Ismael Montero; 134(tr) EcoView; 138(br) cbpix; 148(tr) SLDigi; 153(br) Fabrice Beauchene; 163(br) Snowshill; 171(bl) Abuelo Ramiro; 173(bl) tlorna; 174(tl); 298(bl) Paul Cowan; 312(tr) Patrick Bonnor; 314(cr) Armando Frazão; 321(b) Cathy Keifer; 331(cr) Wong Hock Weng; 333(b) AZ; 335(b) StarJumper; 338(tc) M.A.T.T; 345(t) Claudia Holzmann; 348(cl) Pawel Pietras; 351(cr) Marc Chesneau

Getty
30(tr) Tony Hallas; 69(br) Martin Bernetti/Staff; 88(br) British Antarctic Survey/Science Photo Library; 170(tr) Jacques Pavlovsky/Sygma; 207(br) James L. Amos; 231(c) Roman Garcia Mora/Stocktrek Images; 232(tr) Eric Préau; 234(b) Roman Garcia Mora/Stocktrek Images

Glow Images
89(bl) Vidler Steve; 216(cl) Superstock

iStockphoto.com
9(br) and 18(tc) wynnter/iStock/Getty; 57(b) nicoolay/iStock/Getty; 97(bl) naes; 105(tr) robas/iStock/Getty; 111(tr) graphicjackson; 116(br) titine974; 119(tr) Cinoby; 132(bl); 149(bl) 270770; 152(bl) Andrew_Howe; 174(br) Pareto; 292(br) Tarasovs; 311(t) arlindo71; 320(tr) jeromewhittingham; 324(tr) Cathy Keifer; 325(b) choja; 329(cr) deepblue4you; 344(bl) DavidHCoder; 346(cl) db0973; 350(b) jscalev

NASA
8(tc) NASA, ESA, H. Bond (STScI) and M. Barstow (University of Leicester), (bl) ESA; 9(cr); 10(tr); 11(br); 12(bl);
21(br); 23(bl) NASA/SSC; 24(tc) NASA/George Shelton; 27(c) ESA:NASA:JPL:University of Arizona, (bl) NASA, ESA,
J. Hester, A. Loll (ASU); 29(tr), (bc); 30(bc); 32(br) NASA/JPL/Space Science Institute; 37(tr) ESA/NASA/SOHO;
40(cl); 41(tr) NASA/JPL; 43(br) NASA/JPL; 44(b); 48(bl) ESA/Hubble, NASA; 50(bl) European Space Agency and
Justyn R. Maund (University of Cambridge); 53(tr) NASA/JPL-Caltech; 54(br); 56(t) NASA/JPL-Caltech; 58(tc) ESA/
NASA/SOHO; 59(br) NASA/Joel Kowsky; 60(bl); 62(bc) NASA/JPL-Caltech; 63(cr); 68(tl) NASA/JPL/NIMA;
73(bl) ESA/NASA; 79(cl) Norman Kuring, MODIS Ocean Team; 79(bc) NASA/Goddard Space Flight Center
Scientific Visualization Studio; 85(br) Jeff Schmaltz, MODIS Rapid Response Team, GSFC; 86(tr); 87(cl) Jesse
Allen/ NASA Earth Observatory; 100(t); 102(tr) Jesse Allen, courtesy of the University of Maryland's Global Land
Cover Facility; 103(br) SeaWiFS Project, GSFC/ORBIMAGE; 118(b) Apollo 17 Crew, NASA

National Geographic Creative
203(tc) Pete Oxford/ Minden Pictures; 204(bl) Lowell Georgia; 213(b) Matthias Breiter/ Minden Pictures;
226(br) Xing Lida

NOAA
89(t); 112(tl)

Photoshot
15(cl); 124(bl) Oceans-Image

Rex Features
179(br) Bob Shanley/Rex/Shutterstock

Science Photo Library
14(bl) Andrzej Wojcicki; 15(br) Mark Garlick; 21(c) Rev. Ronald Royer; 22(cl) Dr Juerg Alean; 34(cr) ESA/NASA;
35(tc) Babak Tafreshi; 63(bl) Henning Dalhoff; 93(tr) Claus Lunau; 94(tr) Gary Hincks; 117(tr) Karsten Schneider;
121(b) NASA/Goddard Space Flight Center; 177(cr) Walter Myers; 189(tr) and 221(bl) Mark Hallett Paleoart;
222(tl) Natural History Museum, London; 229(cl) John Sibbick; 236(c) Laurie O'Keefe, (bl) Jose Antonio Penas

Shutterstock.com
5(tr to br) Naeblys, J Palys, Kietr, Michael Rosskothen, Dennis W Donohue, alslutsky; 6–7(bg) Primož Cigler;
20(tr); 25(tr) Triff/Shutterstock Premier; 28(tr); 33(tr) 3000ad/Shutterstock Premier; 36(bl) Vadim Sadovski/
Shutterstock Premier; 38(cr, t) Stephen Aaron Rees; 42(b) John A Davis; 44(tr) muratart/Shutterstock Premier;
45(tc) Arkady Mazor; 46(tr) Joe Gough; 47(cr) Albert Barr; 50(cr) Andrea Danti; 54(cl) Nienora; 66(t) Maxim Larin;
67(b) pmphoto; 69(t) Xavier Marchant; 71(b) Eduardo Rivero; 74(t) bondgrunge; 76(b) Patrick Poendl;
77(cr) RTimages; 80(tr) GybasDigiPhoto; 81(cl) vrihu; 82(b) Incredible Arctic; 85(t) George Burba; 90(bl);
91(tr) Robyn Mackenzie; 93(br) CatchaSnap; 95(tr) dpaint, (bl) Javier Rosano; 96(b) Robert Plotz; 97(bc) EcoPrint,
(br) Mikadun; 98(t) Paul Aniszewski, (bl) Ulrich Mueller; 100(b) Ian Bracegirdle; 101(br) Paolo Gianti;
105(bl) vasen; 106(b) Andrey_Popov; 108(tr) kkaplin, (bl) Lee Prince; 109(t) George Burba, (bl) RIRF Stock;
113(t) Robert Cicchetti, (br) milosk50; 114(cl) evronphoto; 119(br) Joao Virissimo; 120(br) arindambanerjee;
122–123(bg) Vlad61; 125 Steve Allen; 128(bl) dibrova; 131(tr) Andrey Armyagov; 133(m) Sarah Fields

Photography, (bl) Marc Witte; 135(br) Vlad61; 136(c) Ethan Daniels, (bl) John A. Anderson; 137(tr) ILeysen, (br) Amanda Nicholls; 138(cl) Adam Ke; 139(tr) Levent Konuk; 140(bl) Pawe? Borówka; 143(b) Krzysztof Odziomek; 147(br) Dray van Beeck; 149(tr) Natursports; 150(t) BMJ, (b) Maciej Olszewski; 151(br) Jeremy Richards; 153(tl) Attila Jandi; 154(br) Marcos Amend; 157(bl) Kent Ellington; 158(br) Joanne Weston; 161(b) Christopher Meder; 162(tl) Blaine Image, (br) Kristina Vackova; 166(tr) Pincasso; 172(br) Jaochainoi; 175(tr) Arndale, (bl) aquapix; 176(tr) Ethan Daniels; 179(cl) Vladimir Melnik; 180–181(bg), 182(c), 186(tl), 195(b), 209(br), 210(t), (b), 217 and 228(c) Linda Bucklin; 184(b) Ozja; 192(t), 198(t), 208(t) and 224(tr) Catmando; 193(tr), 205(b) and 218(b) Michael Rosskothen; 194(t), 196(bl) and 212(t) Leonello Calvetti; 198(bl) and 200(tl) Ralf Juergen Kraft; 203(br) Kostyantyn Ivanyshen; 206(t) Bob Orsillo; 211(tl) John Kasawa; 213(tr) Catchlight Lens; 215(t) DM7; 219(br) Naypong; 222(bl) DM7; 225(br) Bob Orsillo; 226(t) and 231(b) Jean-Michel Girard; 238–239(bg) Victor Shova; 240(t), 251(b), 252(br), 253(t), 255(t), 280(br) and 284(cr) Eric Isselee; 241(t) Rich Carey, (br) Janelle Lugge; 242(b) JDCarballo; 243(bl) Sari ONeal; 244(m) Riaan van den Berg, (tr) Chris Kruger, 245(b) Karel Gallas; 246(tr) Ethan Daniels; 248(t) Dmytro Pylypenko, (br) sydeen; 249(cl) Meister Photos; 250(t) Wolfgang Kruck, (bl) Csati; 251(cr) EcoPrint; 252(tl) Aaron Amat, (tc) Anan Kaewkhammul, (tr) phugunfire; 253(b) Audrey Snider-Bell; 254(t) TravelMediaProductions, (bl) apiguide; 255(br) Miroslav Hlavko; 257(b) Victor Shova; 258(cr) Zhukov Oleg, (b) Manamana; 259(tc) Bildagentur Zoonar GmbH, (b) Krzysztof Odziomek; 260(tr) Smileus, (cl) worldswildlifewonders; 261(t) Amanda Nicholls, (bc) Jurgen Vogt; 262(br) Ugo Montaldo; 263(c) Jiang Hongyan, (br) javarman; 265(b) krisgillam; 266(b) asawinimages; 267(b) Natalia Paklina; 269(tr) Sekar B, (br) Anna Andych; 270(tr) reptiles4all, (br) Vadim Petrakov; 271(tr) Sergey Tarasenko; 272(c) Andre Dib; 273(tr) Sam Chadwick; 274(t) Johan Swanepoel, (bl) fish1715; 275(tl) Mark Bridger, (b); 276(tr) Brian Lasenby, (cl) Sergei Kolesnikov; 277(t) Eduardo Rivero, (br) wacpan; 278(tr) nialat, (bl) Brian Lasenby; 279(c) Seaphotoart; 280(tr) Steve Byland; 283(tr) Worakit Sirijinda, (b) Matt9122, (b, bg) A Cotton Photo; 284(t) Sergey Uryadnikov, (b) Tony Campbell; 285(tl) D. Kucharski K. Kucharska, (b) Ger Bosma Photos; 286(cl) Nicholas Toh; 287(t) Dennis W. Donohue; 288(t) Cosmin Manci; 289(tr) Eric Gevaert, (br) Eduard Kyslynskyy; 290(t) Iakov Filimonov, (br) Andrea Izzotti; 291(t) Iarus, (br) Rich Carey; 293(t) Bonnie Taylor Barry; 295(tr) Kristina Vackova; 296–297(bg) LilKar; 301(t) vblinov; 308(tl) Decha Thapanya, (br) Eric Isselee; 319(tr) Kjersti Joergensen, (b) Marek Mierzejewski; 321(tr) Noradoa; 331(cl) Cathy Keifer; 344(t) Soyka; 345(b) Eric Isselee; 350(cl) Lee Hua Ming

Superstock
178(bl) Minden Pictures

Every effort has been made to acknowledge the source and copyright holder of each picture. Miles Kelly Publishing apologizes for any unintentional errors or omissions.